KAFKA'S MONKEY AND OTHER PHANTOMS OF AFRICA

WORLD PHILOSOPHIES

Bret W. Davis, D. A. Masolo, and Alejandro Vallega, editors

KAFKA'S MONKEY AND OTHER PHANTOMS OF AFRICA

Seloua Luste Boulbina

Translated by
Laura E. Hengehold

Foreword by
Achille Mbembe

INDIANA UNIVERSITY PRESS

This book is a publication of

Indiana University Press
Office of Scholarly Publishing
Herman B Wells Library 350
1320 East 10th Street
Bloomington, Indiana 47405 USA

iupress.indiana.edu

Originally published as *Le singe de Kafka et autres propos sur la colonie* by Editions Sens Public in 2008 and as *L'Afrique et ses fantômes: Écrire l'après* by Présence Africaine in 2015

This work received the French Voices Award for excellence in publication and translation. French Voices is a program created and funded by the French Embassy in the United States and FACE Foundation (French American Cultural Exchange).

Manufactured in the United States of America

Cataloging information is available from the Library of Congress.

ISBN 978-0-253-04191-3 (hardback)
ISBN 978-0-253-04192-0 (paperback)
ISBN 978-0-253-04195-1 (ebook)

1 2 3 4 5 24 23 22 21 20 19

À Fatima, Khodja, Nadjib, et Marilys.
À Amina, Kérima, Myriam, Élias,
Louis, Wellington, et Zouheir.

CONTENTS

FOREWORD

IT SHOULD BE NOTED AT THE OUTSET THAT Seloua Luste Boulbina's rich intellectual trajectory is not only unique but thoroughly remarkable. A life trajectory mixing familial experience, conscious and unconscious choices, and chance and necessity imposes a rhythm and gives form and matter to a critical project that is without doubt one of the most fertile in the contemporary French intellectual landscape.

Here, we are witnesses to a perpetually wakeful spirit in a state of agility, one open to risk and to the unforeseen, which never stops springing forth and rebounding. This spirit carefully deciphers the multiple meanings of its encounters with all the fragments of a complex personal history, one inscribed at the interface of cultures and societies brought together by the accidents of time as well as the will and the actions of "men." We must understand this initial historical situation, made of prohibitions, juxtapositions, and inversions, as the originating matrix of Seloua Luste Boulbina's theoretical project.

This is what explains her abundant productivity, no doubt the result of circumstances, but also the vivacious expression of an extraordinarily erudite and versatile mind, capable of diverse and singularly creative adaptations because it is endowed with an exceptional gift for identifying and going right to the heart of essential questions, the only ones truly worth the difficulty of being posed.

We would like to highlight above all Seloua Luste Boulbina's decisive contribution to the disentangling of the postcolonial question. Because at bottom, almost everything in her life and in her intellectual quest comes together and leads her to this central subject, which is still theorized far too infrequently and inadequately.

Around the world, the postcolonial turn in the social sciences and the humanities has been at work for almost a quarter century. During that time, the weight of its critique has been felt in many political, epistemological, institutional, and disciplinary debates in the United States, in Great Britain, and in several regions of the Southern Hemisphere (South America, South Africa, the Indian subcontinent, Australia, and New Zealand). Since its birth, this way of thinking has been the object of varied interpretations and has given rise, at more or less regular intervals, to waves of controversy—which continue elsewhere—if not to totally contradictory objections.

Postcolonial critique has also given rise to quite divergent intellectual, political, and aesthetic practices, to the point that one is sometimes justified in wondering wherein lies its unity. Despite this fragmentation, we can affirm that at its core, the object of postcolonial critique is what one could call the interlacing of histories and the concatenation of worlds. Aided, among other things, by a more or less stubborn compartmentalization between the disciplines and between the forms of knowledge produced and disseminated in the Hexagon, France has long remained on the margin of these new voyages in planetary reflection. Such is no longer the case today—or so it seems, from the evidence of the many debates underway and the publication of numerous studies.

In France, meanwhile, the debate suffers from two weaknesses. On the one hand, privileging polemic, it is particularly preoccupied with the syntax and the politics of postcolonial studies, instead of doing postcolonial studies on the basis of empirical cases. On the other hand, this debate has quickly found itself in an epistemological cul-de-sac because it has imported conceptual tools that do not necessarily do justice to the singularity of the French imperial and colonial trajectories.

Africa and Its Phantoms constitutes Seloua Luste Boulbina's response to this double impasse. Her response is hardly a momentary or conjectural one. The ensemble of her work could actually be read as the search for this "third place" (to borrow a term from Derrida), a sort of desert within the desert since it refers neither simply to the "archi-originary," nor simply to the "unarchivable." In this sober and incisive text, history, language, and the colony are put in relation with architecture (interior), politics (internal), sexed space, and unveiled gender.

But what must we understand by *postcolonial*, and how should it be studied? It is a particular historical period, to be sure, but not just that—a heritage from the past, certainly, but not only that either. Much more, it is a rationality that carries within it an imaginary—of what is yet to come. And it is here that Seloua Luste Boulbina distinguishes herself from a whole tradition of critique, which is as much Anglo-Saxon as it is Francophone—or should we say French?

She inscribes her theoretical and methodological effort in the logic of the old injunction to know oneself, which implies recognition of the subject's emergence as the experience of its irruption into speech and into language, passing through the ricochet of the voice. She admits, on the other hand, the centrality of practices of subjectivation inasmuch as they are always singular—in other words, the work of actors situated in time, circumstances, and specific conditions that, for those concerned, make up an event. According this privilege to practice and to experience then permits her to approach colonial situations in their unique qualities and in the way that they become objects of symbolization.

More than a doctrine, what she proposes is therefore a strategy. This strategy gives a large place to indetermination, to instability, to hesitation, and to movement. But it also proposes that the postcolony is, before all else, an "interworld," a relationship that is not just external and objective but also internal and subjective. These claims are realized through a taut and critical articulation of historiography, of psychoanalysis, of philosophy, and of literature.

Many other aspects of Seloua Luste Boulbina's work could be emphasized. One might draw attention to her decisive contribution to resolving the question of method in the apprehension of postcolonial reality, given that this is exactly the point on which the contemporary French debate runs aground. No less important, Seloua Luste Boulbina's works owe their impact beyond any immediate goal to the fact that they have enabled the renewal of critical theory in a singular confrontation with the multiplicity of languages and of discursive forms.

Achille Mbembe
Professor in the Department of Romance Studies,
Duke University
Professor of History and Political Science,
University of Witwatersrand,
Johannesburg, South Africa

TRANSLATOR'S ACKNOWLEDGMENTS

EVERYONE KNOWS THAT WRITING PROJECTS SELDOM MOVE AT the speed originally anticipated, but the perpetual surprise is that even in a translation, different conversations internal to the work move at different speeds. Many problems do not appear until others are cleared away. Some sentences or references take months or years to come into their own. Sections evolve independently like bubbles in broth that eventually join together when moved by a larger theoretical consideration, and periodically the whole thing is stirred up by worry over the flow of English prose apart from sense. Thus materiality disappears into the apparent clarity of form and content.

I want to extend my deepest thanks to those who lived this little drama with me. This includes not only Seloua Luste Boulbina herself, for friendship and encouragement over more than ten years after our first encounter in her seminar on "The Colony," but also my colleague Cheryl Toman, whose expertise in translating has always pushed me to do a more careful job with language and shown me the difference between more and less creative solutions to sentences. I am also grateful for comments from Frieda Ekotto and Ann Laura Stoler, as well as from Gilbert Doho and Thérèse Kuoh-Moukoury, who continue to expand my world—the world of African France as well as Francophone Africa. Megan Weber and Eve Wang provided editorial assistance, as did the Baker-Nord Center for the Humanities at Case Western Reserve University, whose indefatigable administrative director, Maggie Kaminski, was also a source of moral support. Without librarians Carl Mariani and Karen Oye or the outstanding patience and flexibility of Dee Mortensen, Paige Rasmussen, and Leigh McLennon at Indiana University Press, of course, this book would be much less beautiful.

I want to acknowledge Brent Adkins, Andrew Cutrofello, and John Sayer, who read sections and accompanied me through crises of indecision, as well as my parents, for their interest and support. And certainly not last, Joe and CZ, for being thoughtful, resilient, and dancing with me. All of the remaining bad steps and infelicities are my own.

TRANSLATOR'S INTRODUCTION

According to Heidegger, philosophical thought always relates to some world, whose references and ends it complicates. Heidegger was working out the existential-ontological presuppositions of the phenomenology that Edmund Husserl, despite some universalist beliefs, conceived as the only possible response to looming crisis in the "European sciences."[1] But what would it mean to do philosophy that was neither tied to a single world nor global, whether in thought or geography—interworldly, in other words?

In this volume, Seloua Luste Boulbina brings her immense knowledge of political thought and the arts to answer this question. The two texts of which it is composed, *Kafka's Monkey* and *Africa and Its Phantoms*, develop a philosophical metaphorics of the migrant that allows French postcolonial theory to intersect with the Arabic and English-speaking world. This erudite voyage is haunted by the voices of Deleuze, Derrida, and Foucault. But Glissant, Spivak, and Rancière are on board, not far behind Fanon and Said. In France, where postcolonial theory does not have an established academic presence, her work is absolutely new. Its configuration of postcolonial themes is new in the English world as well—and never so timely, for it concerns nothing less than the philosophical subjectivity of a possible interworldly experience.[2]

Thirty years ago, European identity was challenged by the unexpected end of the Cold War division between East and West and the phenomena of migration and ethnic conflict that followed. Today, the challenge to Europe is less intra-European migration than migration from the Arab world, provoked by authoritarian responses to the 2010–12 Arab Spring and the Syrian civil war that has been its most devastating aftermath. To this migration are added refugees from the ongoing American and British wars in Afghanistan and Iraq and those fleeing economic and climate crisis in Africa. The reaction to migration from outside Europe has overdetermined older tensions within European nation-states and increasingly threatens liberalism and the legitimacy of democratic governance in the European Union. This threat seems to be echoed by strains of nativism in the United Kingdom and United States.

In an interview from 1998, Caribbean novelist and philosopher Édouard Glissant suggested that "there are two main types of cultures in the current *tout-monde*": "atavistic cultures" that try to link "their present state to a creation of the world brought about by means of an uninterrupted filiation" and "composite cultures" that "have not had the opportunity or the means to create a myth of the creation of the world because they are cultures born of history," unable to define themselves in exclusionary terms.[3] Such cultures can be found on every continent. Whether tensions between them are the signs of cultural pride or of economic anxiety and competition, this difference between the root and the relation, between societies that embrace tolerance and those that refuse it, poses an unprecedented challenge to the universalism of the human rights agenda that has dominated the global imaginary since 1989. Moreover, even when they come to Europe from Central Africa or arrive in the United States from Mexico and South America, migrants are wrapped in a language of threat that has been associated with Islam and the Arab World since the attacks on New York in September 2001.

Each of the wars producing migration has left unofficial and often unarticulated knowledge in the bodies of its survivors. Uprooted families and ethnic groups found their historical experience and hopes for the future amputated from living reality. Such trauma finds outlets in ideologies of violence, but former colonizers and those whose countries are destinations for the new migration have their own ghosts that must be confronted if they are not to be projected fearfully onto the innocent. In the United States, toleration of difference is shaped by guilt and denial about the theft of wealth from African slave labor and from the Native Americans on whose territory this wealth now exists. New waves of immigration have always been perceived and accepted or rejected against the backdrop of these tensions. Glissant predicts that nothing will change "as long as there is no change, not only in consciousness, but also in the *imaginaire*, the imaginary or deep mentality" of Europeans.[4] Because of its global import, the French contribution to this imaginary must be accurately understood.

Throughout his life, Michel Foucault showed how Western thought was shaped by the division between subject and other, usually as the result of practices and geographical arrangements that did not enter into conscious reflection. In doing so, he drew attention to the modern episteme or interlocking formation of knowledges around which the university is built.[5] These include not just the well-respected natural sciences, human sciences, and mathematics, but also the "minor" disciplines of law, medicine, and administration or management—which often have more impact on the daily thoughts and calculations of individuals and which were particularly important in the colonial context. For "there is thought in philosophy, but also in a novel, in jurisprudence, in law, in an administrative system, in a prison."[6]

According to Foucault's *Les mots et les choses*, time and history on a roughly Hegelian, progressivist model were the unspoken presuppositions for the modern episteme. But as Luste Boulbina argues, history overflows this episteme in the sense that power relations making enunciation possible were not captured in the resulting body of authorized *énoncés*, or statements.[7] "To speak of historical culture," she writes, "is to place oneself beyond the strict domain of the human sciences and to reflect on the ways historical categories 'overflow' the ordinary categories of cognition."[8] The modern arrangement of knowledge in Western universities, as well as universities inherited from the colonial period in Africa and Asia, does not prepare citizens to respond humanely to these rapidly displacing populations. Decolonization, the establishment of independent postcolonial governments, and participation in wider and wider circuits of migration and exchange inadvertently support this arrangement.

In fact, *episteme* is too simple a term for these arrangements of knowledge, and in 1964 Foucault also believed late nineteenth-century episteme was reaching its end—a phenomenon he associated more with structuralism than with decolonization, although their fates were linked in anthropology. Even in *L'archéologie du savoir* (1969), Foucault had begun talking about an "archive" or "regimes of statements" and placed less focus on academic disciplines, pointing to a more complicated relationship between political practice and knowledge. The statements accompanying the military, educational, economic, and cultural policies of colonialists are also intrinsically part of that knowledge, as Olúfẹ́mi Táíwò has shown in the case of Frederick (Lord) Lugard and Uday Singh Mehta has shown in the case of John Stuart Mill.[9] Comparable thinkers, as Luste Boulbina argues, are Louis Faidherbe, who established the basic colonial structure throughout much of the French empire, and Alexis de Tocqueville, who provided many of its rationalizations and strategies.

France was a colonial power from 1605 to 1977.[10] In the 1600s, it had large colonial holdings in Canada and in the Midwest and South of the

United States as well as the Caribbean and coast of South America.[11] Some of these were lost in the course of the French Revolution and Napoleonic Wars (for example, the Louisiana Purchase), but later nineteenth-century holdings in Algeria, West and Central Africa, and Indochina more than made up for their surface area. Algerian colonization was marked by expropriation of land and labor, after a violent struggle with the original Berber and Arab tribes. Most French territories were considered colonies, but after 1848, Algeria came to be considered an integral part of France itself, and after the Crémieux decree of 1870, Algeria was given its own departmental representatives (of European descent) in the National Assembly. In none of these territories, as Luste Boulbina explains, were non-European populations governed according to the same rule of law as French men and women.[12]

Shortly after World War II, revolts against French domination appeared in Indochina, Algeria, Cameroon, and Madagascar. The French were driven out of Indochina in 1954, but the loss of Algeria in 1962 was more difficult to absorb. This was not just because of Algeria's special status as "French," which meant that its independence would considerably reduce the geographical scope of France, but also because the settlers' representatives were willing to topple the Paris government rather than be ruled by a Muslim majority. The Franco-Algerian War was marked by morally repugnant counterinsurgency tactics, including widespread torture.[13] After eight years of bloody warfare, during which the Fourth Republic collapsed and was replaced by the Fifth Republic under the authority of Charles de Gaulle, most of Algeria's European inhabitants emigrated to France, and de Gaulle himself orchestrated the independence of the remaining major colonies. However, the former colonies and territories (*territoires d'outre-mer*) remained economically and politically dependent on France, many to this day.

On the eve of decolonization, knowledge about the Global South in Western universities was shaped by the imperative of training colonial officials and preventing Soviet encroachment on territories, some involved in anticolonial struggle, claimed by the West.[14] Until that moment, the primary anticolonial discourse was Marxist. In this discourse, colonialism was a symptom of capitalist competition rather than a moral and political wrong in its own right. However opposed to colonialism they might be, Marxists and materialist critical theorists tended to share their opponents' view of Western capitalist societies as the most "advanced" and therefore, all things being equal, justified in their efforts to shape the economic future of Africa, Asia, and the Americas, if only in the direction of socialism.[15]

British postcolonial studies, developed largely by literary authors and historians from the Indian subcontinent and the Caribbean, emerged partly in response to the American civil rights and Black Power movements.[16] The prominent British-Caribbean critic Stuart Hall, who applied the Marxist critique of cultural forms to racial expressions in the United Kingdom, was a transition figure to later postcolonial theorists. Historians and archeologists, particularly nonacademic historians such as Basil Davidson, also played an important role in undermining the colonial assumptions of British academic knowledge about Africa and Asia from a standpoint outside the academy.[17] In the United States, postcolonial thought began as one of several critiques of the English literary canon used to instill and justify national identity in university students.[18] It built on a tradition of Caribbean liberatory thought extending back to the eighteenth century and on African American historical studies nurtured in historically black American colleges since the Harlem Renaissance, both of which had been systematized by new black studies departments in major universities. In both the United Kingdom and the United States, postcolonial thought and criticism tried to account for aspects of colonialism and racism that could not be easily reduced to economic class.

In France, where oral sources were mistrusted by most historians, the critique of Eurocentrism began with anthropology, not literature and history.[19] But this did not necessarily entail a reevaluation of Islam, for French orientalist scholarship on West and Central Africa tended to ignore its Islamic culture, much of which was written, just as it demonized Islam in Algeria and the Levant.[20] A significant portion of the French left (as well as the right, of course) had been opposed to Algerian independence, for orthodox Marxism, no less than the official French discourse of republicanism, denied the legitimacy of nationalism or religious particularism.[21] Indeed, it is ironic that in the English-speaking world, so much postcolonial theory relies on French thinkers, for they are less representative of French university life than of tensions in American university life, at least in the humanities.

The trauma of the Franco-Algerian war has made it difficult for academic discourse to connect contemporary French people of African and Caribbean descent to the nation's colonial past.[22] So too does the self-containment of academic disciplines in France.[23] Despite its origins in the

Cold War effort, the phenomenon of "area studies" legitimated interdisciplinary research for Americans, on which later programs such as black studies and women's studies built. This model was never replicated in France. Efforts to link domains of knowledge around the *fait postcolonial* are stifled by suspicions that postcolonial studies is simply a rewarmed anticolonial ideology, excessively and unscientifically partisan (if not antiwhite), and by fear that it may give rise to the kind of ethnic nationalisms that French republicans associate, distastefully, with the United States.[24] Thus, the decolonization of France has largely been studied in France without referring to the history of Algeria written by Algerians or by other scholars from the former colonies currently living in France; and contemporary ethnic minorities are studied by sociologists as if their family histories and communities were isolated from colonial events.

Edward Said and Valentin Mudimbe were among the most significant critics of metropolitan literary studies, history, philosophy, and social science.[25] Said's *Orientalism* critiqued the historical assumptions of American Middle Eastern area studies, just as Mudimbe's *Invention of Africa* critiqued the missionary and anthropological discourse justifying French and Belgian colonialism. Such readings of Africa and the Arab world responded to Western national security and economic interests and contributed to the West's distorted understanding of its own power, as well as a distorted self-understanding among formerly colonized populations. But as African American critics argued with respect to their own canon, these forms of knowledge failed to facilitate the self-understanding of European racial minorities descended from immigration.

Ina Kerner situates postcolonial theory (and more broadly, postcolonial studies) within the historical legacy of European critical theory, which Max Horkheimer opposed to "traditional theory" or the philosophical ground of the modern episteme discussed above, due to its emancipatory orientation.[26] Much critical theory, including its founders in the Frankfurt School, shared the Eurocentrism of its origins in Marx. Having supported many anticolonial liberation movements, if only on the grounds of opposition to imperialism during the Cold War, some Marxist critical theorists accused postcolonial studies of providing the neoliberal university with a safer substitute for political economy. They saw the very concept of episteme as a (defective) replacement for the older concept of ideology, marking a shift from the era of anti-imperialist struggle to one of identity formation within triumphant capitalist liberal societies.[27] And yet Lionnet and Shih propose that class analysis survived in Western universities after 1989 in large part thanks to postcolonial theory, which represented the search for anticapitalist (and antiracist) subjectivities in a post-Soviet world.[28]

Unlike either area studies or the Marxist study of imperialism, however, postcolonial theory has made Eurocentrism and its effects on both liberal and Marxist scholarship the object of study. The Tunisian novelist Albert Memmi argued that European colonial privilege could neither be disentangled from economic interest nor be reduced to it.[29] Immigrant communities in Europe can be sources of such critical insight, as can intellectual communities in the Global South. Some postcolonial authors, particularly from Latin America, have tried to incorporate indigenous and traditional knowledge into their efforts to go beyond Eurocentric visions of the world.

It is important, however, to remember that in practice, postcolonial theory in Western universities may not overlap with literature, history, philosophy, and social science in Asian and African universities, whose existential enterprises are not limited to the critique of Eurocentrism.[30] Nor do writers in the former colonial world necessarily see the same thing as most European or American philosophers in Foucault, Derrida, or Deleuze. The critiques of European subjectivity and knowledge found in these thinkers, as Achille Mbembe explains, were not yet the creation of new philosophical subjectivities by and for non-Europeans.[31] Postcolonial theorists contend that outside the episteme associated with Western historical development there are and will emerge other forms of subjectivity with their own histories, continuous and discontinuous.[32] Intercultural philosophers from both the North and South who draw on their insights, among whom Seloua Luste Boulbina should be counted, are trying to create space for such forms of subjectivity.

The achievement of new subjectivities often takes place in disciplines such as literature, medicine, and the arts. Postcolonial literature does not just illuminate colonial assumptions about subjectivity; it reveals inchoate forms that have counted more as symptoms than as knowledge. In minor literature, for example, languages meet in a heterotopic way.[33] Moreover, according to Deleuze and Guattari, the individuation of the speaker is not stable in the same way as enunciation in a dominant literary language.[34] Since history is difficult to write in a multilingual way and since some events or aspects of events are more frequently remembered or memorialized in some languages than in others, ghosts that elude historians are visible and audible to the novelist, as well as the psychoanalyst.

For Jacques Rancière, born in Algeria, politics emerges when those whom a system counts as subjects, those whose words are worth understanding and contesting, is subjected to pressure and reworking.[35] Rancière began his career as a student and collaborator of structuralist Marxist Louis Althusser, but he later turned his attention to the power relations vested in education and the arts. When those who have never been considered (or even considered themselves) "acceptable" interlocutors make themselves understood and achieve a subject position of their own, this rearranges the boundaries, meanings, and stakes of subjectivity for everyone. This does not, Rancière explains, mean that knowledge becomes partisan, but that the conditions for subjectivity and political agency are made explicit and opened to challenge.[36]

But politics is a rare event, far rarer than academics who accuse each other of "politically" biased scholarship might imagine, for most often we are stuck in a division of roles and categories that police thought just as they police the streets. By insisting on the task of abstractly ordering the just polis, political philosophy in particular refuses the task of actually participating in or encouraging the ferment of politics around signs of equality and inequality. In the United States, decolonial philosophy is the concern of a small number of thinkers, mainly feminist philosophers, whose focus is the "epistemology of ignorance."[37] It is hardly at the forefront like philosophy of science, metaphysics, or even ethics. According to Luste Boulbina, "for a French philosopher, the colony is situated without exception at the limits of philosophical reflection. It is a question simultaneously too empirical and too idiosyncratic to be judged worthy of a 'true' and 'authentic' philosophical interest. It is a question that does not belong, by right, to its political landscape."[38] In French, English, or any other language, philosophy too often ends up justifying various forms of the police—in other words, administration and distribution of goods and social roles.[39] According to Rancière, freedom is the symptom of equality at which genuine politics aims. The form of these colonial thinkers' law courts, immigration procedures, camps in which their opponents are interned, and military strategies, by contrast, are symptoms of the police.

In *Les mots et les choses*, Foucault claimed that literature, with its emphasis on the being of language, had been thrust outside the modern episteme, while philosophy formed a transcendental-empirical fold around it. But as Luste Boulbina argues, it is essential for historians and sociologists to interrogate the concept of the "colony" to which they implicitly refer when describing or explaining what they take to be "colonization" or "decolonization." The interrogation of this concept should be the province of philosophy, just as those who built colonies—their internal juridical system, their distinction from protectorates, or their military corps—were shadow philosophers, even if their work is rarely considered as political thought. To ask about processes of colonization and decolonization rather than the colony, moreover, is to ask about political action—an unfinished and unfinishable action—from the colonizer's point of view, rather than the standpoint of those colonized.[40]

As a philosopher, Achille Mbembe asked "what is the postcolony?" whose relations of power were the implicit object of postcolonial studies.[41] Luste Boulbina takes one step back: what is the *colony*? "What an absurd enterprise this must be: wanting to think the colony! I can already hear the objections: this is neither history nor geography, this is neither done nor something that should be done. The colony exists only in abstracto. In concreto, there are acts of colonization and of decolonization. There are historical phenomena. There are no (valid) philosophical categories. In concreto, above all, there are forms of knowledge, not hypotheses. And yet."[42]

We need to think the colony because it is a philosophical stumbling block that separates the false universalism of European knowledge formations from a general economy of knowledge.[43] It holds France in old patterns of perception and enunciation, despite changing statements (énoncés), and prevents France from acknowledging its own status as a postcolony.[44] But can one think the colony without politicizing philosophy or without deconstructing scholarly history? Can it be done without interrogating our image of the "normal" state?[45] And can it be done without, as Rey Chow notes, changing the relative weight of canonical Western sources and writings from the indigenous or Global South in the academic rituals that legitimate scholarly expertise?[46]

"Politics," Luste Boulbina writes, "involves the encounter between police logic and egalitarian logic, an encounter giving rise to subject positions, or *subjectivation*."[47] Fortunately or unfortunately, asking about the concepts constitutive of but excluded from the modern episteme risks thrusting the one who asks outside of the order of common sense, outside the places and roles through which sensibility is politically distributed. Taking her cues from literature and the arts, therefore, Luste Boulbina approaches these questions by way of a Jewish author of European "minor" literature, Franz Kafka; a philosopher of history, Friedrich Nietzsche; and two

French politicians whose ideas and policies represent the birth and demise of French Algeria, Alexis de Tocqueville and Pierre Mendès France. She does not define a nonpolice philosophy head-on but identifies obstacles to its freedom of movement.

"A way out"—this Kantian formulation of enlightenment resounds through Kafka's autobiography of Rotpeter, the "civilized" monkey whose plea to be recognized as a subject forms the basis for the short story "A Report to an Academy."[48] Rotpeter testifies to the subjectivation of the colonized body in the modern European regime of knowledge. "In the Penal Colony," by contrast, describes the subjectivation of the Western witness to colonial torture who is forced to make an artificial choice between the position of partisan (regarded as unscientific or unreliable) and the position of an impartial (but impotent) witness.[49]

Discourse (communication between individuals) and reportage (*histoire*) are two modes of subjectivation described by the linguist Émile Benveniste.[50] To these, Luste Boulbina adds Nietzsche's affective account of minority subjectivation. She shows how asceticism and bad conscience manifest themselves a series of contemporary events, such as the "veil affair" channeling public outrage against French Muslim high school students and the public humiliation of footballer Zinédine Zidane. Asceticism and bad conscience circulate when people must choose between partisanship and the apparent neutrality of expert knowledge in its most everyday forms—law, administration, education. These challenges are familiar to humanitarians who believe that witnessing suffering is immoral unless accompanied by action. They come to a head in Kafka's story "Jackals and Arabs," in which a traveling European is earnestly interpellated to assume the partisan stance by anti-Arabs who are, in the end, opportunistic feeders on political conflict.

Nietzsche, Luste Boulbina points out, is contemptuous of the historian who confuses scientificity with justice.[51] But does this mean that the work of the historian and the work of the partisan are absolutely distinct? Is it impossible for someone with an existential stake in the outcome of a scholarly inquiry to be just, or even merely accurate? Is history destined to be a purely reactive enterprise? Or is this the effect of a certain historical culture? For insofar as the French recognize that former colonial subjects do have an injury to grieve, they deprive them of recognition as scholars as well as sources of historical evidence, or refuse their experiences as legitimate objects of scholarship. This is particularly ironic given the French focus on the "duty to remember" and the exploration of the nature of individual and collective memory associated with the fiftieth anniversary of the Occupation and Liberation during the 1990s.[52] In fact, the duty was selective, as the new century brought with it, in addition to public condemnation of France's role in the slave trade, official acts of Parliament enjoining schools to teach the "positive" effects of colonization and recognizing the Algerians who fought against independence (*harkis*) without recognizing those Algerians who suffered during France's occupation of their land.[53]

Postcolonial thinkers have criticized Marxist narratives of world history as the history of capitalist expansion, while Marxists, in turn, have criticized postcolonial theory for seemingly refusing to accept the possibility of historical truths.[54] According to Neil Lazarus, postcolonial thinkers slid from a critique of imperialist representations to a critique of representation in general.[55] However, one can argue that Said and Mudimbe interrogate the history of forms of knowledge without abandoning the use of history (including their own) to generate new knowledge. Of course, this new knowledge will not be exhaustive or indubitable. For Michel de Certeau, it refers to a critical standpoint in the Kantian sense. History begins when people debunk the manifest errors in received myths.[56] The given of historical analysis that constitutes its Real is a loss, whether or not the object lost can be precisely identified.[57]

The relationship among philosophy, political philosophy, and the police order is exemplified in Luste Boulbina's case studies of Tocqueville and Mendès France. Americans from the United States think of Tocqueville as a liberal witness to their democracy, but his writings on French Caribbean slavery and the colonization of Algeria are less well known.[58] Indeed, he favored ending slavery in the French Caribbean, but from a colonial standpoint: he suggested the slaves should first be "nationalized" by France. As a witness, Alexis de Tocqueville was immediately shocked by white American treatment of Native Americans. But as a French politician, he recommended the same policy of relocation and expropriation with respect to the Arabs in Algeria. He recognized that Algerians had their own system of property and law, but insofar as they posed a perpetual threat to European settlers, they had to be strictly controlled.[59]

Americans likewise know of Pierre Mendès France as the prime minister who ended the French war in Indochina, leaving unresolved conflict between communist and anticommunist forces that would later give rise to the American war in Vietnam.[60] But because he regarded Algeria—unlike

Indochina, Tunisia, or Morocco—as fundamentally part of France, and because he did not believe that Algerian Muslims' histories or reports of their own needs had to be respected or even known, he could not envision any foreign policy allowing him to engage in true diplomacy with representatives of the revolution. Faced with rising anticolonial sentiment, he recognized that France had put Muslims in appalling social and economic conditions, and he opposed police abuses. He would have tried to satisfy some Algerian demands within the framework of French status if he had not been so strongly opposed by the European residents of Algeria.[61] In this sense, Luste Boulbina points out, he was anticolonial. But he could not think of Algerians as political subjects, and thus he could not even acknowledge the civil war with which he was confronted: all speakers who refused to assume Algeria was part of France were by definition self-contradictory, irrational, and impossible to negotiate with.

For Luste Boulbina, Tocqueville represents Kant's "political moralist" who ultimately puts expediency above dignity, the police before politics.[62] He envisioned neither the slaves, nor the Algerians, nor the insurgent workers of Paris as speakers to be "governed," but rather as things to be "administered." Moreover, Tocqueville was not even trying to add a new colony to France but trying to restore the pre-Napoleonic empire. Like Mendès France's attitude toward the Algerian nationalists, whom he insisted could not be "acceptable interlocutors" because he conceived of them as hoodlums, not politicians, Tocqueville's benevolence toward non-Europeans, whether American or Arab, did not enable him to see them as genuine political subjects. Because he could not imagine the colonial state as abnormal in any way, Mendès France could not understand the National Liberation Front's demand for sovereignty as such rather than as separatism or secession.

The benevolent attitude toward formerly colonized peoples—an "educative" attitude, which turns them into either favored or exploited objects of administration—was criticized even in the 1980s by Édouard Glissant with respect to France's remaining Caribbean territories.[63] As Luste Boulbina argues, this attitude also informs the understanding of "humanitarian intervention" by which continued French interference in African politics is justified.[64] This is why she explores the complicated genealogy of the term *toleration* in liberalism and French republicanism specifically. Such toleration is an ambiguous attitude for depoliticizing a situation, not in the sense (as Marxists protest) that it ignores economic interests, history, and subject positions, but in the sense that it limits consideration of those interests and positions to the racially privileged subjects of political sovereignty.[65] In this sense, although Kant had little sympathy for the kinds of adversarial politics championed by later liberal thinkers, his moral politician would have stood up for the refusal of paternalism implied by *Achtung*, "respect."

Both Tocqueville and Mendès France knew and did not know that the Algerians were subjects, exhibiting what Freud calls "disavowal."[66] But their disavowal was as much the product of the arrangement of knowledge about the colonized as it was the result of personal moral conviction or opportunism. The silence of colonized peoples was a structural condition for the production of administrative statements, discourses, or events—indeed, for the invisible power of administration (with its penal and educational auxiliaries) as a form of knowledge that does not show up in any direct way in the traditional European university. Individuals' memories of the colony, and their selective "duty to remember," have thus been structured by screen memories, which hid painful, incomprehensible, and disabling perceptions behind an apparently anodyne recollection.[67] Tocqueville and Mendès France contributed to that screen through their assumptions about what constituted a colony, what constituted a normal state, and what constituted a war rather than civil unrest or regional separatism.

Thus, a haunted subjectivity corresponds to the evasion or disavowal of politics rather than its engagement. The phrase *phantom Africa* comes from the journals of Michel Leiris, who accompanied the famous Dakar-Djibouti anthropological expedition called for by the French government during 1931–33.[68] The data, narratives, and physical collection of cultural artifacts by this expedition shaped French anthropology for many decades. But as with the Napoleonic expedition to Egypt described by Said in *Orientalism*, the scientists dragged the administrative conditions for knowledge gathering behind them, creating conflict, benefiting from suppressed conflict, and provoking their interlocutors to conceal as much as they revealed.[69] The phantoms of Africa are manifest in the unnatural simplicity of Leiris's travels in colonial space, as well as in the fragmented, frustrated, or panicky experiences of those who endured colonization, anticolonial warfare, and the pressure cooker of postindependence state building. These experiences, bodily but detached from use, take the form of screen memories and phantom limbs. They may not be recoverable, but one can philosophically and psychologically analyze the illusions they produce.

In phenomenology, the medical phenomenon of the phantom limb was enormously instructive for exploring the ontology of embodied subjectivity. The phantom limb testifies to the persistence of a subjectivity identified with bodily integrity even under the most damaging conditions.[70] It is a symptom, an "organ" whose construction allows the analyst to decipher and translate the trauma to which mind and body have been subjected. But in the process, the body to which this phantom belongs is redefined, and aspects of prior normality may come to seem pathological. In a society where the state of exception, particularly the colonial state of exception, has been normalized in relation to the historical past, the "body of exception" (to borrow Sidi Mohammed Barkat's phrase) haunts the structure of contemporary epistemological and economic formations.[71] Such haunting, as in Michael Haneke's *Caché* (*Hidden*), is part of French life, no less than that of contemporary Algeria.[72] France cannot claim to have been unmarked by the loss of its colonial appendages.[73]

But such haunting is also part of the United States, because its heritage is woven from the experiences of European immigrants fleeing poverty and economic uncertainty in Europe and the experiences of transatlantic plantation slavery. These experiences are active in the Caribbean, from which the trauma of bondage in French, Creole, Spanish, Native American, and African languages was exported and then apparently sanitized, forgotten in English. Toni Morrison has foregrounded such ghosts in her fictions, which have inspired and will yet inspire more historiography. These ghosts are also active in South America due to the lasting legacy of dictatorships installed and maintained with the support of covert American and French counterinsurgency experts whose skills were first normalized during the Franco-Algerian war.[74] In *Ghostly Matters*, Avery Gordon connects these two scenes of disappearance in the American sociological imaginary, prepared and reworked through literature.[75] According to decolonial theorists such as Walter Mignolo, the Americas are even less advanced in the process of decolonization than Africa and Asia, despite the growth in radical black and Native American scholarship.

Frantz Fanon, the "hyphen" or *trait d'union* linking France to the Americas, takes medicine and psychiatry seriously as part of the organization of knowledge.[76] A contemporary of Foucault, even in his study of madness, Fanon focused on the way that colonialism anchored and surreptitiously justified the Western episteme.[77] Fanon reads the bodies of his patients as symptoms of a larger reality, one that includes manufactured phantoms, if not the ghosts of popular tradition. The body of the colonized subject, as Luste Boulbina traces its imprint in Fanon, is a body with neither skin nor tongue—its genitals, ears, and eyes are turned against it by both torture and psychological warfare. Using Fanon, Luste Boulbina shows how history functions as an "interior architecture" for the bodies caught in colonial conflict. She compares the subjectivizing, humanizing response to trauma in Europe after its major wars to the neglect of psychiatry in the former colonies. Likewise, language is an "internal politics" because it determines who will be considered an acceptable interlocutor and in what political scenes. In discussing these ideas, she picks up where Fanon left off, between Algeria and the Americas, adding new clinical concepts such as history as "interior architecture" and language as "internal politics" to Fanon's psychoanalysis.

Languages that do not achieve official status, and events lived in languages that cannot connect to the public sphere, are not historical and trap their speakers in a retaliatory cycle whereby, as the analysts Davoine and Gaudillière have argued, what cannot be spoken of must somehow be made physically manifest.[78] At Blida-Joinville, Fanon confronted a French psychiatric practice that literally did not speak its patients' languages. The failure or refusal to hear what is said in another's native language forces him or her to spend valuable time translating and struggling to prove the possession of intelligence itself. To whatever emotional difficulties he or she may have experienced are added the emotional difficulties of struggling with one's image in an imperfectly controlled language.[79] This everyday exhaustion and humiliation is part of the micropolitics of racial and colonial domination.

The official insistence that legal, educational, and medical interaction take place in a certain foreign language, as Luste Boulbina notes, can also be deployed by postcolonial states that wish to restrict discussion of those aspects of national history or those residual aspects of popular imagination lived in unofficial or unauthorized languages and associated with heterodox ideas. Unfortunately, indigenous texts and perspectives can easily be taken over by nationalist or fundamentalist political factions such that the Western episteme and its political and philosophical discourses seem be the only paths to pluralism and egalitarianism.[80] Ideally, the subjectivation that emerges from Rancière's challenge to the existing distribution of roles and perceptions in acknowledged speech should be socially disidentifying rather than a social identification.[81]

Whereas history often attempts to explain, psychoanalysis interprets and translates.[82] Literature, closely linked to the work of analytic narrative, demonstrates the relationship between what is silent and what is audible in a given language, particularly in a multilingual situation. The relationship of both psychoanalysis and literature to what cannot be known historically does produce subjects and public phenomena inasmuch as it alleviates ghosts and makes them once more capable of action. For this to work, of course, doctors and patients, writers and readers, particularly political actors, must speak the same language or have reliable translation mechanisms; but first, they must acknowledge that these multiplicities even exist and do not invalidate speakers. These are the conditions of enunciation that underlie systems of statements (énoncés)—the power relations involved in speaking and hearing, before any arrangement of knowledge, that form the "outside" of history. Eyes, ears, and hands capable of tact must be generated.

In "A Report to an Academy," Kafka's monkey, Rotpeter, reflects on the behavior of his life partner, whose shyness contrasts to his relentless extroversion, and who has "the insane look of the bewildered half-broken animal in her eye." In that phrase, Kafka recognizes that racialization does not happen without sexualization, and one of Luste Boulbina's achievements is her attention to the way that colonization produces sexes of its own. The body of Saartje Bartman was exhibited like the inhabitants of the human zoos referenced by Kafka.[83] It was literally a black body without organs—a body whose organs were removed and put in the museum. In their place, organs were imposed by the racist imagination of her viewers. The Islamic hijab or veil, as Fanon recognizes, is an organ allied with both skin and genitals, protecting but also exposing the wearer to violence.[84] It did so at the time of Algerian colonization, and it continues to do so in the ascetic subjectivation of French Muslim girls held responsible for their parents' decision to allow them or to require them to dress in hijab.[85]

The idea that not just some but all representation is impossible or oppressive is associated, albeit unfairly, with Spivak's "Can the Subaltern Speak?"[86] The topic of this well-known essay is the recognizability of subaltern subjectivity, especially female subjectivity, apart from left-wing fantasies of being able to negate or purify the effects of their own conceptual schemes. In this context, Spivak describes how the Indian practice of suttee was interpreted by a range of British and Indian traditionalists and nationalists, and how those meanings were subverted in the case of at least one female militant from the 1920s. Her point is not that genuine intercultural respect entails respect for what is "unspeakable" in history, for she criticizes the possibility of such authenticity. Nor was she making a radical challenge to the validity of scholarly history (and could only be seen as such by way of an elision with the ideas of radical French psychoanalytic feminists such as Cixous with whom Spivak's intellectual relationship is hardly simple). The problem is that in the absence of mechanisms for social change, equating intercultural respect with respect for the unspeakable rather than with the effort to listen would risk confirming and perpetuating the muteness of the subaltern, particularly women.

Luste Boulbina thus shares Spivak's basic problematic but displaces focus to the famous question rather than to Spivak's answer in the negative. Can the subaltern woman speak? Of course, there are gaps in what can be heard, but the important point for Luste Boulbina is that the subaltern woman is no less qualified to speak than the colonial power or postindependence political actor. Rather than focusing on the fact of silence, as so many of Spivak's readers do, we should ask: How was her silence produced? In what way can theory, too, render silence more totalizing than it needs to be? Or, as Luste Boulbina asks with respect to Saartje Baartman, why should we assume that the woman on display was mute or failed to protest her treatment? Why should she have been any quieter than the male and female American slaves whose rebellions were put down and then minimized or erased from history books?[87] Why should we not rather, with Rancière, assume that her sounds were not understood as words or were deliberately scrambled, that her speech was not received as sense? Just as the subjectivation of French girls in the "veil affair" responded to the bad conscience of certain male school principals, should we not see Baartman's "silence" as a distinct but scarcely audible form of subjectivation? Better yet, how can we see her silence as the effect of a certain configuration or deployment of polyglossia that differentiates identities and enunciations with respect to sacred languages?

Fanon himself participates in these power relations when he is tempted to slip into pidgin with his Algerian patients, but also when he dismisses Mayotte Capécia's memoir of her interracial love story as a desire for whiteness.[88] Luste Boulbina's goal in "having a good ear" for Capécia's story, or rather for that of her creator, Lucette Ceranus Combette, is not to denounce representation or to identify what was unspeakable in her class and racial position. Rather, she wants to hear the author's effort to describe a "sexuality in the first person," to hear her self-assertiveness, and particularly to hear the assertiveness of her intellectual desire alongside her sexual desire. For what differentiates Capécia's novel from her white lover's memoir has everything to do with the point of view and the specific frustrations out of which it emerges.

Neither the subject of Western philosophy nor the subject of Caribbean pan-Africanism was a female subject, and postcolonial theorists vary in their attention to gender. Because of her association with the Vichy government and its representatives in Martinique, Capécia has difficult fitting into the diasporic black women's intellectual tradition represented by the Nardal sisters and later feminist and black radical thinkers.[89] Via suttee, the hijab, and Capécia's inkpot, in dialogue with Spivak and Assia Djebar, Luste Boulbina explores how men give women subject positions—and how women give subject positions to themselves and to one another.

Thus, Luste Boulbina moves from Rancière's analysis of the way that restricting speaking positions limits politics, to considering, with Fanon, specific occasions on which listening and reading could have restructured enunciation. In the psychiatric/political encounter, decolonization is a kind of labor but also a restoration of the capacity for desire.[90] "To speak about the decolonization of forms of knowledge is to interrogate knowledge transfers and to wonder what one has learned, what one is learning, what one can learn from the other—whoever he or she may be and wherever he or she may come from. The decentering implied by this attitude amounts to a new Copernican revolution. In this revolution, Europeans have to know what they are being offered by those other than themselves, non-Europeans."[91]

According to Derrida's *Dissemination*, the origins of Western philosophy position healing and poison in close relation to each other, just as writing is associated with various rituals of ostracism or the scapegoat.[92] Writing, in Plato's *Phaedrus*, was an act of ingenuity offered by a god to King Thamus as a cure for forgetfulness, but the king also worried that it might damage the capacity for memory. If these two achieve a balance, Derrida suggests, it is thanks to another resemblance in the Greek language between *pharmakon* and *pharmakos*, cure/poison and the scapegoat. Now, for Rancière, exclusion is what makes possible the philosophically ordered space of the police, leaving only the roles and groups of sociology.[93]

Derrida's work tries to show that the self-contained space of every language, particularly spoken language, is haunted not only by the ambivalence opened by its written form, but also by the ambivalence opened by the multiplicity of its forms, written and spoken.[94] This polysemy, or, more properly, polyphony, is foregrounded by Assia Djebar, who began in philosophy and migrated to literature, eventually becoming the first Maghrebin member of the Academie Française. For Djebar, the ghosts of precolonial wars, colonization, and the postindependence wars between secular nationalists and Islamists of the 1990s create a cacophony whose affects must be sorted and selected by writing.

Derrida views the haunting of Europe by Marxism as a general effect of closed systems whose most proper phantom, ghost, or revenant today is the *arrivant* or migrant from outside Europe.[95] And perhaps it is appropriate that Derrida's reading of Plato begins with the origin of this difference in Egyptian mythology, given the way that Egypt, a North African country, like Algeria, was taken up by Western historians as a self-enclosed origin of European culture whose connection to Africa as a whole was vigorously disavowed.[96]

As Luste Boulbina says with respect to contemporary migrants, they are "spoilsports" but nonetheless necessary to keep politics going, to prevent the depolitizication of democracy—indeed, though she does not add this, to keep capitalism from coming to seem self-evident within the supposedly closed national space of a welfare state. Although Luste Boulbina refers to psychoanalysis when explaining subjectivation, this subject is revealed through the interstices of a text that fails to nail down its conditions of possibility. How can the Husserlian subject of "European sciences" be open to an outside, to what it cannot hear in spoken discourse? How can it receive stuttering that does not seem to rise to the level of discourse? What would have happened, for example, if Ulysses had been willing to listen to the other language of the sirens, both female and foreign?[97] What kind of subject would this mythical master of ingenuity have become or bequeathed to Europe? And what other conclusions can we imagine for Penelope, who might have gone voyaging on her own?[98]

In a late text, Deleuze draws our attention to the way Foucault's early reference to the Bosch painting of the *Narrenschiff* encapsulates and prefigures so much of his later work on subjectivity: "In all his work Foucault seems haunted by this theme of an inside which is merely the folding of the outside, as if the ship were a fold of the sea. . . . Thought has no other being than this madman himself."[99] For Mudimbe and Said, Foucault is ultimately less a traveler between worlds than an "unhappy 'historian of the Same,'" a "potentate" of the interior, albeit a dissatisfied one.[100] Said, a Palestinian who ultimately made his home teaching European comparative literature in New York, associates the limitation of national exile with the positive condition of critical intellectual subjectivity, and he describes his experience as one between languages. *Orientalism* warned that the object of area studies, and the modern episteme more generally, had failed to connect with the reality of the Arab world and that the very notion of a single, stable "reality" to that world was deeply questionable (a warning echoed by Mudimbe with respect to Africa). But Said also stated that the intellectual's responsibility is to take sides and thus to be a partisan, not merely a witness.[101] What this volume shows is that these are two styles of enunciation, not opposites, and that their respective relation to the truth is not exhausted by "bias" or "impartiality."

By implicit contrast to Foucault, Luste Boulbina observes that Edward Said maps énoncés in relation to their enunciation, rather than to the archive that defines their scarcity.[102] Enunciations are positive acts that escape (for now) the uncertainty of historical interpretation. Enunciations select from polyphony, not once and for all, but in relation to a specific crisis or decision. This raises the inevitable question of what kind of enunciation is performed by Luste Boulbina herself as well as by the translator. In the development of these two books, Luste Boulbina moves from a critique of French philosophy's provincialism to an active, imaginative exploration of the forms of subjectivity it must engender and the organs it must transform, shed, or grow in the process. Her goal is not just to shine a more revealing light on the colonialism of Western knowledge but to participate as a philosopher in the recovery and construction of subjectivities for emerging populations within the West and on its borders.

As an American reader of French philosophy and as a translator, I do not know everything that I do not know, like the driver mentioned by Paul Veyne, "*who does not see that he does not see*, if the dark of night is compounded by rain."[103] This means, among other things, that I don't know the everyday meanings available to Luste Boulbina, who spent part of her childhood surrounded by Arabic, even if she writes in French; nor the way she continually weaves these meanings with those of other French thinkers who were part of her formation and not my own, writers in a language whose meanings change over time without their awareness or intent; nor do I know what associations she imputes to American theorists whom I know well, in an English that has changed even during my lifetime. This is a masterful book with multiple arguments and philosophical narratives, not to mention poetry, that will bear much rereading; only a few come into focus at any given moment. It is also the experimental flight of an interworldly subjectivity.

"French will let me come and go; not just in multiple languages, but in all ways," says Assia Djebar in *Oran, langue morte*.[104] Translation is a network, a transport system; this is why Bruno Latour is willing to use translation as the model for all knowledge.[105] When possible, I have used existing English translations to tie my meaning to the clusters of meaning that other English translators of French philosophy have given certain words, and to make verification or disagreement about those meanings possible for Luste Boulbina's readers. But I also keep in mind that the English terms, particularly in a field so dominated by Anglophone scholarship, have their own clouds of personal meaning that I may read into the French usage, and that even these terms were efforts by scholars and novelists who grew up and formed their imagination in creole, Arabic, Bengali, Wolof, and other languages. I am aware of the global power implicit in the English language, the ideological capacity for depoliticization, particularly in academia. Every act of translation is an act of selection, as well as circulation. Is it really possible for languages to be depoliticized, as Luste Boulbina suggests in a utopian vein?

Luste Boulbina harnesses Said's defense of enunciation to that of Édouard Glissant. For Glissant, a Caribbean novelist, poet, and philosopher who has reflected on the cultural as well as linguistic significance of creolization, the image of the archipelago is paramount. Said's term *interworld*, as Luste Boulbina notes in the afterword to this volume, is a term with a specifically Islamic meaning, having to do with the act of imagination. For Glissant, even Europe can be understood as an archipelago, providing a model for the identity of a subject that need not be self-authorizing or self-contained to be capable of knowledge and action.[106] Glissant's concept of the *chaos-monde* before all territorialization or globalization indicates the larger ontological whole through which a trauma—for example, the middle passage of African slaves—could be transformed into sense.[107] Glissant shows how the Deleuzian concept of the "whole" can play its function in a different key, a different context or continent from the body without organs played in the European context.

Thus, the colony, whose concept was created by practitioners such as Faidherbe (and, in retrospect, Mendès France) as well as philosophers such as Tocqueville, is a repressed or disavowed supplement to the state, one that makes worlds hang together without being interworldly.[108] Its disappearance should be welcomed rather than a source of melancholia. Migrants, particularly women migrants, are the "inside" of a different "outside" than Foucault envisioned. Their subjectivation changes the nature of politics but also frees us from categories of existing knowledge and the philosophy that defines their subject, for a recommencement of politics. In the era of hypercirculating information and easily manufactured simulacra, this need not mean dispensing with knowledge, nor can it mean such a sacrifice. In the epilogue, Luste Boulbina only begins to broach the question of how knowledge might be defined in terms of circulation rather than property, orientation rather than the "zero point" of a single national root, historical "last instance," or fixed cogito.[109]

Seloua Luste Boulbina's demonstration of how to think the colony philosophically is itself a version of the *après* defining a situation as postcolonial. She wants to gamble, as Mbembe suggests in his preface, that the postcolony can be an interworld modeled on something other than the colonial phantom or the normal colonial state whose appendage has been amputated. In these two texts, Luste Boulbina has extended the logic of the phantom limb to the logic of the political cure. The challenge she faces, like many postcolonial and intercultural philosophers, is how to combine liberalism with the nonrooted subjectivity of a thinker like Glissant, without this entailing a simple acceptance of neoliberal capitalism.[110] She uses liberalism against itself, particularly the idea of political self-determination against the paternalism of an ultimately exclusionary colonial order. This means recognizing the political, and not merely humanitarian, stakes for both Europeans and non-Europeans presented by international migration. If migrants are Rancière's "part without part," their presence may be necessary for democratic politics to avoid falling into the "management" against which autochthonous masses then turn in populist fury.

An intercultural philosophy is not a self-evident thing. It is neither comparative philosophy nor postcolonial theory. It hears and responds to Western ingenuity from the sirens' standpoint so as to amplify and elaborate that standpoint. It listens for intermittent sense in the sirens' song, rather than for satisfaction or condemnation. It modulates the signal-to-noise ratio without canceling the competing frequencies altogether. Luste Boulbina ties the stammering, wandering enunciative activity of inquiry to Socrates, whose place in the philosophical canon is both indispensable and unsettled. Socrates, who did not write, is accessible to us only through the *différance* of writing—via both linguistic and historical translation from orality to scholarship. Socrates is neither an observer nor a partisan but is present at their differentiation. This, Luste Boulbina suggests, is philosophy's relationship to the new episteme prefigured by postcolonial studies. Her intercultural philosophy is a figure for the return of politics: the pharmakon or antidote to the police.

Notes

1. Husserl, "The Vienna Lecture," app. 1 in *Crisis of European Sciences*, 281–85; see also Chakrabarty, *Provincializing Europe*, 29.

2. This volume, 274.

3. Hiepko, "Europe and the Antilles," 256.

4. Hiepko, "Europe and the Antilles, 255.

5. See Foucault, *Order of Things*, xxi–xxii. The functions of commentary, authorship, and disciplinarity in recognizing true and false propositions, while rejecting a "whole teratology of learning," are analyzed in "L'ordre du discours," Foucault's inaugural lecture at the Collège de France. So too is the way these functions impose scarcity on the availability of statements (énoncés) at a given historical moment. See "The Discourse on Language," in Foucault, *Archaeology of Knowledge*, 215–37.

6. Michel Foucault, "Order of Things," 267.

7. The concepts *énoncé* (statement) and *énonciation* (enunciation) are taken from Émile Benveniste. Enunciation refers to the act of speaking rather than to the content of what is said. In Meek's English translation of Benveniste, the word *utterance* is substituted for *énonciation*, but the reader must hear this in an active sense. This distinction is also closely related to Benveniste's comparison of *langage*, which consists of the signs or statements that are available for use, and *discours*, the act of using those signs as a subject in communication or, more narrowly, the mode of enunciation that consists in attempting to influence a listener rather than merely report on a situation. See Benveniste, *Problèmes de linguistique génerale*, 80–82; Mosès, "Émile Benveniste."

8. This volume, 65.

9. Táíwò, *How Colonialism Preempted Modernity*; Mehta, *Liberalism and Empire*.

10. Dates for the founding of Acadia in North America and the independence of Djibouti, respectively.

11. For a brief overview, see Aldrich, *Greater France*.

12. See also Le Cour Grandmaison, *De l'indigénat*.

13. Le Sueur, *Uncivil War*. Following Le Sueur's example, I refer to the Algerian War of Independence as the Franco-Algerian War.

14. See Coquery-Vidrovitch, "Francophone African Social Science"; Fyfe, "African Studies"; and Martin and West, "Africanist Enterprise, USA"; see also Harootunian, "Postcoloniality's Unconscious.".

15. See, for example, Chakrabarty, *Provincializing Europe*, 7–9.

16. This literature is now vast. For two historically significant examples, see Ashcroft, Griffiths, and Tiffin, *Empire Writes Back*; and Bhabha, *Nation and Narration*.

17. Fyfe, "African Studies," 55–57.

18. An idea put forward by Gerald Graff, author of *Professing Literature*, but also found in Walzer, *On Toleration*. See also Cusset, *French Theory*, 43–44.

19. Coquery-Vidrovitch, "Francophone African Social Science," 41–42. Lévi-Strauss's *Tristes tropiques* is often cited as a shift in consciousness; Georges Balandier was also an important figure in this turn. See also Richards, "Postcolonial Anthropology," 174–76, 180–81.

20. Islam was perceived as either politically nefarious or historically archaic. Much of Said's *Orientalism* is devoted to the Western (primarily English and French) perception of Islam, which was presented as the essence, however contradictory, explaining all phenomena in the Arab world. The European medieval view was shaped by the image of Mohammed as a "false" messiah, while the mid-twentieth-century view was either erudite but condescending, as with Massignon, or openly hostile, as with Gibb. See Said, *Orientalism*, 59–63, 68–72, 255–328. Anthropologists made efforts to discover or imagine a "pre-Islamic" Africa on which French colonialism could build. See Harrison, *France and Islam*; Amselle, *Mestizo Logics*, 117–35; Le Sueur, *Uncivil War*, 38, 112.

21. Stora, *Algeria 1830–2000*, 55–56, 112; Memmi, *Colonizer and Colonized*, 28–37.

22. Bancel and Blanchard, "From Colonial to Postcolonial"; also Smouts, *La situation postcoloniale*.

23. See de Certeau, *Heterologies*, quoted in this volume, 72–75.

24. Bancel and Blanchard, "From Colonial to Postcolonial"; also Fassin, "Good to Think."

25. Said, *Orientalism*; Mudimbe, *Invention of Africa*.

26. Kerner, "Postcolonial Theories."

27. Lionnet and Shih, *Creolization of Theory*, 12–13; see also Lazarus, *Postcolonial Unconscious*, 9–11. The key voices in this critique were Frederic Jameson and Terry Eagleton, who lumped postcolonial theorists together with poststructuralist philosophers and critics. Bhabha's "The Postcolonial and the Postmodern" (in *Nation and Narration*) was a significant text in this trajectory, along with Young's *White Mythologies*.

28. Lionnet and Shih, *Creolization of Theory*, 13; see also Chakrabarty, *Provincializing Europe*, 95–96.

29. Albert Memmi, *Colonizer and Colonized*, xii–xiii.

30. Kerner, "Postcolonial Theories," 4. Lazarus rightly notes that much of the literature from the former colonial world is modernist and nationalist, and does not have the preoccupation with intercultural identity issues that are associated with "postcolonial theory." See also Loomba, "Postcolonialism—or Postcolonial Studies"; Mohanty, "'Under Western Eyes' Revisited."

31. Mbembe, "What Is Postcolonial Thinking?," 1–3.

32. See Chakrabarty, *Provincializing Europe*, esp. chap. 3, "Translating Life-Worlds into Labor and History," 72–96.

33. A minor language is one constructed "by a minority in a major language," deterritorializing that language away from the concerns of the majority (majoritarian in terms of power, not necessarily numbers). Deleuze and Guattari, *Kafka*, 16; see also this volume, 225–26.

34. Deleuze and Guattari, *Kafka*, 22–23.

35. Rancière, *Disagreement: Politics and Philosophy*, xi–xii. See this volume, 12.

36. Rancière, *Disagreement: Politics and Philosophy*, 35–41. Identities "defined in the natural order of the allocation of functions and places" are transformed "into instances of experience of a dispute" (36).

37. Lionnet and Shih, *Creolization of Theory*, 27. Their primary example is the school of standpoint epistemology associated with Sandra Harding; for another example, see Sulli-

van and Tuana, *Race and Ignorance*, which also draws on the work of Jamaican philosopher Charles Mills. The work of American feminist philosophers, like that of other philosophers whose work tends to be more "critical" than "traditional" theory, has often been best received by and identified with other academic disciplines. See Butler, "The Other of Philosophy"

38. This volume, 75.

39. Rancière, *Disagreement: Politics and Philosophy*, xii, 27–35.

40. This volume, 4, 75, 86.

41. Mbembe, *On the Postcolony*, 102–3.

42. This volume, 4, 75.

43. This volume, 64–65. This is similar to the structuring role played by the "native informant" in the history of anthropology, according to Spivak, *Critique of Postcolonial Reason*, 4 and throughout. On general economy, see Bataille, "Notion of Expenditure."

44. This volume, 72: "Just because minds are decolonized does not mean that *positions* are. People often say certain things because they want to defend their bodies. The unthought gives rise, in other words, to social and political slips. This is not just an affair of *discourse*; it involves *language*."

45. This volume, 76, 80–81.

46. Chow, *World Target*, 13–15.

47. This volume, 13.

48. Luste Boulbina's quotations are taken from Kafka, *Récits, romans, journaux*, but I have used English translations from *Complete Stories*, with some alterations to preserve the connotations of the cited French edition.

49. His story implicitly refers to the Dreyfus Affair, which resulted in the wrongful imprisonment of Jewish/Alsatian officer Alfred Dreyfus on charges of treason. Dreyfus was first sent to New Caledonia and then spent five years in a Caribbean penal colony off the coast of French Guiana. Thus, Kafka's story points to the literal "carceral archipelago" of overseas prisons interwoven with the legal institutions of late nineteenth-century France ("black sites"?), but also to the forms of subjectivity created by the existence of an arbitrary penal apparatus geographically beyond the reach of most citizens' experience or critique. See Spieler, *Empire and Underworld*.

50. Benveniste, *Problems in General Linguistics*, 206–9. However, Luste Boulbina often uses the terms in the sense put forward by Foucault in *The Archaeology of Knowledge*. See "The Formation of Enunciative Modalities," 50–55; and "The Statement and the Archive," 79–125.

51. Most of her citations are to "The Uses and Disadvantages of History for Life," in *Untimely Meditations*.

52. Forsdick, "Colonialism."

53. This history is explained in Le Sueur, *Uncivil War*, 318–20. See this volume, 76–78.

54. Lazarus, *Postcolonial Unconscious*, 124–25.

55. Lazarus, *Postcolonial Unconscious*, 19, 124–27, 131.

56. De Certeau, *Heterologies*, 200–201.

57. For de Certeau, "On the Penal Colony" is a parable about the loss of any transcendent meaning behind the text inscribed by writing or torture; the historian substitutes an institution for this encounter with loss (*Heterologies*, 160–65). Chakrabarty, on the other hand, believes it can also be the starting point for a positive investigation of the past. See *Provincializing Europe*, 112.

58. See the scholarly introductions Luste Boulbina has written to her editions of Tocqueville's collected writings in *Sur l'Algerie* and *Sur l'esclavage*, as well as *De la démocratie en*

Amérique. In the following volume, French references are to Tocqueville's *Oeuvres Complètes*, to *Souvenirs*, and to the Pléïade edition of Tocqueville's *Oeuvres*. Many of these texts were made available to English readers in *Empire and Slavery*.

59. This volume, 117–18.

60. With René Girault and Gerard Bossuat, Luste Boulbina is the coeditor of *Pierre Mendès France et le rôle de la France dans le monde*.

61. This volume, 133–35.

62. This volume, 102–3. See Kant, "On Perpetual Peace," "Appendix I on the Disagreement between Morals and Politics in Relation to Perpetual Peace."

63. This volume, 132–33; Glissant, *Caribbean Discourse: Selected Essays*. Note that many discussions of political economy found in the original French edition are missing from the shortened English translation of *Le discours antillais*.

64. Rancière, *Disagreement: Politics and Philosophy*, 124–27.

65. In addition to Rancière, see Mouffe, *Democratic Paradox*.

66. The best-known explanation is in Freud, "Fetishism."

67. See Freud, "Screen Memories."

68. Leiris, *Phantom Africa*.

69. Said, *Orientalism*, 80–87; and this volume, 189–90.

70. The classic study is Merleau-Ponty's *Phenomenology of Perception*, 76–86. However, the phenomenon of the phantom limb is mentioned in Descartes's *Meditations on First Philosophy* and thus goes back to the origins of French philosophy.

71. Barkat, *Le corps d'exception*.

72. Haneke, *Caché (Hidden)*.

73. Bancel and Blanchard, "From Colonial to Postcolonial."

74. The architects of French military strategy in Algeria acknowledged participating in the training of counterinsurgency military and special operations forces in Brazil and Chile during those countries' respective dictatorships, pioneering certain "disappearance" techniques to demoralize and kill off the political opposition. The CIA has rightly been associated with those deadly policies, but during the early years of American involvement in Vietnam, the French were considered the experts because of their role in Algeria. Robin, *Death Squadrons*.

75. A. Gordon, *Ghostly Matters*. The literature on Morrison and "haunting" is substantial.

76. This volume, 166.

77. Lazarus, *Postcolonial Unconscious*, 161–62. As Lazarus explains in chapter 4, Fanon's legacy is torn between those who claim him for a liberationary political modernism and those who see him as paradigmatically postmodern in his attention to the divided and unstable nature of subjectivity. David Macey's biography *Frantz Fanon* builds on the modernist reading; Bhabha's "Interrogating Identity" (in *Nation and Narration*) represents the postmodern approach. Luste Boulbina's writing contributes to the ongoing reassessment of Fanon's legacy.

78. K. Yacine, "Le cadavre encerclé"; see this volume, 191–92. On postindependence governments' efforts to control history, see this volume, 204–5. Davoine and Gaudillière, *History beyond Trauma*.

79. The project of "decolonizing knowledge," which links it to the revival of indigenous languages as the medium for scholarship, is often associated with the work of Ngũgĩ wa Thiong'o. See *Decolonizing the Mind*.

80. Thanks to Srikanth Mallavarapu for this important observation.

81. This volume, 13.

82. This volume, 195–201. On this point, Luste Boulbina is indebted both to Michel de Certeau and to Dipesh Chakrabarty, for whom history asks questions that cannot always be answered in a historical idiom. As Chakrabarty puts it, disrupting the time of capital but unthinkable except in relation to it, "other temporalities, other forms of worlding, coexist and are possible." *Provincializing Europe*, 95.

83. This volume, 168.

84. See Fanon, "Algeria Unveiled," in *Dying Colonialism*. The critical entry point for such discussions has often been the function of sexual difference in nationalist discourse. This is the context in which it entered French philosophical discourse, introduced by Rada Iveković, a Yugoslav philosopher specializing in Indian thought. See *Le sexe*.

85. See Scott, *Politics of the Veil*.

86. Lazarus, *Postcolonial Unconscious*, 144–47; Spivak, "Can the Subaltern Speak?"

87. This volume, 111, 168; Davis, "Black Woman's Role."

88. This volume, 255, 257–61.

89. The Nardal sisters, Paulette and Jane, were acknowledged as mothers of negritude long after they translated Harlem Renaissance writers for the members of their influential Parisian salon. See Sharpley-Whiting, "Femme négritude," 10. Thanks to Cheryl Toman for pointing out this connection.

90. This volume, 293, 297–99.

91. This volume, 269–70.

92. Derrida, *Dissemination*. Cited in this volume, 11–12, 296.

93. Rancière, *Disagreement: Politics and Philosophy*, 23–7, 69, 116.

94. This volume, 233–34.

95. Perhaps it always was; see Morrissey, "Derrida, Algeria." *L'autre cap* [*The Other Heading*] (1991) addressed the self-definition of Europe after the end of the cold war. *Spectres de Marx* (1993) then foregrounded the relationship between the ghostly and specific historical specters of the East in which the ghostly was (self-preservingly and misleadingly) embodied. *De l'hospitalité* (1997), also inspired by Benveniste, intensified his focus on the immigrant as figure for contemporary Europe's condition of possibility. "Marx remains an immigrant *chez nous*; a glorious, sacred, accursed but still a clandestine immigrant as he was all his life. . . . One should not rush to make of the clandestine immigrant an illegal alien or, what always risks coming down to the same thing, to domesticate him." Derrida, *Specters of Marx*, 174.

96. On debates over the African status of Egypt in Western scholarship, see Davidson, *Search for Africa*, 19–22, 318–33.

97. This volume, 2, 275.

98. This volume, 273.

99. Deleuze, *Foucault*, 97.

100. Mudimbe, *Invention of Africa*, 34; Said, "*Reflections*," 243–44.

101. Said, *Representations of the Intellectual*.

102. This volume, 279; see also Luste Boulbina, *Les Arabes*.

103. Veyne, "Foucault Revolutionizes History," 158. Emphasis in the original.

104. This volume, 223.

105. Latour, *Never Been Modern*, 108–9.

106. Hiepko, "Europe and the Antilles."

107. "The unconscious memory of the abyss . . . the absolute unknown . . . in the end became knowledge." See *Poetics of Relation*, 7–8. See also, Hantel, "Errant Notes." Note that

Glissant thinks Deleuze and Guattari's use of *rhizome* is still too identitarian and prefers the starting point of *relation* (*Poetics of Relation*, 11). On the other hand, relation has much in common with Deleuze's ontological "whole" from which concepts select affects and vice versa in the cinema image (Deleuze, *Cinema 2*, 158–61). See Wiedorn for the possibility of mutual influences between Glissant and Deleuze, in *Think Like an Archipelago*, 69–70.

108. In this volume, Luste Boulbina refers to it as a "space for . . . fantasies and dreams" on p. 5.

109. Mignolo, "Order of Knowing," 160–62; this volume, 293–95.

110. See Bongie, "Édouard Glissant."

KAFKA'S MONKEY AND OTHER PHANTOMS OF AFRICA

PROLOGUE

Thinking the Colony

THERE IS ONE MAJOR DIFFERENCE BETWEEN THE *ILIAD* and the *Odyssey*: "The *Iliad* deliberately ignores the world of everyday things. It uses snow as a pretext for poetic metaphors, not as a physical reality. With the remarkable exception of Thersites . . . or of Dolon, the human world is only made of heroes and these heroes have no relations with the poor humans who are not at all heroic: shepherds, servants, artisans, sailors, peasants. . . . By contrast, in the *Odyssey*, the epic rediscovers flesh, cold, hunger, night, the seasons, ordinary men."[1] The distance between the *Illiad* and the *Odyssey* is nothing less than the gulf between personal experience and its social and above all its political representation, between documents and monuments, or between analyses and judgments (praise or blame). The *Iliad* gives us the world of the powerful, the *Odyssey* the experience of the others.

"The Sirens," writes Michel Foucault, "are the elusive and forbidden form of the alluring voice. They are nothing but song. Only a silvery wake in the sea, the hollow of a wave, a cave in the rocks, the whiteness of the beach—what are they in their very being if not a pure appeal, if not the mirthful void of listening, if not attentiveness, if not an invitation to pause?"[2] They are a kind of Medusa for the ears. "What makes them seductive," he continues, "is less what they make it possible to hear than what sparkles in the remoteness of their words, the future of what they say." Comparing Ulysses's adventure with that of Orpheus, Foucault considers that "each of their voices is then freed; Ulysses' with his salvation and the possibility of telling the tale of his marvelous adventure; Orpheus's with his absolute loss and never-ending lament." And what if Ulysses quite simply had imagined the Sirens' song? What if he heard nothing? He wanted to hear nothing—that much we know—for fear of losing and never being able to recover himself. Ulysses certainly wanted to turn a deaf ear. But what if the Sirens had fallen silent on these Mediterranean shores?

Among Kafka's posthumous papers, Max Brod found a text written in 1917 with the title "The Silence of the Sirens."[3] In another language than his "own" (German), in an "other" version of his own language, Kafka described

Ulysses at sea. In this very short text, he presents us with a remarkable act of resistance: "To protect himself from the Sirens Ulysses stopped his ears with wax and had himself bound to the mast of his ship."[4] Excellent precaution! In fact, "when Ulysses approached them the potent songstresses actually did not sing," but our fabulous hero "was thinking of nothing but his wax and his chains": "Ulysses, if one may so express it, did not hear their silence; he thought they were singing and that he alone did not hear them."[5] The wily Ulysses, for Kafka, was deafened in advance.

What did he think he might hear? He bound himself and immobilized himself. What fright could have moved him? Are there many prisoners like Ulysses? The eyes of Kafka's silent Sirens are filled with tears. Did Ulysses see them? Did he notice what was right in front of him? *Away from home*, was the wily hero afraid of *no longer belonging*?

Kafka continued, "Perhaps he had really noticed, although here the human understanding is beyond its depths, that the Sirens were silent" even though "Ulysses, it was said, was so full of guile, was such a fox, that not even the goddess of fate could pierce his armor."[6] This heroic attitude is all the stronger, or more strongly affirmed, as the Sirens are (by virtue of family roots if not by nationality) Algerian women, Senegalese women, Tunisian, Ivoirian, from Guyana, Martinique, Vietnam, Guadaloupe, Réunion, Caledonia, Cameroon, and so on. "One" stops up one's ears even when "they" neither speak nor sing. As Kafka told the story, if the Sirens are simultaneously neither seen (tears) nor heard (silence), this is primarily because Ulysses defends the depths of his psyche like a besieged fortress. But did the Sirens not suffer anything from this defense?

When Foucault explores the myth, he evokes the "sweet and violent movement intrud[ing] on interiority," a movement that makes the figure of the "companion" rise up: "a form arises—less than a form, a kind of stubborn, amorphous anonymity—that divests interiority of its identity, hollows it out, divides it into noncoincident twin figures, divests it of its unmediated right to say *I*, and pits against its discourse a speech that is indissociably echo and denial."[7] If Ulysses, indeed, had not deafened himself, he would never have been able to tell the tale of his "marvelous adventure." And the Sirens had a certain message: "We know all the suffering, all the suffering inflicted by the gods on the people of Argos and Troy on the fields of Troad." The song of the Sirens, "presented as though in negative outline," Foucault writes, "is but the attraction of song; yet what it promises the hero is nothing other than a duplicate of what he has lived through, known, suffered, precisely what he himself is."[8]

It is imperative that we help Ulysses and his companions to sharpen their ears and give the Sirens a better hearing. Can Ulysses speak in the Sirens' name? This is doubly impossible. Ulysses is deaf. We must therefore ask ourselves what conditions of possibility might enable a kind of hearing that is not just sufficient but also necessary. As Aristotle well knew, no one "can be taught" unless he or she is endowed, even before memory, with the sense of hearing.[9] But the Sirens are also, as in Kafka's text, (relatively) silent. At the same time as we investigate obstacles to hearing, therefore, we must also wonder what conditions of possibility would allow the Sirens to have speech in a full sense. On the one hand, then, Ulysses must be able to hear the Sirens, but on the other hand, they must also speak to Ulysses.[10] Besides, perhaps this will then bring their weeping to an end.

It is a mistake to believe, like Ulysses, that hearing others leads to dying. It is true that, in a way, to listen is to die to oneself. Indeed, to listen one must depart from oneself (Emmanuel Lévinas stresses this when he affirms that listening to someone means to stop looking at them). My proposal is therefore, however strange and uncomfortable this may be, to establish a dialogue in the full sense of the term between Ulysses and the Sirens, between the "ones" and the "others," the two shores of the onetime colony (the expression must be understood philosophically and not geographically). My proposal is to establish this discursively—dialogically. For this, migration is necessary, as is a change of place (common places).[11]

In my opinion, the "spontaneous philosophy" of Ulysses and his contemporary companions involves two grave errors. The first consists in borrowing the keyword "*colonization*" [*colonisation*] from colonial politics, or employing a politically problematic category in a "scientific" manner. Colonization is a project that can be carried out only from the standpoint of the colonizing state. For the colonizing state, it is an indefinite process that cannot be finished while disagreements and differences remain. What is already too much for those colonized will never be enough for the colonizers. Submission is never complete or finished because, in the last instance, the colonized themselves refuse to let it be settled. Thus, if we are rigorous, such a political category can never become a category of analysis.

The second error consists of putting the cart before the horse in making decolonization something that precedes the establishment of independence.

Independence is generally considered to be the endpoint of decolonization. Now, logically, a given territory cannot simultaneously be both a colony and a decolonized space. There we have a contradiction in terms. To make the end of territorial occupation and the birth of new sovereignties into the last word of colonial history is ultimately an underhanded strategy for making a clean slate of the past.[12] It is a way of looking at history as if it were the history of states and not of societies. There we must learn to see things differently: the advent of independence was only the start of decolonization. We must do our philosophical work differently, and think the colony itself.

What an absurd enterprise this must be—wanting to think the colony! I can already hear the objections: this is neither history nor geography; this is neither something one does nor something that should be done. The colony exists only in abstracto. In concreto, there are only acts of colonization and of decolonization. There are historical phenomena. There are no other (valid) philosophical categories. In concreto, above all, there are forms of knowledge, not hypotheses. And yet—on the one hand, there are empires, and on the other, colonies. One can reason about the notion of empire. Can one reason about the notion of the colony?

Meanwhile, the attachment of various colonies to a single state, the one that established them, produces remarkable transitions in space. One example: Louis Léon César Faidherbe, the polytechnic graduate and officer of genius from Lille, operated just as well in Guadaloupe as in Algeria or Senegal.[13] In these travels, but also in the relocations that he carried out, he demonstrated that the primary characteristic of these three places was to be French colonies.[14] The colony-metropole relation can sometimes overshadow the fact that the colonial space is a space of circulation and dissemination.

Jean-Loup Amselle has given us a portrait of Faidherbe as "republican raciologist," as "inventor of the notion of 'black Africa,'" and as "father of French Africanism."[15] For example, today the North/South division of the African continent and its black/white distinction are so well established that one might think there was no religious continuity—such as Islam—between the South and the North, the black and the white.[16] Europeans as well as Africans regard the Sahara as a natural border more than as a space without borders, a space of encounters and crossings. Amselle takes up the idea according to which the colonization of Senegal was carried out on the model deployed in Algeria (transition from restrained occupation to domination, recourse to the raids [*razzias*] so prized by Bugeaud, creation of "Arab bureaus," etc.). Even the Algerian spahis were brought to Senegal.[17] Faidherbe simultaneously employed the Algerian model and used it to differentiate North African and sub-Saharan societies. As applied in Algeria, this strategy involved denying those whom he encountered their status as political subjects, destroying autochthonous modes of government, and, finally, seeking out "acceptable interlocutors" that he thought he could find among those who were mixed.[18]

The vicious circle thereby created is paradigmatic of any colonial situation, despite the differences existing between the various French colonies. In a general sense, the set of colonizing acts contributed to the formation of a colonial language that, like the language of conscience, need not be spoken aloud to exist. This is exactly what Frantz Fanon—like Faidherbe, displaced from one periphery to another, but unlike him, excluded from the metropolitan center—observed in Algeria a century later.[19] Processes of colonization may have been processes of forced territorialization, which rules out neither importations nor exportations, nor all sorts of wanderings, but they also resulted in remarkable movements of deterritorialization.

Perhaps more than anywhere else, the colony is a space for the most audacious and the least censured fantasies and dreams. Speech unravels there, just as social bonds come undone. The situation is shared by colonies everywhere. For the colonizer, a colony is already, more than anything else, an imaginary world and a territory of the imaginary. In this respect, Christopher Columbus could be taken as the paradigmatic colonizer. He did not find what he was looking for, but he imagined and dreamed intensely (of gold, above all). His trajectory traced a path of distress and terror. Indeed, conquest differs from invasion in not being carried out by neighbors; conquest arrives from afar and is secured at close range. Its image is the desert, whether American or Algerian. The desert is the image of unknown desires that are satiated with specific techniques, by means of men and women who can be thrown away, by force, in one's name, for one's use, for one's profit, and for one's pleasure.[20]

Notes

1. Barel, *Le héros*, 59.

2. This and the following quotations are from Foucault's reflection on "La pensée du dehors" which appeared in the review *Critique* in June 1966; see "Thought of the Outside," 160–62.

3. "Silence of the Sirens," in Kafka, *Complete Stories*, 430–32. Translator's note: In some cases the English translation has been altered to preserve the connotations of the French edition. Max Brod (1884–1968) was, like Kafka, a German-speaking Jewish Czech. He was a journalist and a writer, as well as Kafka's literary executor.

4. Kafka, "Silence of the Sirens," 431. In the Homeric text, Ulysses binds himself to the mast, and his sailors are the ones who stop up their ears.

5. Kafka, "Silence of the Sirens," 431.

6. Kafka, "Silence of the Sirens," 432. The French translation reads "ne pouvait pas pénétrer jusqu'en son for le plus profond," which emphasizes the psychological nature of this armor.

7. Foucault, "Thought of the Outside," 163.

8. Foucault, "Thought of the Outside," 161.

9. "Those [animals] which besides memory have this sense of hearing can be taught," Aristotle, *Metaphysics*, 689 (980b).

10. It is a matter of reversing the common attitude: "the strongest" speaks "to the weakest," before opening his ears and closing the mouth. Who is speaking? Of what? How? To whom? The specific positions of interlocution are always worth exploring.

11. See the notion of enunciative third-space in the thought of Homi K. Bhabha: "The intervention of the Third Space of enunciation, which makes the structure of meaning and reference an ambivalent process, destroys this mirror of representation in which cultural knowledge is customarily revealed as an integrated, open, expanding code. Such an intervention quite properly challenges our sense of the historical identity of culture as a homogenizing, unifying force, authenticated by the originary Past, kept alive in the national tradition of the People." Bhabha, *Location of Culture*, 37.

12. For example, hardly had independence been proclaimed when, in the same spaces, the French policy of Francophonie was set in place.

13. He was active in Algeria from 1844 to 1846 and then, after a spell in Guadeloupe in 1848, from 1849 to 1852. Then he was named governor of Senegal from 1854 to 1861 and from 1863 to 1865. After that, he was sent once again to Algeria. In 1857, he was the general commanding the subdivision of Bône.

14. It is not by accident that he imported plants from Algeria or Saint-Domingue into Senegal. Plants from Saint-Domingue were already being imported during the conquest of Algeria. The Antilleans were charged with training "modern" native farmers. Moreover, the Senegalese infantry were created in the model of the Algerian infantry. See also Frederickson, "Identité nationale."

15. Amselle, *Affirmative Exclusion*, 77–78.

16. "It is by playing on a shared but already diversified foundation of customs, practices, and norms that Muslim law brought about a demarcation between related social systems, a demarcation that colonial codification subsequently reinforced. Only by disregarding the influence of Islam were colonial administrators and ethnologists able to divide these systems into a series of discontinuous entities." Amselle, *Affirmative Exclusion*, 30.

17. Translator's note: Spahis were a regiment of Algerian cavalry integrated into the French army. Thomas Robert Bugeaud (1784–1849) was governor-general of Algeria from 1840 to 1846. He had a long career in the French army, including service under Napoleon; served in the chamber of deputies (the lower house of Parliament) during the 1830s; and was known for his antidemocratic politics. Between 1836 and 1837, he essentially accomplished the French conquest of Algeria, although he had to fight repeated uprisings.

18. For a discussion of the French government's perpetual failure to find "acceptable interlocutors" [*interlocuteurs valables*] among the architects of Algerian independence, see pt. 1, chap. 3, of this volume.

19. Frantz Fanon, born in Martinique in 1925, was named medical director of the psychiatric hospital of Blida in Algeria in 1953 after having published *Peau noire, masques blancs* in 1952. He represented the GPRA (Provisional Government of the Algerian Republic) in many African colonies, particularly in Ghana.

20. It is enough to glance at colonial images. See Deroo and Lemaire, *L'illusion colonial.*

PART I

KAFKA'S MONKEY AND OTHER REFLECTIONS ON THE COLONY

1

WITH RESPECT TO KAFKA'S MONKEY

> **There are many who consider as an injury to themselves any conduct which they have a distaste for, and resent it as an outrage to their feelings; as a religious bigot, when charged with disregarding the religious feelings of others, has been known to retort that they disregard his feelings, by persisting in their abominable worship or creed.**
>
> **John Stuart Mill, *On Liberty***

ONE GENERALLY THINKS OF THE POSTCOLONY AS THE situation of states that gained independence after having been colonies under foreign domination.[1] Implicitly, this suggests that colonial space is defined by the colonized territories and excludes the metropole, which is supposed to escape the grasp of colonization. But this is hardly the case. Certainly colonial space is divided, but it is also shared. This is why, like Cameroon, Vietnam, or Algeria, contemporary France can be regarded as a postcolony with respect to its history. It is affected by the advent of independence as well as by its past as a colonial empire. Above all, this means that the political and intellectual work of *decolonization* involves France as much as France's former colonies. The colonizer country is no less thoroughly impregnated by the colony than the colonized country is, albeit in a different way.

We must move beyond outdated representations. The philosopher's task is to flush such representations out of hiding so that we can be freed from them. The point of this chapter is to propose, through a reading of Kafka, a subject-oriented analysis of colonial and postcolonial situations.

Assimilation, Asceticism, Illness

The Greeks knew two forms of spatial exclusion: ostracism, which involved expelling whoever was considered an "evil from above," and the Thargelia ritual, which consisted in expelling whoever was considered an "evil from below." In both cases a human measure was established relative to what is divine and heroic on the one hand and to what is bestial and monstrous on the other. Jacques Derrida analyzed this ancient ritual of exclusion in *Dissemination*.[2] The problem is one of differences and distribution/division [*partage*] implicit in the distinction between the intra muros and the extra muros: "The ceremony of the *pharmakos* is thus played out on the boundary line between inside and outside, which it has as its function to ceaselessly trace and retrace. *Intra muros/extra muros*. The origin of difference and division, the *pharmakos* represents evil both introjected and projected."[3]

Just as in the past, those who are socially excluded today are not exterior to a society; they are outside [*dehors*] while playing an intrinsic part. They are an "inner enemy" whose archetypes can be found in the double figure of the delinquent and the immigrant. More recently, the leper gave rise to exclusionary rituals, but so did madness and poverty.[4] Michel Foucault showed that exclusion was not the same as expulsion. The "great confinement" of the seventeenth century, with its general hospital holding 1 percent of the Parisian population and its houses of correction or work, marked the dividing line between the "good poor" who merited assistance and the "bad poor" who called for repression. It drew a boundary. The great confinement was a matter of preventing every form of mobility or circulation. Indeed, circulation was considered a form of wandering (from whence the prohibition on begging). In the nineteenth century, lepers were treated like plague carriers, meaning that a grid-based technology of disciplinary power was applied to the excluded space whose inhabitants (beggars, vagabonds, madmen, the violent) were symbolized by the leper. Disciplinary power cuts two ways: it individualizes those who are excluded, but its procedures of individualization also stigmatize and serve to mark the fact of exclusion.

Exclusion is an example of what Jacques Rancière calls the *mésentente* (disagreement).[5] If exclusion designates a deprived space, a space of freedom without circulation, this makes it into the object of a genuinely political conflict. Rancière proposes that the ancients (Greeks or Romans) invented politics when they accepted the existence of a faction (*part*) formed by those who have no share in society's goods (*sans part*). Thus, politics emerges when the simple effects of domination are interrupted by an act in which freedom is recognized, understood here as a status of those who lack "status." Socially speaking, there is no faction of those without a share; the only shares that exist are shares in society. But this means that exclusion is the sign of a wrong, a tort.[6]

Politics introduces the tort of incommensurability, the contradiction of two worlds lodged in a single world (with a conflict over the existence of a common scene). One world is occupied by those who count socially, the other by those who do not. The political dimension must therefore be distinguished from that of the police. The *police* refers here to the distribution of places and functions—to redistribution, properly speaking. Politics, on the other hand, refers to the institution of those who by definition lack any place, the institution of democratic equality.[7] Politics involves the encounter between police logic and egalitarian logic, an encounter giving rise to subject positions, or *subjectivation*. But political subjectivation is not social identification with a given place or role; quite to the contrary, it is socially disidentifying.

The moralists known to Nietzsche certainly observed the aggressivity suffusing all social relations, even the most polite and the best policed. "It is monstrous to consider how easy it is for us to ridicule, censure, and despise others, and how we enjoy it," affirmed La Bruyère in *Les caractères* (1688), "and yet how enraged we are when others ridicule, censure, and despise us."[8] But in reality, whatever one might say, the roles of ridiculer and ridiculed are not interchangeable. The moralists were quite aware that civility is a shared illusion that hides differences in the distribution of power and wealth, or more generally in positions and social goods. To put it more simply, it is the valet who must swallow it all [*tout avaler*]. Nothing prevents the master from saying what he likes. Apparent situations of reciprocity dissimulate the profound asymmetry at work in esteem. This is because these situations replace a conflict (of interests) with a play (of appearances).

If some people have the capacity de facto to be "givers" of symbolic gratification beyond the appearances of social play, others are in the position of "petitioners." The individual who must ask waits to be acknowledged, to be admitted. According to Jean Starobinski,

> one suspects that the pleasure is less attached to the persons by whom one is accepted than to the recognition the petitioner asks for, the esteem that he or she is henceforth entitled to feel. It is the pleasure of being "distinguished," of being judged worthy to take part in a "circle." On the other hand, for the one or ones who "receive," who "recruit," who "prefer" to admit others, pleasure comes first and foremost from being able to exercise a choice, feeling able to refuse access, and finally in consulting criteria of similarity which require the petitioner to confirm, by his or her whole being and conduct, the ideal image

> that the members of the "circle" have of themselves: they will only accept someone who resembles them and who, by his or her merits and agreements, offers a reflection of their own value.[9]

This description could serve as a definition of the "complex of the colonized." It could also shed light on the notion of "symbolic violence."[10] Nonetheless, the criterion of admission, being narcissistic, is an image and not a reality—an ideal, not a practice. One has illusions of getting along. Thus Michael Walzer notes, "In ordinary speech, it is often said that toleration is always a relationship of inequality where the tolerated groups or individuals are cast in an inferior position. To tolerate someone else is an act of power; to be tolerated is an acceptance of weakness."[11] He draws an analogy between the majority and government: the majority tolerates "cultural difference" in the same way that the government tolerates political opposition.[12] From this standpoint, belonging to the majority is simply a matter of considering oneself able to judge, to admit, and to exclude: in short, to decide.[13] It is the askers who must demonstrate the appropriate degree of asceticism, even if they ask for nothing strictly speaking and even if the judges themselves must offer similar proofs.

Indeed, asceticism is generally defined as a kind of self-control that is inevitably accompanied by frustrations. But originally *ascèse* (*askèsis*) referred to every form of exercise, particularly gymnastic exercise. It is a type of labor that shapes the body, a discipline in the strict sense of the term. In this sense, the ascetic ideal is both a physical and a moral ideal. To be sure, as Nietzsche has shown, this is why the ascetic ideal is a pillar of mental strength [*morale*] and of morality as practiced.[14] It is altogether noteworthy that in Nietzsche's philosophy, asceticism appears as a subjective tactic of the weak, who seek to carry out in morality what they cannot carry out in reality (socially): the subjective response of a minority who, paradoxically, may be the numerical majority in a population.

For *minority* does not necessarily mean numerically insignificant. In this respect, there are two paradigmatic cases: first, women, whom one may consider a minority historically speaking, as much on the economic and social plane as on the political and cultural plane;[15] second, the colonized. In Algeria prior to independence, for example, former *indigènes* (natives) were an economic, social, political, juridical, and cultural minority although they made up the vast majority of the population. Minority in the largest possible sense exists the moment there is no equality, neither on the political plane, nor the social plane, nor the economic plane, nor the cultural plane. Often equality is also lacking on the juridical plane. Religious minorities (Jews and Protestants in Europe) are a specific kind of minority. What unites all minorities, in their great heterogeneity, is not living under the (bad) gaze of the other; that would simplify things unfairly. Rather, it is living under a gaze one might grant to the other from a ferocious obligation to conform—not to the other him- or herself, but to ideals that are ultimately (if differently) shared. Adepts of internalization . . .

A tyrannical and cruel superego, Freud would say, guards over women, Jews, and other Protestants—a domestic tyrant, in Nietzsche's vocabulary, who administers and domesticates the aggressivity accumulated by what, for simplicity's sake, we call domination, with this caution: that it should be imagined as a *relation* of force, and not as a force exercised by some over others. The older term *power* (*puissance*) could also be used.

If philosophers are not priests, as Nietzsche insisted in his time, they always share with priests a favorable prejudice toward asceticism. It must be said that they are, practically speaking, specialists in asceticism. How should we approach asceticism more generally, particularly the asceticism of minorities? The narcissistic dimension of asceticism is linked to the implicit pursuit of an impossible recognition. Asceticism is an illness, to be sure, but it is also the price of simple survival under conditions of social suffering.

How might we analyze the "last match of a legend," starting from Nietzsche's analysis?[16]

> Like an overly spoiled and badly raised child, he botched his farewell [*raté son sortie*]. During the final match of the World Cup in Germany on Sunday July 9, Zinédine Zidane tarnished the conclusion to his story as a soccer player of genius with an unacceptable, intolerable, unforgivable head butt. . . . A head butt, everything collapses, and forgotten precedents come to mind once again. . . . A head butt, and what reappears is the character's dark aspect, his black face, other side of the rumored image about one of France's favorite public figures. Sunday, the Italians beat the Blues in the World Cup final. But France lost Zizou.[17]

These few lines make the French soccer champion look like a kind of Mr. Hyde hidden behind the good doctor Jekyll, as if this were the nth misdeed (twelfth red card) of a man with no manners. Signs of his "origin"? The mark of his "community"?[18] "He ruined his legend," claimed the journalist in an article that, curiously, said nothing about Marco Materazzi's attitude. Everyone lectured the champion sanctimoniously: "Zinédine," one wrote in an open letter, "do you know that the hardest thing this morning is not trying to understand why the Blues, your Blues, lost the World Cup match yesterday evening. The hardest thing is explaining to tens of millions of children around the world how you could have let yourself batter Marco Materazzi with a head butt ten minutes from the end of overtime."[19] Is it justifiable to throw even one Christian to the lions for the pleasure of so many Romans? At least journalists had a culprit to sink their teeth into (but were they the only ones?). In general, this is what one calls *scapegoating*. Sacrifice or envy? In any case, we have a trial at the end of the game. *Two* players would never let themselves go like that. In the final account, there was only one *bad* player.

Nietzsche would have found such events enjoyable: so many occasions to confirm his intuitions, his hypotheses, his analyses! If Zinédine failed, according to public opinion, it was not in fact as an athlete but rather as an ascetic. From all the evidence, Zinédine Zidane does not embody the ascetic ideal—or this at least is why he is reproached or accused of failing. But this is the ascetic priest's point of view. Is it by chance that conformity to the ascetic ideal should be expected of someone descended from an indigène?

Where do "our" ideas about foreigners come from?[20] In *Le sol et le sang*, Hervé Le Bras shows that the current fear of immigration is "intimately bound up with the colonial adventure" but also "reverses the factors" involved.[21] His book then offers the history of this reversal. Telling his extraordinary story, serious and almost grotesque, the author describes his inner ruminations [*ressort intime*], thereby showing that no history of ideas and opinions holds true without a history of sentiments (fear, hope, etc.). The demographer begins with the historical transformation of emigration into colonization. From the eighteenth to the nineteenth century, a profound mutation took place. If migrations were at first regarded as doomed to failure, a century later migration in the form of colonization became an obvious solution.

In his theory of climates, Montesquieu's characterization of places makes them into roots that cannot be pulled up without damage.[22] The industrialization and economic liberalism imposed during the nineteenth century, however, led to the intellectual neutralization of sites and emphasized space as an undifferentiated and particularly indifferent dimension. It was also a medium of movement—that is, for the transport of commodities and the migration of populations. Finally, the appearance and development of Malthusianism correlated colonization with emigration. The

"Anglo-Saxon race" was "fortifying" itself through emigration; therefore, the French, affected by a lower birth rate, must revive themselves by "bleeding" to the colonies in order to grow in number and power. The premises were in place. The twentieth century did not mark a rupture but continued the prior evolution, notably under authoritarian regimes, such that the "fear of invasion was imposed as the inverse image of the desire for conquest and colonization."[23]

However, showing that colonization has two faces that play against and intertwine with the two opposing sentiments of hope and fear is not even the most trenchant element of le Bras's analysis. For the conceptual frameworks through which we grasp migrations derive from a hydraulic model that, despite its obviously fictive character, still remains in force. Authors who are quite distant from one another, historically as well as politically, approach the facts in the same way. This shows how much the collective vision of "scholars" contributes to the forging of common reference points in their subject matter, or, in the expression Le Bras borrows from Hans Gadamer, to "tradition's founding prejudices."[24] The imaginative matrix of migrations is found in the slippage from a hydrologic metaphor into a hydraulic one, such that the irregularities of landscape, uneven terrains, and dissimilar situations are wiped out and replaced by a single element—pressure—considered less as one factor among others than as essentially decisive. Migrations then exemplify the physics of fluids. All our metaphors come from liquids under pressure, and whatever the nature of the pressure might be, the individuals in this imaginary are irresistibly pushed out of their homes and toward the "French desert" in particular. These visions are underwritten by ignorance of geography.

Many points in the critique of the French political and social imaginary remain in shadow or are passed over silently. Reasoning in terms of pressures and flows excludes any factor other than demographics from the analysis of specific, historically dated migrations. Indeed, although this imaginary may have a chronology, it is certainly lacking in history. In other words, chronology here is nothing but forgotten history. Populations themselves are divided up in crazy ways. Where, for example, does the "European" begin and end? Immigrants and migrants are always put in groups. The migrant, for example, has two sides [*profiles*]: either he is a worker, or he is a resident. The worker is not a resident (right side view of the "good" migrant); the resident is not a worker (left side view of the "bad" migrant).

The causal relationship between the state and the nation is inverted. Because of its past, the nation is supposed to support the state, particularly through colonization. Today, it is the state that takes charge of supporting the nation because of immigration. The construction of the bond between the people and the land that Ratzel established with respect to colonization is henceforth applied, in an inverse manner, with respect to immigration.[25] And when political oppositions are naturalized, as we see today, political positions form around the substantialization of exclusions. Grouping takes place through concentric circles, from the nearest to the farthest, from the assimilable to the irreducible. In the past, one was not supposed to travel too far away; henceforth one must not come from too far away. Given this, are we near or far from the concerns of Bertillon, for whom naturalization was going to give rise to "artificial Frenchmen" sporting "fake French noses"?[26] Every ideology of the nation is accompanied by a representation of the world's nations as a whole. The general grouping of populations is managed by random selection of some "populations," which are then arranged hierarchically against the backdrop of the "rest of the world." There are friends and enemies, there are foreigners, and beyond them, there are peoples who are unknown.

When there is geography, it is a political geography of resemblances [*affinités*] under cover of "criteria," whether these are biological or cultural—because the very same people can become other, and the near can become distant. An example: for France, the Kabyles are placed in the first circle of resemblance/proximity, North Africans in the second, Arabs in the third. This indicates how France locates herself in her dreams. It is also a way of turning what is voluntary (I choose) into something involuntary (the fact is that . . .) and making the arbitrary into the legitimate. Qualities considered "exotic" then indicate the strangeness of the strangest among the foreigners. The sudden appearance of "multicolor populations" shows that France is not in any sense too colorful. What is assimilation, after all? It is the passage from one circle to another, until one reaches the very center: the French "hard core."[27]

The complex of the colonized refers to the impossibility of getting rid of oneself.[28] In fact, there is a manifest contradiction in the fact of being oneself and of wanting, at the same time and place, to be an *other*. The complex of the colonized expresses the passion to be an other. The inability to get rid of oneself reinforces the tyranny that colonized subjects, the candidates for assimilation, exercise with respect to themselves. Would they not have to change skin to change their situation? "The crushing of the colonized," writes Albert Memmi, "is included among the colonizer's values. As soon as the colonized adopts those values, he similarly adopts his own condemnation. In order to free himself, at least so he believes, he agrees to destroy himself. This phenomenon is comparable to Negrophobia in a Negro, or anti-Semitism in a Jew."[29] The complex of the colonized bears witness to the human price required to have, in the best case, an honorable self-image. The complex of the colonized is an expression of the ascetic ideal in which self-esteem and the absence of shame are supposed to (re)compensate for the irrevocable renunciation that is apparently their enabling condition.

Asceticism means you can't let yourself go, can't be carefree. Nietzsche writes in the *Genealogy of Morals*:

> When the oppressed, downtrodden, outraged exhort one another with the vengeful cunning of impotence: "let us be different from the evil, namely good! And he is good who does not outrage, who harms nobody, who does not attack, who does not requite, who leaves revenge to God, who keeps himself hidden as we do, who avoids evil and desires little from life, like us, the patient, humble, and just"—this, listened to calmly and without previous bias, really amounts to no more than "we weak ones are, after all, weak; it would be good if we did nothing *for which we are not strong enough*."[30]

Asceticism grows on the background of impossible vengeance, forbidden reprisals, prohibited violence. It thus appears as the most onerous response as well as the response best adapted to an unfavorable relationship. Making a virtue of necessity: this is the enigma of asceticism, what the Americans call *self-help*—how to redeem oneself in ten easy lessons. Asceticism is the price of dignity; it's an investment in self-esteem, a reactive phenomenon.

Thus, through the effect of an accounting system modeled on the principle of communicating vessels, the magnitude of self-esteem is measured by endurance proportional to the suffering undergone, to patience in the face of felt violence, and so on. An eye for an eye, a tooth for a tooth—for each blow received, asceticism responds by showing merit. A funny calculus. "The slave's eye," writes Nietzsche, "is not favorable to the virtues of the powerful: he is skeptical and suspicious, *subtly* suspicious, of all the 'good' that is honored there—he would like to persuade himself that even their happiness is not genuine. Conversely, those qualities are brought out and flooded with light which serve to ease existence for those who suffer: here pity, the complaisant and obliging hand, the warm heart, patience, industry, humility, and friendliness are honored—for here these are the most useful qualities and almost the only means for enduring the pressure of existence."[31]

All these qualities, one might notice, are also virtues considered feminine.[32] They are even the hallmark of femininity. Egoism, indifference, impatience, negligence, pride, and arrogance have never been considered feminine attributes anywhere. Nietzsche's analysis does not carry over to the benefits gained from such conduct. In fact, those benefits are only secondary. They serve to mask the cost, or rather the sacrifice, implied by such a morality. The supposed advantages are only the trees that hide the forest. What Nietzsche reveals is the control of behavior and, indissociably, thought that is concealed by endurance, humility, and the sense of justice. In his eyes, these qualities are nothing but expressions—first of inferiority, second of powerlessness. This comes down to affirming, in a narrower sense, that being in a minority situation means being in a state of powerlessness, in the grip of distress like a child.

Asceticism goes against nature, but as Nietzsche says, it subjects *ressentiment* to a "positive" transformation. Ressentiment is the counterpart of powerlessness in social relations. Asceticism is a way of *sublimating* this powerlessness. With ressentiment, we see the invention of responsibility. For those who are "weak," ressentiment changes the powerful into those who are guilty. But above all, ressentiment transforms itself: it gives birth to bad conscience. In fact, as soon as one substitutes responsibility for affects (such as anger), one ends by regarding deeds or facts [*faits*] as faults. "It's your fault," cries ressentiment. Accusation is invented. "It's my fault," confesses the bad conscience. Guilt is invented. Henceforth everything is material for a trial.

What goes on in the head of someone who starts the process by making a request? Freud's "dream of the uncle with the yellow beard" appears at the crossroads of ressentiment and bad conscience.[33] This magnificent dream reveals the repression and the censorship at work in asceticism, in the renunciation of our dearest desires, in the prudence that social life imposes on some more than on others, in the disguises imposed on expression. It shows the unconscious accounting that is at the dream's origin. All innocence, like all guilt, needs memory to establish itself.[34]

Freud wished, justifiably, to be appointed extraordinary professor at the University of Vienna.[35] In the spring of 1897, he recalls, he learned that two professors at the university had nominated him for the post. Meanwhile, because he knew that other eminent colleagues were also eager to be named, he forced himself not to believe in it too much. But one day, one of his friends, who was also waiting to find out, visited him and related that someone at the ministry had told him explicitly that "in view of the present state of feeling," certain nominations were prevented by "denominational considerations." Obviously Freud understood right away that, being Jewish, his nomination was not just difficult or complicated but impossible. All hope was pointless.

"It's his fault," thinks the dreamer, searching for an easy way out. In fact, the dream makes Freud's friend an imbecile like his uncle Joseph. It makes another of Freud's colleagues into a criminal, who could never deserve a professorship at this level (unlike Freud, who is personally intelligent and honest!). And Freud continues thus: "I felt obliged to proceed still further with my interpretation of the dream. . . . *I am not yet calm*, I cannot accept my fate in the lightheartedness with which I had degraded two of my respected colleagues in order to keep open my own path to a professorship."[36] To unravel the ruses of this dream, Freud compares psychic to social life: "Where two persons are concerned, one of whom possesses a certain degree of power which the second is obliged to take into account . . . the second person will distort his psychical acts."[37] "A similar difficulty," he adds, "confronts the political writer who has disagreeable truths to tell to those in authority."

As Pascal so rightly put it, there is no arguing with force: action is always wordless.[38] Thought is what needs words. Thus, a discursive dimension that can be difficult to identify is present in asceticism. Asceticism is not only a form of intelligence but also an art of commentary. When cruelty's principal target is the self, for one's greater good, when its pangs [*delices*] are felt every day, then thought and discourse take on the task of transforming this cruelty into justice, torment into morality. It would truly be unfortunate not to notice the speculative dimension of ressentiment, the reflexivity proper to minority belonging (although this word is defective), and, finally, the great spirituality of asceticism. Because hermeneutically, asceticism feeds suffering: it is, in concreto, an interpretation of suffering. The ne plus ultra for the ascetic will be considering (concretely to be sure) the sufferings he or she endures as punishments to which he or she consents.

Nietzsche launched his campaign against morality in 1881, with *Daybreak*. Though he denounces the savagery at work in morality, he has to admit that in morality it is reason that "gains only a hard and bloody victory within the soul" to subdue "powerful counter-drives."[39] Asceticism is thus a victory of rationality over instinct, of humanity over animality. But paradoxically, this rationalization, this humanization, and this moralization take place through stupefaction.[40] Thus, asceticism involves a double paradox: on the one hand because it involves the valorization of a life against life, on the other because it involves dumbing oneself down in order to become intelligent.

No one has better described the complexity of asceticism than Kafka, including the torments of bad conscience and the difficulty of being accidentally but also structurally a member of a minority. The ascetics, these hunger artists, attempt to show that their sufferings are not their own fault. They try to justify themselves. Protesting their innocence, the Nietzschean dog, the Kafkaesque animal, and the wild beast become domestic pet are eager to establish that wrongs are not shared.[41] They want to wash themselves of all suspicion. They will have to prove their asceticism, their purity, their innocence. Next, they will have to gather their memories. In this context, memory is surely the reactive force that animates the weak, those who, in the portrait drawn by the philosopher, appear as slaves of thought (in other words, as artists or philosophers!) while the masters appear as masters of action. For some people, the world is indeed a vista calling for adventures. For others, to the contrary, it is a prison or even a penal colony.

The one text that would ensure that the German philosopher's hammer blows were heard in some other way is "A Report to an Academy."[42] Rotpeter, the humanized monkey, is a monster of asceticism, a masterpiece of humanity and morality. One of this extraordinary character's first declarations consists in explaining that his breathtaking rise was only possible because he forgot his origins and his early years: "In fact," he concedes, "to give up being stubborn was the supreme commandment I laid upon myself; free ape as I was, I submitted myself to that yoke." Thanks to this yoke, the monkey has become foreign to himself. His past is no longer a "strong wind" but a simple "puff of air." Henceforth he is cut from himself. It was only at the price of an Olympian calm, he reports, that he was able to escape from the bottom of his cage. He observes: "Today, I can see it clearly: without the most profound inward calm I could never have found my way out. And indeed perhaps I owe all that I have become to the calm that settled within me after my first few days in the ship."[43]

The ascetic ideal, as Nietzsche says, is "an artifice for the *preservation* of life," although this is a contradiction in terms: "life *against* life."[44] Asceticism makes life possible. But the ascetic lives badly. For Kafka's monkey, the only way out was to be admitted to humanity. The only alternative to the zoological garden was becoming a music-hall star. At a high price, this Guinean monkey reached "the cultural level of an average European." He is almost an artist. He is finally tolerated by society, he has succeeded, but Kafka shows that this requires two conditions: on the one hand, that he hide and remain silent about his wounds, and on the other, that he keep his private life secret.

If then, as in Kafka, asceticism constitutes the only possible way out under certain conditions, apart from taking flight or drowning oneself, this remains nevertheless an exit without a future, a poisoned remedy, a pathological ideal, as Nietzsche demonstrated. The philosopher turns it into a social good without moral value, rather than a moral good lacking social value, as philosophy insisted whenever it idealized asceticism. An ascetic life is in fact a self-negation. It is an ideal for society, but a sickness for humanity. This is where society takes its toll: this is the cost of social peace, which Nietzsche and others after him called the *police*. As for the individual, this Faust, he loses his "soul" or rather his animality, his being. Indeed, ressentiment attains its highest power in asceticism. Dissatisfaction is never so full; self-hatred triumphs. For it is life that the will wants to dominate, in using force to avoid the recourse to force, in using force against itself, life against life. When ascetic individuals find they are their own greatest enemies, the cure is bitter, the consolation very weak indeed. It does no good to make saving one's image a point of honor. Isn't this what Zinédine Zidane understood, finally letting go of his image to save his honor? Recognition is clearly a trap, above all for a "monkey."

Under the philosophical or genealogical scalpel, subjected to internal critique, asceticism cannot claim our commitment, no matter how useful it may be; though fruitful (without asceticism, neither art nor philosophy is possible), it is just too infuriating. Consequently, asceticism raises a problem of conscience. How can we look at asceticism with anything but ambivalence, given that the monkey's questioning is also our own? How (with unequal weapons) can one get out when one is a monkey, and, a fortiori, a little chimpanzee? Must one ascetically keep one's cool at the moment it seems impossible not to lose it? Or is anger a good counselor?

It becomes clear that assimilation is confused with apprenticeship in asceticism. To the contrary, all it takes for assimilation to be judged incomplete is for asceticism to be judged insufficient. The old self must be cast off. This is, in a word, exactly what the Abbé Grégoire sought when he recommended adapting in response to pressure from the dominant norm.[45] This paradigm of assimilation opens the gates to a passion for unmasking: is the asceticism actually real or just apparent? Is it true or feigned? Is it natural or willful, virtuous or self-interested? No inquisition will ever put an end to such suspicions. As Freud said, *I am not yet calm.*

Colonies, Girls, and Men

"Minority religious practices and prohibitions, beyond association and worship, are tolerated or not depending on their visibility or notoriety and the degree of outrage they arouse in the majority."[46] The "veil affair"—the controversy regarding the wearing of the Islamic "headscarf" [*foulard islamique*] in schools—divided French politicians and intellectuals as matters involving young people, particularly young women, rarely do, and riled up almost the entire country.[47] How could children, indeed very young girls, create such passions in such a large part of the population? How could these children have been considered a public danger to such a degree, considered agents transmitting a foreign evil, an almost absolute evil, a permanent menace, a raging epidemic? How could their presence in school have become synonymous with the disappearance of *laïcité* (secularism)?[48]

Today, the "affair" has almost become accepted. It has been regulated, if not resolved, in an authoritarian manner, in the great tradition of the French educational institution, for which diversity—once linguistic, now religious—represents an obstacle to "national education."[49] Just as the patois, the local dialects, the regional tongues (for example Breton or Basque) were actively fought by the Black Hussars of the Republic, today religious signs and visible marks of confessional membership are chased from the immaculate walls of school buildings with the greatest eagerness by virile defenders of laïcité—with this small difference, meanwhile, that the population at stake is not of French "stock" [*de souche*] but comes from the former territories once colonized by France.[50] Another small difference is that "metropolitan" and "overseas" territories do not all have the same standing in such matters. Certain exceptions confirm the rule when it comes to the separation of church and state: Alsace, Guyana, and Mayotte.[51] Today, the rule stipulates that the wearing of the Islamic headscarf is forbidden within the school walls like every other religious sign.

To grasp the postcolonial dimension of the question—which is not its only aspect—we are obliged to return to the start of the "affair." This began in 1989 in the suburbs of Paris, at the *collège* (middle school) of Creil, whose principal, Ernest Chénière, protested at the presence of girls wearing the Islamic headscarf in his establishment. Chénière, whose heritage was French Caribbean, was the first political actor. The second actor was also the principal of a middle school: as director of the Collège Jean Jaurès de Montfermeil, Ali Boumahdi sent home three girls wearing the headscarf. Boumahdi's family was originally Algerian. Both actors had families born in territories that are or were under French domination. They came from the periphery of the French Republic, not from its center. Each belonged to a minority.

How did they approach the question? The first, Ernest Chénière, declared in 1989: "The present texts are sufficiently fluid that *viruses* can get mixed in with them." "The *collège* is French, Creillois and secular [*laïc*]. We are not going to let ourselves get *infested* by a religious problematic."[52] One can hardly help noticing, apart from the singular employment of the verb *infester* along with *virus*, that this school principal organizes his claim in a specific way: the adjective *French* wins out over *Creillois*, which in turn wins out over *secular*. On learning of the November 2, 1992, decree of the Conseil d'État striking down the indefinite suspension [*exclusion*] of three students from the collège of Montfermeil,[53] he added: "In any case, these are not stable families who get involved with fighting against a school, who try to police its administration all the way up to the Conseil d'État. There we have the method of decorated jurists. The girls in question are 'zombified,' transformed into ideological *dupes*, steered from a distance by their parents, who are themselves manipulated by groups colluding abroad."[54] Everything in this statement makes it seem as if he were talking about an attack on state security. Given the symbolic context of the recent bicentenary of the French Revolution and the Declaration of the Rights of Man and Citizen, it is remarkable that he should assimilate recourse to the courts, the personal defense of liberties, with an unacceptable rebellion.

Ali Boumahdi, for his part, stated around the same time that "this decision is only going to encourage the fundamentalists to try and take charge of the situation."[55] This is open war on the girls. It does not matter how often they show their credentials, how much their presence in the republic's schools costs them, or how committed they are to following the collège's curriculum. These children are being asked for a political allegiance that cannot possibly be their business, because they are minors. And with all his scholar's tact, this head of the establishment explains that for him, "as a Muslim, the chador [headscarf] is a rag."[56] Why does he argue on the basis of his religion in such a situation? Isn't he zealous enough? Isn't he a sufficiently avid newcomer? Didn't the two principals show by their attitude, their position, and their decisions that they intended to prove how French they were, how *laïc*, in a word, how assimilated? Must the school wash itself whiter than the whole society?

In 1989, an emergency legal settlement [*dispositif*] was put in place. Drawing on two types of legal texts, the Conseil d'État handed down an opinion that clarified two points in particular.[57] On the one hand, it stipulated that the wearing of the Islamic headscarf is legal: "In educational establishments, it is not necessarily incompatible with laïcité for pupils to wear signs indicating their membership in a religion to the extent that it constitutes the exercise of freedom of expression and manifestation of religious beliefs." On the other hand, it declared that the "ostentatious" character of wearing such religious signs would constitute an act of "proselytism" and would thus tend toward "infringement on either the pupil's dignity or freedom or on that of other members of the educational community."[58]

Put otherwise, the wearing of the Islamic headscarf is *formally* legal but *materially* problematic since it must not disturb the institution's (public?) order. Consequently, all it takes for order to be disrupted is for one person to express his or her distress and to consider his or her dignity or freedom affected by the wearing of this piece of cloth. What better way to take back with the left hand what was given with the right hand? The position is contradictory insofar as ostentation is the act of showing (and thus involves a tautology) and insofar as proselyte is, etymologically speaking, someone newly arrived in a country (thus a second tautology). In sum, the wearing of the headscarf must be neither ostentatious nor proselytizing, but (by definition) it can be nothing else. The double bind decreed by authorities strikes these young students with full force. In a word (or a hundred more), the wearing of the headscarf is not *forbidden*, but it is *intolerable*.

With the notion of public order, in fact, we pass from freedom of expression (for some) to toleration (for others). This displacement is no small thing. First, we are dealing with different subjects: we are no longer speaking of the girls, but of those who mix with them. The principal actors are no longer the same as they were before! Then we have a shift in terrain: we are no longer speaking of right, but of fact. This way of determining how the principle of freedom of expression will be applied, combined with the limitation of its effective exercise, opens a zone of uncertainty as to how order and, eventually, disturbance will be assessed. As a result, Lionel Jospin, the minister of national education, appeared both uncertain as to his right (he clings to the Conseil d'État) and sure about his facts. "When a conflict appears," he contended, "one must immediately engage in dialogue so that, in the pupil's interest and in that of the school's good functioning, the wearing of these signs may be abandoned."[59]

A familiar benevolence rears its head: when it is a question of the young Muslim students' freedom, the educational institution is authorized, per se, to decide on the limitation of the students' freedom for their own good, in their own interest. This proper interest, as quickly becomes clear, follows from the school's "good functioning." The circle is complete. Legal subjects have thus become entirely deprived of rights and submitted, as in the good old days (of the colonies), to the discretionary evaluation of the French administration.

On October 25, 1989, Lionel Jospin held a famous hearing open to questions for the government in the National Assembly, during which two socialist deputies tried to enter the lower chamber with "scarves" on their heads (in fact, *keffiehs*). Jospin began by declaring that "the school cannot exclude, because it is designed to welcome," and that the wearing of the headscarf could not in itself justify exclusion.[60] After that, faced with debate and opposition, which was just as frequently internal to the national education system as external to it, and after a memorandum was further submitted to the Conseil Supérieur de l'Éducation Nationale, a "compromise" text was adopted. At that point, any real compromise between the parties would have given the impression that the authorities were giving in.

At the very moment when the republic was honoring its great men in Condorcet, in Monge, in Grégoire, two hundred years after Abbé Grégoire's "discovery" and "regeneration" of the Jews (showing neither ostentatious signs, nor a unique language, nor public practices), it discovered its Muslims.[61] How? In the form of girls who, entirely despite themselves, were transformed at the age of puberty into enemies of the republic, into adversaries of laïcité. In fact, in this matter, neither age nor family status (father, mother, brother, sister, son, daughter) is apparently important. Nothing counts, on the whole of course, but religious membership and affiliation. This is exactly how the indigènes were considered. Neither old nor young, neither strong nor weak, neither rich nor poor, neither handsome nor ugly, and so on, without individualization of any kind—pure indigènes. In Algeria, they became Muslim Frenchmen. Since 1989, France has been tackling French Muslims (and more importantly, foreigners!) on its own soil. It imports both methods and language from the former colony.[62]

Henceforth, pressure [*contrainte*] can take over from persuasion. Having failed to win the unbeliever's loyalty, "he will be forced to be free," according to Rousseau's slogan.[63] The memorandum clarified that "in evaluating the concrete situation and its context, the director of a school, the head of the institution, or the body of teachers will first have recourse to *persuasion* rather than to *pressure*."[64] Through progressive slippages, political procedures, and sophistical operations, the public expression of a religious affiliation, of a belief, becomes a *fault* to be punished. In this way, the prefect finds himself promoted to the paradigm of judge, and the administrative state is held up as a model for the constitutional state.

The authorities were aware of this, specifying in the memorandum that "in every case, the rights of the defense . . . must be scrupulously respected." "I draw your attention," emphasized the supervisory minister, "to the fact that the disciplinary council is not a tribunal, but an educational body." Correlatively, in the political authorities' preferred doublespeak, the provisional exclusion, in other words the prohibition of a student's access to the school in the name of conservatism, is a measure that "does not present the character of a punishment" [*sic*].[65] Why "respect the rights of the defense scrupulously" if this is not a matter of accusation? And is being evicted from classes "in the student's interest"?

The dispute conceals a *différend*. In fact, the text rests on a circular argument [*une pétition de principe*]. Rather than specifying proselytizing (blameworthy) and proposing criteria by which to evaluate it, which might have been reasonable, the text presupposes that the wearing of the scarf is a scandal to be suppressed. It also subreptitiously reintroduces the "collective responsibility" that the colony reserved only for its Muslims: "One can best evaluate the demonstrative character of clothing or of signs being worn in relation to the attitude and remarks *of pupils and of the parents*."[66] A remarkable turn here: responsibility for the parents' remarks and attitude is borne by the children rather than, as one might logically think where minors are involved, being out of their control. Intention might as well be crime: "All proselytizing behaviors which *aim* to convince other pupils and other members of the educational community and to serve as an example to them are to be prohibited."[67] A scandal is an example that is in fact imitated. This is what explains putting the intention on trial—in other words, evaluating goals rather than acts—since quite simply, it cannot be imagined that these acts will result in conversion (still less massive conversion). The missionaries made no mistake about this: they were not content to recruit adepts by walking around in their robes. They still had to engage in conversation (which they had learned to do in their schools).

As mentioned above, these decisions inherit past representations, attitudes, and repressions proper to the colonies—from "outside." They also inherit—from within—a tradition that is no less republican, because it is that of the Enlightenment, in which tolerance is a combat, not an agreement—a refusal, not acceptance. When Romilly, for example, raises the question of toleration in his article from the *Encyclopédie*, it is with respect to the relationship between the state and religion.[68] In his writings, toleration gains its consistency from the "civil combat," in such a way that toleration winds up belonging to this conflict's victorious side. Why? Because, for Romilly as for almost all of his contemporaries, what has to be tolerated is an error. The error is the other religion, the religion of the other (once Judaism, today Islam). To tolerate, henceforth, is not to accept people but to transform the world.

The result of this is that toleration will be thought of negatively and, by manifest reference to Protestants, as an absence of persecution. In this way of conceiving toleration, whose master-thinker is Voltaire, the question is not about *freedom* but about *truth*. It is not a question of right but of fact. This is how Buisson, one of the most fundamentalist defenders of laïcité, much later referred to "secular faith" (*foi laïque*). In fact, he thinks of laïcité on the basis of yesterday's toleration. This is what, more recently, *Le Figaro* of November 7 and 8, 1992, called the "anti-chador crusade."

Lionel Jospin was not, in this case, being insincere. "It is true," he confessed, "that in this light, the headscarf affair evokes a certain form of religious affirmation that we are not ready to accept, neither as the secular school nor as French society."[69] Recalling his attachment to the "French, individualist model of integration," he clarified his conception: "Now that it has a strong existence in France, Islam must follow a course comparable to that followed previously by other religions. It must consent to remain more within the private sphere."[70]

The explicit reference to Judaism is significant.[71] It is also brought up to date. The way of the cross is already entirely laid out. Pierre Birnbaum has identified its stations. He has shown how, a hundred years after the decree establishing the emancipation of Jews in France and giving them a new status as citizens with full rights, secularization was denounced as de-Christianization and Judaization of the republic.[72] Since then, the inheritors of secularization (its guard dogs?) have examined the "physical, moral and political regeneration of Muslims," the means by which they can be rendered both "useful" and "happy," according to Abbé Grégoire's terminology. They discovered its mystical foundation: private toleration and public order.

Not just because of their confession, but also because of their gender, the girls who interest us are close to the French Jews and French Muslims. Mutatis mutandis, these are to the periphery (the colony) what the others are to the center (the metropole): reprimanded, discriminated against, and fought like powerful enemies. They are also related, through a well-oiled rhetoric, to foreign powers. The refrain is well known to historians. It is less well known to politicians. The era of suspicion is not over. Every index of foreignness is perceived as a sign of exteriority. As for women, whatever their age may be, even very young (above all very young!), they must bend and be quiet, submit and resign themselves, under pain of being sent home. The girls wearing the headscarves are insubordinate [*insoumises*]: they want to prove that they are "neither whores nor submissive" [*ni putes ni soumises*], demonstrating that politics is always—but more or less, for better or worse—sexualized, sexed, differentiated.

This insubordination has been judged all the more severely as the girls were, until that moment, known for their docility. As everyone liked to say, they were well-behaved and disciplined and did not tend to pose the same problems as their brothers. When they kept their headscarves on, their indocility was a veritable scandal. But as we have seen, to prevent their subservience, the educational institution asked them to submit to an authority other than their parents. Meanwhile, was not the "stubbornness" that some of them devoted to keeping their heads covered, that is, their resoluteness, a way for them to avoid *betrayal*?

This affair is a funny sort of lesson in emancipation. If we follow the ultra feminists and secularists, these "little girls" were victims (of familial authority).[73] And in their infinite benevolence (and in the name of political authority), the former found nothing better to do than to sanction said victims of the evil from which they were supposed to suffer (Islam) by excluding them from education. The sign [*l'index*, i.e., the headscarf] thus finds itself blacklisted [*mis à l'index*]. For example, the Association France Plus, along with Choisir and the Club des Égaux, launched an appeal on November 28, 1989, "for the defense of laïcité, for the dignity of women," holding that to authorize "the wearing of the veil or of any religious emblem (Christian, Jewish, etc.) or political emblem" in the "Republican School" "would radically contradict the constitutional principle of republican laïcité."

Notice the progressive slippages of political language. In its September 13, 1990, issue, one year after the start of the "affair," *Le Nouvel Observateur* published a poll that contained these two questions: "Among the differences between French and immigrants, do some render coexistence difficult for you personally?" and "Do you think that it is normal or not normal for girls to be able to wear the Islamic scarf in school?"[74] To the first question, 49 percent of those polled answered that customs were the obstacle, 44 percent religion. To the second question, 14 percent of those asked said that it was normal, 78 percent replied that it was not normal, and 8 percent had no opinion. Without entering into a detailed analysis of the terms of the poll, one recognizes straight off that the questionnaire is addressed to the French and that French Muslims are its object, the absent third party.

Do the "immigrants" get a voice in this chapter? If they had one, they would immediately be judged biased. This was the era in France when politicians "on the left" became "right-wing," in the sense that Pierre Bourdieu used when referring to Segolène Royal.[75] The political divisions had thus changed, and considerations of public order won out handily over the protection of individual freedoms and the absence of discrimination. Today, as one sees with respect to the ground crews at Charles de Gaulle airport, discrimination according to religious confession is institutionalized, legitimated, legalized. Instead of thinking that terrorists hide behind Islam, it is thought that every Muslim may hide a terrorist.[76]

Contemporary France—like laïcité—is still the inheritor of a dominant tradition, which in the eighteenth century was expressed by Romilly as well as by Voltaire. Although they are not the only theorists of toleration, which is to say of religious and political freedom, they are its founding fathers and have inspired all practices that followed after.

In the article that Romilly wrote for the *Encyclopédie*, toleration belongs fundamentally to the political register. There must be no state within the state: the priest must be a citizen before all else. Toleration is aggressive; it is defined in an agonistic manner. Romilly's text presents the proper tactics for bringing off this victory. "Have pity on error," he says, "and never give truth any weapons but kindness, example, and persuasion. In the matter of changes in belief, invitations are stronger than penalties." The victory lies in conversion, the change of belief. Consequently, error belongs to the religion of the other, the other religion, which today as yesterday means Judaism and Islam and, to a lesser extent, Protestantism. If the priest is a citizen before all else, it would also be preferable for the citizen to conceal a priest rather than an imam or a rabbi, for whom such disappearance was long impossible.

To tolerate is to persuade. This is not to pressure [*contraindre*] but still to force. Toleration is a gesture of force. Likewise, in his *Dictionnaire philosophique*, Voltaire poses the question of toleration with respect to the plurality of religions.[77] Here he is writing more in a social than a political register. Toleration is once again conceived on the basis of error. Or, to put it differently, the sole object of toleration is error. The consistency of toleration, on the other hand, comes not from combat but from pardon, which might seem to be more peaceful than Romilly's version. "Let us forgive one another our foolishness; this is the first law of nature": error is human, which means universally shared. No one is privileged in matters of religion, either: if by chance any privileges exist, it is imperative that they be abolished. And Voltaire goes on to propose an eloquent parable: "Will a reed bent by the wind in the mud say to a neighboring reed bent in the opposite direction: 'crawl the way I do, miserable one, or I will ask that you be pulled up and burned?'"

In Voltaire, then, the rational foundation of toleration is not relativism. Quite to the contrary, there are truths and errors, but no one is protected from error, and this, not truth, is what is relative. If toleration is a kind of pardon, does it rest rather in acceptance? It is impossible to give positive acceptance to an error. It is therefore because the object of toleration is defined as error that toleration is defined negatively, in Voltaire, as absence of persecution. Definition by default. Is this not the scheme within which the scarves of these Muslim girls have been apprehended—as the striking manifestation of an error to be corrected, with all toleration, since correction does not signify persecution?

The double key given to us by Romilly and Voltaire consists in two words: coercion [*coercition*] and nonpersecution, which explains in part how fundamentalism (to use contemporary language) or fanaticism (the language of the moderns) can be systematically invoked in the name of justifying coercion, so as to turn error into the enemy. For toleration, there is no question of freedom but only of truth. Now we see the intellectual condition for the possibility of exclusion from the school.[78] But we also see something that illuminates the "disturbance of public order" and the "intrusion on the good functioning of the school" that the wearing of the famous headscarf is supposed to provoke. Meanwhile, in the matter of social relations, if it is truth that counts, freedom is worth pursuing, and if what counts are the facts, then the law still comes first.

In the end, error for toleration, fault for civility (one always finds oneself inside something, whether it is a hat, a scarf, a coat, etc.), the wearing of the Islamic scarf was also treated as a blow against assimilation, a crime toward acculturation, and, as one thing leads to the next, a refusal of France (land of welcome).[79] Everywhere, assimilation is pregnant with a promise: it is supposed to bring personal benefits and social gains to the one who assimilates and who makes the effort to assimilate. On these grounds, assimilation represents a kind of protection against pure and simple exclusion or social disparagement. It is always presented as beneficial, oriented in the direction of history (Enlightenment), inscribed in social progress just as in the progress of humanity in such a way that the end comes to justify its means. This is why refusing or resisting assimilation remains unintelligible, unthinkable, inaudible—for the majority. As for the impossibility of assimilating, that is attributed to a bad will. To wear the Islamic headscarf, in this light, is seen as making a choice for the worse rather than the better, as a refusal of the better.

Tocqueville analyzed this phenomenon quite well in the first volume of his *De la démocratie en Amerique*. There, in fact, he studies "the probable future of the three races that inhabit the territory of the United States."[80] And he notes with respect to blacks that "there is a natural prejudice that brings man to scorn whoever has been his inferior, for a long time after he has become his equal; an imaginary inequality that has its roots in mores always follows upon the real inequality that fortune or law produces."[81] If this is how he distinguishes the imaginary and the real dimensions of inequality (today we would say the subjective and the objective dimensions of inequality), it is to cast a sharper light on the importance and the real effects of the imaginary. Indeed, this double dimension leads Tocqueville to a vicious circle. "In order that the whites abandon the opinion they have conceived of the intellectual and moral inferiority of their former slaves, the Negroes would have to change, and they cannot change as long as this opinion subsists."[82] Moreover, according to Tocqueville, such generosity would offer blacks nothing more, at least initially, than the opportunity to occupy "the lowest rank" in the social hierarchy.[83]

Paradoxically, from this point of view, candidates for assimilation must not conform to the opinion one might have of them. To the contrary, they must go beyond others' natural prejudice against them. Despite appearances, the unremarked affiliations that they transcend when they believe they have succeeded socially lead to the reinforcement rather than reduction of prejudice. In this respect, Tocqueville's paradigm of assimilation is the mixed-race person [*métis*], the model of the very docile young girl who no longer has any exterior sign of belonging to a minority. The mulattos, he writes, "have no force by themselves, and in quarrels of the races, they ordinarily make common cause with the whites."[84] This is exactly what *métis* of France, such as the principals of the middle schools in question, did when they set fire to the tinder. Finally, there remains the thorniest point: the repugnance with which national citizens (or the majority) envisage assimilation, even when they defend it and encourage it. In fact, assimilation happens through mutual consent of two parties. If for some, those "asking," it is a matter of *being assimilated*, for others, those "receiving," it is a matter of *assimilating themselves* to those who are assimilated, which in truth is not always easy.

The question of the Islamic scarf, "this scrap of shadows," to use Sami Naïr's expression, unveils the complexity of social processes that are unknown only due to ignorance and naivete, which then render them unknowable.[85] Meanwhile, obviously, the spatial apprehension of the problem, which is to say of the school's (public/private) space and of the cultural distances that are currently deployed there, should not lead us to forget its temporal dimension or neglect the multiple aspects of its historical weight. At the very least, it is simplistic to believe that assimilation concerns the foreigner without implicating the national citizen, that it is an act and not a process, that it must be free from drama [*sans histoires*] because it is without history [*sans histoire*]. If today Islam is the second religion *in* France, historically it was not the second religion *of* France. The vast majority of French Muslims are actually from families originating in the former French colonies of North and West Africa.

The wearing of the Islamic scarf has upset consciences as much as it has upset the unthought of those consciences. Following from this, it would be normal that, in their own interest—which is to say from the desire for normalization—the very young girls who set this tale in motion should not be Muslim. It would be normal for them to go out everywhere, heads uncovered. It would be normal that they would not want to be noticed.[86] It would be normal that they would become invisible. From that moment on, they would be tolerated.

"When it comes to the principle of laïcité in school," writes David Kessler, "it seems to us that we are bound to reverse the overly rigorous approach of some of its most ardent defenders. Laïcité no longer appears as a principle justifying the prohibition of all religious manifestation. Teaching is secular not because it forbids the expression of different faiths, but because it tolerates them all. . . . This is the point from which a distinction may be deduced, one that in our opinion has not been sufficiently emphasized, between the obligations placed on teachers and those placed on students."[87] Minors have been treated as if they were adults; students have been treated as if they were professors. On November 2, 1992, an injunction from the Conseil d'État annulled the decision to ban the three young girls from the collège of Montfermeil in 1990. In fact, sullied by an abuse of power, the ban had made the prohibition the principle and freedom the exception. And just as when laïcité was first introduced, the government commissioner, David Kessler, was personally called into question (by antisemitism).

Indeed, he had proposed an inversion of the jurisprudence. Until 1992, the Conseil d'État had never ruled on reviews of the legality of internal police measures mainly affecting the army, the prisons and the schools. In *Surveiller et punir*, Foucault had shown the homology between the school, the barracks, the prison, the hospital, and the factory.[88] Once before, the Conseil d'État had been consulted in a case involving the exclusion of a young girl (always the same gender) from a high school [*lycée*] because she was wearing long ski pants, and the council had refused to issue a ruling. In 1992, the Conseil d'État expanded the constitutional state's field of application by reestablishing the right of girls to education and by defending this right in the name of the French constitutional principle of free religious expression in public. In principle, no one might be disturbed for his or her religious opinions on French soil. Nevertheless, on this soil, today in historical continuity with (and not like) yesterday, certain subjects present an exception.

Since the ruling, order has been completely restored. No one continues to hold to the French constitutional principles in individual cases. The school has fortuitously returned to a great silence, becoming a barracks for the teachers and a prison for the students. From one end to the other, it is a space not of liberty but of authority.[89] Henceforth, apparently, order has been completely restored. But since then, the girls' brothers, cousins, or neighbors have also made their indocility known, albeit in a more violent way.

Colonies, Animals, and Men

Kafka undertook to write the colony as a literary enterprise when he drew up three short texts between 1914 and 1917. "In the Penal Colony" was written first but published after the other two. Kafka composed this short story between October 15 and 18, 1914. He finished it in February 1915. It was not published until May 1919, in a deluxe collection by Kurt Wolff Editions. But in Munich on November 19, 1916, Kafka gave it a public reading at the Galerie Goltz, under the rubric of an "Evening of Modern Literature" at which Rilke most likely was also present. The public was shocked. The critics were disapproving. On April 22, 1917, Kafka sent "A Report to an Academy," as well as twelve other texts, to Martin Buber for his monthly review *Der Jude* (*The Jew*).[90] Here, in the October and November 1917 issues, "Report" and "Jackals and Arabs" were published under the title "Two Animal Stories." Kafka sent the following request to Martin Buber on May 12, 1917: "I ask you to not identify these texts as allegories. If you want a title for the two of them, perhaps: Two animal stories." After the monologue of an uprooted monkey, "Jackals and Arabs" proposes a dialogue between the narrator and some jackals. Arabs are the topic of their exchange.

In these texts, Kafka proposes another way of thinking about the colony. Indeed, the two short stories not only present a very original point of view on the subject, but also offer an extremely subtle analysis. This analysis focuses, first, on the speech of someone whose origins are in a colony, subjected and in the end assimilated, and second, on the discourse put forth in the context of a possible colonization, or future colony. In one story, a monkey native to the Gulf of Guinea, henceforth exiled in Germany, makes a speech in the first person before an auditorium of distinguished academicians. In the other story, a jackal's speech is directed at a European Jew traveling in Palestine and passing the night in an oasis. The two short stories describe the gap in perceptions, the differences. They voice a profound dislocation, incarnated in the speakers' specificity: despite all expectations, these are indeed animals. It is the humans who listen. The stakes, finally, are rather different in each situation: knowledge in the first case and power in the second. As a result, the perspective is retrospective in the first case and prospective in the second.

What can be said in the present about the past and the future? This is, in short, the question Kafka raises in these two writings. A gulf separates the animal and the man, the speaker and the listener, the *I* and the *you*—an abyss of differences. Meanwhile, these differences are not givens. They are instituted phenomena whose primary character—more or less—actually turns them into instituting facts. In fact, it is on these differences that the classification of things, the order of the world, and, through this, the division of reason are founded. Such pages do not let themselves be reduced to a single interpretation. The guiding thread I have chosen for my exploration here is the subjectivation of the colonial situation such as one can read it in Kafka's three short stories.

At the end of the nineteenth century, Europeans first encountered the subjects of their colonial empires during exhibitions that took place not only in zoological parks, as in Paris and Hamburg, a city to which Kafka makes explicit reference in "A Report to an Academy," but also in "aquariums" or even in pseudovillages reconstituted in the city center, as in London.[91] In Paris, starting in 1877, the zoological garden was used to show off "exotics" among hippopotamuses, giraffes, ostriches, and palm trees. For example, in a text titled "The Ashantis in the Botanical Garden," published September 19, 1877, Jules Lemaître wrote the following lines: "These exhibitions do not give one a proud idea of humanity. The Ashantis are frightful.—You will say to me that perhaps they find us very ugly from their side, and that they are right, just like us, and that our own beauty is an entirely relative idea, etc. . . .—And still! No, I maintain that they are frightful. . . . In short, these good Ashantis are unpleasant to see, not because they have animal heads, but because, having these heads, they have at the same time the air of being men."[92]

Before the proliferation of images, Achille Mbembe was able to announce his agitation, his embarrassment, and finally, his powerlessness. "What bothers me the most in all this," he declared,

> is that the Other, because he has means that I do not have, is authorized to reduce me to the size of an image he fabricated of me, without my having asked him for anything whatsoever. . . . He wants to oblige me to convince myself that "I am truly in the image of what he has made." Not only does he want to convince me of this, in the sense of persuasion, but he forces me to adhere to what he has decided I am, to repeat this for my own account, to mimic it, as

> a condition for allowing me to live. What irritates and revolts me is realizing this powerlessness; is discovering that, in reality, no matter what I do, he has the means to do what he likes, to "validate" the fables that he tells at my expense, in an authoritarian manner.[93]

"A Report to an Academy" is a text that subverts this principle.[94] It is a text that turns the position of the colonizer inside out like a glove. In short, the monkey says, "If you want to know, then listen to this!" Indeed, Kafka gives him the floor and thereby transforms into a subject someone generally condemned to muteness—someone who, ordinarily, is nothing but an object of discourse, which is the discursive mark of his social, political, and anthropological devaluation. In fact, it is a matter of the speech of someone integrated, or assimilated, delivered in the first person. A humanized monkey, asked to give his report, addresses his words to honorable academicians and provides them with a "report on (his) prior life": when he was a monkey. A speech emerges, therefore, from someone who—finally?—can express himself in his own name, or rather almost his own name because he does it under a surname, and in the first person.[95]

In Kafka's text, this speech is the equivalent of a handshake because it "betokens frankness" [*franchise*]. The handshake, confesses this former monkey, is the first human thing he learned.[96] It marks the beginning of a considerable change within him. Obliged to play a second round, he intends to complete this "handshake" that has now become a principle for him using "frankness in words." Speaking frankly means describing the trajectory of a being excluded from humanity at the start (a monkey is without reason) and then admitted into the community of humans on the condition that he knows how to behave as one must in society. Speaking frankly means summarizing a process of acculturation. No complaint in the remarks, no accusation, neither a defense nor a prosecution: a simple "report." Meanwhile, this poses a great difficulty for someone who, having known two different states, cannot speak of the first without using the words of the second. "Of course, what I felt then as an ape," he explains, "I can represent now only in human terms, and therefore I misrepresent it, but although I cannot reach back to the truth of the old ape life, there is no doubt that it lies somewhere in the direction I have indicated."

The character begins by evoking the marks of the blows inflicted on him: a scar and a limp. This person, this monkey, native of the Gold Coast, then a British colony and now present-day Ghana, recounts his own capture as it was reported to him by witnesses: while he ran with the others, he was hit by two gunshots, two bullets, the one grievously wounding his thigh, leaving him forever lame, and the other hurting his cheek with no serious consequences. Since then, a great red scar remains on his "shaved skin," a red spot on the cheek, as a mark of his difference. This is how he was given the name Rotpeter, Peter the Red.

Kafka's story weaves together all the registers and perhaps all the dimensions of tolerance and of difference. The colony is an elsewhere: the Gold Coast. It is likewise populated by other beings, all more or less monkeys.[97] This is why, in what follows, Kafka mentions the Hagenbeck expedition. In 1907, Karl Hagenbeck (1844–1913), a circus director and animal dealer, opened the zoological park of Stellingen in Hamburg. He invented ethnozoology. Edmund Husserl said, "There is no zoology of peoples."[98] What he meant to say was that no such zoology has a right to exist. In fact, quite to the contrary, the zoology of peoples was one of the masks, one of the expressions, of human blindness and deafness, and also, as Kafka put it so well, of indifference.

Does it matter if certain people are hurt? Here we see someone who feels neither warmth nor coldness toward those who organize and carry out this kind of safari. The Europeans even went so far as to conceive and to establish human zoos to exhibit all these "types" and all the "scenes" associated with them.[99] The Hottentot Venus, "captured" in South Africa, was shown everywhere, even—like Kafka's monkey—on a music-hall stage. In this way, many Africans and Pacific Islanders were uprooted and savagely shown to the blind eyes of Europeans. The colonial expositions were likewise an opportunity for France, in particular, not just to prove its own greatness and its own prestige but also to display the conquered populations as submissive populations.

Rotpeter's "frank words" do not exclude critique. In his mouth, this critique is a defense, the answer to an accusation. What is he being reproached for? For showing the impact "where the bullet went in." In other words, he is expected to act as if he had never been hurt. Or rather, he ought to behave as if he never suffered. He ought to put on a brave face in all circumstances. If he shows the wound's effect on him, he is accused of still having too much of the "monkey" in him and not enough humanity. "I read an article recently by one of the ten thousand windbags who vent themselves concerning me in the newspapers," he declares to the venerable academicians:

> My ape nature is not yet quite under control; the proof being that when visitors come to see me, I have a predilection for taking down my trousers to show them where the bullet went in. The hand which wrote that should have its fingers

> shot away one by one. As for me, I can take my trousers down before anyone if I like; you would find nothing but a well-groomed fur and the scar made—let me be particular in the choice of a word for this particular purpose, to avoid misunderstanding—the scar made by a *criminal* shot.[100]

In fact, the truth can neither silence nor hide the crime. This is why this truly scholarly monkey thinks that "everything is open and aboveboard; there is nothing to conceal; when the plain truth is in question, great minds discard the niceties of refinement." Put otherwise, Rotpeter sustains a non-deceiving discourse against the pretenses inherent in social life, against the blindness—seeing neither the wound nor the scar—that accompanies all vile political and social acts. How can one who is colonized simply by his capture, taken for a parcel of territory, almost a possession, describe his state? An animal in a cage. "For the first time in my life," the monkey continues, "I could see no way out [*pas d'issue*]: at least no direct way out." In one way or another, all movement is constrained. Not only constrained, but for lack of an exit [*issue*], futile and vain. "I am supposed to have made uncommonly little noise," says the monkey, "from which the conclusion was drawn that I would either soon die or if I managed to survive the first critical period would be very amenable to training." The monkey survived and stifled his sobs. Does the monkey feel hate? Not at all. Speaking of the boat's crew, he considers that "they were good creatures, in spite of everything." The "in spite of everything" is what says it all.

The great force of Kafka's text also consists in the way it distinguishes subtly between *way out* [*issue*] and *freedom* [*liberté*].[101] When Kafka tries to identify the difference between a way out and freedom, he has recourse to a metaphor. He assimilates freedom to a "self-controlled movement,"[102] a mastery that one observes among trapeze artists and that elicits peals of inextinguishable laughter at the monkeys. For Kafka, indeed, one can live without freedom, but one cannot survive without a way out. To be without a way out is the condition of someone whose freedom has been taken away, someone who has been, whether literally or figuratively, closed into a cage, placed in a prison. To be *sans issue* is to be unable to go out, certainly, but also means having lost one's origin. To have "come from" [*issu de*] indicates from whom one was born, or from what kind of person, species, and so on. For the monkey, it is a matter of an inhibited filiation, a hampered transmission. An abolition of all difference, the aggression (and intolerance) touches the human being's very heart—in his filiation, in his "ancestral spirits." The monkey is not without identity (he is honestly still too much a monkey for that), but he is without origin: what he is, he is first of all by accident and later by necessity.

Neither choice nor will in his activity—such is the basic constraint. The question posed for him, which raises the issue, is *how to get out of this?* In fact, one lacks a way out whenever one is blocked without being able to discover the reason. Thus the most urgent task is to find an exit. Once again: "All the time facing that locker—I should certainly have perished. Yet as far as Hagenbeck was concerned, the place for apes was in front of a locker—well then, I had to stop being an ape. A fine, clear train of thought, which I must have constructed with my belly, since apes think with their bellies." One can indeed think with various organs: the head, for the luckiest; the heart, for the most sensitive; the belly, for the most experienced.

The only way out for the one who has no way out is thus to transform oneself. The African, the colonized person, is compelled to change. It is imperative that he or she no longer be what he or she is. To survive, he or she must abandon himself or herself. "Today," the monkey confesses, "I can see it clearly: without the most profound inward calm I could never have found my way out." The other option would have been an attempt to escape. But getting out of the cage is not escaping into the world. In the end, therefore, escape represents a desperate act. The monkey describes his great transformation, this passage from one kind to another kind, this elevation into humanity, with detailed force and perspicacity. This ape possesses extraordinary reflectiveness. He does not see himself with the other's eyes, but he sees himself under all the mannerisms, in all his attitudes, his methods, his unconscious ruses.

Thus, the monkey says, "I did not think it out in this human way, but under the influence of my surroundings *I acted as if I thought it out.*" In fact, one must not confuse the calculation of interest with the imperative of finding a way out. To calculate one's interest, one must actually be free. On the other hand, Kafka's monkey does not act on command. He follows his intuition, even if, in the end, he is rather skeptical and incredulous. He clarifies: "No one promised me that if I became like them [the men], the bars of my cage would be taken away. Such promises for apparently impossible contingencies are not given. But if one achieves the impossible, the promises appear later retrospectively precisely where one had looked in vain for them before." In sum, it is a matter of retrospective promises.

The one who does not calculate observes and imitates. Nothing easier. The monkey's confessions go into detail about discreet ways of adapting oneself without being noticed, of integrating oneself without too much effort, of blending in without too much difficulty. These ways are all the more discreet and distant from calculation as they are grounded on no great hopes. When Kafka intends to make himself as clear as can be, he emphasizes that "as freedom is counted among the most sublime feelings, so the corresponding disillusionment can also be sublime." On the other hand, "even should the way out prove to be an illusion; the demand was a small one, the disappointment could be no bigger."[103] Observation thus allows one to become oriented in a precise direction, to organize movement, and thereby to craft a reason for oneself.

Spitting would be the easiest thing to imitate, drinking alcohol the most difficult. To become an experienced drinker actually opens the doors to humanity. The experienced professors are no exception. "I repeat," says the monkey, "there was no attraction for me in imitating human beings; I imitated them because I needed a way out, and for no other reason."

Here we see how the complex of the colonized is fabricated:

> Ah, one learns when one has to; one learns when one needs a way out; one learns at all costs. One stands over oneself with a whip, one flays oneself at the slightest opposition. My ape nature fled out of me, head over heels and away. . . . With an effort which up till now has never been repeated I managed to reach the cultural level of an average European. In itself that might be nothing to speak of, but it is something insofar as it has helped me out of my cage and opened a special way out for me, the way of humanity.

Better to be worth something rather than nothing. This success, relative as it might be, is still undeniable. The uprooting bore fruits. The monkey is henceforth tolerated in society. Just one drawback: private life. This is doubtless one of the most poignant moments in the story, because the monkey lives with a small half-trained chimpanzee. Public happiness, private misery. What does the monkey say to conclude? "By day I cannot bear to see her; for she has the insane look of the bewildered half-broken animal in her eye; no one else sees it, but I do, and I cannot bear it." This is a terrible conclusion to assimilation.

The colony is not just a conquered territory; it can be a dream to come and, as one understands better after "Jackals and Arabs," a utopia.[104] Meanwhile, every colony bears on a territory, and no territory lacks residents. Indeed, the desert does not exist—it is a political category that permits the problems posed by property to be evaded. Thus, it is imperative that the residents of the territory in question be given a *status*.[105] This is the object of "Jackals and Arabs." The text is a dialogue between the narrator, a Jewish traveler or "sir," and the leader of a gang of jackals. The latter expresses his hatred for Arabs. But the story contains a discreet irony, for after having heard the jackals' point of view, the narrator finishes by hearing the Arabs' point of view, to whom Kafka gives the last word.

Everything begins thanks to the narrator's insomnia. Camping in an oasis in Palestine, he is surprised by a pack of jackals. The oldest addresses him. The narrator has apparently been expected for all eternity. But by whom? "I am delighted," says the old jackal, "to have met you here at last. I had almost given up hope, since we have been waiting endless years for you; my mother waited for you, and her mother, and all our foremothers right back to the first mother of all the jackals."

Kafka makes the narrator who hears this prattle into something of a skeptic who, astonished, clarifies that he only came from the great North by accident. He thus opposes chance to predestination and inscribes historical contingency therein. It is then that the old jackal approaches him and, as if to better ground his expectation, sets off to discredit the Arabs living in the area. Can one openly and intelligibly speak ill of them? Does one have the right to slander people without worrying that they will hear? When the narrator insists that the jackal not speak so loudly, the latter expresses his belief that badmouthing Arabs is far better than living with them.

The problematic is palpably different from the one that characterized the "Report." In the "Report," the monkey's speech touched on a social and anthropological subject. It is a speech put forward retrospectively. The monkey's situation is grasped in a return to the past. In "Jackals and Arabs," to the contrary, the dialogue is prospective; it bears on the present (the presence of Arabs) and the future (the presence of the narrator, angel of the good news, a happy arrival). The question raised is neither social nor anthropological; it is political and has to do with the constitution of the enemy. Having arrived on holy ground, the narrator must be informed about and recognize his enemies. Such is the "friendly" position that the jackal leader adopts. As a result, the jackal places the narrator under an obligation to declare himself.

Is the narrator going to agree to this discourse? Is he going to side with the Europeans or with the Arabs? According to the jackal, "not a spark" of the northerners' intelligence is to be found among the Arabs, who are dirty and impure. Their blood must be shed, all their blood. "We know," continues the old one, "that you have come from the North; this is just what we base our hopes on. You Northerners have the kind of intelligence that is not to be found among Arabs. Not a spark of intelligence, let me tell you, can be struck from their cold arrogance. They kill animals for food, and carrion they despise."

This speech puts the narrator in the position of arbitrating a conflict. But the traveler is at once judge and party because he comes from the North and is expected. How could he decide? Is he going to tolerate such hate? "Maybe, maybe," he responds, "matters so far outside my province I am not competent to judge; it seems to me a very old quarrel."[106] No distance can be maintained. Wishing to stand up, the narrator feels fangs pierce his coat so that he is forced to stay and listen to this language.

The traveler's position is also difficult because the jackals' intentions are unclear. Do they want to massacre the Arabs? The old jackal protests against this. He then implores the traveler in these terms: "Sir, we want you to end this quarrel that divides the world. You are exactly the man whom our ancestors foretold as born to do it. We want to be troubled no more by Arabs; room to breathe; a skyline cleansed of them; no more bleating of sheep knifed by an Arab."

The old jackal wants to purify the territory. He wishes that the presence of the Arabs would be invisible and inaudible. To this end, he wishes their throats to be cut. The old jackal asks the narrator to cut the Arabs' throats with a pair of scissors and presents him with "a small pair of sewing scissors, covered with ancient rust." He wishes, to put it bluntly, for a divine intervention that will clear the earth of this bad breed. "How can you bear to live in such a world," cries the old jackal, "O noble heart and kindly bowels? Filth is their white, filth is their black; their beards are a horror; the very sight of their eye sockets makes one want to spit; and when they lift an arm, the murk of hell yawns in the armpit." The Arabs are disgusting; they are repugnant; they stink. They are horrible. How can such a discourse be conveyed?

The truth of Kafka's description is striking. He is describing the ruses, which is to say, the ways and the detours of intolerance. The jackals do not speak—they howl; they fall to crying; they sob. They present their hate as an atrocious suffering. They try to gain the narrator's pity, to bring him over to their side. Meanwhile, the narrator is not moved. The dialogue was a dialogue among the deaf.

At this point an Arab arrives, the caravan guide, setting the pack of jackals to flight. This is the story's twist of fate. Far from being ignorant of the plot being woven against him, the Arab is amused by it and does not take the jackals' hate seriously: "'So you've been treated to this entertainment too, sir,' said the Arab, laughing as gaily as the reserve of his race permitted. 'You know, then, what the brutes are after?' I asked. 'Of course,' said he, 'it's common knowledge; so long as Arabs exist, that pair of scissors goes wandering through the desert and will wander with us to the end of our days.'" And he continues, with as much humor as intelligence: "Every European is offered [these scissors] for the great work; every European is just the man that Fate has chosen for them." Every European therefore appears between jackals and Arabs as the third party that will settle the situation in blood, by making an entire population disappear. Each European is an included third (contradictory as this may be). Every European is supposed to do what the jackals say, charged with fulfilling their wishes as described. As a result, no European can be a third party, properly speaking. Finally, and paradoxically, the Arabs love the jackals for this very reason, because they are crazy and because their hope is senseless.

Addressing the traveler, the guide interrogates him: "Well, you've seen them. Marvelous creatures, aren't they? And how they hate us!" The guide has a dead camel brought to them during the night. Before the dead camel, the jackals "had forgotten the Arabs, forgotten their hatred, the all-obliterating immediate presence of the stinking carrion bewitched them." As long as there will be men, and as long as there will be camels. . .

The third story, on the other hand, interrogates the position of the witness [*le témoin*]—in other words, the third party who may or may not be able to testify about what he has seen. "In the Penal Colony" is a third text.[107] No animal on the horizon—we are entirely among humans. The story raises questions about the possibility of testimony and the intervention of third parties. This is not a monkey who recounts his calvary and his belated acceptance by men. Nor is this an exchange regarding declared enemies. This is the story of a traveler's visit to a penal colony and his discovery of a singular torture.[108] At a moment marked by a world war, Kafka makes his central character a spectator rather than an actor.[109] Is he a witness? Nothing is less certain. In the end, he will flee.

Kafka's text also presents an officer whose task is to ensure that the colony's operations function smoothly. For the traveler's benefit and in hopes of gaining his approval, this officer explains and comments on the performance of an unusual machine designed to inscribe the law on the bodies of those condemned. How would we describe the viewpoint not of settlers but of colonials? Not of civilians but of the military? Not of those who exploit the earth—and humans—but of those who organize and administer the colony? Kafka's text presents a concentrated version of the colony. It is with great subtlety that Kafka, whose inspiration then "broke down," leaving him forever dissatisfied with the story's epilogue, proposes a portrait of the colony—for example, a penitentiary colony. Perhaps there is a sense in which colonial and penal are equivalent.

"In the Penal Colony" appears as a nightmare—the disguised realization of a repressed desire, as Freud would say. This nightmarish effect is reinforced, as everywhere in Kafka, by the story's atopia (relative, as will be seen). The setting is nowhere—it almost doesn't matter where this happens. Marthe Robert has stressed this point: "If the German readers could read *The Country Doctor* or *The Penal Colony* in the original, what they found there was not their national literature, but a *borderline* product in some ways, to which the differences of construction and of temperament gave almost an *exotic* taste."[110] She reminds us that almost all of Kafka's readers, even the most scholarly among them, like Bernard Groethuysen, make this altogether new literary characteristic into something self-evident, inquiring about neither the author nor the context, and thus falling into the trap of abstraction. Indeed, as she says so justly, "Kafka spoke to the 'world' in a language which truly seemed either to precede the *confusion of languages* or to end it. As he maintained no trace of his origin, no sort of terrestrial belonging, he was granted a sort of right to *extraterrioriality*."[111]

In Kafka, extraterritoriality appeared as the colony's most striking characteristic. This does not mean that the colony is not situated on the terrestrial globe—quite the contrary. However, the colony is a location veritably *cut off from the world*. It is even a break in the world, not just a political and social break, but a juridical and economic one as well. For "In the Penal Colony," questions of language and of place are decisive: it is in French, in a tropical region, that the officer expresses himself, just like the visitor, who obviously understands him. The condemned man, on the other hand, does not speak French. The colony is a third place (neither on the national territory nor on foreign soil) marked by a linguistic divorce (the language spoken by some is not understood by others). But French might also be an international language in Kafka's short story, a third language that one uses precisely when one does not want to be understood by third parties, here the soldier and the condemned man. In any case, the colonial and penal language is unintelligible; it is the language of pure force from which right is excluded.

The text does not, as the title would suggest, take the colony as its object. Indeed, the colony is the place or the scene of a confrontation. To begin with, the colony itself is only a landscape: a "small sandy valley . . . surrounded on all sides by naked crags." Only later does the story introduce the "first houses of the colony" and the "teahouse." This description, according to the indications Kafka gave to his editor Kurt Wolff, was supposed to be preceded by "a *white space* of some magnitude, to be filled by example with asterisks." There is, in fact, a blank, a hiatus, a seamlessness, between the sandy desert and the colony's first houses in the port city. What the writer shows is the site and the underside of the colony. The traveler ends up at the port, safe and sound (*à bon port*). He is saved. But from what? A white space separates two worlds: that of the condemned and that of the residents, that of the military and that of the civilians, that of the country and that of the city—ultimately, that of the living and that of the dead (or vice versa).

The colony is the context for an encounter between "a visitor" on a research trip (a "famous investigator," a "great scholar"), and an "officer," a man who solemnly serves at the head of an apparatus whose text is indecipherable. The officer is representing his country, which is why he is in uniform. "'These uniforms are too heavy for the tropics, surely,' said the traveler, instead of making some inquiry about the apparatus, as the officer had expected. 'Of course,' said the officer . . . 'but they *mean home to us*; we don't want to forget about home.'" The traveler feels admiration for "the officer, who in spite of his tight-fitting full-dress uniform coat, amply befrogged and weighted down by epaulettes, was pursuing his subject with so much enthusiasm." The colony, defined as a space of national representation, is thus determined as a territory of the *imaginary*. Indeed, the continuity between the colony and the home country, the absence of any break, is not actually real, even if it is objective—it is merely imagined.[112] The absence of any break is necessarily, if artificially, put into the image.

If the officer is a citizen of the colonial nation [*un national*], the traveler is for his part a foreigner. Because he is doubly foreign, both to the officer's country and to its colony, he is indecisive. What should he do? In fact, the colony rapidly destroys all discernment. "What?" the traveler says suddenly. "Was something forgotten? A decisive word? A manoeuver? A crutch? Who could see clearly in this confusion? Cursed tropical climate, what are you doing to me? I don't know what's happening to me. My good judgment stayed at home, in the North." When Kafka writes these few lines, he is in the process of composing "In the Penal Colony." These lines are in the *margin* of the story and remained unpublished. Clearly what they want to convey is the gulf that separates the North from the tropics: a gulf such that in situ all good judgment is suspended. Weakening his discernment, this gap affects the traveler's subjectivity. Moreover, the traveler is only passing through the colony. He does not live there and will even hasten to leave, after having received an edifying insight into colonial and penal habits and customs.

Who could see clearly in this confusion? What is the tropical heat becoming? As we know, to give the climate the power of influence over human conduct is to make the heavens responsible for human errancy.

But at bottom the encounter fails. The traveler and the officer are in an awkward situation. Properly speaking, they share neither the same time, nor the same place, nor the same action. The time of the officer is that of an eternal *afterward*. The lost paradise of this colony lies in the recent past. Indeed, the officer attributes all his behavior to the heritage of the former commandant. "It isn't saying too much," he tells the visitor, "if I tell you that the organization of the whole penal colony is his work." The coherence of the organization is such that no successor could "alter anything, at least for many years to come." The organization is presented as an infernal machine, an organization with no subject, an empire of administration. But, to the officer's great regret, even if one may do *everything* in a colony, one still cannot do *anything* whatsoever. There is always a limit, even if only a limit on the amount of violence that can ultimately be deployed. A certain measure always ensures that someone's suffering will no longer have the meaning intended by the one who inflicts it.

For this reason, the officer follows a set of extremely complicated instructions. As for the traveler, he is in a hurry. He is impatient to finish with the colony. At the start, with respect to the machine, he showed "almost visible indifference." "He did not much care about the apparatus." As in Camus's *L'étranger*, besides, the sun prevented him from concentrating. Little by little, he begins to take somewhat more interest in the machine. Kafka writes: "The officer had scarcely noticed the traveler's previous indifference, but he was now well aware of his dawning interest; so he stopped explaining in order to leave a space of time for quiet observation."

The first part of the story involves the exchange between the officer and the traveler concerning the *apparatus*. The second part addresses the *procedure*. It is only as an afterthought that the traveler takes interest in the condemned man, whether he is related to the machine or to the procedure. In fact, the officer has every intention of explaining the basis for the procedure. But, paradoxically, he starts with the last step. The judicial procedure closes with a condemnation: "Whatever commandment the prisoner has disobeyed is written upon his body by the Harrow." This condemnation is preceded by a verdict that is unknown to the condemned man. The law is not his own. In the colony, the law is not the expression of autonomy and of natural human freedom, as philosophers from Rousseau to Kant believed it should be. Quite the contrary, the law is the symbol of the heteronomy of the subject to which it is applied. It traces the wall separating some from others, dividing the glorious body, according to Foucault's expression in *Surveiller et punir*, from the "least body" of the condemned. Following the officer's explanation, "there would be no point in telling him [what law he has broken]. He'll learn it on his body."

The condemned never had any rights, not even to defend himself: in short, he was already condemned. "'He has had no chance of putting up a defense,' said the officer, turning his eyes away as if speaking to himself and so sparing the traveler the shame of hearing self-evident matters explained." If all defense is unnecessary, this is because "guilt is never to be doubted." The way Kafka explicitly presents the functioning of the colony thus corresponds, as we know, to his most obsessive fears, to a regime in which ignorance is the rule: everyone is supposed to lack knowledge of the law. The condemned will thus see "honor thy superiors" physically inscribed upon him: something that is not a law but an order, not a rule but a command, an injunction, an imperative. The same for the officer, who maintains the machine and its detailed, almost unreadable instructions for use.

The traveler is staggered not by the apparatus but by the information he receives regarding the procedure. The first sign of his disagreement is the first moment of his transformation into a witness. "But he must have had some chance of defending himself," he says to the colonial officer regarding the condemned. "The explanation of the judicial procedure had not satisfied him. He had to remind himself that this was in any case a penal colony where extraordinary measures were needed and that military discipline must be enforced to the last." In fact, the exception is the rule. Military customs dominate, and civilian customs are almost absent. The traveler would like to refer to a third party to settle the *différend*. He would like to find a witness and an arbiter at his side.

The officer wants to make the traveler into an ally against the colony's new commandant, who disapproves of these judgments and punishments and who thus appears as a progressive character who expects (this has yet to be determined) to be able to end these barbaric and summary procedures. When the traveler, on the other hand, is seated at the foot of the wall by the officer, he is hoping to be able to find an absent third party, a possible or indeed probable virtual ally. He would like to identify a third who would help him evade the disagreements that might follow from being a witness. When the execution is interrupted by a technical breakdown after it has hardly started, Kafka describes the traveler's uncomfortable position (since this was not a leisure trip) in the following way: "The traveler thought to himself: It's always a ticklish matter to intervene decisively in other people's affairs. He was neither a member of the penal colony nor a citizen of the state to which it belonged. Were he to denounce this execution or actually try to stop it, they could say to him: You are a foreigner, mind your own business." There is no witness, in fact, without a case of conscience. And there is no colony without its witnesses. How does the traveler rationalize? Like anyone. How, indeed, could he reply to the objection? "He could make no answer to that," Kafka writes, "unless he were to add that he was amazed at himself in this connection, for he traveled only as an observer, with no intention at all of altering other people's methods of administering justice."

All the variants of the text show how reluctant the traveler is to commit himself as a witness—in other words, to feel himself *implicated* in what he sees. Kafka envisages several possibilities. He thus imagines that the commandant sends someone to fetch the traveler, and he writes: "He leaped to his feet, all agitated. He said, hand over his heart: 'What a dog I would be to put up with this!' Then he took these words literally and set about running to all sides on his hands and knees. But he made a leap from time to time, positively tearing himself from the ground and hanging around the neck of one of these men, shouting in tears, 'Why must all this be happening to me, to me!' and hurried to take up his former stance [*rejoindre son poste*]." Quite simply, the traveler would have preferred not to be there. He would have preferred to act as if nothing were there.

In another version, Kafka envisioned the following way out: "If his boat had glided across these inconvenient sands to pick him up, he would have been overjoyed. He would have gotten on board, but in climbing, he would have made a last reproach to the officer for his cruel execution of the condemned man: 'I will report all this back home,' he would have added, in raising his voice so that the captain and sailors who leaned curiously over the rails could hear him." If he did not intervene, here and now, to prevent the perpetration of a criminal torture, the traveler would like to be able to say what he observed at a later time and place.

The final version of "In the Penal Colony" has the traveler flee as quickly as possible from this deadly place, preventing anyone from following him. He leaves no doubt that the condemned, figure of the colonial subject, is an absent third. Nor is there any doubt that the colony is marked by the absence of the third. The singular but banal attitude of the traveler, the "famous explorer," the "famous Western investigator," the "illustrious foreigner," testifies to this. Instead of taking a side, he takes his own side. Why would the officer have acted this way if it were not just? As naive as it may be, this question is extraordinarily banal. It is even a ritual question that follows every testimony regarding an injustice. One says: "That's how it's been." The other responds: "But why is it so?" Truly, "one can *testify* only to the unbelievable."[113] Is this a way of understanding? Is it also a way of keeping the peace?

Are there eyewitnesses in the colony? Doesn't the confinement that prevails there make it very difficult for the interior of the colony to have any outside? A penal colony is dedicated to surveillance and punishment. But isn't this the preeminent dimension of any colony, in which obedience is aligned not with a law but with a command [*commandement*]? The penal colony lives under military law. What are the consequences of this? Summary justice. Authoritarian verdicts. No legal defense. Unknown law. Kafka invents an impartial spectator who would prefer never to have been present rather than to be implicated in one way or another in what he sees and hears. But he has no desire to speak, to testify. He sees a torture, and he hears the convoluted explications of an officer who ardently defends the colonial tradition ("a handful of generals . . .").[114]

At the same time, it seems that the officer gives the traveler a colonial declaration of the greatest importance. "'I should like to exchange a few words with you in confidence,' he said, 'may I?'" The traveler then listens to him "with downcast eyes." What does the officer say? "This procedure and method of execution, which you are now having the opportunity to admire, has at the moment no longer any open adherents in our colony. I am its sole advocate, and at the same time the sole advocate of the old Commandant's tradition. I can no longer reckon on any further extension of the method, *it takes all my energy to maintain it as it is.*"

Sensitive to aporias, here Kafka makes the officer a second witness, a witness of a wholly different kind. The officer believes, without question, in what he is doing. He will finish by sacrificing his own life (ultimate testimony to his procedure's legitimacy). For the moment, he believes that he is in the same situation as the traveler: alone against everyone else. He presents himself as the only one to have the courage of his opinions. "Even your coming here today seems to me a significant move," says the officer, "they are cowards and use you as a screen, you, a stranger." Thus Kafka sharpens appearances in confronting the traveler's cowardice with the officer's courage. As a result, he systematically inverts the question of the witness according to a procedure he has used before.[115]

The officer is a witness to the past. The traveler is a witness to the present. The officer carries a memory. From the traveler, on the other hand, one expects some action: his future testimony. Two temporalities of witnessing are distinguished: the one places testimony on the side of *history*, the other on the side of *justice*. If Kafka is unsatisfied with the end of his text, it is certainly because it is much harder to write justice than to recount history. It is more difficult to reflect on the conditions of enunciation than on the nature of an *énoncé*.[116]

There are thus two sorts of witnesses: one (the officer) is a *voice* of memory (the interior story); the other (the traveler) is a *gaze*, not the gaze of a judge but of a crusader against wrongdoing (the exterior story). The first is committed; the second ought to commit himself. It is only when the two dimensions and the two temporalities are confused that the *witness* is identified with the *victim*, as happens today, particularly on the subject of the colonies, to such a point that any personal testimony is considered unreliable. It then seems obvious that the desire to bear witness can be reduced to a desire for vengeance, since the one who speaks about the past does so in the name of memory and of justice. The problematic is completely Nietzschean. Bearing witness, on this reading, is an expression of ressentiment.

The only way to escape this circle is to consider the historian as the one who stands in the position of exterior—an impartial or objective witness. François Hartog, who treated the question of the witness as intrinsic to history [*une "evidence de l'histoire"*] recalls a paradox: the ancient Greeks, as in the Homeric epic, used *histôr* to refer to a witness who knows because he has seen, but "the *histôr*, who intervenes in two quarreling situations, has in fact seen nothing and heard nothing."[117] Which matters more: the witness's eyes or ears? (And must the traveler say what he has seen or what he has heard? How to correlate the two?) Hartog shows that ultimately, it to have ears (must the traveler, as one says in French, "close his eyes is moreover the position of Aristotle, who considered that without h g, memory would lead to no knowledge. Hartog thus believes that the histôr is less an arbiter than the one who guarantees whatever the two parties agreed on at the end of their disagreement.

Does this then mean that only the *martus* counts as witness? The histôr is the guarantor; the martus is the one who provides speech that has been authorized.[118] "What changes the one into the other," writes François Hartog, "is the context of intervention and their respective relations to time. The *histôr*, who intervenes in a situation of *différend*, is required by the two parties and listens to both of them, while the *martus* has only to take care of one side; more correctly, there is only one side. The *martus* intervenes in the present and for the future, while the *histôr* must add the dimension of the past, since his intervention today in a quarrel that has emerged in the past (even the recent past) is also committed to the future."[119] For this reason, moreover, testimony and the witnesses who provide it must still be evaluated (through an examination of their relative authority). "The autopsy, one might contend, is a way of removing or silencing witnesses: the eye of the historian against the ears of witnesses."[120] Under these conditions it is hard to avoid being a forensic doctor. To escape this fate, the historians teach, as did Pierre Vidal-Naquet in 1958 with *L'affaire Audin*.[121]

Walter Benjamin said, with justification, that Kafka's texts were "fairy tales for dialecticians."[122] "The traveler wanted to withdraw his face from the officer and looked around him at random. The officer thought he was surveying the valley's desolation, so he seized him by the hands, turned him around to meet his eyes, and asked: 'Do you realize the shame of it?' But the traveler said nothing." The writer does not give the key; he delivers an abyssal enigma. The officer speaks not to try and move the visitor, but he solicits his intervention. He expects that the latter will take his side and not, as he fears, the side of a commandant opposed to another era's practices.

In fact, as we see, the officer orders the traveler to testify on his behalf, tacitly expressing his view that humanism itself makes modern humanists into manipulators. Here one detects the echo of contemporary critics regarding "human-rights-ism." "You are conditioned by European ways of thought," the officer declares to the explorer, evoking several times the pernicious influence of women on opinions and positions when it comes to military and colonial matters. In his eyes, humanism (or human-rights-ism), whose adversaries, it must be stressed, throw out the human with the bathwater, imposes censorship on the expression of opinions. The advocates of this method of execution, he claims, make "ambiguous remarks"; "there are still many of them but no one will admit it." The officer therefore presents himself as a partisan of free expression, excessively constrained by European prejudices that encourage emotionality over what is ultimately simple justice.

Meanwhile, the officer is not bound by this constraint; he is content to assume it. He imagines the traveler's subjective position even though the latter has neither shown nor mentioned it. What in fact does the traveler say? "I am no expert in criminal procedure. If I were to give an opinion, it would be as a private individual." "I can neither help nor hinder you."

> "I do not approve of your procedure," said the traveler then, "even before you took me into your confidence—of course I shall never in any circumstances betray your confidence—I was already wondering whether it would be my duty to intervene and whether my intervention would have the slightest chance of success. . . . You don't know yet what I mean to do. I shall tell the Commandant what I think of the procedure, certainly, but not at a public conference, only in private; nor shall I stay here long enough to attend any conference; I am going away early tomorrow morning, or at least embarking on my ship."[123]

The "witness" is going to look elsewhere. He cannot be both inside and outside. Will history judge?

Notes

1. The term comes from Mbembe, *On the Postcolony.*

2. Derrida, *Dissemination*, 130–33. Translator's note: The religious festival of Thargelia included rituals of purification that involved banishing (sometimes killing) two victims who represented the city's evil and vulnerability. Ostracism was a political tactic for maintaining the relative equality of citizens by banishing exceptionally talented or influential persons for a certain period of time. On the latter, see Aristotle, *Politics*, 1195–96 (1284a–b).

3. The allusion is to Plato's *Phaedrus*, cited by Derrida in *Dissemination*, 133. Derrida also writes, "The city's body *proper* thus reconstitutes its unity, closes around the security of its inner courts, gives back to itself the word that links it with itself within the confines of the agora, by violently excluding from its territory the representative of an external threat or aggression. That representative represents the otherness of the evil that comes to affect or infect the inside by unpredictably breaking into it. Yet the representative of the outside is nonetheless *constituted*, regularly granted its place by the community, chosen, kept, fed, etc., in the very heart of the inside" (133).

4. Foucault, *History of Madness*, part 1, chap. 2, "The Great Confinement," esp. 54; *Discipline and Punish*, part 3, chap. 3, "Panopticism."

5. Rancière, *Disagreement: Politics and Philosophy.*

6. In *Critiques anthropologiques*, Francis Affergan observes that the variations on the couplet "exclusion/inclusion" are subject to intense paralogisms, just like the couplet "conversion/inversion" or "disenchanted/participatory." In this kind of situation, judgments are often self-contradictory (particularly in statements in which the predicate cancels out the subject). Two consequences follow from this. At the level of meaning, there are theoretical paralogisms; at the level of values, practical paralogisms. The discourses of the French colonial period from the end of the nineteenth to the start of the twentieth century are paradigmatic in this respect. "The integration of those excluded" could be their formula, because everything happens as if the excluded party were active in their own exclusion but passive in their integration.

7. Think of the dismay of those police officers dealing with "difficult" banlieues who say that the task is not one for policing but for politics.

8. La Bruyère, "Of Mankind," sec. 78, p. 194. La Bruyère begins by expressing his debt to Erasmus, the theorist of self-effacement before the principle of civility, which is, at bottom, an erotization of social relations and therefore a displacement of pleasures, a narcissization of mirror relations.

9. Starobinski, "Sur la flatterie," 134.

10. Translator's note: In the work of Albert Memmi and Pierre Bourdieu, respectively.

11. Walzer, *On Toleration*, 52.

12. "Intolerance is commonly most virulent when differences of culture, ethnicity, or race coincide with class differences—when the members of minority groups are also economically subordinated." Walzer also observes: "Curiously, this supposedly necessary and necessarily singular culture is often described as a high culture, as if it is our shared commitment to Shakespeare, Dickens, and James Joyce that has been holding us together all these years." Walzer, *On Toleration*, 56, 96–97.

13. "I would consider myself the happiest of mortals if I could make it so that men were able to cure themselves of their prejudices. Here I call prejudices not what makes one unaware of certain things but what makes one unaware of oneself," said Montesquieu in *L'esprit des lois*. See *Spirit of the Laws*, xliv.

14. "Ascetic ideals reveal so many bridges to *independence* that a philosopher is bound to rejoice and clap his hands when he hears the story of all those resolute men who one day said No to all servitude and went into some *desert*." Nietzsche, *Genealogy of Morals*, 107.

15. For Nietzsche, women are the ideal prey for the ascetic priests because they are "prisoners" and "slaves to work." They know the "three great slogans" of the ascetic ideal, according to the philosopher's formula: poverty, humility, and chastity. Nietzsche, *Genealogy of Morals*, 108.

16. Ghemnour, "La finale." The subtitle was "The Kabyle kid who became the best player in the world was held up in Berlin for an expulsion. Trajectory of an idol."

17. Caussé, "Zinédine Zidane."

18. From this point of view, one must ask who the athletes are. "The 2006 Bleues," wrote Chérif Ghemnour for *Libération* on July 10, 2006, "are his [Zidane's] France of the banlieues, of his childhood, with its Afro-Caribbeans and its 'interior immigrant,' Franck Ribéry."

19. Drousset, "Édito."

20. See Weil, *La France*.

21. Le Bras, *Le sol et le sang*, 11. Statistics and demography appeared toward the middle of the eighteenth century, along with what was called political arithmetic. For the latter, it is not the individual who dies, but mortality that strikes the population. On the other hand, natal-

ity is an object of social Darwinism, and today's natalists readily defend what one might call a nationalism of reproduction.

22. Defended in antiquity by Plato and Aristotle, the "theory of climates" was revived by Jean Bodin in the *Six livres de la République* and then by Montesquieu in *L'esprit des lois*.

23. Le Bras, *Le sol et le sang*, 32.

24. Le Bras, *Le sol et le sang*, 115.

25. Friedrich Ratzel (1844–1904) was a German zoologist and geographer who published, in 1901, *Der Lebensraum* (*Living space*).

26. Le Bras, *Le sol et le sang*, 79. The doctor and statistician Louis Bertillon (1821–83) had two sons: Alphonse Bertillon (1853–1914), the creator of judicial anthropometry, who testified against the deportee Alfred Dreyfus at his trial, and Jacques Bertillon (1851–1922), statistician and demographer, author of the above-cited expressions and, like his father, very interested in the "future of the race" and the preservation of "French blood." Here the question of "origins" and "immigration" is central to demography.

27. This passage, for the "good" immigrant, for the worker, can begin legitimately only with the exercise of a difficult manual occupation. The soil is not covered with blood but with sweat.

28. Here we adopt the complex of the colonized as a paradigm and not as an individual case. In part, this is based on Memmi, *Colonizer and Colonized*, 88–89.

29. Memmi, *Colonizer and Colonized*, 121–22.

30. Nietzsche, *Genealogy of Morals*, 46.

31. Nietzsche, *Beyond Good and Evil*, 397.

32. Are they not the ones that were preached to the famous soccer player?

33. Sigmund Freud, *Interpretation of Dreams*, 136–42. The following quotations are taken from these few pages. In some cases the English translation has been altered to preserve the connotations of the French translation.

34. Only the memory preserves a record of offenses. It conserves the memory of offenses with a view to a trial. This is why meanness is, for Nietzsche, the correlate of ressentiment, of bad conscience, and finally, of asceticism.

35. Translator's note: Comparable to associate professor.

36. Freud, *Interpretation of Dreams*, 140 (my emphasis, translation altered).

37. Freud, *Interpretation of Dreams*, 141–42.

38. "Justice without strength is a contradiction. . . . Strength without justice is an indictment. . . . Justice lays itself open to wrangling. Strength is clearly recognizable and cannot be argued with." Pascal, *Pensées and Other Writings*, 34.

39. Nietzsche, *Daybreak*, sec. 221, 225.

40. From the spirit's point of view, Pascal's principle: "Il faut s'abêtir," as Nietzsche writes in French. *Genealogy of Morals*, 131.

41. "Supposing that what is at any rate believed to be the 'truth' really is true, and the *meaning of all culture* is the reduction of the beast of prey 'man' to a tame and civilized animal, a *domestic animal*, then one would undoubtedly have to regard all those instincts of reaction and *ressentiment* through whose aid the noble races and their ideals were finally confounded and overthrown as the actual *instruments of culture*." Nietzsche, *Genealogy of Morals*, 42.

42. "Un rapport pour une académie," in Kafka, *Récits, romans, journaux*, 1084–95. The following quotations are taken from these few pages. The English translation, "A Report to an

Academy," can be found in *Complete Stories*, 250–62. In some cases the English translation has been altered to preserve the connotations of the French edition.

43. Kafka, "A Report to an Academy," 250, 254.

44. Nietzsche, *Genealogy of Morals*, 120.

45. Grégoire, *Essai sur la régéneration*. See also the analysis of Ozouf, *L'homme régénéré*. During the French Revolution, the Abbé Grégoire (1750–1831) defended the abolition of slavery and the equality of rights between Christians and Jews. He was editor of the first article in the Declaration of the Rights of Man and Citizen: "Men are born free and equal in rights. Social distinctions can only be founded on common utility."

46. Walzer, *On Toleration*, 69. "Toleration, remember, is not a formula for harmony: it legitimates previously repressed or invisible groups so enables them to compete for available resources" (107).

47. I use the expression *headscarf [foulard]* for simplicity's sake.

48. Laïcité is a political and legal pact based on the law of 1905 known as the Separation Act. It remains the basis for all relations between religions and the state in France: "The Republic ensures freedom of conscience. It guarantees the free exercise of religions with the sole restrictions decreed hereafter in the interest of public order. . . . The Republic does not recognize, fund or subsidize any religion. . . . State, departmental and commune budgets, together with all expenses relating to the exercise of religions will be abolished." See Legifrance, "Loi du 9 décembre 1905"; also see Saunders, "Knife-Edge of Religion"; Baubérot, "French Laicization"; Balibar, "Dissonances within Laïcité"; and Freedman, "Secularism as a Barrier?"

49. See, for example, Noiriel, "Le jugement des pairs," where the author analyzes the frantic struggle of the educational and university system against accents.

50. One of these, an outraged philosophy professor named Robert Redeker, later got himself renowned for religious neutrality, the chief weapon in his secular combat: "Hate and violence," he has written, "dwell in the Koran, the book by which every Muslim is educated." See Redeker, "Face aux intimidations islamistes." When the author told a television interviewer that he had received death threats, a petition in *Le Monde* on October 2 solicited "unconditional support for Robert Redeker, threatened with death for having criticized Islam," and was signed among others by Bernard-Henri Lévy, Alain Finkielkraut, Pascal Bruckner, Roger-Paul Droit, Claude Lanzmann, Elisabeth Roudinesco, and Elisabeth Badinter.

51. The law separating churches from the state in 1905 (thereby defining laïcité) is not applied throughout all French territories. In Alsace-Moselle, the local law concerning religious groups is primarily the result of the concordat of 1802. In the departments of the Bas-Rhin, Haut-Rhin, and the Moselle, four groups are recognized: the Catholic faith, the Protestant and Reformed faiths, and Judaism. Religious teaching, forbidden in the other French departments, is carried out in public schools.

Guyana remains even today under the rule of the royal act of August 27, 1828. Only the Catholic faith is recognized. The statutes of 1939, called Mandel laws, which allow all religious believers to benefit from public aid, are also enforced. These statutes are also enforced in the overseas collectivities ruled by article 74 of the Constitution (French Polynesia, Wallis and Futuna, and Saint Pierre and Miquelon) except in Saint-Barthélemy and Saint-Martin, as well as New Caledonia and Mayotte.

Mayotte, in the Indian Ocean, is part of the Comoros archipelago, which became the 101st French department in 2011. Its population is 95 percent Muslim.

52. Quoted in *Libération*, October 4, 1989.

53. Three middle schoolers (*collégiennes*) were sent home from their collège on December 16, 1990, one year after the Conseil d'État delivered its ruling (November 27, 1989), and one year after a memo from the minister of national education on December 12, 1989 (see Conseil d'État, "Avis 'Port du foulard islamique,'" and "Circulaire," respectively). They were indefinitely suspended on the basis of a regulation interior to the collège, which followed the cited texts in stipulating that "the wearing of any distinctive clothing or other sign of religious, political, or philosophical belonging is strictly forbidden." On the other hand, on November 21, 1990, the Paris court of appeals stated that an association has the right to make a choice among the forms of racism that it intends to oppose in court. According to Romain Marie, European deputy of the Front National, it was a matter of litigation opposing the General Alliance against Racism and for the Respect of French and Christian Identity (AGRIF—Alliance générale contre le racisme and pour le respect de l'identité française et chrétienne), an association led by Bernard Anthony, and the weekly *L'Événement du jeudi*, pursued by association. The court, in its ruling, said that an association cannot find itself under legal obligation to fight against "racism in its general meaning, without other specification" to exercise the rights reserved for a civil party. The objective of AGRIF is to fight against "anti-French and anti-Christian racism, pornography and attacks on respect for women and children."

54. Quoted in an interview published in *Le Figaro*, November 7 and 8, 1992.

55. Quoted in *Le Monde*, November 4, 1992.

56. Quoted in *Le Monde*, November 7, 1992.

57. On the one hand, texts of domestic law: texts of general applicability, texts relative to the organization of teaching, texts relative to the conditions of visitation and the entry of foreigners into France. On the other hand, international texts.

58. Conseil d'État, "Avis 'Port du foulard islamique.'"

59. "Circulaire," 110.

60. Apart from wearing the scarf, certain students' selective absenteeism (from gymnastics and natural science classes) despite their obligation to attend regularly constituted the submerged part of the iceberg, a less visible but more significant violation of the common rule and ordinary regulations. Paradoxically, what posed the problem and was repressed was not this absenteeism but the exterior sign of (Muslim) religion.

61. See Sahel, "L'Abbé Grégoire." On Abbé Grégoire, see above, note 45. The philosopher and mathematician Nicolas de Condorcet (1743–94) took up the defense of women's rights and the rights of black peoples. He wrote an antislavery pamphlet, "Reflections on Negro Slavery" (1781), and was active in the Society of the Friends of the Blacks (founded in 1788). Gaspard Monge (1746–1818) was a mathematician who joined Napoleon's expedition to Egypt and Syria, participating in the scientific work of the Institut d'Égypte. After returning to France in 1798, Monge was appointed president of the Egyptian commission.

62. The ruling [*ordonnance*] of August 17, 1945, introduced *parité* of representation between the Muslim college and the college of common law, each henceforth represented by twenty-two parliamentary representatives—fifteen deputés and seven senators. See Weil, "Le statut des musulmans." As I have shown, this colonial language recurs in French political life when it comes to women. A paradigmatic example: male-female *parité*. On *parité* between the sexes in electoral lists, henceforth required by a series of laws beginning June 6, 2000, see Luste Boulbina, "Le deuxième sexe."

63. Rousseau, "On the Social Contract," bk. 1, chap. 7, p. 150.

64. My emphasis.

65. "Circulaire," 112.

66. "Circulaire," 111 (my emphasis).

67. "Circulaire," 111 (my emphasis).

68. Jean-Edmé Romilly (1739–79), a Swiss theologian and Diderot's friend, wrote the article on "Tolerance" in the *Encyclopédie*, two years after the appearance of Voltaire's *Traité sur la tolérance*.

69. Jospin, "Le moment ou jamais," 18. An opportunity for the acting minister to settle accounts "with some ideologues who have reaffirmed an ideal laïcité with icy intransigence, but once again without thinking about all the consequences to which their premises lead" (16).

70. Jospin, "Le moment ou jamais," 18.

71. See also the statement made by Lionel Jospin at the Senate during the commemoration of the decree of September 26, 1791, granting emancipation to the Jews of France, partially reproduced in Jospin, "L'émancipation des Juifs."

72. See P. Birnbaum, "Sur l'étatisation révolutionnaire," and *Les fous*, particularly chap. 9, "Les idéologues de la République: La laicisation de la société."

73. See, for example, Kintzler, "La laïcité scolaire," who writes: "It is necessary that things relating to belief and unbelief remain *private*. They must only be made *public* if they are the source of a wrong or of a crime affecting the common law." This is a curious passage from the private to the public, which can only be carried out by way of penalization (where are the terrorists?)

74. At the same moment, SOFRES revealed that 9 percent of French would not vote for a candidate whom "they learned was of the Jewish confession" (poll taken September 20–22).

75. In May 1999, Pierre Bourdieu was interviewed by Pierre Carles and Gaby Reich on the difference between the left and the right, and he said with respect to Ségolène Royal, "She has what I call a habitus, a way of being, of speaking that tells you she is on the right, even if she holds left-wing positions." Ségolène Royal was later a candidate for president of France in 2007. See Bouvier, "Ségolène Royal."

76. This is precisely what political terror means, in the strict sense: a regime of *suspected persons*, as was so well shown by the French Revolution.

77. In June 1764, *Le dictionnaire philosophique ou la raison par l'alphabet (de Abraham à vertu)* was published anonymously in Geneva.

78. An exclusion that we must try to avoid in the meantime: it is not the least of paradoxes in the "scarf affair" that the students were eventually excluded from school due to the desire to better integrate them into French society.

79. We must remember that it was with respect to the classroom that the discussions were the most bitter. Certain young women were admitted with their scarves in the documentation room of their collège, while at the same time being excluded from the classroom and, ipso facto, from the class. The classroom thus appeared simultaneously as a private space (civility) and a public space (tolerance). In the Renaissance, the humanist Erasmus invented civility and indicated some types of clothing corresponding to such states of the soul, thus making the clothes the "body of the body," mirrors of the soul. When a girl wears an Islamic scarf, does she show a body without a soul? A body with no soul: a woman's body!

80. Tocqueville, *Democracy in America*, 302.

81. Tocqueville, *Democracy in America*, 327.

82. Tocqueville, *Democracy in America*, 328n32.

83. Tocqueville, *Democracy in America*, 317.

84. Tocqueville, *Democracy in America*, 342.

85. Naïr, "Ce morceau de ténèbres."

86. In fact, how could one help but notice the hysterization of the wearing of the veil among some of these little ones or these young women?

87. From the November 2, 1992, injunction from the Conseil d'État. David Kessler was government commissioner to the Conseil d'État.

88. Foucault, *Discipline and Punish*, 228.

89. In fact, the disappearance of discipline, a genuine disappearance, is confused with the disappearance of authority, which has simply not taken place. One must read Foucault to understand that discipline is a regime of bodies, which cannot coincide with a society of control, a regime of flows.

90. Martin Buber (1878–1965) was active in the movement *Ihud* (Union), which sought the creation of a binational Jewish-Arab state in Palestine. In 1923, he published *I and Thou* (*Ich und Du*), a book in which he develops the idea according to which a subject maintains two distinct relationships to the world. The I-thou relationship, on the one hand, is rooted in dialogue; on the other hand, the I-this relationship is anchored in monologue. Dialogue opens authentic relations (*Beziehung*) while monologue refers to what is insignificant or to superficiality (*Erlebnis* or *Erfahrung*): "The basic word I-You can only be spoken with one's whole being," whereas "The basic word I-It can never be spoken with one's whole being" (54). In his *Problèmes de linguistique générale*, Benveniste has shown the dissymmetry of the third person with respect to the two preceding persons. The third person, in fact, is not a person—it is only a subject. The third "person" designates the one spoken about, the one who is, in interlocution, absent. The first person designates the one who speaks; the second refers to the one being addressed. Benveniste, *Problems in General Linguistics*, 195–200, 221–22.

91. The most famous of these beings treated as fair animals is without doubt Saartje Baartman, known as "the Hottentot Venus," imported from Cape Town in South Africa, who landed at London in 1810. She died at the age of twenty-six and was dissected by Georges Cuvier, who, like others, was interested only in the evidence she could provide, in herself, regarding her "primitive sexuality." Saartje Baartman's genitals were subsequently displayed at the Musée de l'Homme in Paris. See this volume, pt. 2, chap. 1.

92. Cited in Deroo and Lemaire, *L'illusion coloniale*, 57.

93. Mbembe, "Regard," an article that reconsiders in part the contents of remarks he made at the conference "Images et colonies" in 1993.

94. Kafka, "A Report to an Academy," in *Complete Stories*, 250–62. The following quotations are taken from these few pages. In some cases the English translation has been altered to preserve the connotations of the French edition.

95. The artist Chéri Samba titled one of his paintings *Falsifier un nom, c'est dénaturer son porteur* (1997). He writes: "To falsify a name is to adulterate its owner and his ancestral spirits will turn their back on him. Samba means: to explore, to acquire, to take possession. But someone comes and says that this name must be pronounced Zamba; this changes everything because Zamba indicates a bird or a rat nest. Just one letter is therefore enough to spoil the one whose name it is." This conveys quite easily the importance of transcriptions. See Magnin, *J'aime Chéri Samba*, 86–87.

96. Men taught a monkey to shake hands, but is it not the monkey who taught them to speak frankly? The handshake is the expression of agreement between two parties, in a contract (between fools?).

97. When Voltaire, for example, ruminates on the existence of blacks, in his *Essai sur les moeurs*, he finishes by claiming that albinos, which he judges as being on the last level of the human species, are the fruit of "abominable acts of love between monkeys and girls."

98. Husserl, *Crisis of European Sciences*, 275.

99. Just think of colonial postcards titled "scenes and types."

100. Kafka, "A Report to an Academy," 251–52 (translation altered). In the French edition, the phrase is "*un coup de fusil criminel*.")

101. In the margin of the text, one finds this dialogue: "('I'—'you' . . .): 'A—no way out, then? B—I have not found any. A—and meanwhile, of all of us, you are the one who knows the region best. B—yes.'" Kafka, "Journal de l'année 1917," in *Récits, romans, journaux*, 1108.

102. Translator's note: In French, this is *maîtrise souveraine du mouvement*—"sovereign mastery of movement."

103. "To tolerate life remains, after all, the first duty of all living beings. Illusion becomes valueless if it makes this harder for us," said Freud in "Thoughts for the Times," 299.

104. Kafka, "Chacals et Arabes," in *Récits, romans, journaux*, 1057–61; translated as "Jackals and Arabs," in *Complete Stories*, 407–11. The following quotations are drawn from these pages.

105. This is what can be seen with the naked eye in examining the first phases of French colonization in Algeria and seen with a magnifying glass in reading Tocqueville's reports regarding this colonization. Cf. Tocqueville, *Sur l'Algérie*. Translator's note: Several of these reports are translated into English in Tocqueville, *Empire and Slavery*.

106. In these texts of Kafka's, age [*l'ancienntité*] is a recurrent observation that one also finds in "In the Penal Colony": "Although this tea house was very little different from the other houses of the colony, which were all very dilapidated, even up to the Commandant's palatial headquarters, it made on the traveler *the impression of a historic tradition of some kind*, and he felt *the power of past days*." Kafka, "In the Penal Colony," *Complete Stories*, 166; "Dans la colonie pénitentiaire," *Récits, romans, journaux*, 1014. Moreover, in both texts an elder [*ancien*] is present—jackal in the first case, commandant in the second.

107. "Dans la colonie pénitentiaire," Kafka, *Récits, romans, journaux*, 985–1015; "In the Penal Colony," *Complete Stories*, 140–67. The following quotations are taken from these pages. In some cases the English translation has been altered to preserve the connotations of the French edition.

Three persons are required for rationality to emerge. This is indeed the lesson in legal philosophy Hegel gives us when he develops the difference between revenge and punishment. The gap, in fact, arises because the first is a passionate repair of the passions while the second is a rational and reasoned response. More radically still, it is the existence of a third party, the judge in this case, who permits the passage from one state to the other: one cannot be both judge and plaintiff. This means that punishment can be brought to an end while revenge is an indefinite process.

108. In 1862, New Caledonia became a "deportation" center. The law of May 27, 1885, introduced into French penal law the complementary punishment of "relégation," which consisted in the perpetual incarceration of the condemned persons, in particular recidivists, on the territory of overseas possessions. The penalty of relegation, progressively softened, was definitively suppressed by the law of July 17, 1970. The origin of relegation goes back to Roman law. In Rome, every citizen condemned to relegation was, as formerly in French law, free on the soil where he underwent his punishment. The first and only political deportee to go anywhere but New Caledonia, Alfred Dreyfus, was sent to the Salvation Isles, used as a naval prison first under the Directory and then under Napoléon III, according to a law promulgated February

9, 1895. He was placed on Devil's Island, a former leper colony, and housed in a stone cabin. On September 3, 1896, the false news of an escape mobilized jailers up and down the line. From September 6 to October 20, Dreyfus endured the torture of the "double boucle," which inspired Kafka. Here is how Dreyfus himself described it after his liberation:

> Two irons in the form of a U were fixed by their lower part to the sides of the bed. In these irons an iron bar was locked, to which two rings were attached. At one end of the bar, from one side a stopper, on the other side a padlock, in such a way that the bar was fixed to the irons and thus to the bed. When my feet were then placed in the two rings, I could no longer move around; I was invariably fixed to the bed. The torture was horrible, above all on humid nights. The rings around my ankles were very tight and quickly hurt.

See Turlais, "Alfred Dreyfus," 96.

109. One cannot fail to think of Robert Musil's *Désarrois de l'élève Törless*, which dates from a little after the same time period (1906) and also addresses the question of the witness. While Reiting and Beineberg, "today's dictators *in nucleo*," according to the author's formula, martyr their young Jewish fellow student Basini in an Austrian middle school, Törless says not a word and consents.

110. Robert, "Kafka in France," 3.

111. Robert, "Kafka in France," 4. And at the same time, as she observes, Franz Werfel predicted that "No-one beyond Tetschen-Bodenbach will understand Kafka" (7).

112. This is how, in the colony, one constructs even buildings that represent the (home) country.

113. Derrida, *Monolingualism of the Other*, 20.

114. On April 21, 1961, a putsch took place in Algiers, led by four generals who announced the next day that they had taken control of Algeria and the Sahara. On April 23, de Gaulle delivered a speech in military dress asking soldiers to refuse the coup d'état: "An insurrectional power is being established in Algeria by a military *pronunciamento*. Those guilty of usurpation have exploited the passion of the directors of certain special units, the inflamed commitment of a part of the European-descended population led astray by fears and myths, and the powerlessness of officials overwhelmed by the military conspiracy. This power has a face: a handful of retired generals; it has a reality: a group of partisan officers, ambitious and fanatical." De Gaulle, "Message radiotelévisé."

115. For example, in lectures on Kafka published under the title *Exégèse d'une legend*, Stéphane Mosès has analyzed the text of *The Metamorphosis* in terms of a "subjective story in the third person" and in detaching several fundamental characteristics in this text. "In a general sense, the relations between enunciation and what is said in *The Metamorphosis* can be schematized in the following way: a speaker, whom we call the *narrator*, produces in an enunciative act (E1), an *énoncé* (e1), which we call the *external story*, which has as its object a second speaker, the *protagonist*, who produces in turn and in a second enunciative act (E2), a second *énoncé* (e2), which we call the *interior story*." Mosès, *Exégèse d'une legend*, 56.

116. Translator's note: In Benveniste's linguistic theory, the enunciation (*énonciation*) is the act of speaking, and the *énoncé* is the statement or content of what is said.

117. Hartog, *Évidence de l'histoire*, 199. Significantly, the author stages Ulysses (again!), this time opposed to the bard of the Phéaciens. The latter presents a handsome speech, to which Ulysses addresses a critique: "You sing . . . as if somewhere you had been there yourself or as if you had heard it from someone." See Hartog, *Évidence de l'histoire*, pt. 2, chap. 5, "Le témoin et l'historien," and p. 202.

118. Translator's note: According to Hartog, the Greek term *martus* refers to a witness who can be counted upon to remember: for example, a god to whom one appeals. The martus need not be an "ocular" witness and might only remember on the basis of hearing. By contrast, in the *Iliad*, the term *histôr* referred to someone who mediated and reported the outcome of a struggle in which he or she was not initially involved (Hartog's reference is to Agamemnon, who mediated between two of his warriors), but for Herodotus *histôr* meant someone who *saw* rather than heard; and, by extension, the one who, like Ulysses listening to the Phéacian bard, could *imagine* events and make them *vividly present* on the basis of what he or she had heard. Over time, the function of witness was associated more and more closely with the authoritative voice or "source" than with the one who evaluates and transmits the meaning of an event, whether personally experienced or acquired secondhand.

119. Hartog, *Évidence de l'histoire*, 200.

120. Hartog, *Évidence de l'histoire*, 202–3.

121. Maurice Audin (1932–57) was a French mathematician at the University of Algiers, member of the Algerian Communist Party, and independence fighter. He was arrested on June 11, 1957, in the course of the Battle of Algiers, and disappeared. The official report spoke of an escape. Pierre Vidal-Naquet debunked this account and proposed rather that Audin had died during a torture session. He was able to retrace the complete history later after gaining access to different judicial dossiers, and he published his findings, which were reprinted in 1989. In May 2017, some intellectuals—including Edgar Morin and Benjamin Stora—addressed a letter to the president of France, Emmanuel Macron, asking him to finally (officially) determine the truth about the Audin affair.

122. Benjamin, "Franz Kafka," 117.

123. Kafka, "In the Penal Colony," *Complete Stories*, 159–60.

2

CHALLENGING HISTORICAL CULTURE

LET US THINK THE COLONY: FOLLOWING THE PATH opened by Foucault, think it without rendering it historically present, without representing it. Foucault proposes a singular approach beginning from absence in terms of what, in 1966, he calls "the thought of the outside": "Not reflection, but forgetting; not contradiction, but a contestation that effaces; not reconciliation, but droning on and on; not mind in laborious conquest of its unity, but the endless erosion of the outside; not truth finally shedding light on itself, but the streaming and distress of a language that has always already begun."[1] Absence is an outside delivering neither any essence nor any positivity whatsoever. To give it a voice, one must "accumulate," as Édouard Glissant recommends in his *Discours antillais*—pursue the border between the oral and the written, "abandon the cry," "forge a word."

Rather than recalling the colony as the "origin" of France's contemporary problems or as the "beginning" of new independent states (and the inverse), we must actively forget the colony through an act of deconstruction. This is not about philosophy of history: "Under the sign of history's cross, all discourse became a prayer to the god of just causes."[2] Nor is it about metaphysics—either that of the great cause, or the origin, or the beginning.

The Colony, between the Abuse of History and the Excess of Memories[3]

In France's public debates, the scope of the colony is often reduced to Algeria, which is its unavoidable paradigm. Indeed, Algeria was a settler colony, and the repatriation of European populations left scars over the nation's entire territory. In addition, Algerian independence in 1962 was achieved only after a long war. Independence seems to be a foundational event, almost the alpha and the omega of the historical process. But this way of approaching things involves a mystification, as Foucault has shown. "In short," he writes, "by opposing the philosophico-juridical discourse which models itself on the problem of sovereignty and the law, this discourse that deciphered the permanence of war in society is an essentially historico-political discourse, a discourse in which truth functions as a weapon for a partisan victory, a darkly critical discourse which is, at the same time, intensely mythical."[4] Algeria is the tree that hides the forest of French colonies. Due to its paradoxically "privileged" position, it constitutes an epistemological obstacle. For reasons of historical proximity, geographical proximity, migration, intermarriage [*mixité*]—in short, due to its (false) familiarity—the disquieting foreigner, Algeria, is a stumbling block for thought. On the day when this obstacle is completely overcome, science and politics will finally be decolonized.

For this to happen, though, we must reflect here and now on the abuse of history that produces historical culture. Foucault has shown why history, ethnology, and psychoanalysis do not resemble sociology, psychology, or semiology.[5] The first three discourses animate "the entire domain" of the human sciences across its "whole surface" by "spread[ing] their concepts throughout it," proposing "their methods of decipherment and their interpretations everywhere," as can be seen, moreover, in postcolonial studies.[6] But to speak of historical culture is to place oneself beyond the strict domain of the human sciences and to reflect on the ways historical categories overflow the ordinary categories of cognition. In every given era, there is something that escapes what is knowable. But there are also things that seem to be very well known in a given epoch, simply because they are approached in language that is so familiar. The use of a common language contributes to the production of legitimate discourses. Thus, in France the colony is almost always approached from a historical angle—in histories of colonization, histories of decolonization. The past offers tea leaves to be read.

Literature is out of the picture. So is philosophy. Yet to change this situation, we must begin by interrogating the "historical culture" that conditions our gaze with respect to the colonies of the ex-French empire and, less obviously, with respect to our passions, our interests, and thereby our positions. When a president of the French Republic addresses a specific public in Dakar, he can still see there "the elite of African youth," without apparently finding it odd to amalgamate all the nations and all the nationalities of an entire continent.[7] Is what he lacks historical culture, or is it not rather a matter of critical analysis?

In 1870, at the age of twenty-six, Friedrich Nietzsche signed up as a volunteer in the Franco-German War. In 1872, he published *The Birth of Tragedy*. In fall 1873, he began composing the second *Untimely Meditation*, which he published in February of the following year. It was titled "On the Uses and Disadvantages of History for Life." Indeed, Nietzsche was insightful when it came to (Franco-German) liabilities and disagreements. His critique of historiography and its uses is both severe and ferocious.[8] The philosopher makes academic history into a kind of individual or collective insomnia, thereby showing that the ultimate fate of the past is to be forgotten.[9]

Without a doubt, this places historiography on the side of mourning. For Nietzsche, human health rests on our ability to be ignorant regarding the historical dimension of things. If Nietzsche opposes life to history and its academic writing, this is because a historical phenomenon "known clearly and completely and resolved into a phenomenon of knowledge is, for him who has perceived it, dead."[10] Should we then avoid knowing about it? Or must we, to the contrary, know it so as to get rid of it and bury it in the historians' cemetery? No debate over a politically controversial historical phenomenon can avoid such a dilemma: certain people preach forgetting while others advocate historical knowledge. If we acknowledge the past, what do we do with it? Is it enough to pose memory and history as alternatives? As if in choosing history we could be saved! Foucault, who studied this text of Nietzsche's, saw clearly that beginnings are struck by "dissension" and "disparity" and that history is marked by "the luck of the battle."[11]

When Nietzsche declares his relation (there is no philosophical relation . . .) to a specific form of knowledge, to history, and more generally to an intellectual and political culture, the result is scandalous. "I am here attempting," he writes, "to look afresh at something of which our time is rightly proud—its cultivation of history—as being injurious to it, a defect and a deficiency in it; because I believe, indeed, that we are all suffering from a consuming fever of history and ought at least to recognize that we are suffering from it."[12] We are astonished by Nietzsche's objective in writing the second untimely meditation. For doesn't history produce benefits, and not just for historians? What does the philosopher mean by *historical fever*? To be sure, his hammer blows are intended to reveal the disadvantages of history for life. Here we see a truly iconoclastic way of saying that knowledge has not just a social price but also a human cost.

For Nietzsche, history is a potentially dangerous intellectual fever.[13] Is it not a prison populated with phantoms?[14] Is history not a gigantic nightmare, whose impression is no less forceful for being unreal? Must not the hatchet be buried and the wars themselves forgotten? From this point of view, it is hardly surprising that at the end of the Second World War, the historian Lucien Febvre envisaged the intellectual work before him in the same terms as did the philosopher Nietzsche emerging from the war of 1870. As a historian, what Febvre recommends is forgetting: "Forgetting is necessary for groups and societies that want to live." He sees the historian as the one who must "organize the past so as to prevent it from weighing too heavily on men's shoulders."[15] To forget, meanwhile, is not to be silent—quite the contrary. Forgetfulness in no way resembles silence.

The problem for Nietzsche is not so much the *distance* or the *nature* of the object (history) as the *use* that the subject expects to make of it, or perhaps the advantage he or she hopes to gain. Three relationships to the historical object are possible for Nietzsche, which define three historiographies, three distinct types of history.[16] If it is a matter of acting and of pursuing a goal, history will be monumental. All the same, it takes only a small step to go from a monumental past to a mythical fiction.[17] If it is a matter of conserving and of venerating what has been, history will be antiquarian [*traditionaliste*].[18] If it is a matter, finally, of suffering and of deliverance, history will be critical. It is quite clear that critique is a kind of medicine [*remède*]. Is history then a pharmacy? What to do, but also what to think, when, as the philosopher writes, "the present oppresses"? If the monumentalist historians "pose as physicians, while their basic intent is to mix poisons," if the antiquarians appear basically inoffensive, because the worst they can do is paralyze action, one realizes that the critical historians can also be dangerous in their own way: these are the ones, in fact, who judge and condemn.[19] From their perspective, there is no history apart from fault, and, under the aegis of the all-powerful principle of responsibility, every deed enfolds a doing that is a wrongdoing.

For this reason, the historian appears as someone who rights a wrong. To the extent that they govern over a wrong, historians soothe. It is less a matter of establishing deeds or facts than of determining faults. Thus, academic history is on the side of reactivity, of *ressentiment*, and of bad conscience. How can it escape this fate? Moreover, isn't this what is meant by the reproach "Let us live!"? When someone like Hegel, on the other hand, was interested in a philosophy of history, he was preoccupied with g beyond reconciling himself to the real without illusions. Hegel represents another relation to present suffering—not moral, but theological. Nietzsche, in other words, breaks with all historical theology. The critical historians are not priests. What are they? When one is suffering, the entire past seems brought into question. Nietzsche knows something about that: "Every past . . . is worthy to be condemned."[20]

The colony is no exception. It is not a matter of sorting through the past as if it were an international scrapheap in which some things would be clean, reusable, and recyclable, while others, too dirty, would be abandoned. Indeed, the problem is that the very same person who condemns the confusions, the passions, the errors, and the crimes of the past is their heir and is condemned along with his or her inheritance. The effort appears unnatural. "It is thus," Nietzsche declares, "an attempt to give oneself, as it were *a posteriori*, a past in which one would like to originate, as opposed to that in which one did originate—always a dangerous attempt because it is so hard to know the limit to denial of the past."[21] The critical historian's entire effort is thus essentially one of making a positive change.

What have the historians turned us into? Nietzsche's critique is not addressed directly to the historians, but to the excess of history constitutive of "historical culture," itself characteristic of modernity. First, we have become growling bellies, rumbling between interiority and exteriority[22]—bellies exposed to indigestion. Nietzsche opposes life to history precisely to the extent that historiography disrupts our sense of external reality and distracts us from what is essential. In fact, the essential is like human suffering in being always unhistorical. The philosopher emphasizes the pernicious detachment that can contribute to a true historical culture, because this detachment is the best way to "become insensible to barbarism."[23] Thereby Nietzsche intends to question the objectivity of historical culture and with it the objectivity of the historian, along with his or her concern for justice. Indeed, what the philosopher denounces in objectivity is its tendency to mask weakness and the absence of personality. In the scientific pretention to objectivity, the philosopher sees only an avatar of the "frock coat of bourgeois universality," a kind of good sense adapted to the modern person whose "good sense is more childish than that of the child and more simple than simplicity," the one who is a "walking encyclopedia" and, in some ways, a "concrete abstraction."[24] The historian's objectivity, finally, is his or her form of barbarism.

On the other hand, Nietzsche contends, "A historiography could be imagined which had in it not a drop of common empirical truth and yet could lay claim to the highest degree of objectivity"[25]—from whence the second question addressed to modern persons, that of justice. Charles Péguy is its herald, declaring: "It is evident that historical judgment is not a judicial judgment; we know this from regrettably abundant experience—and the Dreyfus affair was only one illustration of this experience among others, following on so many others—we know because we have sensed how few judicial judgments are based in law, to more or less the same degree in military and civil cases, and above all how unjust they were; now, the first thing we will ask from historical judgments, in admitting provisionally that there are any, is that they be just."[26] Historiography does not merely promote the sense of justice as a striking trait of historical culture but also promotes a meaning of justice it claims is superior to that of past humankind. "Let one now imagine today's historical virtuoso," Nietzsche writes, "is he the most just man of his time?"[27]

Why such a concern for justice? When Michel de Certeau published *Histoire et psychanalyse entre science et fiction* twenty years ago, he showed that contemporary historiography was not finished with its mourning for the real. He writes: "It is not surprising that historiography—which is undoubtedly the most ancient and the most haunted by the past—should become a privileged field for the return of this phantom."[28] In fact, the historian's discourse always has to do with "the other's death"; this other of yesterday, this foreigner of the past, is always dead for us today.[29] But the greatest difficulty, without doubt, is what this discourse has to say at times regarding the foreigner, its specific way of dealing with the other, dead not only today but also yesterday. For there are many ways to die. To die is certainly and in the first place to lose one's life, but this can also be a matter of losing one's being (and becoming a deportee, i.e., a case number), losing ownership of one's body (and becoming a slave), or losing one's individuality (and becoming a native, an example). The reason certain histories are more difficult to write than others is that losses are more serious than clashes.

Felix the Cat runs at top speed. He races over the edge of a cliff. Suddenly he realizes that the ground has disappeared beneath him. He falls. This is the bizarre story told by de Certeau to explain what it means to hear the active *way* in which we are reached by what is said—in other words, what it means to abandon an epistemological base. In fact, truth always proceeds from a change of terrain. This is why it can hurt. It can hurt by bringing out another image of the self even as it reveals another perspective on things. Thus understood, truth is independent of its author's will. It is not a result, properly speaking. It rather appears as an absent dimension of a certain number of discourses, indeed a great number. In fact, one's discourse about others can cause them to die. It suffices to treat them as absent.

The present troubles the past, but the past disturbs the present. At the same time, the past provokes questions concerning the present itself, without producing any lessons. Without a doubt, the current debate in French academic history concerning the war of 1914 raises fewer questions said to be historical than said to be philosophical.[30] In any case, they tend to be conceptual rather than factual questions. Were the soldiers consenting or coerced? Were they heroes or poor bastards? Roland Dorgelès reflects on the Chemin des Dames: "Three hundred thousand dead, how many tears does this make?"[31] One sees immediately that it is delicate to think, and thus to weigh, each person's participation in events.

In any case, this problematic is central. We encounter it again, for example, with respect to the *Judenräte*, the "Jewish councils" in Germany during the Third Reich. We also encounter it with respect to the settlers [*colons*], the colonials [*coloniaux*], and the ensemble of Europeans and their role in colonial Algeria.[32] Consenting or coerced? This inquiry affects, for example, those called up during the Algerian War. Finally, we can pose this question with respect to the indigènes themselves—and they are not, to be sure, undifferentiated. What we are asking about is the nature and the degree of each one's complicity in the operation, and not just the conception and creation, of institutions like war, slavery, imprisonment, segregation, or any other phenomenon of this kind. What is in question is submission, which like rebellion is at once both logical and strange. What is in question is the collective, in the strong meaning of this term. To what extent is a social grouping concrete? On the basis of what resemblances? What differences does it support?

What we owe to yesterday's dead is this truth, which means we ask about them, in their foreignness, as if they were present and yet unknown. As Nietzsche understood so well, we owe them neither memory nor judgment. But we do owe them the truth, because quite simply we owe it to ourselves if we are not to fall into nihilism. Moreover, it this one-on-one intimacy with others, with foreigners, with those who are absent—that renders truth possible. This intimacy has nothing to do with either the scholar's objectivity or the justice of modern man, as Nietzsche would have said. Nor does it have anything to do with the sterile opposition between objectivity and subjectivity. This *principled* intimacy, or intimacy as/of *method*, is evidently opposed to every declared aristocracy of the spirit, for which there exist "small" peoples, "small" people and "great" men, men and women (who, as we know well, don't count). Such intimacy demands a break with anonymity. The democratization of political and social life is accompanied by a profound change of perspectives on the events of the past. It is no longer just the generals and other captains who capture all the attention, but the "people" (in the political sense), if not the population (from the social point of view). It is not just the "powerful" colonizers, but also the "weak" colonized. It is not just the whites; it is the others.

Counting and miscounting [*dénombrer et décompter*] are odd mental operations. On their basis, in fact, nothing would be produced but mythologies or sinister settlings of accounts. On their basis, there would be the colonialists on one side, the victims of colonialism on the other. Looking ahead (and not behind!) on the basis of the past does not mean borrowing the grand inquisitor's role or function. If there is an inquiry, it is, in a different sense, noninquisitorial. What does the prosecutor [*procureur*] actually procure? Meanwhile, it is very tempting to relieve oneself of contemporary suffering due to the past by making some complaints, some heartily felt accusations. Consequently, a part of today's scholarly historical research on the colonies is dominated by such an attitude. It is the same attitude that dominates the political field: for or against France's "positive role"?[33]

The current debates, polemics, and other discussions demonstrate the power of transmission more than they show the significance of memories (and what have been called, on the model of support groups, "memory groups"). When it is founded on the illusion of remembering, the illusion that we remember the past, transmission rests largely on a common unthought, notably a political unthought. Whether they are visual, linguistic, or scholarly, representations are transmitted behind the backs of those who transmit them. For this, all it takes is to "repeat." The door to memories is opened by what remains unthought in representations. This is forgotten far too often.

Republicanism has its share of naivete, which is to say of ignorance—naivete that does not disappear when republicanism takes the side of the colonized or, more generally, of those that the Indian school has for twenty years called the "subaltern." Republicanism has its share of responsibility when it does not want—that is to say, cannot—hear anything from the subaltern. In fact, no society is structured purely by material institutions without also being structured (perhaps more importantly) by immaterial ones. Consequently, there is an extent to which the colony in general and colonial Algeria in particular are immaterial institutions. For example, legitimate alliances are occupied by invisible borders (particularly in colonial society), norms that oblige and forbid, which divide subjects and, in reproducing them, reproduce the endogamy inherent to this kind of society: Europeans with Europeans, natives with natives.

More generally, a society is a "language construct" [*édifice de langage*], in Pierre Legendre's words—something that causes "an unprecedented vision" to surge forth. "Recognizing that a society is a language construct is not self-evident. What is difficult is to conceive how much the emphasis on this approach immediately distances us with respect to the ordinary objectivation by which we grasp social organization, or believe that we grasp it. With language, the subject is brought forth."[34] To consider society as a text, we are led to "conquer the reflective gaze" and to interpret the representations on which the society in question feeds. At that point, we are struck by how little reflectivity they express.

Is it then enough to take refuge in the idea that there is "no salvation outside of science"? Is it enough to oppose history to memory, scholarly discourse to popular discourse, knowledge to opinion? This would be deceptive: it would amount to believing that science, particularly history, is outside of society—in other words, outside the text. What we know about yesterday must also be applied to the present day. We must examine not just the kind of response certain questions elicit, but also and above all the type of question itself—indeed, the absence of certain lines of questioning. Just because minds are decolonized does not mean that *positions* are. People often say certain things because they want to defend their bodies. The unthought gives rise, in other words, to social and political slips. This is not just an affair of *discourse*; it involves *language*.[35] We cannot simply remove a few unhappy words. We must emphasize that certain representations having to do with the colonies are transmitted unwittingly even by those who wish to set them aside.

"No-one can express in words that which gives everyone the power to speak": this remark of Michel de Certeau opens an interrogation concerning what we ordinarily call the "disciplines."[36] This question would not be posed, in fact, if there were no groupings, disciplines, diverse and varied borders, as much or more intellectual than political; if there were no schools or currents; if there were no masters—in short, if letters were a republic. No one would pose the question of a researcher's (academic) nationality. To be sure, whoever says nationality also says rationality. Is one a philosopher or a historian? Is one an anthropologist or a political scientist? What is specific about nationality is that one only declares it in transit, in response to a question. Nationality only has meaning relative to an (academic) territory and to an (academic) sovereignty. Clearly, as the institutional fact par excellence, linked to the arbitrariness of birth and therefore to civil status, nationality generally needs no proof. The question is not "by what right?" but "where?" or "in what capacity?" [*à quel titre?*].

When de Certeau mentions "intellectual geopolitics" of the "disposition of forces at work" in the space of intellectual practices, he distinguishes *place*, *mass*, and *truth*. Place is determined institutionally and becomes for the intellectual a proper site (a natural place in Aristotle's sense). "To start with, place is the post, the institutional situation, the grouping, the social identity, the guarantee offered by a scientific discipline and by a hierarchical form of recognition."[37] Places are often strongholds or impregnable citadels. *Homo academicus* is also a political animal. Contrary to every expectation, and even if language is no guarantee of the ability to decipher situations, in France there still exist specialists in the Arabophone countries of the Levant or the Maghreb, particularly specialists in Algeria, who are neither Arabophone nor Berberophone. Would we find it acceptable for a specialist in France to speak no French? In cases where a specialist comes from a former French colony or from a family with that heritage, it is considered normal for him or her to be Francophone, and no one asks whether the French language might, for this specialist, be only a foreign or second language, even if perfectly mastered.

On the other hand, these days a former indigène of French nationality or the child of an ex-indigène will not be recognized as a legitimate authority when speaking either about the French state (it will be assumed that he or she is biased), or about French society (from which he or she is thought to be alienated), or about French culture (for he or she will be believed ignorant). It will be accepted for an Algerian to speak of Algeria. It will be considered ordinary for a French person to speak of Algeria. It is less easy to admit that an Algerian could be a specialist in French history. A Cameroonian or a Senegalese will have difficulty being accepted. Decolonization will be effective when academic job appointments are finally symmetrical.

Here the taboos are only effects of illegitimacy (or of bastardy). The sacralization of academic identity and the fetishization of national origin leave their combined mark on the places—that is to say, the speaking positions and the (academic) right to speak from them. Place is therefore not science. As we know, disciplinary norms and scientific criteria derive in part from a sociopolitical context, today no less than yesterday. Next comes mass, which is to say the public place from which storms lash at the laboratory windows. Truth, finally, is "an element of interrogation which challenges the configurations of an order of meaning."[38] If you go on a chase, you lose your place!

Challenging the configurations of an order of meaning means displacing them. But whoever does not remain in place will become, under these conditions, the very figure of the rascal whom one does not take seriously. At worst, he or she will be taken for an imposter who must be unmasked. History owns its discipline, its methods, its objectives, and its stakes; the rest is so-called literature. In the meantime, it is not clear that the truth stays put. It is not a real response but yet another challenge. Truth is not, in fact, an answer but a return to the question. The one who crosses boundaries, the questioner, therefore comes off either as a deserter and a traitor, or as an imposter and an ignoramus. In any case, his or her movement appears, to follow the Aristotelian terminology, as a violent movement that pulls him or her away from a natural place.[39]

Michel de Certeau tells how, during a Brazilian speaking tour at Belo Horizonte, Foucault was asked one more time: "So then, in what capacity do you speak? What is your specialty? Where are you coming from? [*Où êtes-vous?*]"[40] We know how Foucault, in *L'archéologie du savoir*, responded that he wrote, like many, to have no face.[41] And still, Foucault was in Brazil only as a traveler and not as a resident, as a distinguished guest and not as an illegal migrant, as a white man and not as a black woman. This is doubtless why he dreamed, in writing, of not having a face or of losing his face—a depth of reflection, as he would have said, from the heart of a painting's depth.

For the resident, the illegal migrant, and the black woman, to have no face is neither an ideal nor a dream; it is an experience, a reality, a nightmare. There are therefore some who express themselves, on the contrary, in order to gain a face. Michel de Certeau adds that at Belo Horizonte, Foucault answered: "Who am I? A *reader*."[42] An *épistémè*, in Foucault's sense, institutes a configuration that makes certain borders appear as natural in a given epoch, makes certain territories seem adjacent and ot This political aspect of knowledge also obeys the rules of its pro other words of politics. Thus, one can retrospectively observe the exercised by certain disciplines on other forms of knowledge. One ke-wise note that certain objects are treated as peripheral. One can see that the geography of knowledge has its history as well.

Not long ago, the colony was treated institutionally as a peripheral and secondary subject, relative to its distance from the centers of power, on whose basis the objects reputed to be henceforth major or minor were ranked hierarchically (the colony is a remarkable example of this). Today, the colony is not studied in its own right. It is rather the processes of colonization and decolonization that interest historians. As for the philosophers, they are almost completely uninterested in it. French philosophers, without exception, regard the colony as an Australia of the spirit—as a question at once remote, distant, and insular, at the antipode of what philosophy is or believes itself to be. For a French philosopher, the colony is situated without exception at the limits of philosophical reflection. It is a question simultaneously too empirical and too idiosyncratic to be judged worthy of a true and authentic philosophical interest. It is a question that does not belong, by right, to its political landscape.

The division of intellectual labor reserves the lion's share for philosophy (albeit a lion who is often old, impotent, and tired): political regimes, the general principles of law, the foundations of justice.[43] From this point of view, academic history is situated in the interval, indeed the wide interval, between facts and principles, between enacting and intending, leading from dispositions and other maneuvers to institutions and constitutions. From the other direction, one sees that, quite to the contrary, historiography exercises a de facto monopoly over the colonial question and therefore treats every wandering philosopher as an intruder, a spoilsport, who prevents things from running as they should. Hybridization is desirable, but up until the present it has been deliberately set aside when the colony was at stake. Why? Meanwhile there exist possibilities for study and studies that situate themselves in the interval—research programs that require more the sense of movement than a taste for dwelling places.

The legitimacy of philosophy is sometimes paradoxical. Indeed, it founds its legitimacy (or authorizes itself) on the basis of ignorance. It claims to know nothing about anything but strives nevertheless to attain what it calls truth. When Socrates places himself on the side of ignorance, this is not one more ruse on his part; it is quite deliberate, because he does not want to be a sophist, which is to say a producer of knowledge. Therefore, he situates himself on the side of desire (and of its cause) when it comes to the "desire to know," rather than on the side of knowledge (and of the object of desire). If he begins from a lack, he does not want to replace it with any specific productivity. "All thought has its truth in a 'thought of the outside.'"[44]

The Colony's Phantoms

One cannot imagine the Bundestag adopting, as a measure with the force of law, certain members' proposal that the positive role of the German Occupation in France between 1939 and 1945 should be taught in Germany. Didn't the Germans bring their famous sense of discipline and organization? Indeed, it would provoke no laughter whatsoever and would produce a scandal in proportion to the enormity of the judgment. Meanwhile, is this a matter of political fiction? Not at all. The French Parliament decided on February 23, 2005, that henceforth the positive aspects of colonization must be taught. Had the French not brought the indigènes piped water and gas on every floor; had they not provided completely destitute populations with culture and civilization? Here we see something that, far from giving rise to scandal, concluded with only a small diplomatic scuffle. The Algerians protested, accusing the French of all evils and, to be sure, all crimes. Intellectuals protested, signing petitions and points of view.

Comparison proves nothing. And here it is not a matter of confusing the two situations—quite the contrary. In what does their real difference consist? The asymmetry is double. On the one hand, insofar as the German Occupation was an exceptional situation, it was the work of a state of exception, which is to say a totalitarian state. On the other hand, that occupation took place between equals. Equals before, equals during, equals afterward. No such thing with the colony—in other words, the occupation of a country (called a territory), resulting from the act of a "normal" state, a "normal" political regime. Nor was the colony a comparable situation insofar as its occupation took place between unequals. Unequals before, unequals during, unequals afterward. This aspect of the colonial occupation was perceived not as exceptional but as a "normal" situation. In particular, this so-called normality causes a problem today in Martinique, in New Caledonia, and elsewhere. This normality must be interrogated. How should the colony be discussed?

Historians have written abundantly about the act or acts of decolonization, confusing them with the events of independence, as if one could make a tabula rasa of the past. We can ask what *decolonization* means. Is it a matter of the colonial power's withdrawal? Is it a matter of independence movements? Is it a matter of France or of the Maghreb? Can a country be "decolonized" in a short period of time? Can a country "decolonize itself" so quickly? In this history, the political break is overestimated while history itself is bizarrely underestimated.

With respect to Algeria, these are the terms in which Daniel Rivet presents decolonization. In 1945, he writes, "It was already too late to envisage a city where there would be room for settlers [*colons*] who could be turned into *privileged foreigners*. It was already clear that the Maghrebins were no longer *colonizable* after 1945."[45] And what was the outcome? "It is hardly exaggerating to say that during this war, the Algerians simply went *from one subjection to another.*" "It was in order *to have the right to be insulted and abused in their own language* and not in the language of foreigners that the Algerians *were caught* in this history, sometimes despite themselves, because the wheels of concrete history miniaturized by Algeria's thousand wars ensured that they *could no longer* do otherwise."[46] One need not have perfect pitch to hear what is being said here, what the author says in defending his body. There is no hope—the Algerians are not persons; they are (subjected) subjects. In other words, the Maghrebins are objects of historical causality. Apparently decolonization refers not to analysis but to assessment. Under cover of impartiality, the practice of history is confused with an international accounting book.

One further glance: Guy Pervillé writes that "one question cannot be avoided: are the peoples who took back their independence through arms happier than those who preserved their close ties with France?"[47]—this is the naive language of the spurned lover. "Decolonization" is not a concept; it is not even a notion. It is a category that the historians use from convenience as if to avoid thinking the colony and, from both sides of the chasm, the postcolonial situation. It is a category lacking in consistency. What does it consist of? One may guess that colonization is a set of methods (raids, etc.) and of procedures (the *code de l'indigénat*); one may guess that decolonization is a process. But which one? Is it a political process? An economic process? A social process? An intellectual process? In most cases, the discourse and the language of history have not (yet) been decolonized. Decolonization has not taken place, at any rate not here. Too often, the language of history is still a language that cannot hear itself, a language of the deaf.

The colony is, in fact, a treacherous subject, a suspect subject, a politically taboo subject. The arguments are legion: One must not reopen wounds. Reconciliation must be possible. The past must be forgotten. To speak of it, but above all to debate it, is to declare war, in this sense—civil war. In an opinion column published by *Le Monde* on May 9, 2005, the minister charged with handling former combatants, Hamlaoui Mékachéra, developed this—quite classic—style of argumentation: "Colonization: reconciling memories."[48] In fact, the argument from national reconciliation was the postwar argument par excellence. It is a political commonplace in France. We must reconsider the minister's *official* prepared remarks. Indeed, he begins by invoking his own history, his own experience. Above all, he reveals the supposed function of reconciliation: to reconcile is to heal. National reconciliation is also the principle in whose name administrative positions have been recycled (a kind of political economy that is not well understood).

On the ideological plane, let us take someone like Georges Mauco.[49] Georges Mauco is one of the ideologues of the interwar period, defending overtly antisemitic positions. Starting in 1932, with a thesis on "Foreigners in France: Their role in economic activity," he was considered the top expert on immigration questions.[50] His proposals were followed first by the Vichy regime and later by General de Gaulle, to whom Mauco was an advisor, integrating the High Commission on Population at the time of the Liberation. The ruling conception at that time was that the influx of Mediterranean and Oriental peoples must be limited. General de Gaulle stated, "It is good that there are yellow French, black French, brown French. It shows that France is open to all races and that it has a universal vocation. But only so long as they remain a small minority. . . . France is a European people of the white race, Greek and Latin culture and of the Christian religion."[51]

On the administrative plane, let us take a Maurice Papon. Maurice Papon, who needs no introduction, was prefect of police in Paris when the October 17, 1961, massacre took place, under his orders.[52] Algerians demonstrated peacefully against the curfew that had been imposed uniquely on "Muslim French from Algeria," who were forbidden to go out between eight thirty at night and five thirty in the morning. As for the "Arab" cafes, they had to shut at seven in the evening. In his days after Vichy and before Paris, Maurice Papon had been sent on a special mission to Constantine as inspector general of administration. One must keep track of this set of trajectories or careers. In France, we see, reconciliation is a political remedy. As a result, there are political subjects so painful that they cannot be discussed freely. The remedy is clearly poisoned. Paradoxically, it is a matter of a memory about which one must not simply be silent but also forget. So is there a "duty to remember"?

To speak of such duties is to misunderstand from the start what psychoanalysis has called *screen memories*—in other words, memories that offer a grasp on the past. Today, the struggle for independence, what Algerians call the "Revolution," functions as a screen memory at times for them and also for others. What the French call the "contribution of overseas fighters" likewise constitutes a screen memory for them.[53] This perspective turns the colony into a site of memory. And what is remarkable in both cases is that the object of this memory is heroism, the safest political value there can be. This memory has to do with what is memorable (the *mirabilia* or miraculous). This is quite simply because, in conformity with the way it was defined by Herodotus, "father" of history, what is memorable makes commemoration possible. We are talking about a memory of the past that is structurally, not accidentally, in the service of politics. As the French expression says so nicely, what counts is the battlefield [*champ d'honneur*].

The Greeks were the first to dematerialize the monument. At that time, memory was oriented by the monument, in the sense that memory was the gravestone of heroes. As Thucydides put it to Pericles, in the funeral oration for Athenians who fell during the first year of the Peloponnesian War, "The whole world is the sepulchre of famous men, and it is not the epitaph upon monuments set up in their own land that alone commemorates them, but also in lands not their own, where nothing is written, each of us is *inhabited by a memory*."[54] This downplays the power of forgetfulness concealed in memory. One finds another formulation among the Greeks in Hesiod's *Theogony*. Mnemosyne gave birth to the Muses "as forgetfulness of evils and relief from anxieties."[55] To praise one's forebears is to construct monuments (signs and emblems of memory) and to symptomatically forget the rest.

Thus, we can speak politically of "good" and "bad" forgetting. Good forgetting is produced by eulogy and the remembrance of glory; bad forgetting is produced by blame, the remembrance of evils. Just as it distinguished two types of forgetting, ancient Greece also distinguished two very different types of memory: the memory of the nation or of the people and the memory of justice. The memory of justice applies itself to the evils that have been forgotten by the national memory or popular memory although they are inscribed in the law. Indeed, there is no justice without memory. It is no longer an affair for Mnemosyne but for the Erinys, whose memory extends beyond a person's life to prior generations in order to uncover the wrong beneath forgetting and to shed today's light, as Aeschylus says, on "the child of ancient murders." Human memory (commemoration) is thus inspired by Mnemosyne, while divine memory (justice) is inspired by the Erinys.

Justice forgets the deeds of arms and restricts remembrance to past wrongs. Given this, it is easy to understand the struggle over memories and the aporia to which this struggle leads, since these two types of memory are not at all on the same plane. To be sure, many historians place themselves on the side of the memory of justice, the side of the memory that judges and not of the memory that enchants. In an opinion piece from *Le Monde* dated May 12, 2005, "The Insults of a Minister of the Republic," Claude Liauzu and Thierry Le Bars hoped to rectify the historical errors they believed were contained in the minister's remarks. But they showed that they did not truly grasp the specific plane on which they were situated when they added, "Our society is crisscrossed by memory wars."[56]

What all these arguments have in common is making the family secret into the paradigm for handling such matters. This is how, in practice and not simply on the plane of representations, nations can behave like families without being like families in any other sense whatsoever. A family secret is something that everyone inside the family knows but nobody truly acknowledges. This does not mean that the nation is a large family any more than it means that the family is a little nation; it simply means that the family is a political site, an insight that despotism has never forgotten. Within the family, there are information politics, communication politics, and politics around transmission. To each his or her regime. Within a state, there are also information, communication, and transmission politics. And this is easily observed: How many French lack any relation whatsoever with some colony or other? Very few of them. Whoever has a settler among his or her ancestors, whoever has an ancestor that served in the army, whoever has ancestors that were among the colonized populations—those for whom the colony is an absolute terra incognita are few and far between. The colony is something familiar. As with everything both *familiar* and *normal*, it is not spoken about. Not to speak about it means not to think about it, not to think it. When one talks about it, as with every subject both familiar and normal, normal because it is familiar, one does so in a positive way.

Thus, what the French *deputés* (members of Parliament) recently expressed was that they considered the colony a normal matter, the act of a normal state. Let's recall the facts. When it was first read on June 11, 2004, the eventual law of February 23, 2005, "conveying recognition of the nation and national contribution in favor of repatriated French," whose goal was to compensate the *harkis* and their families and to grant them the French state's official recognition, contained an article 4, introduced in the form of an amendment.[57] This is the article that provoked the uproar. "University research programs [should] give to the history of the French overseas presence, notably in North Africa, the place that it deserves. School curricula [should] recognize in particular the positive role of the French overseas presence, notably in North Africa, and grant to the history and to the sacrifices of the fighters of the French army coming from these territories the eminent place to which they have a right."

The speech was criticized by historians (with Claude Liauzu in the lead) for two reasons. First for a formal reason, or on principle: law must not impose an official truth. This although the legislature had already intervened at least three times to affirm its position on the historical facts: the Gayssot law (1990) against revisionism, the Taubira law (2001) on the recognition of the slave trade and slavery as a crime against humanity, and the law concerning the Armenian genocide (2001). Second for a material reason, or a question of grounds: "It is not evident that colonization did play a positive role."

This article 4 is interesting not only because of the discourse that is put forward but also because of its object and its language. Its object is concerned not just with teaching but also with research, to which it gives a program, which is to say a direction—in fact, an instruction: "be positive." That the program links teaching and research shows that it is a matter not of education but of transmission. In transmission the fate of our ancestors is played out. In transmission we settle our debt with respect to them. The first article of the same law gives evidence of this: "The Nation expresses its recognition to the women and to the men who participated in the work accomplished by France in the former French departments of Algeria, Morocco, Tunisia and in Indochina as well as in the territories formerly placed under French sovereignty."

The language in which this article is formulated is remarkably revealing: it is quite simply the same language used by the colony. In the colony, the word *occupation* is never used (it is pejorative); rather, one uses the word *presence* (laudatory). One does not say *country* but *territory*. One speaks of "territories formerly placed under French sovereignty." One speaks of "overseas." One says "positive role," but one does not say for whom this role is positive. What is happening is the elision of the subject—the elision of the colonial subject, the elision of the people who were colonized, the elision of the indigène. If he or she was made an integrating part of the republic, it was insofar as absent. When it comes to evoking the positive role of colonization, in fact, it was with respect to the colonizers, not the colonized. There, we see hardly any disagreements.

Christian Vanneste, *député* from the North for the Union for a Popular Movement (UMP), explains: "Our intention was not to rewrite the history books, but to send a message to the *rapatriés*, to solidify France's position with respect to these men and women who lived through a drama, in some cases a tragedy." His position is shared by another member of Parliament, Kléber Mesquida, Socialist (PS) *député* from the Herault, who states: "Today, only the negative side of colonization is discussed. But one forgets the work of *Algerian-born Frenchmen and women*, people born there [*autochthones*] who had to be *repatriated* and many of whom came from modest backgrounds."[58] What happens in these remarks? A great metamorphosis: those who were once French become retrospectively and retroactively noncitizens. This language, shared today by both the PS and the UMP, recognizes only non-Muslims as ever having been Algerian-born French in the past.[59] However, even today, whatever debts France may have are owed to all those who were once French, not just to a select number of them.

It is because the *language* is familiar that everything seems normal. As can be seen, the language of contemporary France is a colonial language, which has its syntax (for the elision of the colonized subject is systematic) and its lexicon: *presence* and *territory* are its key words. In this language, the *colony* does not exist. That word is not a part of the political vocabulary. In other words, one can talk all one wants without saying anything. This is only one of many paradoxes in the affair. The colony is an absent word, a phantom reality.

The first difficulty is therefore a political one: conformism. Conformism is the absence of critical thought, the refusal to critique thought. If it does not have the same nature as censorship, it nevertheless fulfills the same function. Intellectually speaking, conformism is worse than censorship. The latter is repressive, which constitutes both its force and its limit; but one might say the former is preventive, and this is the source of all its singular power. Indeed, the conformism of the majority dries up dissident opinions. It dries them up *ex ante* insofar as it denies almost everyone the effective possibility of expressing a thought that differs from the majority. It also destroys them *ex post* by socially invalidating dissident opinions. Thus, in a passive and apparently inoffensive way, conformism exercises a double censorship: by repression and by resistance. There is no better example than the dissimulation of the massacre of October 17, 1961.

Accusations of exaggeration, partiality, and lack of objectivity are the most widespread weapons when it is a matter of speaking differently about the colony, just as with any subject. It may even be impossible to speak of it. In truth, the colony is a taboo subject. The colonial empires are a major fact of the history of the twentieth century, but in most cases a student at the École Nationale d'Administration will have heard very little *institutionally* on the subject. Who knows what the colony means, apart from, perhaps, the "ex-colonized"? If it is spoken about, it must be done in the standard language, the appropriate language, the colonial language.

That discourses about the colony might be politically alienated, that they might be conformist, that they might exert authority, derives from the (secondary) benefit that false simplicity lends them: as Adorno remarked so well, such discourses and such thoughts "offer explanations thanks to which one can organize a *contradictory* reality *without contradictions*, without making great efforts."[60] In fact, a colony is always a contradictory reality.[61] In a colony, the inhabitants are the intruders. To be colonized is to be in the situation of an invader even at home. Here is a fundamental contradiction if ever there was one. To be an indigène, moreover, is to be deprived of a symbolic existence. It is not to not be a person, but it is to be a person made of nothing. As for the colonists, they are foreigners who feel at home.

To rework the formula offered by Tocqueville, whose colonist opinions are recognized elsewhere, this is "the formidable circle traced by the majority around thought": the border between the politically sayable and unsayable, the frontier between speech [*parole*] and voice [*voix*].[62] The one who is not symbolically inscribed in the city, the one who lacks a name, remains not without voice but rather without speech. To speak, indeed, requires that one can be heard—that is to say, heard as speaking.

At the end of the war against the Volsques, Titus-Livy recounts the episode of the plebeian retreat on the Aventine and, above all, the negotiating team of Menenius Agrippa, and finally, the return both of order and of the plebeians.[63] Between the patricians and the plebeians, no linguistic exchange is possible, just as no linguistic exchange is possible between humans, speaking beings, and simple mortals. "Your misfortune is *not to be*," said a patrician to the plebeians, "and this misfortune is inescapable." With simple mortals, there is hardly any possible contract, hardly any understanding to envision. In 1830, Ballanche commented on this episode: "They had only transitory speech, a speech that is a fugitive sound, a sort of lowing, a sign of want and not an expression of intelligence. They were deprived of the eternal word which was in the past and would be in the future."[64] Deprived of speech bearing on the past and the future means deprived of politics.

Here it must be remembered that, precisely, the Greeks' Mnemosyne was supposed to reveal "what is, what will be and what was." This is therefore another way of saying that the peoples without history are peoples without politics. But at bottom, this shows the political stakes of history. Can there truly be a discourse about the future if there is no discourse on the past? Here we see how much is at stake over history in societies having endured colonial domination. Algeria is just a very telling example. Indeed, until very recently, history in Algeria began on November 1, 1954.

To speak, in the political sense of the term, is not possible for just anybody. All people are not speaking bodies on the same plane. Politics is (also) the art of dividing and hierarchizing human beings with respect to speech. The first political dispute has to do with the unequal distribution of speech. We must recall the imperturbable argument that even the best disposed and most progressive French invoked during the Algerian War: the lack of "acceptable interlocutors" on the other side. They said they could not find people who would talk. Their comment was sheer nonsense. Without speech, a person is only an animated body.

Antiquity invented barbarians, identified linguistically as the ones who expressed themselves without being comprehensible. These barbarians [*barbares*] are the Berbers. The modern world invented its savages, identified by their corporeity since they were humanly nude. It fabricated its slaves, identified by their ownership. Since they were possessed and did not belong to themselves, they had no personal body [*corps propre*]. The contemporary world constructed its indigènes, determined by their personality (this personality made them into subjects without being persons): they not only were unable to govern themselves but, moreover, could not be governed. If they are neither savages nor barbarians, still less slaves, they are at most half civilized.[65]

The Algerians, at that time the Muslim French, were excluded from the judiciary until 1944. They were kept off of juries in criminal cases until 1942. They were reputed incapable of judging. No need to learn their language since, precisely, they did not speak. For these people, emancipation therefore began by taking the floor and, indissociably, by imposing their own language (Arabic in Algeria, Creole in the Caribbean).[66]

After its beginning in Algeria, the mechanism reducing the indigène to immobility and to silence (defined by the law of June 28, 1881) was extended to Cochin China in 1881, to New Caledonia and to Senegal in 1887, to Annam-Tonkin in 1897, to Cambodia in 1898, to Madagascar in 1901, to French West Africa in 1904, to French Equatorial Africa in 1910, to the Somali Coast in 1912, to Togo in 1923, and to Cameroon in 1924. For forty years, with the notable exception of Morocco and Tunisia, the indigènes were forced to be silent. In Algeria, the code of "special infractions" was not abolished until the ruling of March 7, 1944. The truce did not last long: in 1955, the state of emergency was decreed in Algeria, with its subsequent extraordinary measures. It was not for the indigènes but against them that Parliament legislated. If Parliament did so, it was because they considered the indigènes as enemies—not wartime enemies but peacetime enemies, not accidental enemies but perpetual enemies. Perhaps the colonial resemblance was strongest, at least within the French empire, between New Caledonia and Algeria. It was in these two colonies that the repression was most rigorous, the rule of exception affirmed most harshly.

Today no less than yesterday, conformism establishes a policing of thought and speech, which means a great division. Conformism acts on the basis of bodies and not just of minds, thoughts, or opinions. Put otherwise, conformism is also a resemblance between bodies. Even in a democracy, opinions can be judged in bundles. The more physical dissimilarity is visible, the more problematic legitimacy becomes.[67] Like the distribution of the sensible, which means like the police, politics therefore separates those who are from those who are not. This does not mean separating those who exist from those who do not exist, which would really be to misunderstand the situation, but more correctly, those who have existence and those who do not have existence—in other words, those who exist but are inexistent.

All these contradictions boil down to one fundamental contradiction: that of two worlds lodged in a single one, that of two worlds, one existent and the other inexistent, welded together in the same real world. Even if historical discourse is distinguished from political discourse, when it comes to what is essential, they use the same language.

Historical discourse is generally a critical discourse. At the same time, it is not a discourse that systematically reflects on the very categories that it employs in studies and analyses. In this sense, even if its method is rigorous, its reflexivity is approximative. Thus, we do not talk about democratization in America but of democracy in America. We do not talk about the *laïcization* of the French state but of *laïcité*. Meanwhile, most contemporary works having to do with the French colonial empire have titles that use either the word *colonization* or the name of the country concerned.[68] For an example, the book published with Armand Colin in 2004 under the direction of Claude Liauzu is titled *Colonisation: Droit d'inventaire*. As if today the term *colony* were so marked by colonialism that it could not possibly still be used. Banal and used in a specific context, the term has now fallen into obsolescence.

At bottom, saying *colonization* instead of *colony* means one is stuck with an ideological usage of the term *colony*, even if the switch was made precisely in hopes of freeing oneself from it. Meanwhile, the colonies are a major fact in the history of the nineteenth and twentieth centuries. Colonization was not an aborted effort. If the French nineteenth century was the century of colonizations, the twentieth is the century of colonies.[69] To speak of colonization is to insist on the process at work from the colonial state's point of view; it is to admit an eminently problematic division of the world without knowing one does so. Even the best-intentioned historian is more interested in France in Algeria, Morocco, or Tunisia than in Algeria, Morocco, or Tunisia under French occupation. National or foreign subject? This is how a blurring of borders is produced where the colonies are concerned.

There we have one of the reasons for the importance of historical judgments on the question, as if only a judgment—usually moral—would allow one to clear one's name, in the proper sense. When one crosses a border, one pays off one's customs duties; in history, one breaches these invisible borders by pronouncing judgments. The historians have as much trouble escaping the tribunal of history as do the philosophers. The title of a special issue of the magazine *L'Histoire*, "Colonization on Trial," is eloquent. But is it a vulgarization? If no trial (of whom?) is held, then "stock" is taken or an "assessment" carried out. For example, the state of medical progress is reported: the cause of malaria was discovered at Constantine in 1880; 3.4 million "Indochinese" (out of 21.5 million) were vaccinated against cholera in 1931–32. Did the indigènes have to remain ill? Is the progress in medical science or in *care*?[70] More generally, the spread of technologies and their progress are opposed to the political administration and its excesses. Even today, what we have is less a language than a savagely well-oiled rhetoric. "One" constrained them, but "one" also helped them. Thus the scales would be balanced—the positive role displayed. It is not clear that such discourses can be addressed to those who would seem to be affected the most: "But you also got vaccinated!"

There is a structure to such historical rhetoric. It rests on a linguistic unthought. It falls to Émile Benveniste, once again, to shed light on the profound asymmetry at work in our linguistic exchanges.[71] He shows that there is no third *person*.[72] No subjectivity is associated with this pseudo third person. As we see, this corresponds perfectly to the very status of the indigène at the start, to the colonized thereafter, and finally to the underdeveloped, a juridical status in the first two cases and a political status in the last one.

Everything happens (therefore) as if a discourse necessarily had to be about a third person to have any chance of being objective.[73] But one will have understood that this is an illusion. The third person is a phantom. The third person is the obscure object of the discourse, because one does not hear this person speak (even if he or she speaks, to be sure!), and because he or she is not addressed. The third person is tacitly a subaltern.

At minimum, a discourse about someone is only viable if it can also be addressed to that person. Sometimes the French accuse one another (among themselves), but then nothing remains of the third person, the third subject, the slave, the indigène, the colonized, except for the humiliated victim, the passive subject, to whom all the evils happened. The victim, another commonplace of our representations, is a mute body. At best, one lets the victim talk or one tries to acknowledge what he or she has gone through. But is genuinely hearing people the same as letting them talk? Is validating their experience the same as giving their life back to them? What a heavy burden the white man carries! For some, "the Republic doubtless has no need to apologize for its colonial past."[74] But "must one, at any cost, deny *millions of individuals* who testify today regarding the Republic's century-long connection with empire the *right to a history*?" Hell is paved with good intentions: How can the historians place history on the side of *right* and not on the side of *fact*? How can they place a scientific discourse on the side of people's rights and not on the side of the written record? Like the stolen letter, a certain history is missing/suffering [*en souffrance*].

France is well and truly a historical country: in France, political questions are posed in historical terms.[75] But this happens in both voluntary and involuntary ways. The return of the repressed still has many fine days ahead of it. The states of emergency and other exceptions to the common law, and thereby to the constitutional state, were decreed on the basis of a significant historical forgetting and on the basis of a certain history, as well as a certain politics. Stigmatizations, in fact, do not disappear immediately when political conflicts end, or when the historical problems seem settled. The bad political conscience often masks the absence of a real sentiment of guilt and blocks out the past.[76]

Nietzsche picked up the opposition between "an interiority to which no exteriority corresponds" and an "exteriority to which no interiority corresponds."[77] As one knows, today, interiority would be sensitivity, and exteriority would be objectivity. Everything happens as if talking about the negative aspects of colonization would show one's sensitivity and subjectivity, and on the other hand, as if speaking about the positive aspects of colonization would also manifest one's objectivity and impartiality. Such are, at least, the principles of the "handbook of subjective culture for outward barbarians" that prevails under our skies.[78] We do not have a choice about condemning the past or making it into a tabula rasa. "National reconciliation," far from transcending this alternative, is a proved political technique. There is no national reconciliation without the organization of a certain forgetfulness—that is, without either the creation of totems or the construction of taboos. If the subaltern(es) could speak . . .[79]

Some resurgences are curious indeed. Sometimes it is said, "It's just natural" [*ça coule de source*]. Indeed, it can happen that new streams appear from insufficiently explored springs. For example, the right to humanitarian intervention [*droit d'ingérence humanitaire*] rests on intentions that are both honorable and praiseworthy; it also rests on a very unique conception of humanity. In 1968, famines devastated Biafra. Some doctors intervened to come to the aid of the famished and damaged population. In 1987, a conference took place in Paris on the duty to intervene. In 1988, on December 8, the UN voted on resolution 43/131 on the "new humanitarian world order" at France's initiative. It was titled "Humanitarian Assistance to the Victims of Natural Catastrophes and Emergency Situations of the Same Order."

The following day, an earthquake ravaged Soviet Armenia. International aid missions were organized. The duty to intervene promoted by Bernard Kouchner and Mario Bettati was consecrated by this resolution under the title of "right to humanitarian assistance," improperly but commonly called the "right to intervene."[80] Thus emerged "a new norm of international law according to which the protection of the individual, a collective human heritage [*patrimoine*] given the same importance as the environment, no longer depends simply on the authority of the state of which he is a member, but interests the entire international community."[81]

The goal of the right to intervene is clear; it was explicitly formulated by Kouchner: "Save bodies."[82] This seems very far from imperial and colonial goals, from crusades and other civilizing missions that sought to "save souls." Humanitarian effort seems a world away from the care for humanity animating former crusaders, since the objective is no longer to convert but to preserve. However, we do not yet know whether the protection of some is not the salvation of others. The individual is supposed to be given the status of a common human heritage with the same importance as the environment because it is a matter of saving the bodies of individuals who are victims of natural catastrophes and emergency situations. In Roman law, in the narrowest and oldest sense, the *patrimonium* designates the corporeal things that are the property of the paterfamilias. By extension, it comes to designate someone's rights and actions, like goods. Property, the most absolute right over things, has long been confused with things themselves—in other words, with the objects of property.

The object of the right to intervene is therefore the bodies of others. The individual is placed on the same plane as the environment and under the same sign: life. If it is a patrimony, this signifies properly that humanity possesses individuals as goods, which can only be meant in one of two ways: either humans possess themselves, or some humans possess other humans. . . . Humanity is buried under the patrimony. The right to intervene appears not as a personal right, but as a real right (right *in rem*). There is a significant theoretical and practical risk involved in considering the objects of the right to intervention as corporeal things and not as people—in privileging, correlatively, the cry (inarticulate sound/voice) over the appeal (articulated sound/speech).

"Right to humanitarian assistance": the assistance designates both a set of subjects that one calls the public and the action itself, the aid that someone can receive.[83] The whole logic of the right to intervene states that it is insufficient to be a spectator; one must also be an actor. Put otherwise, one cannot rest content with looking; one must act. This leads to the classic criticism aimed at the humanitarian, namely that humanitarianism constitutes humanity as a spectacle. To what in fact does assistance respond? To images of suffering bodies. Without doubt, the *image* prevails because the *body* is what counts. For Bernard Kouchner, "Information and humanitarian action are the remedies against extreme suffering. Without an image, people lack indignation: only the unfortunate are struck by misfortune. So one cannot extend the hand of rescue and fraternal impulse toward them. Photography and the leap to action that it triggers remain the essential enemies of dictatorships and of underdevelopment."[84]

The image is therefore supposed to render possible this paradox (or if you like, this miracle): that misery strikes those who are happy. By being displayed, the atrocious sensations of some people have to produce sentiments in other people. Thanks to images, these bodies must strike at hearts—from whence the hypothesis that these images make people into simple bodies. Indeed, the images present persons not as speaking beings but as mute (photographed) bodies. And this explains how the right to intervene reemerged from what we call the *right to look*.

To clarify these problems, we have to go back to a prior state of places and things. Let us recall the association Doctors Without Borders. Observe that they are known (in English) as the "French doctors." This is not an accident. It institutes a *France des hommes*, a "manly France." To make doctors without borders into French doctors effectively encourages the breaching of borders other than one's own from the very start. There are two processes going on at the same time: on the one hand, the shrinking of the right to asylum, notably in the European countries, and the struggle against the porousness of borders, in the name of imperatives that are at once economic, political, and social; and on the other hand, the institution of the right to intervene and the demand for total permeability of borders, in the name of a humanitarian imperative. The doctors are without borders in a world that preserves its own.

It has been claimed that this was an ethical imperative before it was a juridical one. Thus Bernard Kouchner established an analogy between assistance to someone in danger and humanitarian assistance, called intervention. Assistance to someone in danger is a categorical and not a hypothetical imperative (it is not conditional). If this is true on the national plane, Kouchner asserts, it must also be true on the international plane. "What would you say," he asks, "of an internal law that would protect property to the point of making the inviolability of the home prevail over the protection of childhood and would let your neighbor down the hall rape his child or break his son's limbs even when the victim's screams are audible? Of a law which would forbid you to kick down the door?"

The analogy seems manifest, but in reality it confuses the subjective and the objective meanings of law. In its objective meaning, law is *norma agendi*; it is a rule of action (law, or *loi*). In its subjective meaning, law is *facultas agendi*; it is a capacity to act (right, or *droit*). In its objective meaning, law is singular (*jus*) and is expressed in particular laws. In its subjective meaning, laws are plural (*jura*) and are established positively by the law. Thus, assistance to someone in danger is a legal obligation, an element of the *norma agendi*. One is in the domain of the common law. With the right to intervene, a subjective right is established, a new *facultas agendi*. One is no longer in the domain of the common law established in and by international law. Put otherwise, the right to intervene is an entirely discretionary capacity. This is a troubling rupture of the analogy, one that elevates an exception to the law to the rank of a rule of law.

Thus, contrary to what is sometimes affirmed, we are not dealing with a new international juridical norm. Nonintervention is neither punishable nor even condemnable, since the beneficiaries of the right to intervene are not those responsible for acting. Put otherwise, if the appeal and the consent of victims constitute a foundation for the right to intervention, they still do not provide its principle. "Everything truly rests on the imminence of danger," said Bernard Kouchner; "urgency prohibits complicated procedure, composed deliberation, graduated meditation. It commands action." The principle is neither ethical nor juridical; it is pragmatic. But to reduce the other to the other's body, more precisely to the image of the other's body, comes down to neglecting the person. Such an ardent defense of the body's life cheats the person of his or her personhood [*laisse l'homme en souffrance*].

"Practice is not some mysterious agency, some substratum of history, some hidden engine." Indeed,

> we are often aware of it, but we have no concept for it. In the same way, when I speak, I am generally aware that I am speaking and am not in a hypnotic state; on the other hand, I do not have a conception of the grammar I am using instinctively. I think I am expressing myself naturally, in order to say what needs to be said; I am not aware that I am applying restrictive rules. Similarly, the governor who gives his flock free bread or who denies it [to] gladiators believes he is doing what every governor has to do, when dealing with the governed, owing to the nature of politics itself; he is not aware that his practice, observed in and of itself, conforms to a specific grammar, that it embodies a specific politics,[85] just as, while we believe we are speaking without presuppositions, in order to say what has to be said, what is on our minds, when we break the silence we can only speak a specific language, French or English or Latin.[86]

Paul Veyne discussed Foucault's work at great length; he supported its approaches, its simultaneously precise and humorous manner. He defended it against the accusations of historians, which he began by reworking, as if the trial of Foucault were that of a historiographical Socrates.[87] After asking where "practice itself" came from, "with its inimitable contours," Paul Veyne proposes the following response: It comes from

> historical changes, quite simply, from the countless transformations of historical reality, that is to say from the rest of history, like everything else. Foucault has not discovered a previously unknown new agency, called practice; he has made the effort to see people's practices *as they really are*; what he is talking about is the same thing every historian talks about, namely, what people do. The difference is simply that Foucault undertakes to speak about practice *precisely*, to describe its convoluted forms, instead of referring to it in vague and noble terms. He does not say: "I have discovered a sort of historical unconscious, a preconceptual agency, that I call practice or discourse, and that provides the real explanation for history. Ah yes! But how am I going to manage to explain this agency itself and its transformations?" No: he is talking about *the same thing we talk about*, for example, the practical conduct of a government; only he shows it as it really is, *by stripping away the veils*.[88]

Notes

1. Foucault, "Thought of the Outside," 152.
2. Foucault, "Ways of Writing History," 280 (translation altered).
3. This text in this chapter comes from a contribution to the conference "Au-delà des pressions officielles et des lobbies de mémoire, pour une histoire critique et citoyenne, le cas de l'histoire franco-algérienne," which took place at ENS-Lyon on June 20–22, 2006. This contribution was not published in the proceedings. It was refused by the organizers, Frédéric Abécassis and Gilbert Meynier. The position of Frédéric Abécassis can be summarized thus: "What pushes me to react is that your text is founded on a posture that, viscerally, I refuse,

because it claims to make a judgment about the manner in which I exercise my profession (along with others, I am happy to say). . . . This is to make an assault, in a totally unjustified way, on our credibility, to give the impression that the profession in its totality (apart from a few elect members) is content to reproduce either unknowingly or willingly, a colonial vulgate."

4. Foucault, "Defendre la société," 128.

5. Foucault, *Order of Things*, 344–87.

6. Foucault, *Order of Things*, 379. The fecundity of this field is evident. We might think of approaches to the colonial situation by Frantz Fanon, Octave Mannoni, or, to a lesser extent, Albert Memmi.

7. On July 26, 2007, Nicolas Sarkozy delivered a speech at Cheikh Anta Diop University that resulted in many sharp reactions and contained these words:

> The African peasant who has lived with the seasons for millennia, whose ideal life is to be in harmony with nature, knows only the eternal recommencement of time as marked by the endless repetition of the same acts and the same words. In this imaginary, where everything continually begins again, there is no place for the human adventure nor for the idea of progress. . . . Here lies Africa's problem, if you will permit a friend of Africa to say so. Africa's challenge is to enter more fully into History. It must draw from its depths the energy, the force, the desire, the will to hear and to embrace its own history. Africa's problem is that it must stop endlessly repeating and ruminating, and must liberate itself from the myth of the eternal return, recognizing that the golden age that it never ceases to mourn is not going to return, for the reason that it never truly existed. (Sarkozy, "Le discours de Dakar").

8. Translator's note: The French term *historiographie* tends to mean the scholarly writing of history rather than the study of research methods used by historians (cf. the English term *historiography*).

9. Nietzsche, *Untimely Meditations*, 62.

10. Nietzsche, *Untimely Meditations*, 67.

11. Foucault, "Nietzsche, Genealogy, History," 372, 381.

12. Nietzsche, *Untimely Meditations*, 60.

13. Nietzsche, *Untimely Meditations*, 60.

14. Nietzsche, *Untimely Meditations*, 61.

15. Febvre, *Combats pour l'histoire*, 436–37.

16. Nietzsche, *Untimely Meditations*, 67.

17. Nietzsche, *Untimely Meditations*, 70. The history of the establishment of independence in the concerned countries is often monumental.

18. Nietzsche, *Untimely Meditations*, 72–75. One can equally say this about philosophy. The philosophy of Republican laïcité often falls under the stroke of Nietzsche's critique.

19. Nietzsche, *Untimely Meditations*, 72. "If the man who wants to do something great has need of the past at all, he appropriates it by means of monumental history; he, on the other hand, who likes to persist in the familiar and the revered of old, tends the past as an antiquarian historian; and only he who is oppressed by a present need, and who wants to throw off this burden at any cost, has need of critical history, that is to say a history that judges and condemns."

20. Nietzsche, *Untimely Meditations*, 76.

21. Nietzsche, *Untimely Meditations*, 76 (translation altered).

22. Nietzsche, *Untimely Meditations*, 78.

23. Nietzsche, *Untimely Meditations*, 79 (translation altered).

24. Nietzsche, *Untimely Meditations*, 84, 79, 86 (translation altered).

25. Nietzsche, *Untimely Meditations*, 91.

26. Péguy, *Oeuvres en prose complètes*, vol. 1, 1222.

27. Nietzsche, *Untimely Meditations*, 89 (translation altered).

28. De Certeau, *Heterologies*, 214.

29. Michel de Certeau, showing that absence is the condition for the possibility of historiography, writes: "The death of the *other* puts him beyond reach, and for this very reason, defines the status of historiography, which is to say of the historical *text*." "Histoire et structure," in *Histoire et psychanalyse*, 190. Translator's note: This essay is not in the 1987 edition of *Histoire et psychanalyse* and is not translated in *Heterologies*.

30. J. Birnbaum, "Guerre de tranchées."

31. Dorgelès, *Reveil des morts*, 180.

32. The settlers are at the heads of industrial, commercial, and above all agricultural companies. The colonials are the agents of the colonial state, who administer the colony, often (but not always) without any qualms.

33. Legifrance, "Loi no. 2005-158 du 23 février 2005." Article 4, line 2 prescribed that "educational programs in particular should recognize the positive role of the overseas French presence, particularly in North Africa, and give the history and the sacrifices of the French soldiers coming from these territories the eminent place that they deserve." This line was revoked by the decree of February 15, 2006.

34. Legendre, *La société comme texte*, 17.

35. Translator's note: Referring to Benveniste's distinction between *discours*, the act of conversation in a given context, and *langage*, the signs available for reference and persuasion.

36. De Certeau, *Heterologies*, 172.

37. De Certeau, "Le rire de Michel Foucault," in *Histoire et psychanalyse*, 148. Translator's note: This passage is not included in the English translation, *Heterologies*.

38. De Certeau, "Le rire de Michel Foucault," in *Histoire et psychanalyse*, 148.

39. In his time, Nietzsche was accused of being unscientific. What was his academic position? He was ordinary professor of classical philology at the University of Basel. His colleague, Ulrich von Wilamowitz-Möllendorff, who would later be an authority on the subject, said of him, "Let Mr. Nietzsche keep his word, let him take his *thyrse*, let him travel from India to Greece, but let him leave this chair where he is supposed to teach science; let him reunite the tigers and panthers at his feet, if he can, but not the young philologists of Germany." Not only was Nietzsche, for this "savant," a pseudophilologist, but he was also considered a pseudophilosopher. He had such a bad reputation that one of his classes attracted only two students. Wilamowitz-Möllendorff, "Philologie de l'avenir (Deuxième Partie)" (1872), cited in Nietzsche, *Oeuvres philosophiques complètes*, vol. 1, 126.

40. De Certeau, *Heterologies*, 193.

41. Foucault, *Archaeology of Knowledge*, 17.

42. De Certeau, *Heterologies*, 194.

43. Between history and philosophy, there is a reciprocal interest and a respective indifference. History and historiography are the grain against which the philosopher scratches. Facts put principles and other speculations in a bad light. Certain scholars, such as Pierre Hadot or Mona Ozouf, emigrate and leave their native (institutional) country. Born philosophers, they become historians by naturalization. Exile is their kingdom. Others become binationals, keeping their original passports.

44. De Certeau, *Heterologies*, 182 (translation altered).
45. Rivet, *Le Maghreb*, 373 (my emphasis).
46. Rivet, *Le Maghreb*, 377.
47. Pervillé, *De l'empire français*, 244.
48. Mékachéra, "Colonisation."
49. See Weil, *Qu'est-ce qu'un Français?*
50. Mauco, *Les étrangers*.
51. See Peyrefitte, *C'était de Gaulle*.
52. Maurice Papon was put on trial and found guilty of crimes against humanity in 1997 for allowing 1,560 Jews to be arrested and deported from Bordeaux between 1942 and 1944. Papon was regional prefect in Constantine at the start of the Algerian War and prefect of the Paris police from 1958 to 1967, during which time he was proved responsible for the repression of Algerians in Paris during the October 17, 1961, demonstration and the Charonne demonstration in February 1962. Further government posts included serving as *député* of Cher and as national budget minister from 1978 to 1981. Maurice Papon thus had a very "good career" in France. See Le Cour Grandmaison, *Le 17 octobre 1961*.
53. Translator's note: In psychoanalytic theory, a screen memory is a relatively benign or even self-affirming memory that replaces and thus represents a traumatic, inchoate experience that has been repressed. See Freud, "Screen Memories."
54. Thucydides, *History*, 337 (2.43; my emphasis, translation altered).
55. Hesiod, *Theogony*, 7 (55).
56. Liauzu and Le Bars, "Insultes d'un ministre."
57. Legifrance, "Loi no. 2005-158 du 23 février 2005." See Hautreux, "L'engagement des harkis": "During the war of Algerian independence, these [the *harkis*] formed a category of auxiliaries to the French army, 'irregular' soldiers recruited to help with the war. With independence, the word took on two new meanings: traitors in Algeria, 'repatriated Muslim Frenchmen' in France" (33).
58. See Van Eeckhout, "Une disposition."
59. Given this, we see the singular position (and the absence of place) given to the *harkis*. In 1962, Muslim French were called "repatriated Muslims" and became, at the recommendation of a report by the coordinating commission for the reinstallation of overseas French, "Algerians of Muslim origin." For the French bureaucrats, "Muslim French of Algeria" is supposed to be an expression with no religious meaning. In principle, they were supposed to be treated like the other Algerian-born French. In fact, very rapidly, the French government stopped respecting the Evian accords: the "Muslim French" who were supposed to be automatically repatriated became "Algerians of Muslim origin" (according to de Gaulle, they could claim the status of refugees only if the French authorities agreed to it). In France, the independence of Algeria consecrated the notion of origin. Thus the term *Muslim* came to mean "of Algerian origin" in the vocabulary of the French state.
60. Adorno, *Modèles critiques*, 119.
61. Consider today the case of Mayotte and its exceptional legislation.
62. See for example Tocqueville, *Sur l'Algérie*.
63. See the analysis of this proposed by Rancière, *Disagreement: Politics and Philosophy*, 23–25.
64. Rancière, *Disagreement*, 26, 24. The original source is Pierre-Simon Ballanche, "Formule générale de l'histoire de tous les peuples appliquée à l'histoire du people romain," *Revue de Paris*, September 1829, 94.

65. At the start of their conquest of Algeria, the French distinguished between the Kabyles, savages, and the Arabs, half-civilized. In the following century, during the 1950s, they spoke again of "advanced fringes" [*franges evoluées*] of the population in contrast to "backward mentalities" [*mentalités arriérées*].

66. In Algeria the question of *language* was posed starting from the fall of Algiers in 1830. It was raised by teachers. Jomard, director for the Egyptian school of Paris, wrote to the minister of the navy to offer his support. He was told that a linguistic problem must be surmounted. Between Arabic, Turkish, Franque (Mediterranean pidgin), and French, which should be taught? The doctrine of the duke de Rovigo (1832) was as follows: "I see the propagation of instruction and of our language as the most efficient means to ensure progress in our domination of this country . . . the real feat to be accomplished would be replacing Arabic little by little with French." In fact, nothing was required to dominate other than to oblige everyone to express himself or herself in a different language than his or her own, another language than his or her maternal language, and finally, a language that one could not learn. The first public schools, opened starting June 1, 1833, in Algiers, did not accept any Muslims. As for the Arabic courses intended for the French, there were no students during the first years.

67. It is not accidental that the effective eligibility of women in French political life was treated in terms of *parité*, which was the term employed with respect to the Muslim French, a term that actually indicated an impossible equality. See Luste Boulbina, "Le deuxième sexe." It was thus that one matched the situation of blacks and the situation of women. Like race, gender is not a scientific but a political category.

68. A remarkable exception: Manceron, *Marianne et les colonies*. On the other side: Hanotaux and Martineau, *Histoire des colonies françaises*.

69. In 1914, the French colonial empire was almost entirely built. Only the Sahara (1934), the Rif (1926), and the Atlas (1930s) remained to be pacified. The empire covered twelve million square meters (ten million square meters in Africa). The African continent alone was entirely colonized by 1914. The Europeans divided up the totality of Africa, primarily to the benefit of the French and the British. Morocco, Algeria, Tunisia, the territories of the south (the Algerian Sahara), Mauritania, Senegal, Guinea, the Sudan, Côte d'Ivoire, Niger, Chad, Oubangui, Gabon, Congo-Brazzaville, and Madagascar were French colonies.

70. The example of AIDS today indicates that these cannot be confused. The scientific and technological advances are not necessarily political and social advances, and health, as all studies show, is one of the most unequally distributed social goods in the world.

71. "Along with the pronoun," the verb is "the only class of words embodying the category of person." The Arabic language distinguishes "the one who speaks" (*al-mutakallimu*), "the one who is addressed" (*al-muḫāṭabu*), and finally "the one who is absent" (*al-yā'ibu*). Benveniste, *Problems in General Linguistics*, 195, 197.

72. "One should be fully aware of the peculiar fact that the 'third person' is the only one by which a *thing* is predicated verbally. The 'third person' must not, therefore, be imagined as a person suited to depersonalization . . . it is exactly the non-person, which possesses as its sign the absence of that which specifically qualifies the 'I' and the 'you.' Because it does not imply any person, it can take any subject whatsoever or no subject, and this subject, expressed or not, is never posited as a 'person.'" Benveniste, *Problems in General Linguistics*, 199–200.

73. In his Second Untimely Meditation, "On the Uses and Disadvantages of History for Life," this is how Nietzsche criticizes objectivity: "These naive historians call the assessment

of the opinions and deeds of the past according to the everyday standards of the present moment 'objectivity': it is here they discover the canon of all truth; their task is to adapt the past to contemporary triviality." And he adds: "Thus man spins his web over the past and subdues it, thus he gives expression to his artistic drive—but not to his drive towards truth or justice. *Objectivity and justice have nothing to do with one other.*" *Untimely Meditations*, 90–91 (my emphasis).

74. Thus the historian Daniel Lefeuvre published *Pour en finir avec la repentance coloniale.*

75. Laïcité is a textbook case.

76. We must remember the antisemitic campaigns led against Pierre Mendès France after the Liberation and after the liberation of the camps—as if there were nothing, as if nothing had taken place.

77. Nietzsche, *Untimely Meditations*, 78 (translation altered).

78. Nietzsche, *Untimely Meditations*, 79.

79. See Spivak, "Can the Subaltern Speak?"

80. Humanitarian assistance rests on a particular conception of sovereignty. It is because, in this conception, sovereignty is an absolute that an exceptional right to intervention is necessary. Now, there are a multiplicity of states and therefore relative sovereignty (to put it otherwise, the principle of sovereignty is unconditional, but sovereignty itself is limited).

81. Bettati, "Le droit d'ingérence."

82. Kouchner, "Introduction."

83. The misadventures of Zoe's Ark (l'Arche de Zoé) are eloquent on this point. Zoe's Ark is a French humanitarian association (NGO) created in 2004, whose officials tried, in 2007, to extract 103 children from Chad to France, presented as orphans of Darfur. The problem was that these children were neither Sudanese, nor orphans, nor victims of the Darfur massacres. Those responsible were later convicted by the French courts. See Jablonka, "L'Arche de Zoé."

84. Kouchner, "Le mouvement humanitaire," 28–36. The following quotations are taken from the same article.

85. As an example of this politics, consider the French Communist Party's call to resistance according to Jacques Duclos and Maurice Thorez (1940): "France wants to live free and independent. Never will a great people like ours be a people of slaves." Still on display at Bobigny (Seine-Saint-Denis). Translator's note: This note is added by the author, not by Veyne.

86. Veyne, "Foucault Revolutionizes History," 153–54.

87. "That Foucault reifies an authority which escapes human action and historical explication, that he privileges breaks or structures in relation to continuities or evolutions, that he is not interested in the social . . ." Veyne, "Foucault Revolutionizes History," 154.

88. Veyne, "Foucault Revolutionizes History," 156 (my emphasis).

3

THE COLONY, MIRAGE AND HISTORICAL REALITY

THE POINT OF THIS CHAPTER IS NOT TO attack two idols: Alexis de Tocqueville and Pierre Mendès France. Its goal is to interrogate the complexity of two distinct positions, incarnated in two figures, both of whom are celebrated and respected. The first is a position on the colonies, whether the older colonies such as Martinique and Guadeloupe or the new colony yet to be created in Algeria, held consistently by a theoretician who was also a politician. Like others, Tocqueville envisages the abolition of slavery almost exclusively through a colonial lens. It astonishes me that the very numerous French works dedicated to this illustrious thinker, even the most recent, make little of Tocqueville's colonial ideas. A century later, an upright politician, a fearless and irreproachable republican, almost an intellectual of political practice, confronted the fratricidal wars of independence opposing colonizers and colonized. He was not a colonialist, but his conceptual schemes contain what Susan Buck-Morss calls "islands of blindness," which prevented him from correctly diagnosing the Algerian situation.[1] Two republicans with a century between them, two democrats grappling with the colonies.

Tocqueville and the Colonies: America, Antilles, Algeria

Alexis de Tocqueville became famous on January 23, 1835, when he published the first part of *De la démocratie en Amerique*. The book encountered clear success and gave rise to lively polemics. A legitimist newspaper, the *Gazette de France*, released an anonymous article containing these lines: "Monsieur de Tocqueville is a lawyer and, as such, he pleads the case of democracy in America. It is with a very unique predilection that this author encourages the peoples of Europe to admire . . . a country of tri-colored humanity where the red men who are its natives see themselves exterminated by white men who are seizing it from them, and where black men are sold pell-mell along with animals in the public square."[2] Tocqueville was not blind to this, but he did not make it the central object of his inquiry, which was democracy. He devoted much of his study to the analysis of this "tri-colored humanity" and the relations that its colored components entertained with one other.

His analyses are perceptive. One may therefore be astonished to read the reports that Tocqueville prepared on Algeria during the colony's beginning phases, in 1841 and 1847, which do not show Arabs the humanity he felt for blacks and native peoples in America. If, in fact, he seems sensitive to questions of equality between blacks and whites—because for the Native Americans, the question is posed not in terms of equality but of banishment—he remains completely indifferent to the lot of this multicolor population (Kabyles, Arabs, Moors) who people the territory of Algeria.

In a letter to his mother from December 25, 1831 (on the Mississippi), the traveler makes the following observations: "You know then that the Americans of the United States, reasonable and unprejudiced people, the greatest philanthropists, imagined like the Spanish that God gave them the New World and its inhabitants as simple property. They have moreover discovered, as was proven—listen well to this—that a square mile can nourish ten times more civilized people than savage people, and thus reason indicated that everywhere the civilized people could establish themselves, the savages had to give way. You see how beautiful logic can be."[3]

Tocqueville then follows with a sadly ironic observation: in fact, the Indians, the Chactas (or Choctaws), were deported "into a desert where the Whites would not leave them in peace for ten years. See what comes from an advanced civilization?"[4] Further, one must recognize the different modalities of the complete expropriation of the Native Americans, or in other words, the white appropriation of lands. If the Spanish, indeed, are "truly brutal, let their dogs loose on the Indians as if they were ferocious beasts," "[if] they kill, burn, massacre the New World," the Americans of the United States, for their part, who are "more humane, more moderate, more respectful of law and of legality, never bloody, are more profoundly destructive to their race."[5] The philosopher is thus an observer with a distant gaze but a sensitive heart. His perception is not political; it is human. This is why he writes, "There was, in the whole of this spectacle, an air of ruin and of destruction, something that smelled of a final farewell with no return; one could not watch it without a torn heart."

On the other hand, when in October 1841 he reflects on ways to make war against the Arabs in Algeria, the writer recommends the same methods that he disapproved of in America. "The means second in importance, after the interdiction of commerce, is to ravage the country. I believe that the right of war authorizes us to ravage the country and that we must do it, either by destroying harvests during the harvest season, or year-round by making those rapid incursions called razzias, whose purpose is to seize men or herds."[6] "I have already said," he adds, "that what most worried and irritated the natives, reasonably, was to see us take and cultivate their lands. This irritates not only those we dispossess but the entire country. For three centuries the Arabs have been accustomed to being governed by foreigners. As long as we take over only the government, they are well enough disposed to let us do so. But the moment the laborer appears behind the soldier, they will conclude that we mean not only to conquer but to dispossess them. The quarrel is no longer between governments, but between races."[7]

Such is the difference between a *conquest* and a *colonization*. Conquest is about the government of people; colonization about the administration of things. Perhaps any territory in which all matters are referred to the administration of things, moreover, is a colony. Henceforth, what is being expressed is no longer the sensibility of the thinker but what is supposed to be his reason. In fact, if to colonize is to dispossess men and to appropriate things, only violence can bring this about. This is why Tocqueville believes that it is necessary to cut to the chase, so to speak, once and for all, and to take the coveted lands away definitively. He considers as follows:

> In general, nothing is more dangerous in a new country than the frequent use of forced expropriation. . . . But in the present case, and in the prodigious disorder of property, such a remedy, administered once and for all in a single dose, is necessary. It is absolutely necessary that we manage to fix property and its boundaries using a summary procedure and an expeditious court established for that sole purpose. Having thus created a certain landowner and an alienable property, we should declare that if, after a term we indicate, the recognized owner does not cultivate his land, this land will fall to the state, which will secure it by paying the purchase price. These are undoubtedly violent and irregular procedures, but I defy anyone to come up with another way to extricate ourselves from this problem.[8]

Was it due to his tender age (he was twenty-six years old) that Tocqueville empathized with the Native Americans' fate? He was a mature man (thirty-six years old) when he examined the case of the Algerian Arabs. How many observations go into making a political gaze? How should we explain, and eventually understand, that he successively defended two contradictory positions? What he condemns in America, he recommends in Algeria.

It is shortsighted to decide that Tocqueville simply finds the Native Americans interesting and remains indifferent to the Arabs. His position is both more complex and more eloquent. Tocqueville had no interest at stake when he observed the deportation of Native Americans on a boat crossing the Mississippi. Then, he was a simple detached spectator who, powerless, contemplated a spectacle that he found both horrible and atrocious. He was a disinterested witness who, moreover, observed a scene that he judged deplorable in moral terms. From his point of view, the Americans of the United States were politically deserving of critique, if not morally condemnable, in their colonizing practices. When, on the other hand, he was an engaged actor, he was no longer a legalist, and raison d'état struck him as superior to principles. The gap is not so much between theory and practice as it is between inquiry and expertise. This split within a single subject is also found in Tocqueville's treatment of slavery. Indeed, like Broglie, Tocqueville belonged to the abolitionist society.[9] In 1833, Victor Schoelcher had already published his work *De l'esclavage des Noirs, et de la législation coloniale.*

If one compares Tocqueville's different statements about slavery, one might remark a certain gap between different texts with respect to their intended audience. In 1843, the newspaper *Le Siècle* published in its columns anonymous articles preceded by the notice: "A man, who owes his pure reputation and his high position in letters and politics only to his painstaking works, addresses us on the grave question of the emancipation of slaves in a series of articles, which we recommend to the total attention of our readers."[10] Tocqueville does not express himself in his own name but uniquely in the name of his authority—that is, his reputation and his position. He does so as an author. He does nothing of the sort when he reports the work of the "commission charged with examining M. de Tracy's proposition concerning slaves in the colonies."[11] It is as a member of Parliament that he presents conclusions for the approval of his peers. Tocqueville argues *in his own name* and as a representative—doubly, of the people and of the commission. He is an agent of the first rank. Politics is occupied with the question of means, not that of ends. What interests him is a technical question: "The commission," he declares, "does not have . . . to establish that servitude can and must come to an end one day. Today it is a truth universally recognized, and one that slave owners themselves hardly deny. The question which we must address is therefore how to get out of the sphere of theories in order to finally enter the field of practical politics. It is hardly a matter of knowing whether slavery is bad, and whether it must end, but when and how it is best to end it."[12] Several years later, this "universally recognized truth" remained the site for a *struggle of opinions* among the readers of *Le Siècle*.

Tocqueville the orator [*tribun*] does not use the same language as Tocqueville the member of Parliament. He writes: "France possesses 250,000 slaves. The colonists declare unanimously that the emancipation of these slaves would be the colonies' ruin, and they pursue all men who express a contrary opinion with their abusive clamor."[13] In 1839, therefore, the colonists were political partners if not allies in the Assembly chamber. In 1843, in the columns of a newspaper, they are ideological enemies. For Tocqueville, they do not have the same status when he places himself on a strictly technical plane as they do when he occupies a more generally political plane, or when he takes the terrain of action rather than that of opinion.

Tocqueville is a political moralist. It is to Kant that we owe the distinction between two political types, two ways of doing politics.[14] The political moralist adapts his maxims to circumstances while the moral politician models his actions on his principles. Kant stresses the relation each style of doing politics maintains with history. The political moralist is the one who thinks he knows the course of events. He is the one who sees politics as a technique—in other words, as a production of effects that are all the more predictable as they reflect a familiarity with things. What gets called the *way of the world* is meaningful for him.

By contrast, the moral politician is the one who sees in politics a practice from which one hopes for certain results. He is the one who believes history does not allow the future to be judged in advance. Sometimes, the moral politician is maladroit and, with respect to actual experience, despotic. When he neglects the force of things, indeed, he does violence to experience and imposes principles with neither discernment nor prudence, the political virtue if ever there was one. However, and without doubt most important, in this case, Kant believes that the "moralizing politicians, for what they are worth, try to cover up political principles which are contrary to right, under the pretext that human nature is *incapable* of attaining the good which reason prescribes as an idea. They thereby make progress *impossible*, and eternalize the violation of right." "These worldly-wise politicians," he continues, "resort to despicable tricks, for they are only out to exploit the people (and if possible the whole world) by influencing the current ruling power in such a way as to ensure their own private advantage. They are just like lawyers (i.e., those for whom law is a profession, not a matter of legislation) who have found their way into politics."[15]

The portrait that Kant paints of this kind of political man resembles, trait for trait, Tocqueville himself.

Tocqueville is well aware of this. In his "Lettres sur la situation intérieure de la France," he poses a classic question in political thought: "What exactly is meant by these words, repeated every day: that the opposition lacks the practical spirit?" His response:

> It is a maxim widely touted among men of government and generally among all those who have possessed or want to possess power, that in politics there is nothing true about principles in themselves, and that they must be considered as various means appropriate to the various ends that may be proposed. This confusion in the general notions of good and evil where government is concerned and this scorn for rules are what they ordinarily call the practical spirit. They regard this vast love for the human race, this immense desire for men's freedom, this respect for their rights which have given so much power and so much force to the first efforts of the French Revolution, as so many literary exaggerations. Scorn for these disinterested and generous feelings in politics, this too they call the practical spirit.[16]

One might say that in a sense the political moralist, or the man of government, remains with the administration of things while the moral politician, or the man of the opposition, prefers the government of persons. This is not through any political accident but is a fundamental structure of politics. The political scientists oppose government parties and activist parties, but within each party one also observes governmental and activist wings. The former are associated with measures proposed; the latter result from the critique of others' political measures. From whence it appears that one can, at the same time (it depends!) be a technician and an ideologue in politics. This combination is even the hallmark of conservative attitudes. However much Tocqueville may be a moral politician on French soil, he remains a political moralist in the overseas territories. Thus the political split can also divide humanity.

If there is one fundamental point on which Tocqueville has a practical sense, or is a conservative, and *ipso facto*, a political moralist, it has to be property ownership. Property is the center of gravity in the analyses that he proposes when it comes to the situation of the Native Americans, as likewise for the slaves in the English and French colonies, and finally, the Algerian Arabs. Property and property owners must be respected, even if they are Native American and frightful—this is a political principle. But one must expropriate and dispossess property owners, particularly Arabs—this is a political technique, even the best-tested political technique when colonization is in question. It is impossible to bring these two positions into harmony, because they involve different indigènes. From afar, Tocqueville defends the Native Americans and condemns the Americans. Up close, he defends the French and hardly ever condemns them in their persecution of Arabs.

In an analogous fashion, for Tocqueville, slavery must be abolished in the name of freedom, a political principle. But at the same time, the masters must be reimbursed—the political technique at work in numerous reforms. It is not the slaves who need to be reimbursed for the injustice they experienced, but the masters for the loss they suffered. Reparation is not about freedom but about property ownership. If some people paid for this with their lives, too bad. Property is certainly one of the belated motivations for efforts at reparation. The *pretium doloris* is worth much less than material losses.[17] "It is unworthy of France's greatness and generosity," Tocqueville declares, "that the principles of justice, humanity and reason, which she and her overseas children have so long misrecognized, should be made to triumph exclusively at the expense of the latter; to take the honor of such a belated reparation only for herself, and to leave the colonists with nothing but the work. . . . When this way of thinking is not indicated by equity, interest alone will make of it a law. To arrive without trouble at the happy results that emancipation must produce, the active cooperation of the settlers must be gained and preserved."[18] There are worse things than slave revolts, such as the revolt of settlers. Turn necessity into a virtue. Is this political realism? Doubtless, Tocqueville wished to avoid making irreducible enemies out of the settlers, more concerned, in politics as in business, about their returns than about their principles. To ruin the settlers, indeed, would be to ruin the colonies. This is the real reason why the social question and the colonial question intersect.

In fact, emancipating the slaves posed no political danger either for Tocqueville or for the commission that he represented. In his eyes, Saint-Domingue was the exception that confirmed the rule. But whether Tocqueville said nothing about it or did not know, Saint-Domingue was also the place where slavery was the most demanding, the most implacable, the most ferocious. It was the place where color prejudice, as one said in the eighteenth century, was associated most strictly with slavery, forbidding mixed unions with the most extreme rigor.

There was nothing like it in the English colonies, where the abolition of slavery was pronounced August 28, 1833, and was enforced starting August 1, 1834.[19] The British prohibition on the slave trade dated from 1807. In 1815, the Congress of Vienna had confirmed the will of participating states to abolish the trade. In the French colonies, according to Tocqueville, "slavery, moreover, has become mild enough for a long time now."[20] This is why the rapporteur believes that "the greatest fear from emancipation is not the violent death of our colonies but their gradual deterioration and the ruin of their industry by the stoppage, the considerable reduction, or the high cost of labor."[21]

Thus, what calls for reflection is logically labor and property ownership. If slavery is a matter of work and of property, abolition must also be a matter of work and property. The English example is instructive for him, because Tocqueville believes that the difficulties encountered after the abolition of slavery derive, on the one hand, from the fixing of the price of work (the black demands too much; the settler does not offer enough) and, on the other hand, from the fact that the former slaves are also, generally, small proprietors in their own right (of gardens) who prefer to work for themselves rather than for others.

What conclusions are drawn by Tocqueville and the members of the commission to which he belongs? To a man, they defend the necessity of establishing "an intermediary and transitional state between slavery and freedom." What is that state? Quite simply, nationalization of the black people! "The State alone would become the guardian of the freed population, and it is the state that would, as it wished and on conditions it would establish, lend the services of blacks to the colonists, while keeping the use of disciplinary measures in its own hands."[22] This is the compromise that the French members of Parliament found to reconcile the interests of colonists, slaves, and the French state.

Colonial interests predominate.[23] Slavery must be abolished, perhaps, but in a way that preserves the colony itself, which means both its existence and its structure. "I recognize, however," Tocqueville writes in one of his articles, "that the principal merit of our colonies is not in their markets, but in the position they occupy on the globe. This position makes several of them the most precious possessions France could have."[24] The distance between the analyses that Tocqueville devotes to the Native Americans in *De la démocratie en Amerique* and the position he takes with respect to the Arabs in Algeria is the same as the distance separating the reflections that he devotes to the blacks in *De la démocratie en Amerique* and the measures that he proposes for them in the Caribbean colonies.

When he considers America, in fact, Tocqueville pays attention to the mode of government, democracy, and to the limits of democracy. In the famous chapter on "the future of the three races that people the territory of the United States," he emphasizes that he is attacking a subject that is at the limits of democracy in America, thereby showing that not everything in a democracy is democratic. When, on the other hand, it is a matter of the territories placed under French domination, or English as the case may be, Tocqueville is *attentive to the interests of the state*, and even if he is republican, he prefers to defend the state (which sometimes includes critiques of its government) rather than the interests of the diverse inhabitants of the territories concerned. In this, he is a true colonist. This is why his writings reveal a partisan of the colonial state, with a double standard for different cases.

In his biography of Tocqueville, André Jardin contends that "the immediate conclusion of the first part of *De la démocratie en Amerique* is the need to get into the Chamber to apply its directives."[25] But this continuity is meaningful only on the plane of institutions and the organization of the state. Otherwise, the solution of continuity differentiates Tocqueville's views on America from his views elsewhere on the French colonies. Democracy, in fact, is a government of similar people. Similarity is the basis for the interchangeability of citizens. Any differences (of ethnicity, of race, of religion) break this supposed interchangeability by imposing places to which citizens belong. Put otherwise, by believing that each must be in his or her place, socially, one loses sight both of the republic and of democracy and retains only the social order, which continues to rest on property ownership. In a colony, what is vital is property.

Describing the transformation of the British Caribbean colonies, Tocqueville makes the following observation: "The apprenticeship was a preparation for freedom; when it was completed, complete freedom was granted, and colonial society entered into the same conditions of existence as European societies. Whites formed the wealthy class, Negroes the working class. . . . The workers of the colonies had precisely the same rights those of the metropole enjoyed."[26]

The problem produced by the transformation of the colonies was the considerable increase in the *cost of labor.* "The cause of the problem being well known, what were the remedies?" Tocqueville asked himself. "Many presented themselves, but one in particular would have been very easy and very effective. . . . It would be enough to prohibit them [the former slaves] for a certain period from becoming landowners."[27] After enduring the prohibition of freedom, the blacks could expect prohibition from property ownership. To be nonproprietors—such is the trait common to French workers and to former colonial slaves. Dissimilar on numerous points, they resemble one another in possessing nothing apart from, at best, themselves.

The only difference was the cost of land, higher in France, where the market was better, than in the colonies. Due to this fact, the French workers could only gradually become (small) proprietors while the blacks were able to suddenly change their condition. This is why, to ensure that the former slaves were forced to remain workers, they had to bc prevented—through legal means—from becoming property owners. There was no other way to prevent wages from rising. Tocqueville's argumentation here comes down to a simple calculation. A worthy point of principle: "The English government," he claims, "should thus have refused, at least for some time, to grant Negroes the right to acquire land; but it never had a very clear idea of the peril when there was still time to avert it. At the moment when slavery was abolished, such a restriction of freedom would have been accepted without murmur by the black population; later, it would have been imprudent to impose it."[28]

Other places, other customs—it is out of the question that a colony, whichever one, might resemble its metropole. Abolish slavery, maybe, Tocqueville writes, "but this does not mean that colonial society must all at once take on exactly the same appearance as greater French society, nor that the emancipated Negro is to enjoy on the spot all the rights that our worker possesses. The English example is there to prevent us from making such an error."[29] Thus, what blacks must be granted is a different freedom, which is to say an unequal freedom: a freedom within an assigned residence (a black person cannot leave the colony), a freedom that obliges them to work and forbids them from working for their own benefit (which will inevitably lower the cost of labor), a freedom, finally, in which wages will be fixed by the government.

Liberalism, as much economic as political, is limited. It is limited by the state's superior interests, the state's political interest in possessing colonies.

The settlers would not have been able to endure the freedom of blacks; the author's argument is that the settlers did not *establish* slavery even if they *profited* from it. This is the argument from attenuating circumstances: slavery was not the fruit of the settlers' will, but of a historical sequence that went beyond them. The settlers are not to be put on trial. One must not present them with an indictment.[30] Tocqueville thus pleads here on behalf of the masters, those very owners who, in Martinique, in Guadeloupe, in Réunion (Bourbon), considered slavery as an absolute or relative benefit. Thus the state will have to recompense them for half of their losses, and the blacks' free labor will also be a partial compensation. This means that for Tocqueville, the blacks must pay for their own emancipation. Because for him, "however important the position of the Blacks may be, however sanctified their misfortune must be in our eyes, for it is our doing, it would be unjust and imprudent to be concerned with them alone. France cannot forget those of her children who live in the colonies, nor lose sight of her greatness, which demands that these colonies progress."[31]

Meanwhile, not everything can be explained by the colonial cause. At root, Tocqueville is rather indifferent to black people, just as he is rather indifferent to Arabs. During his trip to America, he was able to carefully observe the condition of blacks, whether slave or free. He was able to produce a subtle theory of assimilation, in which he shows that it cannot be a unilateral movement bringing blacks toward whites but must be a mutual process of intersecting identifications, such that the failure of assimilation cannot be blamed on the incapacity of black people, as ordinary hasty judgment might have it, but on whites' refusal to identify with some or all blacks. Finally, he was able to analyze with great perspicacity the dangers that the fate of black people posed for Americans. But what preoccupied him was the population, not the individuals.

When Tocqueville conducts his inquiry, it is exclusively with respect to whites. He never met a black person during his year of traveling in the United States. He reports on no revolts. He mentions no freed black, no black abolitionist. The paradox is that black people themselves are absent from his study although they are, as slaves, present in his thought, since slavery is one of the most important subjects of which traces remain in his travel notebooks. Black people remain invisible and mute . . . On the other hand, he does recount how the Native Americans disappointed him.[32] In other words, the indigenous Americans are exotic and constitute objects of curiosity while the blacks, more familiar, do not interest Tocqueville in themselves. His observations are sparing. He tells an anecdote and foregrounds a black servant.[33] He is present at a scene in which a black person is kicked out, which he mentions in passing.[34] He is struck by the madness of a black person.[35] He visits a plantation in Louisiana.[36] He discovers the small white landholders of Kentucky and of Tennessee with their slaves.[37]

Whatever diverse horizons it may come from, all the testimony that Tocqueville gathers and that he has retranscribed in his notebooks agrees on one point, which is that whites and blacks in America cannot possibly finish by forming a single people. Thus, Tocqueville gives a first interview, on September 18, 1831, to a planter from Georgia, Mr. Clay ("I have rarely seen a man more amiable and better educated"). What does he say? That America will finish by being divided into two zones, the whites in the North and the blacks in the South. "In this way, a people entirely descended from Africans will be formed there, which will be able to have its nationality and enjoy its own laws. I cannot see another solution to the great question of slavery. I do not believe that the Blacks will ever mix sufficiently completely with the Whites to form a single people with them. The introduction of this foreign race is, moreover, America's great blemish and its only one."[38]

The French scholar with whom he was speaking on October 27 of the same year, M. Duponceau, is of the same opinion: in his view, slavery is America's plague not only in itself but also because of a consequence he believes is inevitable: segregation.[39] Thus, slavery appears, in the testimony taken as a whole, whether by abolitionists or supporters of slavery, to be at once a political evil, a social evil, an economic evil, a moral evil, an evil at present, and an evil to come: a complete and thorough evil.[40] To be sure, this American evil is not exclusively perceived as damaging to black people; it is apprehended first as an evil for America, an evil for whites, an evil for the masters! This is why it constitutes a peril.[41]

The free blacks of the North numbered only one hundred thirty thousand in 1830, when Tocqueville discovered America. Two hundred thousand of them were counted in 1850. They fought for the abolition of slavery. They created the first black abolitionist newspaper, *Freedom's Journal*. A white abolitionist journal already existed, the *Liberator*, edited by William Lloyd Garrison. Moreover, numerous slaves tried to escape their condition and reach the northern states.[42] In 1829, David Walker, born free though he was the son of a slave, published a pamphlet that created much noise: *The Walker's Appeal*. Georgia promised a $1,000 reward to anyone who would take Walker dead or alive. Walker was killed a year later, in the summer of 1830.

What did he write? "Show me a page of history, either sacred or profane, on which a verse can be found, which maintains, that the Egyptians heaped the *insupportable insult* upon the children of Israel, by telling them that they were not of the *human family*."[43] He also declared: "I would wish, candidly . . . to be understood, that I would not give a *pinch of snuff* to be married to any white person I ever saw in all the days of my life."[44] And then he announced: "Our sufferings will come to an end, in spite of all the Americans this side of eternity. Then we will want all the learning and talents among ourselves, and perhaps more, to govern ourselves.—'Every dog must have its day,' the American's is coming to an end."[45]

In 1831, the first National Negro Convention took place. The most celebrated of these northern black people was Frederick Douglass. A slave, he nevertheless succeeded in learning to read and to write. In 1838, at the age of twenty-one, he fled to the North and became a journalist and writer. In his autobiography, published under the title *Narrative of the Life of Frederick Douglass*, he wrote:

> *Why am I a slave? Why are some people slaves, and others masters? Was there ever a time when this was not so? How did the relation commence?* . . . Once, however, engaged in the inquiry, I was not very long in finding out the true solution of the matter. It was not *color*, but *crime*, not *God*, but *man*, that afforded the true explanation of the existence of slavery; nor was I long in finding out another important truth, viz: what man can make, man can unmake. . . . I distinctly remember being, *even then*, most strongly impressed with the idea of being a freeman some day. This cheering assurance was an inborn dream of my human nature—a constant menace to slavery—and one which all the powers of slavery were unable to silence or extinguish.[46]

Fantastic testimony from this man. For the commemoration of independence, July 4 1852, he gave the following speech:

> Fellow-citizens, pardon me, allow me to ask, why am I called upon to speak here to-day? What have I, or those I represent, to do with your national independence? Are the great principles of political freedom and of natural justice, embodied in that Declaration of Independence, extended to us? and am I, therefore, called upon to bring our humble offering to the national altar, and to confess the benefits and express devout gratitude for the blessings resulting from your independence to us? . . .
>
> What, to the American slave, is your 4th of July? I answer: a day that reveals to him, more than all other days in the year, the gross injustice and cruelty to which he is the constant victim. To him, your celebration is a sham;

> your boasted liberty, an unholy license; your national greatness, swelling vanity; your sounds of rejoicing are empty and heartless; your denunciations of tyrants, brass fronted impudence; your shouts of liberty and equality, hollow mockery; your prayers and hymns, your sermons and thanksgivings, with all your religious parade, and solemnity, are, to him, mere bombast, fraud, deception, impiety, and hypocrisy—a thin veil to cover up crimes which would disgrace a nation of savages. There is not a nation on the earth guilty of practices, more shocking and bloody, than are the people of these United States, at this very hour.
>
> Go where you may, search where you will, roam through all the monarchies and despotisms of the old world, travel through South America, search out every abuse, and when you have found the last, lay your facts by the side of the everyday practices of this nation, and you will say with me, that, for revolting barbarity and shameless hypocrisy, America reigns without a rival.[47]

The mute (and consenting . . .) victim is a myth. It is at best a cause to defend, but never *someone*, never a *person*. In reality, here, as in every other case, some victims denounce, refuse, and revolt. The slaves in America were not submissive. On August 30, 1800, for example, a young slave aged twenty-four, Gabriel Prosser, took the lead of one thousand blacks to occupy Richmond, Virginia. Betrayed, he failed and was hung with fifty other insurgents. In 1811, a revolt of four hundred to five hundred slaves took place in New Orleans, on the Andry plantation. The army intervened, killing sixty-six slaves and condemning sixteen others to death. In 1822, a conspiracy implicating thousands of blacks was thwarted. The thirty-five organizers were judged and hanged at Charleston. The trial transcripts, judged too dangerous, were immediately destroyed. In the year 1831, when Tocqueville found himself in the United States, Nat Turner led a revolt of seventy slaves in Southampton County, Virginia, destroying everything in his path. Captured, he was hung with eighteen of his companions.[48] Tocqueville makes no mention whatsoever of all these facts. He doesn't *know* about them.

It is also quite clear that the fight Tocqueville led against slavery in France drank from the same springs. It was a *political fight* more than a *social question*. There is the same indifference—in other words, the same ignorance—in the way he writes about French workers, more generally anyone who could be called "the little people." His *Souvenirs* show this: when the July Monarchy collapsed on July 24, 1848, Tocqueville judged that "it was this mixture of greedy desires and false theories that engendered the insurrection and made it so formidable. These poor people had been assured that the goods of the wealthy were in some way the result of a theft committed against themselves. They had been assured that the inequalities of fortune were as much opposed to morality and the interests of society as to nature."[49]

But he recounts that George Sand opened his eyes. "Madame Sand gave me a detailed and very vivacious picture of the state of the Parisian workers: their organization, numbers, arms, preparations, thoughts, passions, and terrible resolves. I thought the picture overloaded, but it was not so, as subsequent events clearly proved."[50] What we see admirably in Tocqueville, when it comes to the blacks in the colonies, the workers in France, and the Arabs in Algeria, is at once his political clairvoyance and his social deafness. The theme is classic.

This is why Tocqueville's attitude faced with the conquest of Algeria is coherent with respect to his other commitments. He is not so much inhumane as he is realist. How can one be a Persian? This is by way of an allegory that Tocqueville uses to open his second article on Algeria.[51] If the emperor of China landed in France, if he destroyed everything he encountered in traveling there, if he deported all the authorities "to some far off country," one would see up close the damage produced by conquest.

For all that, in Algeria, Tocqueville adopts precisely the position that he condemns among the Americans. He is at once favorable to expropriation, and therefore to violence, and legalist. It is a common situation where colonies are concerned. In a colony, contraries are supposed to be able to get along. From the American point of view, the expropriation of Native Americans is grounded on the fact that they are not cultivators and that on this basis, one cannot consider them true proprietors of the territories on which they live and hunt. Thus, in keeping with the Lockean theory that only work founds property, one is the owner of whatever one farms. At the same time, the colonists who appropriate these spaces in the South contend that the climate does not allow them to work personally and that they must absolutely have recourse to an African workforce—who should then logically be proprietors of these lands.[52] The Native Americans hold neither legal nor legitimate property ownership.

According to Tocqueville, the case is different for Native Americans than for the Arabs. In the evident conflict between legality and legitimacy, where property ownership is concerned, Tocqueville opts for legitimacy in America, for legality in Algeria. Sensitive to some, such as the Native Americans, he is indifferent to others, the Arabs. But if he is indifferent, this is because colonization is at stake, and there is no territory under domination without land under colonization. It will be understood that the colonial enterprise begins, therefore, as an effort at desertification. To hunt the Native Americans and the Arabs is to render the property owners absent. It is a simple formality, then, that legality becomes a mere affair of titles—a simple political technique. The Arabs will then resemble blacks in certain ways: they will become wage earners, like farm workers.[53]

Just as he pushed rapidly in his parliamentary action against slavery, Tocqueville moved quickly in his parliamentary defense of Algeria's colonization. He dealt with the colonies (old and new) for the same length of time, almost ten years, between 1839 and 1847 (or 1849 if one considers his nomination to the foreign affairs office). Then they ceased to interest him—at least explicitly.

In his preface to Tocqueville's *Souvenirs*, Claude Lefort traces a great line of division between Tocqueville's two monuments (*De la démocratie en Amerique* and *L'ancien régime et la révolution*) and the rest of his texts, except *Souvenirs*.[54] What Lefort appreciates in *Souvenirs* is that it offers a mirror of its author. In fact, on the literary plane nothing compares to Tocqueville's two great books, except, as he contends, for the recounting of his memoirs. Nonetheless, all Tocqueville's texts can be situated politically on the same plane, which is at once a mental geography discoverable in his work, with all its distinctions and categories, and a political geography that allows him to move from America to the Caribbean (English as well as French), from the Caribbean to Algeria, and finally to an unfinished project, a study of India.

From this perspective, the colony is decisive: all its forms or all its stages can be found therein. America is the colony emancipated from its metropole. The Antilles are former colonies (the French swore to remain there forever) to be transformed profoundly by the abolition of slavery. Algeria is a colony yet to be established and to be created top to bottom. To read Tocqueville in this light is to discover a colonial panorama in all its variety, its differences and, sometimes, its similarities (slavery, indeed, is a common point in America and in the Caribbean).[55] But if Tocqueville is read in a literary way, this essential dimension of his work will be missed.

Starting in 1828, Tocqueville, who was then a twenty-three-year-old civilian officer, came out in favor of the military expedition in Algeria. His older brother Hyppolite had also wished, unsuccessfully, to participate in the landing. In 1833, with his cousin Louis, who was knowledgeable about agronomy, Alexis de Tocqueville imagined leaving for Algeria and acquiring some land in the Mitidja. They knew General Lamoricière.[56] The philosopher himself was probably in touch with Genty de Bussy, who was the civil quartermaster in Algiers. He hoped to obtain information about Arabic from Sylvestre de Sacy (Is it a difficult language to learn? How much time should he expect it to take?) and about books that could help him.[57]

Four years later, it was with the gaze of a parliamentary representative that his interest turned again to Algeria. At that time, what and whom did the inhabitants of Algeria resemble for Tocqueville? Were they other Native Americans? In the picture of the country he presents in the first *Lettre sur l'Algérie*, published June 23, 1837, Tocqueville recounts the singularity of the Kabyles in relation to the Arabs. The division between "good" Kabyles and "bad" Arabs that we find in the most common representation of the Algerian population tends to be hidden by the common status of indigène, which was later imposed on them. "If Rousseau had known the Kabyles, sir, he would not have uttered such nonsense about the Caribs and other Indians of America; he would have sought his models in the Atlas."[58] Since the start of the conquest, in fact, the Kabyles were considered a separate case: "The Kabyles speak a language entirely different from the Arabs', and their mores are not at all alike. The only point of contact between these races is religion."[59]

For Tocqueville, Islam is not an admirable religion. The following year, he dove into a reading of the Koran.[60] Later, he sent the following observations to Gobineau, author of the *Essai sur l'inégalité des races humaines*: "I have studied the Koran extensively, above all because of our position vis-à-vis the Muslim populations in Algeria and throughout the East. I confess to you that I am emerging from this study with the conviction that on the whole, there were few religions in the world as deadly to men as the religion of Mohammed."[61] Apart from the defect of being Muslim, the Arabs also have "a multitude of vices and virtues that are not peculiar to them but belong to the stage of civilization at which they find themselves. Like all half-savage peoples, they honor power and force above all else."[62] They are pleasure-seekers, not thinkers.

In Algeria, one therefore finds "savages," the Kabyles; the "half savage" or "half civilized," the Arabs; and finally, the Turks.[63] Tocqueville writes: "These Turks thus formed an aristocratic corps and they possessed the faults and virtues of all aristocracies. Filled with immense pride, they also displayed a certain respect for themselves that made them speak and almost always act with nobility."[64] Still a little later, on May 7, 1841, Tocqueville visits Algeria in the company of Gustave de Beaumont. He finds Algiers spectacular: "I have never seen anything like it. Prodigious mix of races and costumes, Arab, Kabyle, Moor, Negro, Mahonais [Balearic Islanders, from Port Mahon on Minorca], French . . . it is Cincinnati transported onto the soil of Africa."[65]

In 1837, not long after his trip to America, Tocqueville seems firm on principles and hardly ready to accept expropriation of the Arabs without qualms. Is Algeria a desert, as many represent it? In a desert, in fact, "no more borders, no more boundaries to the fields, no more titles of land-ownership."[66] Apparently a desert is a zone of nonlaw. Far from rallying behind this commonplace, to the contrary, Tocqueville wants to debunk it. "Europeans in general believe that all Arabs are herdsmen, and we like to picture them spending their lives driving large herds through immense pastures that are no one's property or that, at least, belong to no one."[67] Only cultivation of the soil gives ownership of the land. The representation is reliable and efficient: does the earth belong to animals? Look for the shepherds, and you will find lands without owners. From this start, the temptation is great to consider the Arabs, like the Native Americans, as hunters or as shepherds.

Refuting the received idea, Tocqueville begins by stressing that this is a matter of an anachronism (at best, this representation might have been valid three thousand years before). Then he defends the existence of an autochthonous ownership: "Can you believe, sir, that there is not an inch of land in the area around Algiers that does not have a known owner, and that there is no more vacant land in the plain of Mitidja than in that of Argenteuil [just northwest of Paris]. Each owner is provided with a title drafted in good form before a public officer. These, you will agree, are singular savages. What do they lack, if you please, to resemble civilized men entirely, but constantly to dispute the boundaries indicated by their contracts?"[68]

In 1837, before becoming a member of Parliament, Tocqueville showed himself concerned for truth and facts where Algeria was concerned. The North of Algeria is not a desert. The Arabs are not savages. Meanwhile, it will be necessary to expropriate them and to thumb one's nose at all their property titles. Starting in 1841, Tocqueville's position begins to bend: He no longer reasons as a thinker but as a politician. He no longer thinks coldly but heatedly. He no longer feels himself to be a man but a statesman. Before doing the "zoology of peoples," according to Husserl's formula, it would be better to establish a zoology of individuality. . .[69]

In 1842, Tocqueville and Beaumont are named members of a special commission charged with examining the colonization of Algeria.[70] Before taking off to Algeria for the first time, Tocqueville scrutinizes collections of articles and official texts.[71] One point that particularly holds his attention in the *Tableau* is, quite rightly, the constitution of property. Ownership, in Algeria, rests on Muslim law, which imposes on the individual proprietor the obligation to pay the *achour* (tithe) on his harvest, given that the only true proprietor is God. What attracts Tocqueville's attention above all is the importance of *habous*, religious lands, which "greatly trouble the development of colonization" because they are inalienable.[72]

Tocqueville continues, "One could not imagine anything more opposed to colonization than such a state of property ownership. What a colonist needs first and foremost is free ownership of land which will belong to him both in the present and the future." Now, the majority of the lands are *habous*, which suggests that many difficulties are ahead. And even in the cases where this is not true, collective property is often predominant. In this case, "the land belongs to no one in particular, but to the tribe as a whole." One can guess at the author's bitter conclusion: "This is a deplorable combination of affairs: in the cities and around them, reigns the *abuse* of individual property which is very inopportune for us; among the tribes, individual property does not exist, which is even more troublesome for us."[73]

The set of notes Tocqueville took constitutes the framework for what he will develop later. What interests him are the pious and benevolent foundations in Algiers, the taxes and the revenues of the regency under the Turks and the French, the state of commerce and industry before the conquest, why one does not encounter a priesthood among the Muslims, the civil state, justice (and particularly the study of the constitutional ruling of August 4, 1834), and many other things besides. "Expropriation in Algeria," Tocqueville notes on the review itself, "is carried out as if by savages. Everywhere buildings are pulled down to make streets and plazas, without yet knowing if one will hold onto the city, without knowing who owns them and what their value is."[74]

These proceedings cannot help but offend Tocqueville's legalism, but very quickly he will agree to methods that are far more summary and also far crueler. Considering in fact that forced expropriation as it has been carried out in Algeria is abusive and dangerous, he nonetheless considers it absolutely necessary—because otherwise, domination will not be accompanied by colonization—and thus, it is also inevitable. "One of the first tasks of government, henceforth, is to consolidate property ownership, weakened by the very procedures of appropriation."

The problem will last for some time. In 1847, Tocqueville wonders in the name of the commission "how we should proceed regarding land." He writes: "But the vital question for our government is that of land. What, in this matter, is our right, our interest and our duty? . . . Does it follow that we cannot take possession of the lands necessary to European colonization? Undoubtedly not; but it strictly obliges us, for the sake of justice and of good policy, to indemnify those who own them or enjoy their use. Experience has shown that this could easily be done, either in concessions of rights, or in an exchange of lands, without costing anything, or for a little money."[75]

The way Tocqueville argues is very interesting. In fact, as with respect to slavery and the reimbursement of the settlers, Tocqueville does not seek to *legitimate* the measures he recommends through reasons; he tries rather to *justify* the means by reference to the ends.[76] What counts is success. In the whole of his political action, he places himself not on the plane of justice, but on that of the police. If in fact he recognizes the irregularity and the illegality of the means, he still believes they are imposed by necessity.

This is the discursive structure typical of raison d'état. This is why, in his thought, the approval of violence against goods is accompanied by consent to violence against persons. Domination requires the first, and colonization the second. Whoever speaks of domination is actually talking about war. Whoever speaks of colonization is talking about occupation and, eventually, settlement. Now, he contends, "colonization without domination will always be an incomplete and precarious work, in my view."[77] Correlatively, in his eyes, "domination . . . is only a means to achieve colonization."[78] The consequence is clear: "I have already said, and I repeat, that until we have a European population in Algeria, we shall never establish ourselves there but shall remain camped on the African coast. Colonization and war, therefore, must proceed together."[79] To colonize is to replace some with others. There were individuals; there will be other individuals in their place—this means deportation.[80] There were property owners; there will be other property owners in their place—this means expropriation.[81] There were, finally, persons; there will be other persons in their place—this means subjection.

For Tocqueville, the difficulty in this whole affair is that domination remains irremediably uncertain. And if such is the case, this is because, like other countries, Algeria is not deserted! It is neither an indeterminate land nor an empty one. "Domination over semi-barbarous nomadic tribes, such as those around us, can never be so complete that a civilized, sedentary population could settle nearby without any fear or precaution."[82] He is arguing less from the security of Europeans than from the securing of the settlers. The realist argument is therefore (always?) an argument from fear. The logic of this uniquely colonial police order is to ensure in some way that the new arrivals fear nothing from the first inhabitants.

The police are therefore established for some against others, law is therefore made for some against others, and justice is therefore done for some against others. The resulting situation is thus the well-known right of the strongest, "never strong enough to be master all the time, unless he transforms force into right and obedience into duty," according to the apt formula of Jean-Jacques Rousseau.[83]

In this properly colonial logic, war can no longer be anything but a total war, a war whose horizon is *extermination*, in the sense of this time period.[84] Today the term is polemical and overdetermined by its contemporary referent.[85] What did extermination mean in a very different context? It signifies simply that where people were once, they will be no longer; the place will be scrubbed clean so that others can move in, whatever the cost. In the end, in this colonial logic, war can have no conclusion, since it is impossible for domination to be total while any indigènes remain. War is endless, peace impossible. Henceforth colonization will be an indefinite process.

The parliamentary commission for which Tocqueville was the rapporteur had eighteen members. Only two of them, Desjobert and Tracy, a very small minority, were unfavorable to colonization. Tocqueville summed up their opposition: "The country to be colonized, they said, is not empty or populated only by hunters, like certain parts of the New World; it is already occupied, possessed, and cultivated by a population that is agricultural and often sedentary. To introduce a new population into such a country is to lengthen the war and to pave the way for the inevitable destruction of the indigenous races."[86] How did the parliamentary majority, via Tocqueville, respond to their objection?

The response, titled "Reasons That Ease the Introduction of a European Population," is detailed. If the country is undeniably occupied, it is so only in a scattered way. "You will see," claims the commission, "that greater and more remarkable means for leading such an enterprise peacefully and to good result are nowhere to be found."[87] Algeria is therefore the royal road to settler colonization [*colonisation de peuplement*]. Algeria, and Africa along with it, is the new New World. Then follow considerations according to which property law is so obscure in Africa that the expropriation and installation of Europeans cannot encounter serious obstacles, at least not juridical obstacles. "These questions are obscure in themselves, and they were further obscured and muddled by the attempt to impose a single, common solution, which the diversity of facts resisted."[88] It must therefore be concluded that the introduction of European farmers will be the easier as it is accomplished "delicately, humanely, and competently."[89] Meanwhile, one must not hope that the two populations will produce a happy mixture: Tocqueville believes, to the contrary, that the division between Europeans and Arabs is so profound that in the future it will only be possible to soften the hostility of Arabs, without being able to suppress it entirely. "It would be unwise," he writes, "to believe that we shall manage to tie ourselves to the indigenous population through the community of ideas and practices, but we may hope to do so through the community of interests."[90]

It was in November 1841, just when he dedicated himself to Algeria, that Tocqueville began reading a history of India. The reading note he then composed remains preoccupied with the very same questions.[91] Like the residents of Algeria, Indians are used to being governed by foreigners. But their system of property ownership is very different from that of Europeans. He writes, "It is a very peculiar thing that the *individual property* that we regard almost as a quasi-natural institution only truly exists in Europe. When one examines all the legal systems of Asia, in the end, one sees that the prince is the owner of the land, if not in fact at least in theory."[92] Property ownership is a very complicated subject. "The English find the question of property undecided in India."[93] In other words, in India, as in Africa, the government of people and domination are far easier than the administration of things and colonization in the proper sense.

In India, what fascinates him is the "grandeur of the English." In Algeria, what concerns him is the grandeur of France. Is India an example to follow? Are the English good colonizers? "This subject," he writes in one of his letters, "which has been of interest in all ages, is extremely so now that all the great European affairs find their kernel in Africa. It is particularly interesting for us since we have the colony of Algiers."[94] Indeed, with Algeria as in other matters, what is at stake is France's rivalry with England. On a geopolitical map of the world, the colonies are the multitudes empires need to exist. If not? If not, then we have decadence.

For Tocqueville, France's decadence began not with Waterloo but with the Treaty of Paris in 1763, which ended the first French colonial empire.[95]

Furthermore, this loss was one of the reasons why his family hated Louis XV. Tocqueville visited Louisiana with nostalgia. When, with Beaumont, he composed *Le système pénitentiaire aux États-Unis*, he blamed France's inability to have colonies on its centralization. In his examination of the Algerian situation, centralization is one of the problems he evokes most regularly because it is an obstacle and a brake on colonization. In his eyes, as he will maintain later in 1856, in *L'ancien régime et la révolution*, centralization is not in fact "a conquest of the revolution," as is sometimes incorrectly believed, but "a product of the *ancien régime*." Thus, for Tocqueville, the colonial enterprise represents a restoration of France's former power, which had been lost. As he claims in his *Souvenirs*, 1830 represents the end of "the first period" of the revolution, but also "a marked lull . . . in every political passion, a sort of universal shrinkage."[96] It was also the year of the conquest in Algeria, the antidote France found to revive its passions and expand its interests. The year 1830 was the beginning of the last French colonial empire.

Pierre Mendès France and the Eruption of Independence: Indochina, Tunisia, Algeria

Here we reflect on the French perception of the colonies in the middle of the twentieth century, beginning with the political position of Pierre Mendès France.[97] In fact, Mendès France was involved with and committed to the independence of Indochina and later to the autonomy of Tunisia. He was the first to have sought an end to the constant use of torture in Algeria. Under the Fourth Republic, he is without doubt the politician who imagined the colonial situation in the most republican manner.

Now, if we analyze the position adopted by Pierre Mendès France, which was in a sense the best of the government's positions, we find a constitutive blindness in his vision of Algeria. On the French side, Pierre Mendès France was the "artisan" of the events of independence. For this reason, his road crossed that of outrageous adversaries, notably—this is just an example—in the person of René Mayer, parliamentary representative [*député*] from Constantine and defender of colonial interests. But what vision of the French colonies did he develop? Was he not more interested in peace than he was friendly to the establishment of independence? Here we propose the philosophical analysis of a structural frame that made Pierre Mendès France and French politicians capable or incapable, in the strong sense, of coming to terms with new political conjunctures and with a new historical context.

One might say that the second Algerian war began in the immediate postwar period, in 1945 (the first Algerian war refers to the conquest, 1830–57). In North Africa, Vichy found a site for the application of its "national revolution" founded on the division of people into two hermetic groups: those who are destined to command and those who are destined to obey. In his *Politics*, Aristotle defined the citizen as the man capable both of commanding and of obeying and believed, therefore, that a city composed on the one hand of men who command, and on the other of men who obey, is not a city of free men but, politically speaking, a city of masters and slaves.[98] The Vichy regime had reinforced this split, abolishing the Crémieux decree after the law of October 7, 1940, and relegating around 117,000 Algerian Jews to the status of indigène (a French subject without citizenship).[99]

Particularly in North Africa, the colonies were more than ever lands of political servitude during the 1940s. On February 10, 1943, under the leadership of Ferhat Abbas, a Manifesto of the Algerian People was sent to the general government and to the United Nations: "The systematic or disguised refusal to give Muslim French access to the French city has discouraged all advocates of the politics of assimilation. . . . Henceforth, a Muslim Algerian will ask for nothing but to be an Algerian Muslim."[100] Under the influence of General Catroux, the ruling of March 7, 1944, put an end to the *indigénat*. Abbas set up the Association of the Manifesto and of Liberty (AML).

The battlefield [*champ d'honneur*], on the other hand, does not foster servitude any better than servitude adapts to the battlefield.[101] It is estimated that 132,000 Algerians, 90,000 Moroccans, and 22,000 Tunisians served under Allied flags from 1939 to 1945. Of these, 13,500 perished.[102] Mohamed Boudiaf and Ahmed Ben Bella, for example, were survivors from the Fifth Algerian Infantry Division, which participated in the battle of Monte Cassino.[103] How many of these men were going to accept becoming "former fighters" like their fathers who were veterans of the Great War? The Maghrebin soldiers, particularly the Algerians, had been defenders of freedom against oppression. On returning home, they had to forget both the freedom they had defended and the oppression to which they were subjected. One can imagine the rupture.

At the time, Algerian nationalists were lumped together with objective allies of Hitler. It is true that on April 10, 1941, Ferhat Abbas had addressed a report titled *L'Algérie de demain* to Marshal Petain, in which he asked for a plan of administrative, educational, and financial reforms, after which he was named to the finance commission of Algeria. One year later, he resigned. But during the Anglo-American landing of November 8, 1942, he put his faith in (more than he received support from) Robert Murphy, personal representative of President Roosevelt in Algeria. In Tunisia, Habib Bourguiba had alerted his "fellow citizens": "The naïve belief that the defeat of France is a punishment from God, that its domination is finished and that our independence will come from a victory of the Axis considered to be certain, is anchored in many minds and this is understandable. And yet I tell you that this is a mistake, a grave impardonable mistake."[104] At the start of 1943, meanwhile, Bourguiba had just been liberated from French prisons by the Italians. . .

In another way, the war also produced effects in Southeast Asia. The Philippines were witness to the Bataan "death march" (1941) imposed by the Japanese on their American prisoners. The Vietnamese saw the French enclosed by the Japanese in cages of less than one cubic meter. The French administration remained operational until March 9, 1945. But the Japanese recognized the independence of the Philippines and of Burma, starting in 1943 (the year in which the Moroccan Istiqlal party was founded). Bao Dai, emperor of Annam, proclaimed the end to the French protectorate and independence with their support, and he was imitated by the kings of both Cambodia and Laos. At Potsdam, the partition was accomplished: confiding the north of Indochina to Chiang Kai-Shek and the south to the English, with the border at the famous sixteenth parallel. On August 13, 1945, after the Japanese surrender, after Hiroshima, Ho Chi Minh, who had never recognized Bao Dai's regime, issued a command for a general uprising. Bao Dai abdicated, recommending that France recognize the independence of Vietnam. On August 25, 1945, a huge demonstration took place blessing the Viet Minh. Independence was proclaimed once again, as well as the democratic republic.

The Indochinese federation was reestablished with its five territories and its high commissioner. De Gaulle, at the head of the Provisional Government of the French Republic (GPRF), wanted to send troops. He named Admiral d'Argenson high commissioner. On March 6, 1946, an accord was signed making the "Free State" of Vietnam one component of the Indochinese federation. The first French troops landed with Leclerc at Hanoi, others at Saigon. When France proclaimed the creation of an autonomous republic of Cochinchine during the summer of 1946 (confirmed in the Fontainebleau accords), the Viet Minh went into action. General Valluy ordered the bombardment of Haiphong. Twelve hundred French were attacked, forty massacred. On December 21, 1946, the Ho Chi Minh government declared a general uprising from exile. "This will be the war between the tiger and the elephant," declared Giap. "If the tiger ever stops, the elephant will break through his powerful defenses: but, the tiger will not stop, he lies low in the jungle during the day to go out only at night; he will throw himself on the elephant and tear his back to shreds then disappear, and slowly, the elephant will die of exhaustion and hemorrhage."[105] In 1949, Mao Zedong took power in China and helped Vietnam. "Henceforth," said Ho Chi Minh, "we have a border with the socialist world."[106]

The colonial conflict intersected with the Cold War. But France remained attached to its colonial empire and feared that the member countries of the French Union would follow the Vietnamese example. This is why France constantly stated that the Destour party in Tunisia and the Istiqlal party in Morocco were paving the way for communism. In fact, the Moroccan and Tunisian leaders used the international scene to ensure the advancement of their interests, taking the internationalization of the Indochinese question as their example. As Ferro recounts, "When in November 1952 the Haut Conseil de l'Union Française, under the presidency of Vincent Auriol, met with Antoine Pinay, then president of the Conseil, and representatives from Vietnam, Laos, and Cambodia, one of them, Nhiek Tioulong, proposed to invite the sovereigns of Tunisia and Morocco to participate in their work."[107] Although Antoine Pinay saw no formal objection, Vincent Auriol, like others, made no secret of his refusal.

On January 30, 1944, De Gaulle gave a speech in Brazzaville in which he stated his desire to "establish the exercise of French sovereignty on new bases."[108] (Were they really so new?) He decided to introduce 63 "overseas representatives" (*députés d'outre-mer*) into the constituent Assembly, out of a total of 522 members, of whom 25 would represent the colonies (women therefore arrived at the same time as the colonized peoples!) Among them were Félix Houphouët-Boigny, Léopold Sédar Senghor, and Aimé Césaire.[109] In March 1945, Cheikh Ibrahimi, president of the Oulémas association, announced at Tlemcen that President Roosevelt had been asked for Algerian independence and that this was to be granted during the conference of San Francisco in 1951, when the peace treaty with Japan was to be signed.[110] For him, "Muslims do not ask to elevated to French citizenship, they already consider themselves quite distinguished by virtue of their status as Muslims."[111]

On March 2, 3, and 4, 1945, the central meeting of the Friends of the Manifesto and of Liberty (AML) took place. On April 29, Ferhat Abbas stated that the meeting of the United Nations was going to assure the freedom of all peoples, thus including the Algerian people. The preceding June 15, he had declared at Khenchela that it was necessary to "force the hand of the French, to make them understand our will while looking at each other eye to eye."[112] Members of the Algerian People's Party (PPA, the Parti du Peuple Algerien) wanted to organize a general uprising, despite the AML's appeals to calm.[113] On March 31, the prefect of Constantine had already judged that it "was best to watch out lest some bloody event definitively separate French from Muslims."[114] The secretary-general of the general government, Pierre-René Gazagne, decided on April 19 to have Messali Hadj arrested. He had him transported to El Goléa and then to Brazzaville.

On May 1, the nationalist organizations demanded Messali's freedom and the independence of Algeria. Demonstrations took place throughout Algeria. At Algiers, clashes with the police left thirteen wounded and three dead among the demonstrators. There were also wounded at Bougie (Béjéïa) and at Oran. Some thirty "preventive" arrests took place from May 3 to 6. Troops were sent to the region of Constantine. The rebellion was supposed to begin on Armistice Day, May 8. The PPA periodically gave its militants the order to arm themselves and to fight back when confronted by police.

In Algiers, demonstrators had raised the green-and-white flag marked with the star and crescent. At Sétif, the demonstration was authorized on condition that there would be no nationalist banners. The demonstration turned into a riot starting the moment that the police tried to take away the banners and the Algerian flag. Between eight thousand and ten thousand demonstrators had come armed with batons, knives, and revolvers. There were twenty-nine deaths and many injured. The insurrection expanded into the countryside, in the centers of colonization between Bougie, Djidjelli, and Sétif, to Bône (Annaba), Guelma, and Batna, leaving one hundred French victims, sometimes violently mutilated. Telephone lines were cut; houses in the woods were burned. General Duval, commander of the Constantine division, sent thousands of men to repress and carry out "search and sweep" [*ratissage*] operations: Senegalese infantry, Moroccan Taborists, and Legionnaires, using both the air force and the navy. Six thousand to eight thousand Algerians lost their lives. At Guelma, five hundred to six hundred Algerians were shot after a farcical trial. Order was reestablished on May 13, but the seats of rebellion remained in the mountainous uplands. The AML was dissolved.

The "sweeps" continued until June. Eighteen planes bombarded 44 *mechtas* (3,000 inhabitants).[115] The cruiser *Duguay-Trouin* also bombed the foothills of Babor. To the military and police repression was added civil repression led by self-defense groups. The judicial repression led to the arrest of 5,460 suspects (of whom 3,696 were from Constantine). The military tribunals pronounced 1,307 of 1,476 condemnations, of which 99 or 121 involved the death penalty. There were 20 to 28 executions. The PPA spoke of "genocide." Starting May 10, the French radio stations of North Africa attributed the riots to "troubling elements with a Hitlerian origin" (Radio Maroc) or to "Hitlerian terrorists" (Radio Alger).

A comparable situation was found in Madagascar, where, as in Algeria, France turned a deaf ear. In March 1946, Joseph Raseta and Joseph Ravoahangy, two young Malagasy representatives who were members of the Democratic Movement for Malagasy Restoration (MDRM), presented a bill to the office of the National Assembly in Paris asking for the island's independence within the framework of the Union Française. Vincent Auriol, then president of the Assembly, refused to have the text printed, because "it was an act of accusation against France and, in short, a call to revolt." The bill was rejected. In the subsequent legislative elections of November 1946, the three seats of the second college (reserved for "indigènes") were won by the leaders of the MDRM: Joseph Ravoahangy, Joseph Raseta, and Jacques Rabemananjara.

In 1947, the Great Red Island counted four million inhabitants, of whom thirty-five thousand were European. On March 29, 1947, the island rose up. At Diego-Suarez, Fianarantsoa, and Tananarive, the rebels were held back. Elsewhere they enjoyed some success before being repressed. Isolated European plantations were attacked. Starting in April, the authorities sent an expeditionary corps of eighteen thousand men to Madagascar—essentially colonial troops, eventually numbering thirty thousand men. The French army carried out typical acts of repression: summary executions, torture, forced resettlements, burned villages. They experimented with a new technique of psychological war: suspects were thrown alive from a plane in order to terrorize the inhabitants of their region. The fight continued in the east of the country, where two zones of guerrillas resisted in the forest for more than twenty months.

In France, some newspapers mentioned the uprising, but the government and the various media minimized its importance and said nothing about the repression. In twenty months, according to the official reports from the French chief of staff, "pacification" had produced 89,000 victims among the Malagasy. The colonial forces, for their part, hung 1,900 men. The death of 550 Europeans, of whom 350 were military, was also reported.

From the start, the government of Paul Ramadier had placed responsibility for the insurrection on the three Malagasy representatives of the MDRM. These three, aware that a project of insurrection was underway, had sent all the villages a telegram asking immediately that each one avoid violence. Their appeal had no effect, but for the French government, this telegram was in fact a coded text that put their signature on the "crime." Their parliamentary immunity having been lifted, they were arrested and tortured. Insisting on the thesis of an MDRM conspiracy, French justice found them guilty. Two of them were condemned to death before finally being pardoned. On July 10, 1947, President Vincent Auriol wrote, "There were apparently cruelties and they were punished. There were equally excesses of repression. A few of the wrong people were shot indiscriminately."

Albert Camus protested in an article of *Combat* dated May 10, 1947. Acknowledging that "we are doing what we reproached the Germans for doing," he continued: "If, today, Frenchmen learn of the methods that are sometimes used by other French toward the Algerians or the Malagasy and if they do not revolt, it is because they live in the unconscious certitude that we are superior in some way to these peoples and that the choice of proper means to illustrate that superiority is of little consequence." Regarding Morocco, on September 20, 1947, Paul Ricoeur published in *Réforme* an article titled "La question coloniale." "The fanatical and often premature appetite for freedom which animates separatist movements," he wrote, "is the same passion that is at the origin of our own history of 1789 and of Valmy, of 1848 and of June 1940."

In Algeria, an amnesty law was passed on March 16, 1946. Ferhat Abbas founded the Union démocratique du manifeste algérien (UDMA). Messali Hadj was freed in November 1946 and returned to Algeria. He created the Mouvement pour le triomphe des libertés démocratiques (MTLD). After the election of President Auriol, the newly created institutions of the Fourth Republic discussed a new status for Algeria. The governmental project defended by the interior minister, Edouard Depreux, which reworked Bidault's propositions, was adopted on September 20, 1947, by 322 votes for and 92 votes against. The existence of two *collèges* (one for fully vested French citizens, plus 58,000 Muslim citizens with local status and the other for 1,300,000 Muslim voters) reworked the decree of 1944.[116] What was new: to elaborate a new community structure, to organize the vote of Muslim women, to define a new structure for Muslim worship, to expand teaching in Arabic. This law was never put into effect.

After eight years of war between French forces and the Viet Minh of Ho Chi Minh, supported by Communist China, the Geneva accords signed on July 20, 1954, marked a decisive step in the process of French disengagement from Asia, which had begun in 1945, and in the progress of the Soviet camp within the Third World. The former metropole, weakened by the defeat of Dien Bien Phu (May 7, 1954), gave complete independence to Laos and Cambodia in the course of a full peace conference and, after obtaining an armistice, withdrew its troops to the south of Vietnam. The latter was divided at the seventeenth parallel between thc pro-West South and the communist North. This effective division of the newly independent Vietnamese nation soon led to the resumption of hostilities and then the direct intervention of the United States. For France and the Fourth Republic, the loss of Indochina represented a French defeat. The French colonial empire, almost reduced to Africa, was challenged in 1955 at the Bandung conference.

The year 1954 was a year on the brink of flames. Indochina was covered in blood; Algeria was catching fire.[117] The defeat of Dien Bien Phu was on May 7. Dien Bien Phu was, according to Ferhat Abbas's expression, "the Valmy of colonized peoples."[118] On April 7, before the debacle, General de Gaulle had recommended negotiation. General Ely followed General Navarre as commander in chief and high commissioner of France in Indochina. It was also a year tasting of ashes. Although peace was concluded with Indochina, the war was only starting in Algeria. On November 1, thirty attacks took place simultaneously in many regions of Algeria. The National Liberation Front (FLN) was created. On November 2, military reinforcements were sent to Algeria. The Arab and Asian countries asked that the questions of Tunisia and Morocco be placed on the agenda of the General Assembly of the United Nations.

Pierre Mendès France challenged the Laniel government over its Indochinese policy. When he was presented by President René Coty to preside over the Conseil, he declared that "Indochina is at the center of all preoccupations." During his inaugural speech on June 17, 1954, he identified his three objectives. Peace was his first political objective, the most important, but also the most urgent. "And here we see a new and fearful menace appearing today: if the Indochinese conflict is not brought under control—and brought under control very soon—we need to worry about the risk of war, of international and perhaps atomic war."[119] The problem here is a classic problem of government in general and of republican government in particular: that of war and peace. Although all politicians did not share the same analysis or the same opinion—far from it—they all had a clear picture of the question. In fact, this question is the political question par excellence. It is the question for which they were all prepared by function and, at that time, by experience. In the end, this question cannot be managed anywhere but on the strictly political plane. War and peace are haggled over but neither bought nor sold. Meanwhile, this is what Pierre Mendès France was blamed for. It was a logical accusation for his adversaries, since it was a way—ultimately an antisemitic way—to deny him the status of politician, of a man capable of reasoning politically—in other words, in everyone else's name.

Europe was his second objective. The third objective was "the reestablishment of agreement and security in the two North African countries that are suffering from fanaticism and terrorism at this very moment." He did not intend to tolerate "hesitation and reticence in making good on promises": "Make it possible for (these populations) to govern their own affairs themselves."[120]

Accompanied by Marshal Juin, Pierre Mendès France arrived in Tunis on July 31 and delivered his Carthage declaration, in which he proclaimed the internal autonomy of Tunisia. His action was swift: it was not lightning war; it was lightning peace. On August 1, the cease-fire was concluded in central Vietnam. On August 6, in Laos. On August 7, in Cambodia. On August 26, the four-part conference (France, Vietnam, Laos, and Cambodia) opened in Paris, charged with organizing the transfer of expertise after independence. On August 10 and 11, the government's policy in Tunisia and Morocco was approved (361 votes for, 90 against, 143 abstentions). On August 26 and 27, the government's North African policy was also approved (451 for, 112 against, 77 abstentions). On September 4, negotiations on the Franco-Tunisian conventions were opened. The Néo-Destour party was once again made legal. On October 21, an accord was signed with India regarding the French trading posts that had voted to rejoin the Indian Union on September 18. On June 1, 1955, Habib Bourguiba entered Tunis on horseback, as he had promised. On July 25, 1957, Tunisia proclaimed itself a republic. Bourguiba was its first president.

Although it had been a French colony, for Pierre Mendès France, Indochina was part of France's foreign policy. Even today, the Algerian War, an *anticolonial* war, eclipses the war of Indochina.[121] Everything seems to happen as if the reasons for the war in Indochina had nothing to do with those that led to the Algerian War, or as the Algerians say, the "Algerian Revolution." In Indochina, the French did not face the Indochinese alone with their cause or with its stakes. Starting in 1950, the Indochinese war seemed to be both an East-West international war and a North-South civil war. At that moment, during the parliamentary debates of October and November 1950, Pierre Mendès France was already proposing a solution negotiated with the Viet Minh—a position totally opposed to that of his irreducible enemy René Mayer, who, having become head of government in January 1953, transformed the army into a national industry. . .

On October 30, 1954, Mendès France stated, "Let us therefore recognize our country as it is: immense and varied. It is the French Republic such as it is proclaimed in our laws. Over its entire territory, the same principles of progress and liberty are applied. Everywhere the historical inhabitants enjoy civic rights. In Parliament, the overseas populations are represented by representatives and senators who have acquired a great deal of influence."[122] Such a declaration can only elicit astonishment. How could Pierre Mendès France have held to such soothing ideas during such a troubled period? In this type of case, psychological arguments are always invoked: he had to show himself as reassuring, not throwing fuel on the fire, calming spirits. The vocabulary is perfectly codified.

In fact, Pierre Mendès France was careful to address "the whole nation's heartfelt recognition from afar" to the "pioneers, both metropolitan and African—administrators, doctors, teachers, missionaries, engineers, farming specialists—who gave themselves without reward in the cities or in the back country." This is the language of the military chief who unconditionally supports his troops, translated for the civil landscape. It brings the battlefield to those outside the military, fighters from civilian life and in civilian life, courageous pioneers of modern times.

Indeed, in the best of cases, benevolence was able to motivate men on the ground as well as politicians. But it is a political trap well known to philosophers, notably Kant, who since the eighteenth century have seen it as a discreet form of political despotism, because this type of attitude works very well for minors (in a family) but could not be appropriate for relations between equals—in other words, majors. Pierre Mendès France was therefore reasoning on the basis of the commonplace according to which the overseas populations were populations whose autonomy and political majority are lacking. "There are peoples who are condemned to be eternal minors," Louis Bertrand affirmed in 1926.[123] Rare were those who did not make these populations into minorities, or as one would say today, "welfare populations."

Paradoxically, the discourse of firmness went along with the soothing discourse. It is a tried and true tactic to couple pacifying statements with actions that, as one says, show political firmness. Thus it is that, speaking at the National Assembly several days later, on November 12, Pierre Mendès France made the following remark: "You can be sure, in any case, that there will be on the part of the government neither hesitation, nor procrastination, nor half-measure in the actions it will take to assure security and respect for the law. There will be no moderate policy against sedition, no compromise with it, and each person here and over there must know this."[124] Iron fist in the velvet glove: "The departments of Algeria constitute a part of the French Republic." François Mitterrand, for his part, declared on November 5, 1954, before the Interior Commission of the National Assembly that "the action of the fellaghas does not permit us to imagine any form whatsoever of negotiation. It can only lead to a terminal form, war."[125] And circular 333, in which he clarifies his instructions, indicates that the measures for surveillance and the "re-establishment of order" "must not lead to errors that, in the past, have made it possible to believe that the law safeguards the Muslim French citizens to the least degree."[126]

Here Algeria is the exception that confirms the rule. It is a unique colony to the precise extent that it is *not* integrated de facto into the colonies. A contradiction in terms—Algeria is a colony that is also France. Nothing is more glaring than this negation of the fact of the colony in Algeria. It is constantly affirmed that Algeria is the most "assimilated" colony—but it is so in a regime of exception that is constantly denied. As the parliamentary summary mentions: "Applause from the left, the center, the right and from the extreme right."

Militants of the MTLD, such as Moulay Merbah, Benyoucef Benkhedda, and Abderrahmane Kiouane, were arrested.[127] Nationalist newspapers were seized. The police proceeded to carry out two thousand arrests in November and December 1954. Police reinforcements as well as six battalions of the

Twenty-Fifth Airborne Division were sent to Algeria, under the orders of Colonel Ducournau. For all that, Pierre Mendès France could not consider repression as a policy, any more than the continuation of politics by other means. Furthermore, reassuring the European representatives about the nature of his policy, he also complied in part with the request for reforms coming from the Muslim representatives, a request that would fit perfectly into his views.

Pierre Mendès France is thus totally unaware of colonial questions, he is distant from them, and he is also very badly informed. He is ignorant like many of his contemporaries, except for those who made common cause with the colonies. "I do not know the Algerian file, I have not had the time to open it," he said to Ferhat Abbas, whom he met in the fall of 1954. "Algeria is not my thing, go see Mitterrand," he also said to his friend Roger Stéphane, cofounder of *L'Observateur*.[128] In his archives, one finds the "Notes Pelabon": "Why is Algeria calm? Perhaps it will stay that way?"[129]

The reason he is distant from these questions is that, in the words of Henri Borgeaud, a large owner of cork and tobacco plantations who knew what he was talking about, "Algerian political cuisine is cooked in an Algerian pot, by Algerian cooks. Meaning, to be sure, by Algerian Europeans."[130] Pierre Mendès France is completely ignorant of colonial realities, in the strong and radical sense of the term, because at that time those realities did not interest anyone. They were realities known only by those who had no existence, those who were inexistent, who were therefore neither seen nor heard, the "Muslim French," or by those who, in Léon Blum's words, confused sovereignty and domination—in other words, most of the "Algerian-born French," like the "radicals" Henri Borgeaud and René Mayer, former representative from Constantine. These two personalities, moreover, appealed to Mendès France to warn him how imprudent the immediate implementation of administrative reforms would be.

Finally, Mendès France was badly informed, particularly by François Mitterrand, who was more up-to-date on these matters, largely thanks to Georges Dayan.[131] In fact, on an official trip to Algeria on October 22, 1954, Mitterrand sent a telegram in which he told Mendès France about "the great hope that his government elicited among the loyal and faithful populations" and "the confidence that they have in his person."[132] Mitterand confided later to journalist Franz Olivier Giesbert that Mendès France had asked him why he wished to be interior minister, and Mitterand had responded, "I think we must take care of Algeria right away if we want to avoid an explosion."[133] Meanwhile, on March 23, 1954, Mohammed Boudiaf, Mostefa Ben Boulaid, Mourad Didouche, and Larbi Ben M'hidi founded the Comité révolutionnaire pour l'Unité et l'Action (CRUA), quickly joined by Krim Bel Kacem, Hocine Aït Ahmed, Ahmed Ben Bella, and Mohamed Khider. On October 10 and 24, they took the initiative to dissolve the CRUA and to found the FLN, in anticipation of an armed insurrection.

"With the overseas territories, France is a great State."[134] During these affirmations of national union, everything happened as if Pierre Mendès France had to give tokens of his attachment, not to the republic and to its principles, which was unquestionable, but to France and its grandeur, an attachment that had been called into doubt. Antisemitic campaigns had been extremely virulent since the relinquishment of Indochina. "The Jew Mendès" was a "bargain basement Jew." Far from being a political asset, Mendès France's Jewish status, which he never mentioned (quite the contrary, since he only once, and very belatedly, identified himself as a "marrano"), was a sizeable handicap. Is this to say that Mendès France gave in to his adversaries? Not at all. But he had, at least, to reckon with the profound opposition that his actions in Indochina and in Tunisia had encountered. Thus, one realizes the complexity of the conditions that shape a policy and, at the very least, that determine a point of view.

We must pause, meanwhile, on the question of minority, or of the subalternization of populations. There is an overlap between two distinct ways of seeing. In the first, there are peoples who bring enlightenment because they are enlightened and shadowy peoples grappling with darkness. In the second, which Pierre Mendès France defends, history is everywhere that of progressive access to the Enlightenment. But the zoology of peoples, according to Husserl's expression, and the defense of progress coincide in what they imply—namely, that right ultimately proceeds from fact, and facts are modified very slowly.

The theory of "educative peoples" is ancient. It is related to the right of the elder, a right of advanced age applied not to families—with landed estate at stake—but to populations, understood in a familial way. The supposed right of advanced age is perfectly adapted to justify and legitimate the colonial situation. An eloquent example of it can be found in the report made by a high civil servant in Algeria in March 1954 (surely Maspétiol), which contains these eloquent lines:

> It is hardly possible to institute an absolute distributive justice between populations that are separated by such a difference of evolution, any more than one can balance the favors done for small children in a family with the greater freedoms given to their elders. What is necessary is that eventually they attain the age of reason, the young benefiting in their turn from freedoms and responsibilities larger than their age justifies, that they are progressively treated as adolescents and then as adults. In a united family, such questions are not posed and no jealousy is conceivable: the elders know quite well that they were formerly indulged just as their younger siblings are now; the younger ones sense confusedly that the tighter discipline to which they are subjected is in their own interest, and that, when the time comes, they will quite naturally accede to the situation of their older brothers. These are the kind of sentiments that we must promulgate here between those of French origin and the autochthones. The administration could do much in this direction, but on condition that they ensure humane considerations always prevail over the scruples of pure administrative technique, in short, that the spirit which enlivens takes the lead over the letter which kills.[135]

The difference between the two ways of seeing is that the age of reason, in one case, depends on anthropological and ethnic factors while, in the second case, it depends on economic and social conditions.

Pierre Mendès France never again challenged the mode in which Muslims were represented. Like the colonies, the Enlightenment imposed a (more or less) hidden tax [*cens*] on the double plane of intellect and politics—not with respect to money (an economic threshold) but with respect to merit (a cultural threshold). This shocks no one. There are philosophers who, even today, share this representation of humanity. When Mendès France proposed to offer Muslim women what one might call active citizenship, he meant it only for the most "advanced" [*évoluée*] among them, as one said at the time.

One of the paradoxes proper to the Enlightenment is this refusal in reality of what is prescribed as an ideal: since the rational citizen is formed by education, citizenship reveals itself to be not only conditioned, which is a matter of fact, but also rightfully subordinated—primarily to education, but also to tests of patriotism. Citizenship is then acquired by spirit and by the shedding of blood—suffrage for those who paid the tax. But unlike many others, Mendès France never mentioned Islam as an objective as well as subjective obstacle to the exercise of democracy. He simply never put it on trial; to the contrary, he defended the republican principle of not distinguishing with respect to confession.

This is why Mendès France's approach to citizenship is distinguished by the importance he accorded to education. He also recommended an emergency plan to accelerate the rate of public schooling in Algeria. As finance minister, he had already taken credit for having contributed to the plan of compulsory schooling begun in Algeria in 1944. In ten years, the total number of children sent to school went from less than two hundred thousand to five hundred thousand (out of two million educable children, however). All of this meant that despite his principles, for the reasons indicated, Mendès France could not imagine the end of a system of political, juridical, social, and cultural organization founded on discrimination.

This also meant that Mendès France never approached the Algerian question as a genuine *political question*. He intended to treat it, and to manage it, as a *social question*, putting off a genuine political solution to the indefinite future. He repeated this in 1955: "At bottom, there is a social problem, and as always at the basis of a social problem, we find an economic problem."[136] What speaks to him in Algeria is actually the inequality. Is the reduction of inequality a matter of sovereignty for him? No. On the other hand, it is a matter of sovereignty for the Algerian independentists (or "nationalists"). The Algerian Europeans generally refused any effort to reduce the considerable gap between the Muslim population and the Jewish and European population. Pierre-Henri Teitgen therefore stated during a debate in the Chamber: "We need the courage to say what we are not ready to give: assimilation in standard of living."[137] In 1952, the SMIG[138] in France was raised to around 240,000 francs per year, but the average individual income in Algeria was between 40,000 and 51,000 francs per year. Three-quarters of the population lived on less than 20,000 francs per year.[139]

This is one sense in which Pierre Mendès France is anticolonialist. Contesting the very notion of French presence, it is clear that on this point he shares the opinion expressed by Ferhat Abbas, appearing June 25, 1954, in *La République Algérienne*, and also found in his archives: "France is absent in North Africa. Its laws are mocked, its will contravened. Paris is only there to entertain a fiction from which Algiers, Tunis and Rabat draw an exorbitant privilege."[140]

Mendès France is anticolonialist in another sense. In May 1954, the secretary-general of the Arab League sent a note on human rights in Algeria to the accredited ambassadors in Cairo, intending that it would be forwarded to delegations at the United Nations. In it, the three Algerian departments were accused of being "legal fictions." The notion of collective responsibility entailed by the *code de l'indigénat*, which justified the punitive expeditions being carried out at that time, was denounced.[141]

On the other hand, article 80 of the penal code was also denounced. Called the "Daladier decree," this article defined violation of the state's security in terms of any violation whatsoever of the integrity of the French territory, including the subtraction of a part of that territory from France's authority. Between April 1948 and January 1953, 393 condemnations were pronounced in the name of this article. In October 1953, Cheikh Zermki, who had opened an Arab school without authorization, was condemned to four years in prison for violating the state's security. Attacks on freedom of the press, which were numerous, were also justified as punishments for violation of the state's security.[142]

Now, soon after taking over the command of government, Pierre Mendès France was forced to bring an end to what he called, in a confidential note to Jean-Jacques Servan Schreiber, "bad habits" "which have always had an unofficial and clandestine character" but that were always officially tolerated. This is the standpoint from which he decided, with the support and indeed the compulsion of François Mitterand, to merge the metropolitan police and the Algerian police into a single corps so that changes would become possible. Henri Borgeaud was violently indignant when senior officers of the police were recalled to France in January 1955 at the request of Jacques Chevallier, the mayor of Algiers, who judged inadmissible proceedings against the members of the MTLD in whom he had placed his confidence. During the summer of 1955, Bourgès Maunoury, who had followed Mitterand in the office of the Interior, was struck by an official report recommending recourse to torture in order to confront the rebellion. Mendès France is anticolonialist to the very extent that he opposed the most traditional and most habitual colonial procedures.

November 1, 1954, posed a problem for all French politicians. Some of them saw it as a "tribal" affair.[143] Roger Léonard, still governor general, denounced a conspiracy fomented in Cairo. At Constantine, Prefect Dupuch and General Spillman accused Tunisia. Attacks were credited either to a peripheral (tribal) element or to an external power. On November 12, in the chamber, some European representatives from Algeria blamed the Tunisian policy of Mendès France. The latter was then forced to reassure them: "Many representatives made connections between the French policy in Algeria and in Tunisia. I believe that no connection is more erroneous, no comparison more false or more dangerous."[144] For Mendès France, French Algerian policy and French Tunisian policy were totally incomparable. When Algeria was in danger, the republic was in danger. Independent Algeria would mean an amputated republic. In Tunisia, unlike Algeria, the question was broached not in social terms but rather in political terms. In Tunisia, what was at stake in 1954 was not equality but sovereignty, and freedom along with it.

In his November 12, 1954, address, Mendès France committed himself to destroying all possible comparison between Tunisia and Algeria. Like Morocco, Tunisia had always enjoyed a more favorable status than Algeria. The framework defined by the law of June 28, 1881, constituting the indigène (as immobile and silent) was extended to other colonies starting with Algeria. For forty years, with the notable exception of Morocco and Tunisia, the indigènes were kept silent. In Algeria, the code of "special infractions" was suppressed by the ruling of March 7, 1944. But in 1955, the state of emergency was declared in Algeria, along with new exceptional measures. Protectorates are very different from the French departments in Algeria. They were colonies, but of a different type. In the protectorate, integration and (more or less relative) respect for local particularities prevail. In the department, by contrast, the model of *assimilation* is promoted, but in reality it hides the model of *segregation*, particularly on the political and civil plane. In the department, local particularities are denied.

During the hundred-year anniversary of (French) Algeria, Georges Hardy, director of the École Coloniale, claimed that "profound differences still exist between conquered, annexed Algeria, and Tunisia or Morocco, which were simply pacified and protected."[145] At the end of the nineteenth century, a protectorate was imposed by the French Republic on Tunisia, on Annam, and on Madagascar, and later, in 1912, on Morocco. The term *protectorate* is an inversion of the notion of protection (*himâya*) exercised by Muslims over the Jewish or Christian "infidels." The semantic inversion repeats the political reversal since, in a protectorate, it is the Muslims who are supposed to be found under the protection of those they protected. The term was introduced by the convention of La Marsa, in 1881.[146] In a protectorate, sovereignty is not purely and simply confiscated. The sovereigns of Rabat and Tunis, for example, continued to make laws. To dress up colonial domination in a juridical vocabulary, France argued for the theory of the delegation of powers from the caliph to his servants, forged by Imam Ibn Malik, the founder of the Maghrebin legal school. Meanwhile, the protectorate establishes subalternity in political and civil affairs.

There are four fundamental differences between a protectorate colony and a department colony.[147] First, colonization in the form of a protectorate is the institution of a state of civil domination by a sovereign power. Colonization in the form of a department never completely abandons military domination. It is not a handful of retired generals who make the protectorate, but men whose model of action is more like that of the diplomat or prefect.[148] This does not mean that the military are absent. In Morocco, for example, the African army, assisted by Senegalese, kept colonial order. In Tunisia, Cambon, resident from 1882 to 1886, succeeded in ensuring that the administration of the country was in the hands of civil inspectors rather than officers from the Arab bureaus, as in Algeria.

The second fundamental difference is that in the protectorates, the colonial and colonizing power does not establish a system of concessions, which, as in Algeria, are only a mode of more or less violent expropriation of local owners. The gap is therefore one separating respect for local private property from its pure and simple negation (as was largely the case at the time when Algeria was conquered).[149]

A third fundamental difference between the protectorate colony and the department colony is that the occupation of a protectorate is carried out with an economic goal in view; in a department, on the other hand, the goal is political. In a department, the government of people is referred back to the administration of things. In a protectorate, at least in the Maghreb, the government of people is local and rests on the "indigène" state, while the administration of things is colonial and refers to the imported technostructure.

Finally, a fourth fundamental difference can be found in the colonial power's relationship with the Jews. Tunisia and Morocco had no equivalent of the Crémieux decree—in other words, no statutory differentiation between the Jewish population and the Muslim population. To be sure, this does not mean that the Tunisian or Moroccan Jews were well treated—as Pierre Birnbaum has shown, the Third Republic did not like its Jews.[150] Paradoxically, it is in Algeria, the place where France claimed to be exporting its most republican values, that it introduced the sharpest form of discrimination on the basis of religion. Meanwhile, these differences often remain misunderstood, even today. Thus, the Algerian War is blamed for phenomena that actually go back to the difference between the colonial regimes characterizing one country under French domination as opposed to the other.

This discrepancy between the Tunisian situation and the Algerian situation was one of the unknowns working, to a greater or lesser extent, against Pierre Mendès France and his contemporaries. What he was ready not just to accept but even to promote in Tunisia, he categorically refused in Algeria. The "internal autonomy" of Tunisia was recognized by his Carthage speech on July 31, 1954. "Independence within interdependence" was announced in Morocco in November 1955. Because the contexts were distinct, the implications were not the same.

Mendès France also fell victim to many beliefs that the majority of his fellow citizens held to be self-evident. While he was ready to grant autonomy to the Tunisians, he hoped to promote not the independence of Algerians, but their progress. Another element in the explanation of Mendès France's position was strong international pressure. Thanks to the states of the Arab League, the United States voted in 1952 to include the Tunisian question on the agenda of the UN.[151] The UN recommended "the development of free institutions in both protectorates." But this international pressure did not really contribute to the *interpretation* of his position. When it came to Tunisia, Mendès France was liberal. On the other hand, he did not simply regard Algerian nationalism as illegitimate; it was a contradiction in terms and thus did not exist. No one wanted to hear the voice of French Muslims of Algeria in the elections (Naegelen); their cries could not be heard in the uprisings (Mendès France). Definitively, as subalterns, the Algerians could not speak. . .

They lacked speech even more so, inasmuch as the French neither could nor wanted to understand their language. The Algerian is Camus's Arab: a silent and mute foreigner, under the sun, holding a knife. In Morocco and in Tunisia, classical Arabic was taught in the Muslim middle schools [*collèges*]. In Algeria, even in 1954, those who were most opposed to this kind of teaching were those who claimed to oppose it on republican grounds. For example, the *Bulletin* of the Algiers section of the Syndicat national des instituteurs de l'Union française (National Teachers Syndicate of the French Union) held the position adopted by the inspectors of primary teaching in Algeria, which called for an end to the teaching of Arabic that had been rendered obligatory by the statute of 1947. Meanwhile, the UDMA's request for the teaching of Arabic had never really been taken seriously.

In Algeria, thus, there could be no "acceptable interlocutor" [*interlocutor valable*]. In his letter to Guy Mollet on April 21, 1956, Pierre Mendès France returned to the question of acceptable interlocutors in these terms:

> But, it is said . . . there are no acceptable interlocutors and representatives, and those who claim to count as such refuse all discussion, animated as they are by a totalitarian sectarianism, a limitless fanaticism which refuses any transaction: what they demand is independence and nothing else, and with it the pure and simple departure of the French and of France. Others admit that some day it will be necessary to talk, but first, they say, some victories must be achieved to change the climate, so that the moderate elements can abandon the wait-and-see attitude in which they are hiding and dialogue with us. Still others denounce interventions from abroad.

Mendès France concluded this review of the situation in the following way: "Today we know what these arguments are worth and where they have taken us. We will not repeat the same errors."[152]

Mendès France's insistence on speaking only with his own chosen interlocutors is well known. It is also known that he always defended discussion with enemies. One is reminded of the thesis according to which there were no "elite" in Algeria, unlike Tunisia, and therefore no "interlocutors." All the same, while he was president of the Conseil, Mendès France would not receive Ferhat Abbas and Ahmed Francis, although they made great efforts to obtain a meeting with him, according to the testimony of Mohammed Harbi.[153] The liberal character of Mendès France's position, Harbi writes, troubled the Algerian radicals, but the moderates "expected help from him which never came."[154]

In fact, if dialogue such as Mendès France understood it could be carried out only with enemies, then dialogue ultimately assumed the existence of war. Now, his republican perspective as well as his diagnosis of the situation did not permit him to imagine any response to the Manifesto of November 1. This response would have counted as recognition of the rupture of internal peace (in other words, recognition of the Republic's disintegration) and, *ipso facto*, as a constitution of adversaries or of sides opposed in enmity. Thus it was belatedly, in his letter to Guy Mollet, that he recommended dialogue, but only to immediately invalidate the only interlocutor whose republicanism seemed to render him legitimate: Ferhat Abbas. "Ferhat Abbas," he wrote, "is the symbol of these elements who formerly made claims within the French framework, but who disappointed us and went over to the other side."[155] Pierre Mendès France also considered that the issue rested with the "indispensable acquiescence of the masses" to "a new state of things."

Despite all this, as contacts became absolutely inevitable, Jacques Soustelle handed over the task to Vincent Monteil, who, starting in February 1955, met in Tunis with the head of the Aurès zone, Mostefa Ben Boulaïd, who had just been arrested by the French Directorate of Territorial Surveillance.[156] But on the one hand, contact meant information much more than it meant negotiation, and on the other hand, what was *done* unofficially could not be officially *mentioned.* On October 25, 1956, about two years after the start of the insurrection, three days after the plane containing four historic leaders of the FLN, including Ben Bella, was intercepted, Mendès France still refused all negotiation.[157] "Would it then be a matter of opening direct negotiations with those who fight us or with those whom we have just captured?" Mendès France asked himself. "I believe for my part that these negotiations would be untimely. They would create, they would crystallize a situation to which I, for one, cannot resign myself."[158]

Algerian nationalism could only be French or could not be at all, hardly the least of its paradoxes. From this point of view, France is its own proper interlocutor. "The Republic is one and indivisible. The Governor General represents the one and indivisible Republic and there would be no question of his having a policy other than that of the Republic," declared Pierre Mendès France with respect to the nomination of Jacques Soustelle.[159]

Mendès France established a curious analogy between "independentist" Algerians on the one hand and Alsatian/Lorrainian "autonomists" on the other hand. For him there were truly no Algerian nationalists; there were only Algerian autonomists.

> Let no one say that elections could bring men into the Algerian Assembly and, perhaps, into the National Assembly, whose tendencies and opinions would risk offending us or violating this unity that we want to reconstitute between Algeria and the Metropole. Unity is threatened more by the disorders and bloody troubles we have seen than by the appearance, within the framework of our republican legislation generously open to all, of a certain number of new men capable of announcing even their feelings of opposition. After the other war, there were moments when we also suffered from the presence of Alsatians and Lorrainians, happily a small number, elected to the National Assembly who expressed autonomist sentiments. Their speeches at the tribune of the Assembly often pained and offended us. But it was far better to have such men in our Parliament and speaking freely there than to know they were in the bush, leading a revolt against us in the Vosges![160]

Algerian nationalists would all be Alsatians from the South. This comparison had already been made by Naegelen, at the end of the 1940s.

What is frequently called "common sense," or indeed, "good sense," is determined by what is collectively unthought. Whether they are visual, linguistic, or scholarly, representations are transmitted invisibly. Revisiting the notion of the "advanced Muslim" [*musulman évolué*] comes down to naively reopening the colonial opposition between the "advanced" (Francized) native and the "backward" one (the one whom eternity changes into himself, as the poet would say). In truth, the colonial state never finished colonizing both the territories and their populations. Even the most virtuous and most honorable political positions, such as those of Pierre Mendès France, could not avoid this problem.[161] Instead of opening up solutions, his republican spirit and his representations led him into a political impasse. As for the Algerian politicians, they were aware of the French wish to engage in a dialogue of the deaf. When the French heard neither their intentions nor their positions, the Algerians understood the positions and intentions of their adversaries perfectly.

To follow Carl Schmitt, the "friend/enemy" couple structures political relations and therefore also the way relations are treated politically.[162] The implicit "friend/enemy" division articulates blood and soil politically. This is how immigration can appear as an invasion: by definition, an invasion is the work of enemies. An imposture and an apocryphal citation testify to the importance of this dimension.[163] The imposture: in the nineteenth century, a Frenchman (Pernessin) had himself taken for German (Rommel) when he published *Le pays de la revanche* (The country of revenge), in which he declared that Germany would eventually overcome France by the force or rather the great power of numbers. The apocryphal citation: a prophecy that Alfred Sauvy attributed in a 1978 issue of *L'Expansion* to Houari Boumédiène, then president of the Algerian Republic, to the effect that a North poor in numbers but rich in capital would be invaded by a South rich in men but poor in capital. The enemy of the day, German at one moment and later Algerian, can be made to say whatever one would like to prove. The constitution of the enemy appears clearly. The enemy is the one who is said to have declared war—invasion sensu stricto in the first case, immigration in the other.

The complex of the colonizer is that colonizers do not see themselves in the eyes of the colonized people who look at them and whom they cannot, therefore, perceive as they are. The complex of the colonizer is the colonizers' failure to understand that the colonized can speak and consequently can be a "political body." In fact, as Aristotle has taught us, speech is what gives access to politics because speech is, as such, rational. In this sense, to find no acceptable interlocutors, to consider the colonized as incapable of being political enemies and to judge that they are not sufficiently "advanced"—that is, rational—comes down to one and the same thing. To speak of war as an art is to speak of rationality; it means to articulate ends and means theoretically and to bring the means into practical alignment with an end. If it is said following Clausewitz that war is the continuation of politics by other means, then logically the Algerians could not be at war in terms of the colonial gaze (understood here as benevolently as possible).[164]

The aptitude for war is not equally shared, according to the complex of the colonizer. This aptitude must be associated with the constitution of regular armies. In this way of thinking, war is truly war—in other words, the continuation of politics by other means (i.e., equally rational)—when it is waged by a rational political body: the army. This is why Clausewitz wonders whether one can speak of a small number of isolated partisans as an army. His conclusion was affirmative, based on the civil war in the Vendée during the French Revolution. The question results from Clausewitz's way of envisioning agents' motives in a war: the people are moved by hate and animosity, the military command by courage and talent, and the government by intelligence.[165] In this respect he remains Platonic.

As Raymond Aron relates, Clausewitz, who subordinates the military to the politicians, was read not by politicians but by the military.[166] In Algeria, it was the military who considered seriously what was denied by the politicians. Their reasons for this denial were both theoretical (because of their training and sometimes their reading of Clausewitz) and practical, particularly for those who had discovered "popular" and "revolutionary" war with its new methods and procedures in Indochina. Carl Schmitt writes: "The analogy between the Spanish guerilla war experienced by the Prussian General Staff (1808–13) and the partisan warfare in Indochina and Algeria experienced by the French General Staff (1950–60) is striking."[167]

In this context, Schmitt offers as an example the attitude and the behavior of Raoul Salan.[168] Indeed, according to Schmitt, Salan led a partisan war (particularly a psychological one) against the partisans. During his trial, Salan contended that the Organisation de l'armée secrète (OAS) was a "response to the most odious of all forms of violence, the one that consists of ripping away the nationality of those who refuse to lose it." Then he announced that he would henceforth be silent.[169] Examining the respective positions of a military figure (Salan) and a politician (Mendès France) in Algeria, one realizes that the soldier was informed about war while the politician was less conscious of what politics itself required. This does not mean, to be sure, that one must think Salan was right and that Mendès France was wrong.

The colonial world is thus a divided world, both in its experience and in its representations. In it, oppression consists in, on the one hand, legally relegating certain people to the world of needs and desires, the world of particularities (tastes and colors), while, on the other hand, lifting other people (identified in advance) to the possibility of an ethical life and a political existence—in other words, to the possibility of universality (on the intellectual plane) and of war and peace (on the political plane). For the French government to accept talk of war in Algeria would have been for them to recognize a civil war, given the singular situation of colonial Algeria. So much for the context. But the structure is one of a formal division between those who are supposed to announce, and make, war and peace and those (unacceptable interlocutors) who are reportedly unable either to make it or to put it into words.

If the French could have recognized hatred and animosity toward them in Algeria, if they could have glimpsed courage and talent, still it would have been impossible for them to see that intelligence at work in a partisan guerilla. Pierre Mendès France, like the majority of French politicians, was unable to break with this fundamental prejudice. For a long time, and after having employed the language of conquest, the French colonizers employed the terms of domination, pacification, and the preservation of order rather than speaking of war. A whole world order was thus established, sketched out, and affirmed. One must defeat a whole world order if one wants to decolonize thought.

Epilogue

People more happily situated, who sometimes hear their opinions disputed, and are not wholly unused to be set right when they are wrong, place the same unbounded reliance only on such of their opinions as are shared by all who surround them, or to whom they habitually defer: for in proportion to a man's want of confidence in his own solitary judgment, does he usually repose, with implicit trust, on the infallibility of "the world" in general. And the world, to each individual, means the part of it with which he comes in contact; his

party, his sect, his church, his class of society: the man may be called, by comparison, almost liberal and large-minded to whom it means anything so comprehensive as his own country or his own age. Nor is his faith in this collective authority at all shaken by his being aware that other ages, countries, sects, churches, classes, and parties have thought, and even now think, the exact reverse. He devolves upon his own world the responsibility of being in the right against the dissentient worlds of other people; and it never troubles him that mere accident has decided which of these numerous worlds is the object of his reliance, and that the same causes which make him a Churchman in London, would have made him a Buddhist or a Confucian in Pekin.

John Stuart Mill, *On Liberty*

In a colony, the colonized never have their "own world": they live in a world that is not their own. Their subjective experience is that of a decentering that cannot be lifted merely by their country's political independence.

Notes

1. Buck-Morss, *Universal History.*
2. Jardin, *Alexis de Tocqueville*, 216.
3. Tocqueville, *Lettres choisies, souvenirs*, 254–59.
4. Tocqueville, *Lettres choisies, souvenirs*, 254–59.
5. The Spanish, for Tocqueville, are the worst when it comes to the Indians, but the best when it comes to the blacks. See the "Rapport fait au nom de la commission chargée d'examiner la proposition de M. de Tracy relative aux esclaves des colonies": "The Spanish, who showed themselves so cruel toward the Indians, have always governed the blacks with a singular humanity. In their colonies, the black man has been much closer to the white than in all the others, and the authority of the master in these colonies often resembled that of a family father." Tocqueville, *Oeuvres Complètes*, vol. 3, 52–53.

   Translator's note: French citations to Tocqueville are given along with the pages to the following English translations: *Writings on Empire and Slavery, Democracy in America*, and *Recollections.* All English translations not found in these texts are my own.
6. Tocqueville, "Travail sur l'Algérie," *Oeuvres Complètes*, vol. 3, 228; *Empire and Slavery*, 71.
7. Tocqueville, "Travail sur l'Algérie," *Oeuvres Complètes*, vol. 3, 242; *Empire and Slavery*, 83.
8. Tocqueville, "Travail sur l'Algérie," *Oeuvres Complètes*, vol. 3, 248–49; *Empire and Slavery*, 88.
9. Gustave de Beaumont, certainly Tocqueville's best friend, published a fiction in 1835 on returning from their voyage together: *Marie, ou L'esclavage aux États-Unis: Tableau des moeurs américaines.* The author's preface contained the following remarks:

   > Readers do not know that there are still slaves in the United States; their number has grown to over two million. It is assuredly strange to find so much servitude in the midst of so much freedom: but what is perhaps more extraordinary still is the violence of prejudice which separates the race of slaves from that of free men, i.e.,

the blacks from the whites. For the study of this prejudice, the society of the United States offers a double element that one would have difficulty finding elsewhere. Servitude rules in the south of the country, while the North no longer has slaves. In the southern states, one sees the wounds inflicted by slavery when it is in force, and in the North, the consequences of servitude once it has ceased to exist. Slave or free, the blacks form everywhere a people different from the whites. To give the reader an idea of the barrier placed between the two races, I must cite an event in which I participated. The first time I entered a theater in the United States, I was surprised by the care with which the spectators of white color were distinguished from the public of black faces. The whites were in the first gallery, in the second gallery were found the mulattos, in the third, the blacks. An American near my own seat pointed out to me that the dignity of white blood required these classifications. Meanwhile, my eyes were drawn to the gallery of mulattos, where I saw a young woman of stunning beauty, whose perfectly white skin announced the purest European blood. Entering into all the prejudices of my neighbor, I asked him how a woman of English origin was so shameless as to mix with the Africans.

"That woman," he told me, "is colored."

"How? *Colored?* She is whiter than a lily."

"She is colored," he responded coldly; "the tradition of the country establishes her origin, and everyone knows that one of her ancestors was mulatto."

He pronounced these words without further explications, as one imparts a truth that need only be uttered to be understood. (v–viii)

10. When Tocqueville thought about getting himself elected parliamentary representative of Versailles in 1837, he published two *Lettres sur l'Algérie* in the *Presse de Seine-et-Oise*, a newspaper in which he was a shareholder, on June 23 and August 22, 1837 (found in *Oeuvres Complètes*, vol. 3, 129–53; *Empire and Slavery*, 5–26). In 1845, he represented Valognes, and he was codirector with Corcelle of the newspaper *Le Commerce*. But it was Corcelle who set the paper's tone on Algeria. When, finally, Tocqueville turned in his two reports on Algeria, they appeared in *Le Moniteur* of May 24, 1847. For Tocqueville, therefore, the press was a considerable means of expression and vector of opinion.

See Tocqueville, "L'émancipation des esclaves," *Oeuvres Complètes*, vol. 3, 79–111; *Empire and Slavery*, 199–226. The articles appeared in the issues of October 22 and 28, November 8 and 21, and December 6 and 14, 1843.

11. "Rapport . . . relative aux esclaves," Tocqueville, *Oeuvres Complètes*, vol. 3, 41–78. Tocqueville's intervention took place on July 23, 1839, but Tracy's proposition was never discussed in Parliament.

12. Tocqueville, "Rapport . . . relative aux esclaves," *Oeuvres Complètes*, vol. 3, 42.

13. Tocqueville, "L'émancipation des esclaves," *Oeuvres Complètes*, vol. 3, 80; *Empire and Slavery*, 200.

14. Kant, "On Perpetual Peace," "Appendix I on the Disagreement between Morals and Politics in Relation to Perpetual Peace," 116–25.

15. Kant, "On Perpetual Peace," 119.

16. These articles appeared in *Le Siècle* of January 1–14, 1843, and are published in the *Oeuvres* by Pléiade, vol. 1, 1085–113; see 1108.

17. In 1804, France had demanded the sum of 150 million francs in gold from Haiti in reparation for its lost plantations. It was not until 1916 that Haiti finished paying off this debt. See Vergès, *Abolir l'esclavage*.

18. Tocqueville, "Rapport . . . relative aux esclaves," *Oeuvres Complètes*, vol. 3, 56.

19. Despite this, the slaves were not free. In fact, apprenticeship followed slavery. Children of more than six on August 1, 1834, became either apprentice or predial farmers, obliged to

work without salary until August 1, 1840, or personal domestic servants obliged to serve for free until August 1, 1838. The sole benefit that they could thus draw from the abolition of slavery was the legal limitation on the duration of work. "Moreover," Tocqueville claimed, "experience has shown that the difficulty was not that of preventing freedmen from revolting, nor of punishing or preventing their crimes, but of making them bend to laboring habits." "Rapport . . . relative aux esclaves," *Oeuvres Complètes*, vol. 3, 63. On the other side, the colonists showed their discontent by behaving with the freedmen as they had with their former slaves, and "then tried to avenge the acts of resistance that were provoked by these ways of behaving" (64). Moreover, in 1833 Lord Grey introduced a clause according to which slavery would cease to exist in India starting in 1837.

20. Tocqueville, "Rapport . . . relative aux esclaves," *Oeuvres Complètes*, vol. 3, 59.

21. Tocqueville, "Rapport . . . relative aux esclaves," *Oeuvres Complètes*, vol. 3, 59.

22. Tocqueville, "Rapport . . . relative aux esclaves," *Oeuvres Complètes*, vol. 3, 74.

23. One of Tocqueville's arguments in favor of the abolition of slavery was the unshakeable loyalty felt by former slaves of the English colonies toward their metropole. See "L'émancipation des esclaves," *Oeuvres Complètes*, vol. 3, 83; *Empire and Slavery*, 202.

24. Tocqueville, "L'émancipation des esclaves," *Oeuvres Complètes*, vol. 3, 85–86; *Empire and Slavery*, 204. In terms of market, the measure is not interest but stability: a colony is a captive market. In Algeria, Tocqueville also reasoned in terms of the market.

25. Jardin, *Alexis de Tocqueville*, 214.

26. Tocqueville, "L'émancipation des esclaves," *Oeuvres Complètes*, vol. 3, 97; *Empire and Slavery*, 214.

27. Tocqueville, "L'émancipation des esclaves," *Oeuvres Complètes*, vol. 3, 98; *Empire and Slavery*, 215.

28. Tocqueville, "L'émancipation des esclaves," *Oeuvres Complètes*, vol. 3, 99; *Empire and Slavery*, 216.

29. Tocqueville, "L'émancipation des esclaves," *Oeuvres Complètes*, vol. 3, 102–3; *Empire and Slavery*, 219.

30. See "Intervention dans la discussion de la loi sur le régime des esclaves dans les colonies" of May 30, 1845, Tocqueville, *Oeuvres Complètes*, vol. 3, 117.

31. Tocqueville, "L'émancipation des esclaves," *Oeuvres Complètes*, vol. 3, 105; *Empire and Slavery*, 221.

32. Tocqueville, *Oeuvres* (Pléïade), vol. 1, 217.

33. See Tocqueville's description of January 1, 1832 (at Mazureau's), *Oeuvres* (Pléïade), vol. 1, 187. Etienne Mazureau (1777–1849) was a Frenchman who moved to New Orleans in 1805 and became attorney general for Louisiana on three occasions. He met Alexis de Tocqueville in 1832 and gave him a great deal of information about the city.

34. Tocqueville, *Oeuvres* (Pléïade), vol. 1, 173–74.

35. Tocqueville, *Oeuvres* (Pléïade), vol. 1, 175–76.

36. Tocqueville, *Oeuvres* (Pléïade), vol. 1, 258.

37. Tocqueville, *Oeuvres* (Pléïade), vol. 1, 285. See also his portrait of Charles Carroll, owner of three hundred slaves (101–2).

38. Tocqueville, *Oeuvres* (Pléïade), vol. 1, 64.

39. Tocqueville, *Oeuvres* (Pléïade), vol. 1, 85.

40. Here, the moral evil is to be found in black women (!). See Tocqueville, *Oeuvres* (Pléïade), vol. 1, 122, 180, or 280.

41. *An evil for the masters*: they are lazy (it is the lazy ones who judge the lazy slaves, as if they were specialists in work!), violent, and backward. Discussing with Mr. Latrobe, a Baltimore lawyer, on October 31, 1831: "Slavery is in general a costly way to farm." Tocqueville, *Oeuvres* (Pléïade), vol. 1, 91. See above all his conversation with Mr. MacIlvaine, one of the biggest merchants in Louisville, on December 9, 1831 (115), or another grower (117); see also significantly (287). *An evil for the whites*: slavery "dulls the black population and aggravates the white population" (282). This is also the opinion of Mr. Guillemin, French consul in New Orleans (122–3), and of Mr. Poinsett on January 12 to 17, 1832 (132–33). The end of slavery, in fact, brought out the question of equality (243–44) since free blacks remained without rights. In Ohio, for example, the laws were very hard on blacks (113–14). *An evil for America*: this is the North-South divide and the internal division of the United States.

42. In 1850, the United States passed the Fugitive Slave Law, which allowed owners from the South to pursue and recapture not only those of their slaves who had managed to flee to the North, but also blacks whom they claimed were fugitives.

43. Walker, *Appeal*, 12. See also Zinn, *People's History*, 175–76.

44. Walker, *Appeal*, 11.

45. Walker, *Appeal*, 17.

46. Douglass, *Bondage and Freedom*, 52–53.

47. Douglass, "Fourth of July," 367, 371. Slavery was not abolished in America until 1863.

48. Certain historians claim that four of every five cotton-picking slaves participated in at least one act of rebellion between 1840 and 1841. Confronted with this resistance, the slave owners organized repression. One of them, James Hammond, declared in 1845: "But if your course was wholly different—If you distilled nectar from your lips and discoursed sweetest music . . . do you imagine you could prevail on us to give up a thousand million of dollars in the value of our slaves, and a thousand millions of dollars more in the depreciation of our lands?" Zinn, *People's History*, 170.

49. Tocqueville, *Recollections*, 136–37.

50. Tocqueville, *Recollections*, 135.

51. Published on August 22, 1837, in *La Presse de Seine-et-Oise*. Tocqueville, "Seconde lettre sur l'Algérie," *Oeuvres Complètes*, vol. 3, 139–40; *Empire and Slavery*, 14.

52. Conversation with Mazureau, January 1, 1832, from Tocqueville, *Oeuvres* (Pléïade), vol. 1, 118. The argument from climate did not, meanwhile, enjoy unanimity. See conversation with Adams, October 1, 1831, *Oeuvres* (Pléïade), vol. 1, 75.

53. In February 1842, two colonists, Vialar and Saint-Guilhem, defended the employment of native labor before the chamber. Tocqueville listened to them and understood. "Our agriculturalists," he writes, "gladly make use of indigenous manpower. The European needs the Arab to make his lands valuable; the Arab needs the European to obtain a high salary. In this way, two men so widely separated by education and origins are naturally brought together in the same field, and united in the same inevitable conclusion by their interests." Tocqueville, "Rapport sur le projet de loi relatif aux credits," *Oeuvres Complètes*, vol. 3, 329; *Empire and Slavery*, 145.

54. Tocqueville, *Souvenirs*.

55. It is also, in a different way, common to Algeria. In 1847, Tocqueville asked: "France does not only have free men among its Muslim subjects. Algeria also contains a very small number of Negro slaves. Should we allow slavery to continue on soil we control?" In fact, a petition circulated in France in 1849 called for the emancipation of Algerian slaves. See Tocqueville, "Rapport sur le projet de loi relatif aux crédits," *Oeuvres Complètes*, vol. 3, 330; *Empire and Slavery*, 146.

Finally, when Tocqueville took an interest in India and read extensively on the country in 1841, he tended toward the subject: "It seems somewhat difficult to separate slavery properly speaking from many things in India that resemble it, such as the constitution of the lower castes." *Oeuvres* (Pléïade), vol. 1, 1052.

56. General Lamoricière arrived in Algeria in 1830. Named marshal in 1840, he governed Oran until 1848.

57. Antoine-Isaac Sylvestre de Sacy (1758–1838) was a linguist and polyglot (Hebrew, Persian, Turkish, Arabic, etc.) philologist. He taught Arabic at the School of Oriental Languages, created in 1795, and then, in 1806, he was named professor of Persian at the Collège de France.

58. Tocqueville, "Première lettre sur l'Algérie," *Oeuvres Complètes*, vol. 3, 131; *Empire and Slavery*, 6.

59. Tocqueville, "Première lettre sur l'Algérie," *Oeuvres Complètes*, vol. 3, 131; *Empire and Slavery*, 6.

60. Tocqueville, "Notes sur le Coran," *Oeuvres Complètes*, vol. 3, 154–62; *Empire and Slavery*, 27–35.

61. Tocqueville, letter to Gobineau, *Oeuvres Complètes*, vol. 9, 69.

62. Tocqueville, "Première lettre sur l'Algérie," *Oeuvres Complètes*, vol. 3, 135; *Empire and Slavery*, 9–10.

63. "Muslim society in Africa was not uncivilized; it was merely a backward and imperfect civilization." Tocqueville, "Rapport sur le projet de loi relatif aux crédits," *Oeuvres Complètes*, vol. 3, 323; *Empire and Slavery*, 140.

64. Tocqueville, "Première lettre sur l'Algérie," *Oeuvres Complètes*, vol. 3, 136; *Empire and Slavery*, 10.

65. Tocqueville, "Notes du voyage en Algérie de 1841," *Oeuvres Complètes*, vol. 5, pt. 2, 191; *Empire and Slavery*, 36.

66. Tocqueville, "Première lettre sur l'Algérie," *Oeuvres Complètes*, vol. 3, 133; *Empire and Slavery*, 8.

67. Tocqueville, "Première lettre sur l'Algérie," *Oeuvres Complètes*, vol. 3, 132; *Empire and Slavery*, 7.

68. Tocqueville, "Première lettre sur l'Algérie," *Oeuvres Complètes*, vol. 3, 132; *Empire and Slavery*, 7.

69. Husserl, *Crisis of European Sciences*, 275.

70. The commission was composed of Dufaure, Morny, Allard, d'Oraison, Tracy, Corcelle, Lasteyrie, Schneider, Plichon, Oudinot, Desjobert, Boblaye, La Guiche, Béchameil, Chasseloup-Laubat, Beaumont, and Abraham Dubois. Desjobert was a well-known anticolonialist. It was also in 1842 that Gustave de Beaumont had a series of anonymous articles appear in *Le Siècle* under the title "État de la question de l'Afrique" (November 26 and 30, December 3, 7, and 11, 1842). Bugeaud believed, incorrectly, that these texts were penned by Tocqueville.

71. This is what we find, on the one hand, in the "Tableau de la situation des établissements français dans l'Algérie" (June 1838, June 1839, June 1840), and on the other hand, in the *Actes du gouvernement*. It is the "Tableau" that contains a study (1838) titled "Constitution ancienne de la propriété."

72. "An example. I give the bare property of the Bourg farm to the church of Tocqueville as *habous*. From that moment forward, I cannot sell this farm. But if it later happens that from lack of resources, I allow the buildings to deteriorate to the point that it compromises even the bare property of the church of Tocqueville, I can be authorized or forced to sell. Only the buildings can be sold . . . but in their place, the church is guaranteed income." Such

is the practical exercise to which Tocqueville devoted himself to better comprehend the functioning of *habous* property. Tocqueville, "Tableau de la situation . . . ," *Oeuvres Complètes*, vol. 3, 165.

73. Tocqueville, "Tableau de la situation," *Oeuvres Complètes*, vol. 3, 166–67.

74. Tocqueville, "Tableau de la situation," *Oeuvres Complètes*, vol. 3, 180. See "Travail sur l'Algérie" for Tocqueville's critique of the usage made of the October 17, 1833, decree on expropriation for the purpose of public utility. "Travail sur l'Algérie," *Oeuvres Complètes*, vol. 3, 264–65; *Empire and Slavery*, 102–3.

75. Tocqueville, "Rapport sur le projet de loi relatif aux crédits," *Oeuvres Complètes*, vol. 3, 326; *Empire and Slavery*, 143.

76. Here one is reminded of one of the sophisms that Kant considers characteristic of political moralism: "*Fac et excusa*. Seize any favourable opportunity of arbitrarily expropriating a right which the state enjoys over its own or over a neighbouring people; the justification can be presented far more easily and elegantly and the use of violence can be glossed over far more readily *after the fact* than if one were to think out convincing reasons in advance and then wait for counter-arguments to be offered. . . . Such audacity itself gives a certain appearance of inner conviction that the deed is right and just, and the god of success (*bonus eventus*) will then be the best of advocates." Kant, "On Perpetual Peace," 120.

77. Tocqueville, under the heading "La domination totale et la colonization partielle," in "Travail sur l'Algérie," *Oeuvres Complètes*, vol. 3, 218; *Empire and Slavery*, 63.

78. Tocqueville, under the heading "Colonisation," in "Travail sur l'Algérie," *Oeuvres Complètes*, vol. 3, 239; *Empire and Slavery*, 81.

79. Tocqueville, under the heading "Colonisation," in "Travail sur l'Algérie," *Oeuvres Complètes*, vol. 3, 239; *Empire and Slavery*, 81.

80. "In Algiers, as elsewhere, we cannot settle without taking territory from the tribes, but in Algiers, at least, we shall only be dispossessing tribes that have always been at war with us." Tocqueville, under the heading "Colonisation," in "Travail sur l'Algérie," *Oeuvres Complètes*, vol. 3, 244; *Empire and Slavery*, 85.

81. "In the vicinity of Algiers itself, the very fertile areas were torn from the hands of the Arabs and given to Europeans who, not being able or not wanting to cultivate them themselves, rented them to these same indigenous people, who thus became the mere farmers of the domains that had belonged to their fathers. Elsewhere, tribes or factions of tribes that were not hostile to us, or even more who had fought with us and sometimes without us, were pushed off their territory." Tocqueville, "Rapport sur le projet de loi relatif aux crédits," *Oeuvres Complètes*, vol. 3, 322–23; *Empire and Slavery*, 140.

82. Tocqueville, under the heading "Colonisation" in "Travail sur l'Algérie," *Oeuvres Complètes*, vol. 3, 240; *Empire and Slavery*, 81.

83. Rousseau, "On the Social Contract," bk. 1, chap. 3, 143. The chapter opens with this equation.

84. See le Cour Grandmaison, *Coloniser/Exterminer.*

85. In France today, the term *extermination* refers in everyday language exclusively to the Shoah, the extermination of Jews in Europe.

86. Tocqueville, "Rapport sur le projet de loi portant demande," *Oeuvres Complètes*, vol. 3, 380; *Empire and Slavery*, 174.

87. Tocqueville, "Rapport sur le projet de loi portant demande," *Oeuvres Complètes*, vol. 3, 380–81; *Empire and Slavery*, 175.

88. Tocqueville, "Rapport sur le projet de loi portant demande," *Oeuvres Complètes*, vol. 3, 381; *Empire and Slavery*, 175.

89. Tocqueville, "Rapport sur le projet de loi portant demande," *Oeuvres Complètes*, vol. 3, 382; *Empire and Slavery*, 176.

90. Tocqueville, "Rapport sur le projet de loi portant demande," *Oeuvres Complètes*, vol. 3, 329; *Empire and Slavery*, 145.

91. Tocqueville, "Notes sur l'Inde," *Oeuvres Complètes*, vol. 3, 511–35.

92. Tocqueville, "Notes sur l'Inde," *Oeuvres Complètes*, vol. 3, 514–15.

93. Tocqueville, "Notes diverses sur l'Inde" (November 1842), *Oeuvres Complètes*, vol. 3, 485.

94. Letter of October 3, 1840, cited in Tocqueville, *Oeuvres* (Pléïade), vol. 1, 1555.

95. The Napoleonic conquests ended with the French defeat at Waterloo, June 18, 1815. The army of Emperor Napoleon I was defeated by the Anglo-Prussian coalition led by the Duke of Wellington and Field-Marshal von Blücher. The Treaty of Paris put an end to the Seven Years' War among France, England, Spain, and Portugal. As a result, France lost "New France" in Canada, Louisiana, and its trading posts in India, but kept Martinique, Guadeloupe, and its trading posts in Africa. England subsequently became the leading colonial power. See also Benot, *La révolution française*.

96. Tocqueville, *Recollections*, 5.

97. Pierre Mendès France (1907–82) became a radical parliamentary deputy in 1932 and, in 1938, entered the Blum government of the Popular Front. He joined de Gaulle in London during the Second World War and became the national economic minister in 1944. In 1954, he was president of the Conseil for a little more than seven months. In 1956, he resigned from the Guy Mollet government because of his opposition to French policy in Algeria. Subsequently banned from the Radical Party, he joined the PSU, whose majority was anticolonialist, in 1960. After 1972, he dedicated himself to the resolution of the Israeli-Palestinian conflict.

98. Aristotle, *Politics*, 1180–82 (1277a–b), 1185 (1279a1–20).

99. In response to many requests, the Crémieux decree of October 24, 1870, granted full and complete French citizenship to Algerian Jews (excluding Jews of the Sahara) on the condition that they renounce Mosaic law and any of its prescriptions that might conflict with civil law in matrimonial affairs, a renunciation confirmed by French consistories during the First Empire. Isaac Adolphe Crémieux (1796–1880), who gave his name to this law, was the founder and leader of the Alliance Israélite Universelle (1860) and minister of justice during the early Third Republic. However, the law led to the division of Algerians between those eligible to become French citizens (Jews) and others who remained indigènes (Muslims). The law was opposed by the Catholic Church; by the Republicans, who in 1865 had allowed Muslim indigènes to ask for French citizenship; and by Muslims who considered the law discriminatory and rebelled. Adolphe Thiers, head of the provisional government, proposed to repeal the decree in 1871 but was defeated by the opposition under pressure from Alphonse de Rothschild. The leaders of the insurrection were deported to another French colony: New Caledonia. See Amson, *Adolphe Crémieux*; and Taïeb-Carlen, *Les Juifs*.

100. Cited by Rivet, *Le Maghreb*, 369. Ferhat Abbas (1899–1985): president of the Front de Libération Nationale (1954–62), president of the provisional government of the Republic of Algeria (1958–61), president of the constituting National Assembly of the Democratic People's Republic of Algeria (1962–63). Opposed to Ben Bella, he would be imprisoned (1963–65) and withdraw from political life.

101. In Algeria, Muslims were enlisted during the First World War thanks to the Lessimy law of 1908 on the extension of conscription to native subjects.

102. Numbers provided by Levisse-Touzé, *L'Afrique du Nord*, 366, and discussed by Rivet, *Le Maghreb*, 364. See also Coldefy, "Une éducation brusque."

103. Mohamed Boudiaf (1919–92): minister of state of the provisional government of the Republic of Algeria (1958–61), vice-president of the GPRA (1961–62). Condemned to death in 1964, he left Algeria. He later became president of the Haut-Comité d'État; in 1992, he was assassinated.

Ahmed Ben Bella (1916–2012): vice-president of the GPRA (1958–62). After six years in prison, he became president of the FLN (1962–65) and was removed by Houari Boumediène's coup d'état. He was then imprisoned until 1979 and assigned to a one-year house arrest. He lived in exile from 1981 to 1990.

104. Cited by Ferro, *Histoire des colonisations*, 358.

105. Ferro, *Histoire des colonisations*, 353.

106. Ferro, *Histoire des colonisations*, 354.

107. Ferro, *Histoire des colonisations*, 358. The Fourth Republic (1946–58) was a bicameral parliamentary regime with a president of the republic, elected by Parliament, who proposed to Parliament a president of the Conseil. Thus, it was the president of the Conseil who exercised executive power.

Samdech Chakrei Nhiek Tioulong (1908–96) was a Cambodian politician who played numerous official roles both in the French context and in independent Cambodia. First general of the royal Khmer army, he became Cambodia's military representative at the Geneva Accords (1954).

108. The Defferre outline-law to grant autonomy to the French territories of black Africa was only passed on March 23, 1956. *Mutatis mutandis*, on February 22 of the same year, in the United States, Martin Luther King called for a boycott of buses in Montgomery, Alabama, to protest against racial segregation. The first independent African states were Ethiopia, Liberia, the Sudan, Togo, and, in 1957, Ghana (formerly "Gold Coast"). In 1960, Dahomey, Niger, Upper Volta, Côte d'Ivoire, Chad, Central African Republic, the Congo, Gabon, Somalia, and Madagascar became independent.

109. Translator's note: Félix Houphouët-Boigny (1905–93) was the first president of Côte d'Ivoire, governing from 1960 to 1993. Léopold Sédar Senghor (1906–2001) was the first president of Senegal. An internationally recognized poet and first African member of the Académie Française, he also wrote numerous theoretical essays on negritude and the idea of African socialism. Aimé Césaire (1913–2008) was another founding member of the negritude movement, as well as a surrealist poet, playwright, and politician from Martinique.

110. Founded in 1931 at Constantine by Abdel-Hamid Ben Badis (1889–1940), it initially gathered ten Algerian graduates from Cairo, Damascus, and above all Zaytuna in Tunis and had the goal of reviving Arab and Muslim culture in Algeria. In 1940, when its founder died, Bachir Ibrahimi followed him in the role. The association opened primary schools and offered Arabic courses. Ben Badis considered the education of girls essential and opened the first girls' school in 1919.

111. Cited by Ageron, *Histoire de l'Algérie*, 566.

112. Ageron, *Histoire de l'Algérie*, 570.

113. In 1937, Messali Hadj founded the Parti du Peuple Algerien—in France—after the Étoile Nord-Africaine was banned by the Popular Front.

114. Ageron, *Histoire de l'Algérie*, 571.

115. Translator's note: Small groupings of brick houses.

116. The Algerian Assembly established by the new law was composed of 120 members. Sixty members were elected by each of two electoral colleges: The first college consisted of male and female citizens with full French civil status (around 470,000), plus 58,000 additional Muslim citizens with some professional or military qualification giving them civil status under local law. The second college consisted of more than one million Muslim men, with plans to include Muslim women starting in 1958. Clearly the "Europeans" were overrepresented and the "Muslims" underrepresented. The items prioritized for the new assembly were a vote on the budget and authorization for public financing. This was a mere sham of autonomy. The "Europeans" were opposed to the introduction of any Muslims at all in the first college; the nationalists rejected this doubly discriminatory law. The first elections were marred by fraud.

117. See Harbi, *La guerre commence*, 11. "Under the pressure of catastrophe, Mendès France acted quickly. In Indochina, the situation of the French army called for rapid decisions." At the moment when he opened negotiations over internal autonomy at Carthage, "the fighting capacity of the French army had fallen from 18,370 men in July 1954 to 43,112 men in January 1955. His goal was to prevent the partisans of internal autonomy from eventually overflowing [state borders] and to establish a protective barrier [*cordon sanitaire*] around Algeria" (12).

118. Cited by Rivet, *Le Maghreb*, 382.

119. Mendès France, *Oeuvres Complètes*, vol. 3, 51.

120. Mendès France, *Oeuvres Complètes*, vol. 3, 55.

121. This expression is preferable, from my point of view, to "war of decolonization." In fact, decolonization is a process that no war can accomplish on its own, because this would imply that decolonization can be resolved through a simple transfer of sovereignty. This is a very shortsighted and reductive way of understanding the term *decolonization*. Decolonization is a process, grounded in actions, which take place not only in the colonized country but also in the country that colonized it.

122. Mendès France, *Oeuvres Complètes*, vol. 3, 419.

123. Cited by Rivet, *Le Maghreb*, 215.

124. Mendès France, *Oeuvres Complètes*, vol. 3, 455.

125. *Fellaghas* is the French name for the Algerian and Tunisian partisans who rebelled against French authority for the sake of independence. They were considered cutthroats. The term was used starting at the turn of the century during the uprising of Khalifa Ibn Askar in the south of Tunisia. Then the French press used it to designate any and all nationalists. Finally, it was applied to guerrillas (*maquisards*) and other Algerian fighters.

126. Cited by Rivet, *Le Maghreb*, 34.

127. Moulay Merbah (1913–97) was an *oukil* (defense attorney appointed to practice in French jurisdictions). Militant of the PPA and then the MTLD, he was detained in 1944, deported to an assigned residence in 1945, imprisoned in 1948, and condemned once again in 1953. In October 1954 he was arrested, tortured, and returned to prison. Beginning in 1956, he represented the Mouvement National Algérien (MNA) in delegations of the United Nations.

Benyoucef Benkhedda (1920–2003): second president of the GRPA (1961–62). He was a member of the PPA in 1942. A year later, he was arrested and tortured for having spoken against the conscription of Algerians. Arrested again in November 1954, he was freed a year later and joined the FLN. In 1976, like Ferhat Abbas, he was placed under house arrest.

The lawyer Abderahmane Kiouane (1925–2014) was a member of the PPA in 1939 and then of the MTLD, from which he was later expelled. He too was arrested in 1954 and imprisoned until 1955. He was more open to giving Algeria internal autonomy. "Ambassador" of the GRPA, he was known for being the head of the GRPA's diplomatic mission in Asia, whose offices were in Tokyo. He published *Débuts d'une diplomatie de guerre (1956–1962).*

128. Cited by Ferro, *Histoire des colonisations*, 298.

129. Ferro, *Histoire des colonisations*, 299.

130. Ferro, *Histoire des colonisations*, 299.

131. Georges Dayan (1915–79) was an Algerian Jew. A lawyer, he was a friend and collaborator of Mitterand and a member of his cabinet at the time.

132. Telegram dated October 22, 1954. Mendès France, *Oeuvres Complètes*, vol. 3, 414–15. François Mitterand returned to Algeria from October 16 to 22, after an earthquake in Orléanville.

133. Giesbert, *Mitterrand*, 120. On September 3, 1953, François Mitterrand had resigned from the Laniel government to protest against the policies of Resident General Voizard in Tunisia and against the overthrow of the Moroccan sultan by General Guillaume.

134. Pierre Mendès France, radio broadcast speech on October 20, 1954.

135. Report titled "Pour une administration plus soucieuse des problèmes humains," in *Archives IPMF*, Algérie III D, 18–19.

136. January 26, 1955. Mendès France, *Oeuvres Complètes*, vol. 3, 690. Inversely, in improving the country's conditions of production, "economic progress leading as always to social progress, the profound causes of political trouble will gradually be eliminated" (691). For Mendès France, order "is not a notion that can be dissociated from political, economic, and social progress." Speech at the National Assembly on February 3, 1955. *Oeuvres Complètes*, vol. 3, 711.

137. *Journal Officiel*, session of March 20, 1956, 1073.

138. Translator's note: Salaire minimum interprofessionnel garanti (guaranteed minimum wage).

139. The first evaluation had been made by Delavignette, the second by Maspétiol. Pierre Mendès France merged these numbers and mentioned them in his speech on November 5, 1955, during the Congress of the Radical Party. See *Oeuvres Complètes*, vol. 4, 127.

140. *Archives IPMF*, Algérie, II C.

141. In the Aurès, public tortures took place on January 28 and 29, 1953.

142. See review no. 1432/232 of June 18, 1954, *Archives IPMF*, Algérie II C.

143. Translator's note: Referring to the thirty simultaneous attacks on military or police targets that marked the start of the Algerian Revolution and the formation of the FLN by younger nationalists, at a moment when Messali Hadj's MTLD (Mouvement pour le Triomphe des Libertés Democratiques) was internally conflicted. See Stora, *Algeria*, 35–36.

144. Address before the National Assembly on November 12, 1954. Mendès France, *Oeuvres Complètes*, vol. 3, 455–56.

145. Rivet, *Le Maghreb*, 211.

146. The treaty of Fès, signed March 30, 1912, repeated word for word the treaty of Bardo (1881) and the secondary convention of La Marsa (1883).

147. There are three departments in Algeria (but the whole of the territory was never entirely departmentalized): that of Algiers (91), that of Oran (92), and finally, that of Constantine (93). The "9/3," as one says today to designate the department of Seine-Saint-Denis, already existed in Algeria.

148. Translator's note: The *préfet* represents the French state in one of its departments, or major administrative units.

149. See Droz, "Main basse," 71–83.

150. P. Birnbaum, *Les fous*. The state Jews whose history Pierre Birnbaum retraces showed themselves "mad" for the republic that had emancipated them; but within the state itself, they encountered administrative authorities who were not always free from antisemitic prejudices, which ended up presenting incontestable career obstacles. These internal forms of ostracism were a hidden face of the republic.

151. If this was not done for Morocco, it is because France gave them its military bases. For this reason, therefore, the Americans did not react to the sultan's overthrow.

152. Mendès France, *Oeuvres Complètes*, vol. 4, 175–76.

153. Ahmed Francis (1912–68) committed himself very early (to the AML and then the UDMA). He joined up with the FLN in Cairo in 1956 and became finance minister of the GRPA (1958–61), then minister of the economy (1962–63).

154. Harbi, "Pierre Mendès France," 372.

155. Mendès France, *Oeuvres Complètes*, vol. 3, 177.

156. Jacques Soustelle (1912–90) began as an ethnologist, specializing in the Lacandon people of Mexico. In 1940, he joined the Free French Forces (Forces Françaises Libres or FFL) in London. This inaugurated a second, political career. Pierre Mendès France named him governor-general of Algeria (1955–56), but he proved to be completely partisan on behalf of French Algeria.

Vincent-Mansour Monteil (1913–2005) was a French military officer who then became a well-known orientalist. With Soustelle he assisted the information service of the Free French Forces and was imprisoned at the same time as Mendès France during the Second World War. In 1955, he was head of the military cabinet for the governor-general in Algeria: Soustelle. He resigned when Soustelle's politics became officially militarist.

Mostefa Ben Boulaïd (1917–55) was one of the "new historical leaders" of the war for Algerian independence and, on November 1, 1954, the head of the wilaya (substate) of the Aurès-Nemencha in the south of the Constantine region. Arrested at the Tunisian-Libyan border in 1955, he succeeded in escaping and died the following year while opening a parcel bomb.

157. Five leaders of the FLN were traveling together on October 22, 1956, when their plane from Rabat to Tunis was hijacked by the French army and forced to land in Algiers, resulting in their capture. They were Ahmed Ben Bella, Hocine Aït Ahmed, Mostefa Lacheraf, Mohamed Khider, and Mohamed Boudiaf. This was the first act of international piracy in which a civilian passenger airliner was prevented from reaching its destination.

158. Mendès France, *Oeuvres Complètes*, vol. 4, 225.

159. January 26, 1955. Mendès France, *Oeuvres Complètes*, vol. 3, 692.

160. Mendès France, *Oeuvres Complètes*, vol. 4, 126–27.

161. Philosophical critique is not reducible to a simple evaluation of virtue and of honor, to a moral judgment. As we know, the latter is a question only for the valet (no man is great in the eyes of his valet, said Goethe, to which Hegel added: no man is great in the eyes of the schoolmaster, the specialist in morality).

162. Schmitt, *La notion de politique* and *Théorie du partisan*; translated as *The Concept of the Political* and *Theory of the Partisan*.

163. See Hervé Le Bras, *Le sol et le sang*, 50–52, 56.

164. Clausewitz, *De la guerre*. In his reading of Clausewitz (*Theory of the Partisan*), Carl Schmitt raises a very interesting question, although he leaves it unanswered. He wonders,

with respect to the French officers in Indochina, whether one must not see in their conceptions, as in Clausewitz's thought, the "intellectual type" of the "colonel" rather than the *general*. Later, we spoke about the "Algeria of the colonels."

The language is therefore one of revolts, riots, uprisings, incidents, attacks, and aggressions rather than of "war" (a term that cannot be logically used here): at most, the language of the "guerrilla." Correlatively, the language cannot refer to "fighters": it can only refer to "rebels," "fellaghas," "terrorists," and so on. On October 5, 1999, French representatives adopted a bill officially recognizing the "state of war in Algeria" between 1954 and 1962.

165. This did not prevent him from writing to Fichte in 1809 that "there was infinitely more to gain from stimulating individual forces than from cultivating an artificial formalism," "particularly in the most beautiful of all wars, that which a people wages on its own land for its liberty and its independence." It is in that tradition—the true war is the revolutionary war in which absolute hostility is incarnate—that the Algerians' way of referring to "their" war is ultimately inscribed: revolution.

166. Aron, *Sur Clausewitz*.

167. Schmitt, *Theory of the Partisan*, 64.

168. Between 1940 and 1944, Salan (1899–1984) was appointed to the army staff of the colonies and sent to Africa. He was responsible for the command of French troops in the North, in Indochina, in 1948. In 1951, he was high commissioner of the Republic of North Vietnam and directed the investigation into the defeat of Dien Bien Phu in 1954. In 1958, he was named commander in chief of the military forces in Algeria. In 1961, he became the declared head of the Organisation de l'armée secrète (OAS). He participated in the putsch. Arrested in April 1962, he was condemned to life in prison (with attenuating circumstances) by the high military tribunal of Paris in May 1962. In 1968 he was granted an amnesty.

169. *Le procès de Raoul Salan*, 88.

PART II

AFRICA AND ITS PHANTOMS: WRITING THE AFTERWARD

INTRODUCTION

WHILE MUSING OVER THE BEST WAY TO INTRODUCE a reflection on decolonial becoming, it seemed to me that a personal account would undoubtedly be the best kind of approach.[1] People's lived experiences, the things they carry within but also between them, are often imperceptible; all the same, this does not mean they are inaccessible. Colonial upheavals, postcolonial outcomes, and decolonial becomings are not just historical events or political phenomena. They are also disruptions or improvements in communication, in themselves and among themselves.

"It's a land of lunatics!" This judgment was the everyday expression of coloniality. It testified to the colonizers' ignorance and incomprehension. But there is another way to understand this outburst. Certain countries are marked by a disturbed self-understanding due to colonialism. Individuals are affected as much as societies, which often devote themselves to searching for an identity—one forever lost, given how thoroughly colonial relations were able to modify the forms in which individuals and collectives lived and perceived themselves.

As a child in Algeria, I gazed with fascination at the men without noses who had been mutilated during the war and forever after bore its stigmata. The FLN had waged war on the consumption of tobacco and had forbidden smoking and the taking of snuff. The disobedient found themselves sanctioned by the savage amputation of their lips and particularly their noses. The *nif*, the nose, is the very symbol of honor, and someone who has lost his nose has also lost his honor. He no longer has *horma*, or respectability. At that time, however, I did not understand what I was seeing, and the information available to me was neither enlightening nor comforting.

Other phenomena were also disconcerting. Ben Khedda's house was next door to ours, but he was said to be under "house arrest." It seemed that Ferhat Abbas could no longer be officially named. I had never known the father of one of my best friends, either. Her home, an apartment at the center of Algiers where she lived with her brother, was filled with Russian literature but also, if I remember correctly, the complete works of Kim Il Sung and many other things besides. Her father, a communist, was imprisoned somewhere in the South. Where exactly? I am not sure that anyone ever really knew.

Her father, whose first name was Nasser, had been registered by the French authorities under the family name Naceur. In French Algeria—in other words, colonial Algeria—certain people were simply saddled with new names. No one knows why the Aït Kaci Ouyahia became Yakhou. Ordinary civil servants entered certain colonized persons in their registers as SNP or "without surname" (*sans nom patronymique*). What could you do but give in, even if only partially or disingenuously, to the imposition of your own name?

On French soil, candidates for naturalization also had new names imposed on them—but in a different way. Thus it happened that Ezra Benveniste, who was born in Aleppo and had not yet become the great linguist that we know today, later bore the official name Émile. He always signed his name E. Benveniste. Clearly these events had psychic consequences.

The personal, the historical, and the cultural dimensions are so intertwined in experience that they are difficult to disentangle. Being born to a father who was denounced by a compatriot and slaughtered by French soldiers, as one of my friends was born, forges a personality. He was orphaned by a war with no name. In fact, Algerians have always used the terms *struggle for independence* and *revolution* although the French referred to "Algerian events" before recognizing, in 1999, that what had been going on was really a war.

Moreover, the age of reason becomes a singular adventure for anyone who has to change countries at the age of seven, like this friend, who learned how to speak, think, indeed dream in another language than the one he had spoken until that moment. Placed in the care of a granduncle, owner of a hotel for immigrants in Paris, the young Berber-speaking boy was then handed over to a French nanny in the countryside. He received a Catholic education and learned French with her.

In Algiers, I remember how difficult it was to speak colloquial Arabic (*darija*) because the little blond girl ("visibly" foreign) who tried to use her rudimentary phrases upon arrival met answers only in French. Today, the spoken language has turned out to be something almost like a third language, embedding French within Algerian. "I want to reserve a seat for Algiers" ("*Je veux réserver une place pour Alger*") is said "*Habith n'reservi plaça li dzaye.*" "The children in the building have broken the elevator like they always do" (a recurrent complaint) ("*Les enfants du bâtiment ont cassé l'ascenseur, comme toujours*") turns into "*Louled tàa l'batima fassdou l'ascenseur comme toujours.*" To drive (*circuler*) becomes *circuliche*, and so on.

Discovering Algeria led me to encounter my grandmother for the first time. She lived in Annaba, which everyone was still calling Bône. When she went out, she wrapped herself in a large black veil made of thick cloth, very structured, which covered her entirely from head to foot. A small white veil masked half her face. Not a hair escaped. What a contrast between the way she appeared inside the house and the image she offered to the outside world—she was almost impossible to recognize.

In Algiers, the white haik was worn much less seriously. This was a large piece of white cloth, rectangular in shape, and more or less delicate. The way some women wore it was fairly sexy, showing the form of a leg or a high-heeled foot in the slit between layers. Others, walking differently, buried themselves almost entirely under the fabric. Always, the little veil, attached by strings, hid the wearer's nose and especially her mouth. Men dominated the space of the street and cafés. They were saved by their gender, free to come and go where they wanted and dress as they pleased.

In the city center, the Milk Bar—where the attacks of September 30, 1956, took place during the Battle of Algiers—was the only place where orange juice, a lemon tart, and other equally delicious things could be enjoyed in peace.[2] It was one of the rare spaces where women and young girls could take a break. It still exists, in Emir Abdelkader Place. Not long ago, one of the servers from the 1950s was still working there. This kind of context is fundamental in any human existence even if it seems tiny and insignificant when seen from afar.

The festivals staged just after the new states established their independence, such as the 1966 festival of black African arts (Festival Mondial des Arts Nègres) in Dakar and the 1969 pan-African festival in Algiers, showed how urgently people needed to restore their self-images when anticolonial victories had brought neither freedom nor wealth nor happiness.[3] For Senegalese president Léopold Sédar Senghor, it was a matter of "achieving a better international and interracial understanding, of affirming the contribution of black artists and writers to the great universal currents of thought and of allowing black artists from all horizons to confront each other with the results of their research."[4]

In Algiers, the public demonstration immortalized in film by William Klein was intended to have an international and revolutionary spirit.[5] For example, it affirmed Algeria's support for Frelimo, the Mozambique

Liberation Front, which won the country's independence in 1974, as well as for the American Black Panthers. At that time, Black Panther spokesman Eldridge Cleaver had been hiding in Algiers for a year. He learned French from Daniel Boukman, a Martinican who had taken the side of the Algerian FLN at the time. The capital of Algeria welcomed refugees from a great many countries. The Arraès had fled the Brazilian dictatorship, the Da Silvas the Portuguese regime, and so on.[6]

The single television station broadcast concerts of Arabo-Andalusian music or *chââbi*, recitations of the Koran and Muslim sermons, Egyptian and Indian musicals, animated Czech shorts, and American and French drama series. Without leaving home, we were plunged into the world's internationality—except that the love scenes were always cut. Characters pulled toward one another for an embrace in which the lips never touched. They were brutally separated from one another without the slightest contact. When I go to Tunisia today, by contrast, I often have a choice among several religious stations and others devoted exclusively to ads for paid encounters with supporting photos.

Our telephone line was tapped, and children as well as adults were careful not to say anything that could be politically compromising. We all knew that the telephone had ears. Before arriving in Algeria, I lived in Marseille, where my family was guarded day and night by French police. The OAS, the secret army organization dedicated to fighting against the Evian accords and to struggling at any cost for French Algeria, had bombed the consulate where my father was consul general of Algeria at that time.

Today it seems to me that I forged a child's theory of nationality. Just as one imagines sexuality in various ways that leave their mark on fantasies and affects as well as on styles of thinking and intelligence, I strove to pierce the mystery of nationality, whose how and why remained elusive to me. Where do children come from? Where does nationality come from? In Algeria, I and others were classified among the "mixed": neither truly Algerians nor truly French, in an indeterminate no-man's-land, an indefinable and deterritorialized third space. Those of us with French mothers and Algerian fathers were a small minority in this unstable position, created by a politically contradictory genealogy.

This, then, is how my *Wissendrang*, my drive for knowledge, was awakened. Since knowledge is a matter of desire, to satisfy this drive (at least partially), in this book I have struggled to add to my self-knowledge. I have tried both to shed light on the self's relation to itself and to resolve it. From my point of view, particularly in the colonial and postcolonial context, this relation is traversed by history, language, and gender. In fact, nothing human happens without the involvement of subjectivity.

From this perspective, the decolonization of subjectivity is also at stake in any decolonial politics, even a theoretical politics like the one here. Decolonization is a challenge meaningful only for subjects—that is, for human beings as bearers of a singular subjectivity, which would have been called *spirit* or *soul* in another age. *Décolonialité* is a becoming that has no meaning apart from the subjects whom it defines. In terms of space, it is a third place: neither that of the colony nor that of the postcolony.

The idea of becoming does not mean we are assessing and examining either the past and the present or the present and the future. It is not a question of establishing continuities. Whether one likes it or not, action, like thought, proceeds by leaping. There is no determinate beginning because neither the start of an anticolonial struggle nor the date of independence can be identified as such. Nor is there any clear end, a finish line that one would progressively reach.

Subjectively, we have only the present and becoming, through continuities and discontinuities. The subject's time is neither clock time nor calendar time. The subjective present is fundamentally marked by heterochronies. This means it is a mode of existence, not a time period. It is not a uniform or homogenous block. It is characterized by relative powerlessness as well as by real possibilities. Becoming means simultaneously coming (from) and going (to). It is a matter of starting to be what one was not and passing from one situation or state to another. The only decolonial becoming is an open one.

"Let us step up the pace in order to finish: in view of a *third place* that could well have been *more than* archi-originary, the most anarchic and anarchivable place possible, not the island nor the Promised Land, but a certain desert—and not the desert of revelation but a desert in the desert."[7] Certain formulas are as enticing as they are enigmatic. Such is the case with this passage from Derrida. To be sure, there are many ways to understand it. The afterward [*après*], in light of which one would wish to step up the pace in order to finish, is a third place. It is neither the site of the colonial past nor the site of the postcolonial present, but that of an approaching decolonial future—an afterward to decolonization.

Neither an island where the shipwrecked of the earth might find refuge nor a promised land, the future is a certain kind of desert teeming with winds and sands, dunes and mountains, stingy with its landmarks and resources. This is why one can reach the third space only with makeshift means. But someone who does not know that he or she is in a *sahara* (the Arab word for desert) will never be able to orient himself or herself. As we already know, it is in the sky and thanks to the stars that nomads trace their paths.

Notes

1. Decolonization is a becoming. *Devenir*, or "becoming," is a Deleuzian term. As Deleuze says, to start with, "becoming is always 'between' or 'among': a woman between women, or an animal among others" (*Essays Critical and Clinical*, 2). Further, this becoming inevitably remains incomplete. It is not a present endowed with a future that would have an end and would be an *avenir*. It is a continuous present deprived of any teleology. In becoming, one is like Kafka's champion swimmer, who does not know how to swim. This becoming remains to be thought in a specific context, that of Africa, and particularly in the countries of the former French empire: "a witch's line that escapes the dominant system" (5). Following this line, one witnesses the appearance of visions and voices: "They are not interruptions of the process, but breaks that form part of it, like an eternity that can only be revealed in a becoming, or a landscape that only appears in movement" (5). From my point of view, a decolonial becoming is both a critique and a clinic.

2. Yacef Saadi (b. 1928) and Larbi Ben M'hidi (1923–57), the principal leaders of the FLN in Algiers, had decided to attack the places where young middle-class Europeans gathered, the Cafeteria and the Milk Bar as well as the Air France hall of the Mauritania Hotel. Yacef Saadi had the idea of using three young women from "good families": Zohra Drif, Samia Lahkdari, and Djamila Bouhired. Many victims lost their limbs. Arrested in 1957, Ben M'hidi was killed. Sentenced to death, Saadi was freed after the Evian Accords.

3. This festival, strongly influenced by the idea of negritude, "had four goals: to make the contribution of *négritude* to universal civilization known to all the youth of Africa and the world who were seeking their path, to all persons of good will, and to all friendly peoples; to permit black artists from across the Atlantic to periodically make a 'return to the sources'; to ensure that all the contributions of *négritude* referred to the great currents of thought and numerous forms of art; to give African artisans the opportunity to meet publishers, film producers, and members of the international elite, in order to make their talent known." See "Le festival."

Three years after Dakar, Algiers demonstrated its own pan-Africanism in what was called a "third-world opera": the pan-African cultural festival of Algiers. Notably, the Black Panther Party and the Palestinian Fatah were represented. Myriam Makeba was a stunning success there. Jazz (e.g., Nina Simone, Archie Shepp) had a place of honor. The anticolonialist struggle was still going on in the Portuguese colonies (Mozambique, Angola, Guinea Bissau) and the South African colonies (Namibia) as well as against apartheid in South Africa. This festival was a way of affirming the central role that Algeria wanted to play in the nonaligned movement.

4. Brunet and Hourdeaux, "Retour sur le Festival."

5. Produced by Algeria, William Klein's film *Festival panafricain d'Alger* has become a cult item. Filmed in 1969 as close as possible to the artists and the performance troupes of a truly historic festival, it features archival footage from independence struggles and interviews with the representatives of liberation movements, as well as with African and Caribbean writers and essayists such as the Haitian poet Rene Depestre and the Senegalese linguist Pathé Diagne.

6. After the coup d'état of 1964 carried out by Marshal Castelo Branco, many Brazilians were exiled. Algeria was one of their destinations, the only one in Africa. The Brazilian dictatorship lasted until 1985. In Portugal, Antonio de Oliveira Salazar's dictatorship lasted from 1932 to 1968; that of his successor, Marcelo Caetano, ended with the "Carnation Revolution" in 1974.

7. Derrida, *Acts of Religion*, 55 (translation altered).

1

SAVING ONE'S SKIN

FRANTZ FANON WAS BORN AS A MARTINICAN ON July 25, 1925. He died in Washington as an Algerian on December 6, 1961. He was laid to rest in the soil of his compatriots, buried in the plot reserved for martyrs (*chouhadas*) in the township of Aïn Kerma. Between 1949 and 1950, he wrote three plays—*L'oeil se noie, Les mains parallèles,* and *La conspiration*—of which only the first two survive. He published *Peau noire, masques blancs* in 1952, one year before his fellow Martinican Édouard Glissant published *Un champ d'îles.* He was not even thirty years old. Soon followed *L'an V de la révolution algérienne,* in 1959, and *Les damnés de la terre,* in 1961. His political writings, gathered under the title *Pour la révolution africaine,* appeared posthumously in 1964. At once Martinican and Algerian, he is a mediator [*trait d'union*] linking the islands of the Americas to the African continent. He turns our common humanity into a universal rather than dissolving it into skin-based figures of the visible such as "the black" or "the Arab." For racialization turns the universal into a particular and humanity into a privilege.

Fanon entered writing through the theater and discovered the colony through psychiatry. He approached medicine as a reparative discipline. Fanon's intellectual action can also be read as restoring and repairing the skin, his own and that of others—blacks on the one hand, those colonized on the other. Before being any color, the skin (*peau*), from the Latin *pellis,* is a film or pellicule. It is the organism's first protective barrier, a complex organ involving many layers of tissue.

Figuratively one uses the phrase "getting out of one's skin": ceasing to think only about oneself. One also speaks of "getting into the skin" of a character: representing him or her vividly, naturally, as if one were playing one's own life. Whoever mentions skin has "epidermal reactions" in mind. An epidermal reaction is one that is hypersensitive [*à fleur de peau*], strong, or immediate. Thus, showing a visible reaction indicates that one is really affected; otherwise, one remains "stony," impassive, as if nothing had happened.

Do Blacks Have Anatomy?

In Europe, when skin is white, one is tempted to remove it like a garment to see what lies beneath. At least this is the lesson of anatomy's famous écorchés. With the publication of *De humani corporis fabrica libri septem* in 1543, Vesalius founded the art of the écorché, this anatomic map on which swelled muscles leap to reveal themselves. Anatomy proceeds in a specific way: by incision, dissection, intrusion, penetration. By subordinating the profanation of cadavers to an imperious desire to know, to see, to possess, anatomy testifies to an obsession with death. It reveals an obsession with the underside.

Historically and anatomically, however, we find a profound dissymmetry between the white skin that must be lifted if we are to see what lies beneath and the black skin that remains a surface covering nothing. This gaze and this desire to see beneath the skin deny blacks any anatomy. Apparently they are not organisms. They are only skin. For color prejudice, what anatomy teaches us is identical beneath every human skin has no significance. To the contrary, everything is reduced to this fleshly difference. Anatomists could only preserve this difference by transforming it into a fetish. The skin becomes the organism itself: it is the part that stands for the whole. The anatomist Ruysch removed a "*reticulum mucosum*" from a "negro."[1] This was kept in the curiosity cabinet of the Russian tsar whom Voltaire mentioned on several occasions.

In the article of his *Dictionnaire philosophique* titled "Ignorance," Voltaire responds to the argument that skin color depends on climate: "You are ignorant that the *reticulum mucosum* of the blacks [*nègres*] is black, although I have mentioned the fact innumerable times. No matter how many children you might have with your Welsh wife in Guinea, they will never have that black skin, those thick dark lips, those round eyes, or that frizzy wool on the head, which make the specific difference of blacks. Put down roots in America and your family will always have beards, while no native American has one. Now see if Adam and Eve can get you out of this one."[2] If color prejudice has disappeared today, racialization remains hard at work.

The perennial tendency to deduce the whole of an organism from its skin was recently debunked, discreetly but effectively, by a young Nigerian artist who had the contrary intuition, since she was born in 1985. Toyin Odutola drew paradoxical, black-skinned écorchés.[3] For example, the 2011 work *A.O.*, an intense face in black and blue, and the 2012 works *The View from Behind* and *Adeola in Abuja*—an almost invisible drawing—show interlacing muscles that are at once dark and luminous, spindles of flesh making a human being out of a mere body. In 2013, she introduced colors into the bodies of her subjects. This specialist of portraiture turns all her models into écorché(e)s. Given that the history of Western art has long pitted draftsmen against colorists, it is interesting to find blacks placed on the side of drawing this time rather than that of color.

A body without organs, the black is therefore no organism. Does it have a gender? The history of the Hottentot Venus, Swatche or Saartje Baartman, turns gender into an anatomical characteristic and turns that anatomical characteristic into a monstrosity. In 1810, Baartman was shipped by a surgeon of the Royal Navy to Europe, where she died five years later at the age of twenty-six. After having been dissected alive, so to speak, her lifeless body was handed over to two great names of the period, first the naturalist Geoffroy Saint-Hilaire and then the anatomist Georges Cuvier.[4]

Is this past truly over and done with? In 2010, Abdellatif Kechiche made the film *Vénus noire*, which revisits the tragic story of Saartje Baartman.[5] The first scene shows a woman presented to the gaze of foreign men. Her sexual organs are exhibited, sacrificed on the altar of science. She is alone against them all. Until 1974 the real Baartman's remains were on view at the Musée de l'Homme in Paris.[6] It was only in 2002 that the "scientific" relics of this woman were repatriated to South Africa, eight years after the Khoikhoi asked Nelson Mandela to reclaim them.[7] In the film of a director who identifies with his heroine, Saartje Baartman is mute. But why would she not have spoken? Would she really have submitted without saying a word?[8]

Sex dominates. Whether masculine or feminine, the black is therefore nothing but exteriority. The "negro's" skin blots out his subjectivity. The "negress's" sex negates her will. The white has a soul, while the black has a skin and a sex. Fanon observes an "epidermization of inferiority."[9] "Lactification" is thus understood as an effort to win back an organism, a gender, and a subjectivity lost to color. This is why Fanon integrated the case of women into his analyses of both Martinique and Algeria. He introduced sexual difference onto the map of bodies and of subjectivity.

In racialization, the skin metonymically becomes the black man's objectivity just as subjectivity, inversely, is the burden of the white man. We owe the expression "white man's burden" to Rudyard Kipling; this was his title for a poem published in 1899 with the subtitle "The United States and the Philippine Islands," in which he defends the colonization of the Philippines:

> Take up the White Man's burden
> Send forth the best ye breed—
> Go bind your sons to exile
> To serve your captives' need
>
> To wait in heavy harness
> On fluttered folk and wild—
> Your new-caught, sullen peoples,
> Half devil and half-child.[10]

"The black man is attacked in his corporeality."[11] His skin is a prison: "The black physician will never know how close he is to being discredited. I repeat, I was walled in: neither my refined manners nor my literary knowledge nor my understanding of the quantum theory could find favor."[12] Because Fanon offered these considerations in the first person, they were not immediately accepted.[13] Fanon apprehends the world beginning from his subjectivity. This is why he can understand an unknown situation (Algeria) as well as the one he knows (Martinique). It matters little that the terrain is foreign or familiar to him because he is the line that joins them.

Being Flayed Alive

Fanon was said to be a tortured soul—an *écorché vif*, flayed alive. The standard image of the *écorché vif* comes to us from Valverde.[14] In this sixteenth-century anatomical representation, a flayed figure dangles his own skin from one hand. The skin has no use and, in the drawing, resembles a phantom. This remnant is no longer a container because it has been opened out. Its eyes, nose, and mouth are holes. *Écorché vif*: this is the expression one uses for an extremely sensitive person who cannot tolerate others' suffering, finding it a torture. Tortured soul Fanon might be, but he is no less a doctor and psychiatrist. A doctor—namely, someone familiar with anatomical images. A psychiatrist, who takes more of an interest in what the skin protects than in what it projects. We have yet to explore Fanon's thoughts on anatomy.

The moralists of the eighteenth century spoke of the mind as an "interior anatomy." "Few people, nevertheless, have taken the trouble to anatomize the soul; and this is an art at which no one blushes to be perfectly ignorant," said Shaftesbury in his *Inquiry Concerning Virtue or Merit*, translated by Diderot in 1745.[15] Indeed, anatomical knowledge served for a long time as the paradigm of knowledge about humankind. But Diderot mistrusts anatomy's virtues: "Doubtless the study of the *écorché* has its advantages, but one fears that this *écorché* remains perpetually in the imagination," he said in *Essais sur la peinture*.[16] Again in *Héros et martyrs*: "In painting as in morality, peering under the skin is very dangerous."[17] For Diderot, the écorché under the skin is not the same as a nude under the drapery.

There is a sadistic aspect to revealing or flaying someone's skin, whether literally or figuratively. In the *Cent vingt journées de Sodome*, Sade identifies this as the fifty-second passion.[18] Fanon's effort to draw up an inventory and an analysis of the real remains distant from all sadism as well as eroticization, but without applying the methodological rules proclaimed by specialists of anatomy. Fanon indicates that a researcher can approach this in two ways: "describe" in the manner of the anatomists, or else, after having described the real, propose to "change" it oneself. This project was already taking shape in *Peau noire, masques blancs*.

Fanon prefers the clinic to anatomy. The clinic supports the living person while anatomy dissects the dead one. There are no écorchés in Fanon, apart from *écorchés vifs*. "Analyzing the real is always a delicate task," he confesses in *Peau noire, masques blancs*.[19] "A researcher can choose to adopt either of two attitudes towards his subject. First, he can be content with a description—like the anatomist who, in the middle of a description of the tibia, is surprised to be asked how many fibular depressions he has. This is because his research always focuses on others and never on himself."

What would be the colonial analogue for anatomy? Official literature. Fanon adds: "There are too many official and unofficial stories about black people [*nègres*] that cannot be swept under the carpet. But putting them all together gets us nowhere as regards the real job, which is to demonstrate their mechanism."[20] Tales about black people are fundamental to the colony because they allow distinctions to be made between "native" Senegalese and the Europeans of the French Caribbean. First Césaire and then Fanon introduce a decisive symbolic reversal. They see that an Antillean is a contradiction in terms: he or she is a black European.

Paradoxically, the only way for Césaire and Fanon to deracialize and to liberate the Antilleans was to transform these Europeans into *nègres*. The decentering is striking but subtle. Instead of "lord[ing] it as uncontested master over this black rabble," the Antillean of the new generation, according to Fanon, "is a black person [*nègre*]."[21] Rather than telling tales about black people, one must deconstruct the mechanism of such stories and change their discursive regime. This is a revolution. Dissection is a form of rumination. Now what interests Fanon is not so much dissection as mental illness. And it is because of his interest in mental pathology that he takes an interest in racism and the colony, for they are a part of it.

Those who have been colonized prioritize saving their skin above all else. This can be understood in two distinct ways. For the Algerian, it means living with less than nothing; it means going so far as to risk one's life in combat. For the person from Martinique, however, things are different. They are epidermal. The Martinican's skin is also a mask in its own right. It troubles interpersonal relations, whether between Martinicans, between blacks and whites, between Martinicans and Senegalese, or between Martinicans and North Africans. The skin of the Martinican is "saved" by lactification. Is this a way out?

One might reconsider Fanon's analysis of these questions from his first book in terms of the "false self." A concept borrowed from Winnicott, the false self is a mask: it dissimulates and it protects.[22] Saving one's skin means undoing the fatal link that asymmetrically unites colonizer and colonized, whites, Arabs, and blacks. For Fanon is not just talking about the black skin for which white masks are prescribed and in the end proscribed. He is referring to the skin of the colonized subject as such. This he says explicitly. In planning to write a book on language and aggressivity, he emphasizes that "going beyond [the black Antillean], we shall enlarge the scope of our description to include every colonized subject."[23]

This includes not only every colonized man but also every colonized woman . . . When he analyzes the forced unveiling of Algerian women, Fanon shows how much the veil functions as a second skin holding the whole body together.[24] For women who have always worn a veil, unveiling is corporeal dismemberment. According to him, insofar as these unveiled women are exposed to everyone's gazes, they find themselves paradoxically dispossessed of their own bodies.

"One must have heard the confessions of Algerian women," Fanon writes, "or have analyzed the dream content of certain recently unveiled women to appreciate the importance of the veil in the woman's lived bodily experience. Without the veil she has an impression of her body being cut up into bits, put adrift; the limbs seem to lengthen indefinitely . . . the unveiled body seems to escape, to dissolve."[25] Everything indicates an impact on the corporeal schema. For women who traditionally cover themselves completely and comfortably with a white or black veil, the intolerable effect of being bared contrasts with the swelled garments of the women carrying bombs. Embodiment is then involved with everything.

Tearing into the Skin, Caring for the Body

Saving one's skin: the skin is the metaphor for the body itself. Hence the expression "to tear [*trouer*] into the skin"—in other words, to kill [*tuer*]. It can be understood literally or figuratively, as a material or a mental intrusion. From this point of view, the colonized person is a weakened being whose skin preserves neither physical nor mental integrity. But, contrasted with other colonized people, the skin of the Antillean is torn or is killed because it is black. One finds in Fanon a keen interest in life and death and, above all, in the living and the deadly elements that each of us contains.

The Antillean "discovered himself to be a transplanted son of slaves; he felt the vibration of Africa in the very depth of his body and aspired only to one thing: to plunge into the great 'black hole.'"[26] This hole refers to the feminine as much as it evokes the phenomenon of being "silent like a grave"—in other words, incapable of speech and obliged to remain silent. In the originary colonial vision, the hole is torn by a colonial gaze that associates its object with waste. This gaze, in the strict sense, is what does him in [*lui fait la peau*]. It is, as one says, murderous. Although, therefore, the colonized person must live under this gaze, what really interests Fanon is that he or she must also live without it. Decolonization and deracialization involve nothing other than conditions sine qua non for being comfortable or at home in one's skin [*être bien dans sa peau*].

On several occasions, Fanon insists on the corporeal schema, the constriction, confinement, but also the dispersion of being. In fact, the white gaze performs a dissection, as if bodies with black skin were dead. "The white gaze, the only valid one, is already dissecting me. I am *fixed*. Once their microtomes are sharpened, the Whites objectively cut sections of my reality. I have been betrayed."[27]

The description of "the Black's lived experience" shows the extent to which the skin exposes more than it protects: "The Other fixes me with his gaze, his gestures and attitude, the same way you fix a preparation with a dye. . . . I explode. Here are the fragments put together by another me."[28] "The body schema, attacked in several places, collapsed, giving way to a epidermal racial schema."[29] "My body was returned to me spread-eagled, disjointed, redone, draped in mourning."[30] The skin is no longer a psychic or physical container, no longer the wrapping of a self.

Achille Mbembe did well to note the contradiction confronting every colonized person when he is both required and forbidden to resemble the colonizer. "If there is one domain where all these paradoxes can best be seen," he holds,

> it is, as Fanon says, in the relation between medicine (care) and colonialism (hurt). The body which is sometimes closed in, "stripped, chained, constrained to labor, struck, deported, put to death" in one context is the same body that elsewhere is "cared for, educated, dressed, fed, and paid." In the colony, the subject destined for care is no different than the one that elsewhere becomes the object of disfiguration. In the context of healing, he or she appears as so much human waste, scum, and residue, since, as a subject who has been deprived and ceaselessly exposed to injury, he or she would have been technically dishonored.[31]

The gaping chasm of contradictions separating each person from himself or herself is a kind of Acheron, the mythic river transporting the souls of the departed towards the underworld. Hades? The very place where souls, separated from their bodies, endure extreme suffering, whether temporary or eternal. To speak of the "damned of the earth" is to evoke hell—in other words, the hell of the colony. Everyone knows that hell is a fiery inferno.

Its first sign is a burn. A burn is a partial or total destruction of the skin, the soft parts of tissues, and even the bones. The severity of a burn depends on its location, its depth, the extent of the damaged surface, and the nature of its origin. Severe burns present a threat to life. The victim must therefore be protected and the burn cooled back down, a difficult matter in the case of bombs or nuclear tests. From this point of view, independence resembles a care unit for acute burns. Thus the last lines of *Les damnés* speak of making "new skin."

In the colonial system, the physician is an armed agent of French power. His Hippocratic oath is beside the point. We know of countless denunciations, false death certificates, and cases of failure to provide care. Colonial violence passes through medicine, which, however unwillingly, is one of its vectors. At least this is the rule, which, as always, had some fortunate exceptions. So often is the doctor regarded as a colonial agent that the local people lump him together with the administrator, the mayor, or the military police: no one trusts him, everyone is wary around him, and no one wishes to tell him the truth. The bond made with him is deceptive; he must be distracted from the real problem and put on the wrong path. Medicine too is in occupied territory—a no-man's-land.

What consequences follow from this? "From this point on, the real values of the occupied quickly tend to acquire a clandestine form of existence. In the presence of the occupier, the occupied learns to dissemble, to resort to trickery. To the scandal of military occupation, he opposes a scandal of contact. Every contact between the occupied and the occupier is a falsehood."[32]

What develops is a culture of opportunism in which one's interior dialogue correlates with a deceptive response to the other's address, in which secrecy becomes a value. It is a culture in which falsehood is put at the service of truth. Thus, one must find true words for what is true. In turn, Fanon will force himself to speak truthfully with those whom he recognizes are right to lie to him, in principle, because their lying reveals the truth [*ils mentent vrai*]. Because "in answer to the lie of the colonial situation, the colonized subject responds with a lie."[33]

We know how much significance Fanon gave to the therapeutic relationship. Every word that removes skin can be a wound. Moreover, the observations he provides in his first book must be carried over to those that, horrified, he gathered later in Algeria. Fanon offers a clinical description of colonial medicine from which no pathology is excluded. How can consultation take place when the black mask weighs on their conversation, when the Arab's face is veiled by his skin? "Twenty European patients come and go: 'Please have a seat. Now what's the trouble? What can I do for you today?' In comes a black man or an Arab. 'Sit down, old fellow. Not feeling well? Where's it hurting?' When it's not 'You not good?'"[34] Fanon is so acutely conscious of the possibility of such derailment that he confesses: "At a personal level, during certain consultations, I have felt myself lapsing."[35]

Colonial medical practice is characterized largely by corruption. In a chapter of *L'an V de la révolution algérienne* dedicated to medicine and colonialism, Fanon offers the following claims:

> Medical practice in the colonies very often assumes an aspect of systematized piracy. . . . It even happens that doctors in rural centers (several examples of this in Algeria are known) boast of taking X-rays with the aid of a vacuum cleaner. We may mention the case of a European doctor practicing in Rabelais (in the region of Orléansville) who explains how he manages, on market days, to earn more than 30,000 francs in the course of a morning. "I fill three syringes of unequal size with salt serum and I say to the patient, 'which injection [*piqûre*] do you want, the 500, the 1000 or the 1500 franc one?' The patient," so the doctor explains, "almost always chooses the most expensive injection."[36]

Is it not meaningful that we are talking about piercing [*piqûre*]?

Organic Symptoms and Death Reflexes

One must, according to Fanon, begin with the body and interpret its organic troubles. It is hardly simple to destroy the "core of despair crystallized in the body of the colonized."[37] We have a clinical description of these kernels: stomach ulcers, renal colic, menstrual irregularities in women, "hypersomnia due to idiopathic tremors," early whitening of the hair, cardiac spasms, generalized cramps, muscular stiffness. In this case, "the sick person seems unable to 'demobilize his nerves.'" He is constantly tense, alert, between life and death. Thus one of them tells us: "You see, I am already as stiff as a corpse."[38]

Indeed, colonization appears not just as depersonalization but also as self-dispossession. The colonized person's body does not belong to him or her. Not that it belongs to the colonizer either, which is why he or she differs fundamentally from a slave. But it belongs to no one; it is property in escheat. This is, moreover, why it can form neither a social nor a political body. This phenomenon is both individual and collective. Henceforth, whether among slaves or colonized people, struggle resembles hand-to-hand combat. They die to their own bodies, ready to sacrifice their lives in order to preserve their selves. To fight is to "allow death to enter into [one's] soul."[39]

The psychoanalyst Didier Anzieu spoke of the "ego-skin" (*moi-peau*).[40] Certain psychoanalysts also believe there exists, psychically as well as physically, a second muscular skin. It would provide protection, a limit between the outside and the inside, when the epidermis can no longer fulfill this role—for example, in the case of physical aggression. In Algeria, Fanon observes the function of muscular reactions. Muscular contractions appear as a substitute for action itself. Tensed, the body acts without doing anything, obeying the double bind that characterizes colonial existence.

In dreams, therefore, animation and physical movement are the very figures of freedom. Whereas colonial oppression immobilizes, emancipation is all about moving. This is why Fanon brings up the odd tension of his colonized patients' sleep: "During colonization the colonized subject frees himself night after night between nine in the evening and six in the morning" in "muscular dreams," "action dreams," "aggressive dreams"; "I dream I am jumping, swimming, running, and climbing. I dream I burst out laughing, I am leaping across a river and chased by a pack of cars that never catches up with me."[41] In this unexpected first-person passage, Fanon presents the portrait of the colonized as fugitive, or in other words, as an escaped slave [*marron*]. This suggests that, as he sees it, the Algerian situation resembles what he knew of the history of Martinique, his home country. Although there remain considerable objective differences between Algeria and Martinique, the subjective reactions to oppression are similar. They are quite simply human reactions.

But not only that. Night contaminates the day just as myth contaminates experience. The aggressivity demonstrated in action dreams is also expressed in broad daylight. Internalized and repressed anger reappears in sensational ways. Murders, fights, and other crimes observed among the colonized people themselves are negations of reality within reality. They go so far as killing one another to show that they are free and alive, without knowing that this is why they do it. One passage from *Les damnés* is completely dedicated to extracting the internal logic from this mad phenomenon. We are very far from good sense, because it is good for nothing.

Consider one paradox: "Whereas the colonist or police officer can beat the colonized subject day in and day out, insult him and shove him to his knees, it is not uncommon to see the colonized subject draw his knife at the slightest hostile or aggressive look from another colonized subject."[42] The colonized person throws himself into acts of vengeance, Fanon says, "with his last muscles," the way one says "with all his might" ("*à corps perdu*"). These and other individual or collective forms of behavior or conduct that he witnesses are "reflexes of death in the face of danger."

Speaking of death reflexes is even more paradoxical because the very term implies that their goal, as reflexes, is to protect life. Myth is the only protection against this invasive aggressivity that affronts the colonized person's objective interests but also permits him or her, subjectively, to hold up and to continue hanging on to life. Only monsters and chimeras allow the colonized person to relativize the settler's power, insofar as this power always manifests itself in attitudes of omnipotence. "Zombies," writes Fanon, "believe me, are more terrifying than colonists. And the problem now is not whether to fall in line with the armor-plated world of colonialism but to think twice before urinating, spitting or going out in the dark."[43]

In his clinical approach, Fanon applies medicine to the colonized: the prone man exposed to everyone's looks. The etymological definition of the term *clinic* situates it in the same family as *bed* [*lit*], *resting*, and *leaning* [*incliné*]. Fanon applies it to the upright person, the fighter, who, in dreams or in reality, gets up to see a new day. "Relations with conflict, with life, all that I would like to call clinical psychology," said Freud.[44] Quite simply, the Algerian is on the ground instead of in bed. This is also expressed in the form of emotional trouble. A young man of twenty-two explains what is or what was on his mind in this way: "All I wanted to do . . . was to die. Even at the police station I believed and I hoped that after they tortured me they would kill me. I was happy to be beaten because that proved they considered me to be one of the enemy as well. . . . I am not a coward. I am not a woman. I am not a traitor."[45] Sometimes picking oneself back up has an exorbitant cost.

Making One's Voice Heard

Fanon makes the skin a complete organ to be restored and protected in both the physical and psychic senses, at once psychiatric and political. But he succeeded in this project through the voice, a phallic organ if ever there was one, and through what one might call the *invocative drive* [*pulsion invocante*]. Invocation is not demand: "In demand, the subject is in an absolutely dependent position relative to the Other, because he lends the Other the power to fulfill him or not. Demand is understood here as an absolute requirement placed on the Other to manifest himself here and now. On the contrary, the subject of invocation is removed from this dependence because he or she is no longer addressing a question to an other who would be there. Rather, what is invoked is an alterity whose emergence might summon a subject, a pure possibility, to take up the process of becoming."[46]

Fanon installed himself in the voice, the symbolic place par excellence. He dictated all his texts out loud while walking and moving, except his plays, which, strangely enough, he wrote down. The texts that made him an author were therefore written by others, always women taking dictation. In short, he "told" his texts and responded to a (bad) gaze with a (good) voice. This is how he successfully escaped the problematic of recognition. If the gaze cuts up the body and objectivizes it, the voice unifies it and gives it subjectivity. This response to the gaze constitutes an effective counteroffensive. The introduction to *Peau noire, masques blancs* reveals how much the shout [*cri*] is related to writing [*l'écrit*]. "I honestly think . . . it's time some things were said. Things I'm going to say, not shout. I've long given up shouting. A long time ago. . . . Why am I writing this book?"[47]

Thus in Fanon we find a double envelope, one written (like a skin) and one oral (like an invisible wrapper) that gave him back to himself in his ego and in his being, at the level of the universal. Fanon's intellectual style is one of tactfulness. Tact? The only one of the five senses that belongs to the cutaneous organ, that lets us judge certain qualities of bodies, such as their solidity or their fluidity, their humidity or dryness, their temperature, and so on. Tact includes two fundamental sensations: the sense of contact or pressure and the sense of temperature. From *tangere, to touch.* Medical touch—the ability to judge the character of a sickness and the appropriate responses.[48] This sense is unique in taking the place of sight for those who cannot see.

The black person is a body without organs, unless they are visible and therefore sexual. The colonized is a person without subjectivity. The black person and the colonized subject are nothing but exteriority. Their identity is declined in the third person, without making them into real subjects. With tact and hearing, necessary for any examination or consultation, interiority reappears, along with its dark humor or its bad blood. Organs and words take on meaning. Subjectivity is reborn from its colonial ashes. The first person can revive.

"I sincerely believe," Fanon confides, "that a subjective experience can be understood by someone else, and I dislike having to say that the black problem is my problem, and mine alone, before I set myself to studying it. . . . I am bound in this study to touch on the misery of the black man. *Tangibly and affectively.* I did not want to be objective. Besides, that would have been dishonest: I found it impossible to be objective."[49]

Notes

1. Translator's note: Voltaire's belief in the *reticulum mucosum*, a layer of tissue between the muscles and skin, discovered by seventeenth-century anatomist Marcello Malpighi and supposedly responsible for darkening the skin of Africans, is discussed in Curran, *Anatomy*

of Blackness, 121–22, 145–46. On Ruysch and the Russian legacy of his collection of specimens, see Kooijmans, *Death Defied.*

2. *Works of Voltaire*, chap. 267. See Voltaire, "Ignorance," in *Philosophical Dictionary.*

3. See her site, "Toyin Ojih Odutula." She presents her work in these terms: "Where some may see flat, static narratives, I see a spectrum of tonal gradations and realities. What I am creating is literally black portraiture with ballpoint pen ink. I'm looking for that in-between state in an individual where the overarching definition is lost. Skin as geography is the terrain I expand by emphasizing the specificity of blackness, where an individual's subjectivity, various realities and experiences can be drawn onto the diverse topography of the epidermis. From there, the possibilities of portraying a fully-fledged person are endless."

4. Geoffroy Saint-Hilaire (1772–1844) held the chair of zoology at the National Museum of Natural History starting in 1793. The following year he began a correspondence with Georges Cuvier, equally renowned founder of comparative anatomy. Eventually Saint-Hilaire switched from zoology to anatomy and, in 1815, asked for permission to examine the "Hottentot Venus." He wanted to observe "the distinctive traits of this curious race." For him, she had no face since he continually referred to her "muzzle," which was even larger than that of the red orangutan who inhabited the "greatest islands of the Indian Ocean." He compared "the prodigious size of her buttocks" to those of the mandrill ape. See Le Garrec, *Rapport*, 6–7.

Cuvier, who was named to the Collège de France in 1800, learned about Saartje Baartman's death before she could be buried by the civil state and had her body brought illegally to his anatomy laboratory, where he made a mold of her body, preserved her genital organs and her brain in formaldehyde, and finally carried out the extraction of her skeleton.

5. Kechiche, *Vénus noire.* Abdellatif Kechiche was a French filmmaker born in Tunisia. He made *La faute à Voltaire* (2000), *L'esquive* (2004), *La graine et le mulet* (2007), *Vénus noire* (2010), *La vie d'Adèle* (2013), and *Mektoub Is Mektoub* (2017).

6. In 1937, the mold of Baartman's body, her skeleton, and her organs (preserved in jars) were transferred to the Jardin des Plantes at the Trocadéro during the foundation of the Musée de l'Homme in Paris. The skeleton and the preserved organs were displayed to the public in the gallery of physical anthropology until 1974 among other skeletons, molds, and photographs of human beings from every continent. Then the mold was put on display for two years in the hall of prehistory. Stored after this in the warehouse, it came out one last time in 1994 on the occasion of the presentation of an exposition on "Ethnographic Sculpture in the 19th Century, from the Hottentot Venus to the Tehura of Gauguin," first at the Musée d'Orsay and then in Arles.

7. Loi no. 2002-323 of March 6, 2002, concerning France's restitution of the mortal remains of Saartje Baartman to South Africa. The demand for repatriation came from the organization representing the descendants of Khoisans, starting in 1994, during the Griqua national conference, whose president had called on the authorities of South Africa to this end. In 1999, during an archeology conference in Cape Town, he described the French intent thus: "The exhibition of her posterior and her genital organs to entertain the crowds of people having no heart violates the dignity of my people" (See Le Garrec, *Rapport*, 9). The descendants of Hottentot (Khoi) and Bochiman (San), former aboriginal tribes decimated by the Dutch, count no more than a few thousand citizens living, under precarious conditions, in the Kalahari Desert and in Namibia. Meanwhile this claim is largely shared within South African populations. Although the president of France, François Mitterrand, promised President Nelson Mandela to resolve the issue during his official visit to South Africa in 1994, the

repatriation was not carried out. In 2002, a precedent had been created by the repatriation of the mummy "El Negro" to the government of Botswana by Spanish authorities.

8. Perhaps the answer can be found the travel reports of a Frenchman, François le Vaillant (1753–1824), who visited the Hottentots (1783–85). At first, what interested him was the hypertrophy of the bottom lip and the steatopygy of women in the region. Later, he was interested in a certain Narina, and finding the local language very minimal, he explained that it was unnecessary to learn it, since the "pantomime" (*sic*) of natives permitted them to be understood well enough. When Saartje Baartman arrived in Paris, she was therefore preceded by a double representation that—as if by chance—associated women's sexual organs and muteness. To all appearances, women's sex was a mouth without words. See Ricard, *Le sable de Babel*, 50–2.

9. This is a chief concern of *Peau noire, masques blancs* (1952). See Fanon, *Black Skin, White Masks*, xv.

10. "The White Man's Burden: The United States and the Philippine Islands, 1899."

11. Fanon, *Black Skin, White Masks*, 142.

12. Fanon, *Black Skin, White Masks*, 97.

13. In fact this was his thesis in psychiatry, a thesis that was refused for its purpose and that was later published in 1952, under the title *Peau noire, masques blancs*. The book had a preface by Francis Jeanson (1922–2009), who, like Fanon, had fought during the Second World War alongside the Free French Forces. The work opened with a quotation from Aimé Césaire (*Discours sur le colonialisme*, 1950): "I am talking about millions of men whom they have knowingly instilled with fear and a complex of inferiority, whom they have infused with despair and trained to tremble, to kneel and behave like flunkeys" (Fanon, *Black Skin, White Masks*, xi).

14. In 1560 Juan Valverde published *L'anatomia del cuerpo humano*, a book born of double inspiration: on the one hand by Vesalius's *De humani corporis fabrica* (1543) and on the other by Michelangelo's painting of the torture (by flaying) of Saint Sebastian. In the image under discussion here, the écorché remains expressionless because his very face has been flayed.

15. "Personne, dit-il aussi, ne prend le scalpel et ne travaille à s'éclairer dans les entrailles du cadavre: on en est à peine, dans cette matière, aux idées de parties et de tout." Shaftesbury, *Essai sur le mérite*, 328.

16. Diderot, *Essais sur la peinture*, 13–14.

17. Diderot, *Héros et martyrs*, 431.

18. Sade, *Les cent vingt journées*.

19. Fanon, *Black Skin, White Masks*, 145.

20. Fanon, *Black Skin, White Masks*, 146.

21. Fanon, *Black Skin, White Masks*, 10.

22. Donald Winnicott (1896–1971) was an English pediatrician and psychoanalyst who is well known for his ideas on the true and false self and the transitional object. The false self is a defensive facade, a compliance with others' expectations (initially those of parents). "Other people's expectations can become of overriding importance, overlaying or contradicting the original sense of self, the one connected to the very roots of one's being." Winnicott, quoted in J. Klein, *Our Need for Others*, 241.

23. Fanon, *Black Skin, White Masks*, 2 (translation altered).

24. This discussion is found in the first chapter of *L'an V de la révolution algérienne (ou sociologie d'une révolution)*, published in 1959 by Maspero and translated as *A Dying Colonialism*.

25. Fanon, *Dying Colonialism*, 59 (translation altered).
26. Fanon, *Toward the African Revolution*, 27.
27. Fanon, *Black Skin, White Masks*, 95.
28. Fanon, *Black Skin, White Masks*, 89.
29. Fanon, *Black Skin, White Masks*, 92.
30. Fanon, *Black Skin, White Masks*, 93.
31. Mbembe, "De la scène coloniale," 40.
32. Fanon, *Dying Colonialism*, 65.
33. Fanon, *Wretched of the Earth*, 14.
34. Fanon, *Black Skin, White Masks*, 15.
35. Fanon, *Black Skin, White Masks*, 15.
36. Fanon, *Dying Colonialism*, 133.
37. Fanon, *Wretched of the Earth*, 219.
38. Fanon, *Wretched of the Earth*, 217–19 (translation altered).
39. Fanon, *Dying Colonialism*, 57.
40. Anzieu, *Le moi-peau*.
41. Fanon, *Wretched of the Earth*, 15.
42. Fanon, *Wretched of the Earth*, 17
43. Fanon, *Wretched of the Earth*, 19.
44. Letter to Fliess on January 30, 1899. See Roudinesco, *Jacques Lacan and Co.*, 218.
45. Fanon, *Wretched of the Earth*, 203–4 (translation altered).
46. Vives, "Pulsion invocante."
47. Fanon, *Black Skin, White Masks*, xi.
48. *Littré*, s.v. "tact," accessed November 3, 2018, https://www.littre.org/definition/tact.
49. Fanon, *Black Skin, White Masks*, 67 (my emphasis, translation altered).

2

HISTORY, AN INTERIOR ARCHITECTURE

Historiography, Psychiatry, Subjectivities

History with a Big H?

The practice of distinguishing "small" from "big" history might have been useful. However, it treats phenomena that can only be conceptually distinguished as if they were separate kinds. Historiography as we know it identifies the "great men" and leaves human beings anonymous. It rises above blood and tears to deliver a rational discourse on what has taken place. In scholarly history, everything happens as if the earth could be correctly apprehended only from a standpoint in the sky.

This is why it is so easy to say that one must not look at things through the wrong end of the telescope. It is also why we talk about history "with a big *H*." It might seem to be a question of scale. Since the seventeenth century, one speaks of scale in a figurative sense. Apart from cartography, *scale* means a series of levels and evokes the image of an army organized into hierarchical units. An army is composed of grades in which subgroups of a higher level contain others that are subordinate. Discrete ranks are involved: we find nothing between two rows.

This is the hierarchical model on which we have envisioned the history of humanity—from generals to infantry, from heroes to the unknown soldier, from subofficers to women in the field brothels. Of course, we cannot say how much general history owes, in its approach, to military history. Nor can we really measure the consequences of this bias. Without a catastrophe, the Jewish victims of the Third Reich would never have been named. Reference to the war ensured they were not buried under a number. Counting, in fact, amounts to forgetting.

Only after the demise of the colonial empires did people agree that individuals could no longer be entirely reduced to populations. This is a way of restoring life to subjects who had experienced complex situations that they both interiorized and transformed, usually without knowing they did so. Literature took responsibility for those who were easily ignored by formal history [*historiographies*], including the way they were psychologically affected by events and the consequences for their life trajectories, representations, practices, and customs.

Changing Scales

These effects and consequences were varied, numerous, unpredictable. A painter's agitation is explained by his father's antisemitism. In *L'intranquille*, Gérard Garouste tells how his father participated in the Aryanization of property during the Second World War. He unwinds the sinuous political and familial paths that led him to painting as well as to madness. The cover of his book reproduces a self-portrait. The author faces the reader. His red shirt is swelled as if he were concealing a hunchback. He carries a wolf's head in his right arm, while his lower body is reversed and advances from behind. "I am the son of a bastard who loved me. My father was a furniture salesman who collected the goods of deported Jews. Word by word, I had to disassemble the enormous lie of my education. I had my first attack of madness when I was twenty-eight, then others. I made regular stays in a psychiatric hospital. . . . For a long time I was nothing but a pile of questions. Today, I am sixty-three, I am not wise, I am not cured, I am a painter. And I think I can pass on what I have understood."[1]

A father's nationalism can also become a son's lasting exile. Thus in *L'écrivain*, it is with great accuracy that Yasmina Khadra describes "an Algerian childhood" among his cohort of junior officers at the very start of a former French colony's independence—one that, in his own terms, "deported" him to literature.[2] In a country that rested many of its hopes on its future army, because this is the indisputable proof of sovereignty, a child, submitted to severe discipline, separated from his loved ones, took shelter in the imaginary. The narrator confides: "I will rebel neither against the abuse of authority—which, moreover, could never make the officer I had become bend in any way—nor against the twist of fate that lavishly torments the novelist I am trying to be; in return, to the bitter end, I will have the titanic patience to always accept the arrival of whatever I cannot seek out."[3] Both respond to the question "Who am I?" and wonder about their own subjectivity. Khadra also writes: "My father replied with his Olympian calm that life was not just weeding, pruning, watering, and harvesting; that it was also painting, singing, and writing; and teaching; and that the most beautiful vocation was healing. His dearest wish was that I should become a doctor."[4]

We could thus examine what happens historically from above as well as from below, in a vertical and hierarchical way or one that is horizontal and democratic. A change of scale is needed: humanity is not a by-product of the army; it is not made of ranks. What has been surgically severed in a certain vision of events and subjects must be sutured back together. Thus, memory and history are not opposed to each other like subjective and objective perspectives.

In fact, objectivity is nothing without subjectivation.[5] But what does subjectivation mean? Autobiography, like history, can refer to fiction. But fiction is indissociable from the facts that it elaborates. This formulated or unformulated elaboration is what makes someone a subject. Subjectivation is a seam, a crossing of the border. In this sense, it creates an interworld [*entre-mondes*] that includes the facts outside a subject as well as the emotions found within.

Continuities are revealed at the level of subjects even when the most profound upheavals are taking place in the exterior world. From the pen of authors such as Yasunari Kawabata, Yukio Mishima, and others, lovers of Japanese literature were able to read the weight of a past that did not pass after the bombs of Hiroshima and Nagasaki, the defeat of 1945, the emperor's overthrow, and the advent of a new demilitarized country. The same thing happens everywhere.

Edward Said was right in saying that "to have been colonized was a fate with lasting . . . results."[6] In fact, fate was the perspective from which the ancient Greeks learned about the effects of history and of histories. Approaching historical facts not from on high and far off but from below and up close allowed their tragic dimension to be revealed. The Greeks uncovered the repetitions that are the most characteristic sign of history's unknown aspect.

The Oresteia: A Tragic Reversal

For example, Aeschylus dissects the sacrifices required by war in the trilogy of the *Oresteia*: *Agamemnon*, *Libation Bearers*, and *Eumenides*. The first performance took place in 458 BCE, just when Athens was becoming democratic and moderate democrats were being opposed to radical ones. It was by following the latter that Athens broke with Sparta. Thus, the theater was a social institution standing alongside political and judicial institutions. In theater, myth looks at itself through the citizen's eyes, but also through the eyes of a subject.

According to the myth, Agamemnon had to sacrifice his daughter Iphigenia so that the gods would send the starting wind enabling his fleet to sail to Troy. The playwright holds on to the familial dimension of the situation and portrays a father who has taken his daughter's life. The modernity of Aeschylus consists in his staging of history starting from the subjects themselves rather than, as in the myth, presenting the subjects on the basis of a history that goes beyond them. To be sure, the Greeks knew their myths. When they went to see noble actions and listen to lofty speeches at the theater, they already knew the tormented genealogy of Agamemnon and his cousin Aegisthus.

Thyestes, the father of Aegisthus, had seduced the wife of his brother Atreus, Agamemnon's father. In revenge, the latter made Thyestes eat his own children during a banquet. Repeating his father's act, Thyestes's son seduced Clytemnestra, the wife of his second cousin, Agamemnon. In the myth, Aegisthus assassinates Agamemnon with Clytemnestra's complicity. In the *Oresteia*, he is only Clytemnestra's passive accomplice. Orestes, Agamemnon's son, then avenges his father. He ends up with bloody hands before a "truth and reconciliation" commission, defended by the shining Apollo, judged by a jury over which Athena presides.

All of this shows that wars are also family conflicts. By inscribing individuals within a genealogy they have not chosen and within situations over which they are not masters, the Greeks explored the way that History (with a big *H*) is lived, not the way it looks. Today, more weight is given to the way that history is seen, except—paradoxically—in film. But history cannot be reduced to memories or to memory.[7]

The historical fact is something invisible to witnesses themselves. When the writer Malek Alloula recalled the independence of Algeria and Ben Bella's triumphal arrival in Oran, he added that the vast number of people prevented him from seeing anything. In its place, something is produced that goes far beyond perception.[8] The author dwells there, in the crowd and in the rejoicing—in an event that picks up and dashes away in one stroke all of French colonization, suddenly reduced to a dead letter.

The incarnation of a human life in historical temporality cannot be contained by what we usually call "historical context," unless what we mean by this expression is a surrounding and not a setting, an environment and not a background. A historical context exists only for the historian, the sociologist, or the philosopher. In experience, and subjectively, we are dealing with something completely different. If there is context, it is not just exterior and objective; it is above all interior and subjective. It is imaginative.

War Neuroses

But how is context inscribed in the subject? Historical facts register in the subject as an interior architecture. They do not spare the intimate sphere. "War neuroses" were discovered after the First World War. What became of the soldiers once peace was concluded? They no longer needed to face the enemy's image. Fear or horror no longer shielded them from reality, and the prospect of dying or of being hurt no longer blocked out the whole of experience. Demobilization was therefore a major event, and war left significant physical and psychological marks on those who participated in one way or another.

Colonial violence and the violence of the struggles that led to independence are inscribed in the flesh and blood of individuals who lived these situations. The psychiatrist Frantz Fanon was one of the first to discuss this, with reference to Algeria.[9] He paved the way for serious accounts of pathologies in the context of the colonies and during anticolonial warfare. He showed how muscular stiffening is a way of "playing dead" [*faire le mort*] when normal possibilities for living have disappeared. He does not treat Algeria as cardboard scenery with its sand dunes and its Bedouins, its beaches and cliffs, its *fatma* and leaden sun.[10] An active witness, Fanon sizes up the real country. Meanwhile, how many people recognized the mental wounds among those who were colonized?

After the First World War, physicians and psychiatrists, especially those in the military, were able to help those who had been damaged by combat and privation, even if only in a partial way. No such hope in a newly independent country: neither physicians nor psychiatrists were available. No theorists of psychic trauma. In Cameroon, in Algeria, everywhere that the struggles had been particularly long and especially bitter, there were no professionals who could manage the distress of the present on the basis of an accumulated body of knowledge. Winding down a war is both difficult and damaging. The junior officers whose conditions of existence Yasmina

Khadra described in postcolonial Algeria were for the most part war orphans. What became of them?

Colonization operated on the presumption that conquered lands were deserts belonging to no one and empty of any living souls. This schema is at work in every instance of colonization, past and present. Nomads are invented to get around the landowners. On the eve of independence, scorched-earth policies are among the colonizer's last weapons. They ensure no one will be available to govern, care, or educate—the three professions that are the most essential and most impossible because they rest on nothing but transmission. When the former military leaders take power, they run the country like a battalion and enlist absolutely everyone. Each opponent is considered as an enemy. Discipline must reign, just as during combat. Memory or history? Here one sees clearly that history is being not memorized but subjectivized.

To speak of history as an interior architecture is to speak of history without reducing it to memory, while extending it to imagination, perception, sensibility, and reason. If we were drawing up a geography of the faculties, the mind without memory might seem mutilated. But the silence of conquerors and victims shows that forgetting is the way life returns to those who believed they had lost it.

If history is to be an interior architecture, one must suppose the existence of an unconscious. Thus, representations also refer to drives. At the end of the First World War, Freud and others such as Karl Abraham, Ernest Jones, and Sandor Ferenczi distinguished banal peacetime neuroses from traumatic neuroses of wartime, the old peaceful ego from the new warrior ego.[11] What happens to the new warrior ego when peace returns?

It is wounded. The broken mouths [*gueules cassées*] must be heard in both the literal and the figurative sense. At the end of his studies in 1914, Otto Dix entered the artillery. He was designated a "degenerate artist" in 1933. *The Skat Players*, which he painted in 1920, shows three human beings seated at a café table playing cards. Every line in the painting is broken. The bodies are terribly decrepit. Shattered jawbones, ruined skin, various prostheses—a yellowish light shines over the suffering of these soldiers returned from the charnel house. Survivors, definitely, but also handicapped. The artist shows veterans with mutilated lower limbs—men who can no longer stand up on their own. He paints individuals with amputated upper limbs—these can no longer take anything in hand. Their movements are governed by the appliances they wear.

History need not be memorized to find a place of definitive inscription in the body. The psychoanalyst Karl Abraham drew attention to the case of a man psychically incapable of standing up (astasia) and of walking (abasia). Sandor Ferenczi conveyed his deep surprise at entering a hospital room reserved for victims of war neurosis. In the lecture he gave on the subject in 1916, he said he had the impression that every one of the fifty patients he encountered was an invalid. Moving about was very difficult for them.

The doctor emphasized that this symptomatology suggested the existence of serious damage to the central nervous system. Yet rigidity and muscular contractions were not always effects of a cerebral lesion but of an affective phenomenon—namely, terror. Hysterical conversion can be considered a manifestation of history once we conceive history as a way that subjectivity is structured. As Freud put it, "the one typical, that is regular—representation of the human person as a whole is the *house*."[12] Sometimes, however, it is more like the Tower of Pisa.

Because it was a political and sometimes military victory, independence from colonialism concealed the prior era's miseries and sufferings behind triumph, joy, and relief. In Indonesia, four years of armed conflict (1945—49) pitted the Dutch against their colony. The Indonesians refer to this war as *Revolusi*. Cameroon went through seven years of war (1955–62) before winning its independence. In Algeria, it took eight years of fighting (1954–62) before sovereignty was achieved. In Indochina, eight bloody years (1946–54) passed before a peace treaty was signed. In Angola, Guinea-Bissau, and Mozambique, conflicts broke out in 1961. They did not end until 1974, with the fall of the Portuguese dictatorship.[13] Thirteen years of battle—without leaving a trace?

The Army in Subversive War (*O exército na guerra subversiva*) is a collection of manuals providing guidance for the psychological war that the Portuguese were trying to wage in certain regions where "winning the population" (*conquista das populaçoes*) was crucial. Manipulation was thus established as a military strategy. These methods were conceived and set in motion precisely to reach subjects susceptible to different forms of pressure. In every case, the goal of the colonial power was to persuade targets that "the others" were lying, whether Frelimo or the FLN.

It takes a lot of effort to resist the intellectual uncertainty that this kind of operation can provoke. Today's Algerians accuse the *harkis* less of betraying the revolution than of showing weakness, for believing the political lies they were told.[14] "Stick with us, and you will be our equals": their later fate in French society showed how little these promises were worth.

Colonial violence, violence in the state of nature, reigns during war but also precedes it. It works through intrusion and intimidation. Even surveys, which seem to be peaceful, have an inquisitorial side. Colonial ethnography expects that the people it encounters will give themselves up, that they will completely hand over their subjectivity. Any refusal suggests an inclination to resist, and every evasion, treason. The survey becomes a kind of psychological war for appropriating information that can be gotten only through speech.

Several Forms of Intimidation: Threats and Retaliatory Measures

On the above point, there is no testimony more obvious than that found in Michel Leiris's *Afrique fantôme*. Here, the desire to know legitimates the wish to see others submit.[15] Like Marcel Griaule, Michel Leiris is impatient with his inability to get explanations for the meaning of masks he has just acquired. Questioning the guides does not really produce the desired information, and this irritates the interrogators. The fact that certain sites are sacred does not stop them from wanting to penetrate, observe, photograph, and record them.

The field journal of the expedition, which took place from 1931 to 1933, mentions the retaliatory measures that researchers took toward recalcitrant informers. At Fodébougou, Griaule reports the guides' behavior to the village chief. They lied to him, which he finds intolerable. He was looking for painted grottos (which Leiris calls "holes" in his text). First the guides said that none existed, and then they said that they were impossible to reach. Griaule therefore decided to give them only a very modest tip for their assistance, instead of paying fifty francs as he had intended.

These are clearly not commercial relations we are talking about here. These are power relations. Again, we see Griaule wanting to buy some slippers for twelve francs. One of his assistants has them made by a cobbler, who asks 12.50 francs instead. The assistant then discusses this with the cobbler since Griaule does not want to pay one penny more than he had decided on. The tone rises; the two negotiators come to blows. Griaule hints that they must resolve this conflict elsewhere, but they refuse. As a result, he lashes out with kicks at a witness and chases him away. The witness was a station employee who wanted to reconcile the two others. This scene reported by

Leiris repeats itself long afterward, even today, in the tourist zones of contemporary Tunisia and Morocco, very often during bitter discussions in which no more than a few centimes are at stake that the local merchant does not want to concede because he knows what they represent to the customer: almost nothing. But we are not actually talking about money. As a subject, Griaule is also a vector of power.

This anecdote shows the general nature of their exploratory mission from the Atlantic to the Red Sea, from Dakar to Djibouti. The slippers were forgotten in the course of travel across fifteen countries, but thirty-five hundred objects that the ethnologist brought back in his luggage were preserved at the ethnographic museum of the Trocadéro. In the course of the journey directed by Griaule, every step was marked by a cocktail or congratulatory meal with a colonial administrator and accompanied by informers.

When he was not doing ethnology, Griaule was making war. He enlisted for aviation in 1917, at the age of nineteen. Then he remained in the air force and participated from 1920 to 1921 in the Syrian campaign, whose goal was to place the region under French rule. In 1939, he was forty-one years old; he reentered the service to defend his country and returned to ethnology after demobilizing. He was remobilized from 1944 to 1946. Progressively he became, as was said at his death in 1956, the "friend of black people."

Did Africans Have a Postwar Period?

In Europe, one speaks of the immediate postwar period [*l'après-guerre*]. Can the same be said for Africans? Is their nature so different that they cannot also be affected by war neuroses? Freud characterized war neuroses, which he distinguished from traumatic neuroses, by the presence of an "inner enemy."[16] In the same era, Karl Abraham emphasized that identical symptoms need not correspond to identical processes. According to him, the survivors suffered from tremors, worries, irritability, vulnerability, insomnia, headaches, anxieties, depressive moods, and feelings of inadequacy. The test of an absolute self-sacrifice did not have the same consequences for everyone. Soldiers had to renounce all their narcissistic privileges. On the other hand, they had to show themselves prepared to kill.

This is a classic motif: the horrors of war must not conceal the honor in and of war. Thus, there were many soldiers from the colonies who ardently defended France against her German enemy and returned ready to lose their lives for their own freedom. For the historian Frederick Cooper, this indicated an opportunity:

> It was the Second World War that triggered the radical change in imperial structure. Even without the war, the system could have not have lasted indefinitely, but the scenario would have been very different. Hitler was the last of a series of emperors who tried to dominate Europe. Now the colonization of Africa was a consequence of the competition between Europeans. After 1945, this rivalry was weakened to the benefit of conflicts between the North and South and the East and West. All the uncertainties of the postwar moment opened the way for the political mobilization of Africans. The continent's political and social movements seized the chance.[17]

On May 8, 1945, Kateb Yacine was sixteen years old and in the *troisième* when he participated in nationalist demonstrations at Sétif.[18] At that time Sétif was a city with a majority Muslim population, just like Constantine, although this was not the case in Oran or Algiers. Three days later, the young man was arrested and detained for three months. He watched his mother go mad. Since he was expelled from his lycée, his father sent him to the lycée at Bône (Annaba).

There, he met "Nedjma" (the star), a married cousin with whom he had an affair lasting several months. In 1946, he published poems under the title *Soliloques* (in Bône) and then, in 1948, *Abdelkader et l'indépedence algérienne* (in Algiers). As Derrida says, "A hyphen is never enough to conceal protests, cries of anger or suffering, the noise of weapons, airplanes, and bombs."[19]

The struggle for independence and Algeria's effort to decolonize itself politically (as independence was established) constituted a real crisis of possession. Colonial occupation does not just take hold of the land and the body but is also, and maybe foremost, an occupation of the soul. The colonized subject must therefore take himself or herself back by reappropriating that land, body, and soul. In this sense, a crisis [*crise*] of possession is also an act of taking [*prise*] possession, which does not happen without evil, damage, or loss. While indispensable, independence should not be idealized and considered a solution in its own right. It is only the precondition for decolonization. When it is not a ritual, a crisis of possession is madness.

May 8 was also the day the Algerian writer was born. The French repression was merciless. "I was born to a wonderful mad mother. She was generous, simple, and pearls dropped from her lips. I gathered them without knowing their value. After the massacre, I watched her lose her mind.

Her, the source of everything. She threw herself into the fire, everywhere she could. Her legs, her arms, her head, were nothing but burns. I lived through that, and I flung myself straightaway into the madness of an impossible love for a cousin who was already married."[20]

Kateb Yacine published *Nedjma* in 1956; *Le cadavre encerclé* appeared in the journal *Esprit* in 1955.[21] In this play "in memory of a fallen youth," the wounded come to die in heaps of undifferentiated bodies in the street. An officer says: "One could say he lost his mind." His superior adds: "He is hopeless. He will have visions his whole life. He shouts like one possessed. When they see him, they will understand." Both are speaking of the play's hero, Lakhdar, who talks out loud to himself.

"Look at Lakhdar!" says a woman, who immediately adds: "I would have preferred to sit on his gravestone than to see him wander like a blind person or a madman. Pray to God that night finally closes over him."[22] At this moment, Kateb Yacine notes the stealthy approach of Tahar, who is hidden in the scene's background. He leaps on Lakhdar and stabs him.

Lakhdar's voice rises to save him: "I go down into the earth to revive the body that has never belonged to me, but in waiting for the resurrection, so that now Lakhdar has been killed, I can return from beyond the grave to give my funeral oration . . . so that the pull of the moon might raise me above my tomb with the widest possible wingspan."[23] If there is no war without a heap of bodies on the altar, neither is there war without madness and fury. To each his or her phantom.

Literature abandons the divine point of view and, schematically, that of reason in history. This loss is made up by an emphasis not so much on the viewpoint of hypostasized "Man" but rather on that of one man—or better, one human being in the grip of his or her demons. In countries where intellectual debate and academic criticism still lack a rightful place, historical questioning and reflection on historicity find their royal road along literary paths.

Yacine speaks through his megaphone, Lakhdar: "I feel universal oppression more keenly. Now that the least word weighs more than a tear, I see this country and I see that it is poor, I see that it is full of headless men. And I encounter these men one by one in my mind because they are ahead of us and there is no time to follow them."[24]

While critics cite Sophocles, Aeschylus, and Claudel, Kateb Yacine declares himself inspired by Shakespeare, because the latter put history onstage along with the incarnation of his own visions.

Decolonizing Psychiatry

In dedicating himself to psychiatry, Fanon entered into one of the most disreputable areas of practice in the medicine of his time. He transformed it from the inside, from the periphery. Thereby he showed that decolonization must be the work of subjects, and he introduced a subversive dissociation between political crime on the one hand and the psychiatry of order and social defense on the other. In *Damnés de la terre*, published in 1961, he observed the following fact: "Confronted with a world configured by the colonizer, the colonized subject is always presumed guilty."[25]

The criminalization of natives was institutionalized by the *code de l'indigénat*—improperly named, since in fact it was a list of measures [*mesures d'exception*]. Once it was codified, criminalization could be naturalized by psychiatry and managed jointly by the prison and the local authorities [*préfecture*]. Thus, this classificatory scheme had a policing side and a psychiatric side. Psychiatry took over from the police. Starting in 1834, administrative internment became the rule. It was applied, for example, to those trying to make their pilgrimage to Mecca without prior authorization.

In his 1974–75 course at the Collège de France, Michel Foucault highlighted the features of modern racism.[26] In Europe, this generic racism toward "abnormals" relied on psychiatry at the start of the twentieth century. It was dominated by an obsession with degeneration and the transmission of defects. One could easily read in this obsession the secular heritage of the problematic of original sin. Mental impairments, gullibility, suggestibility, weakness of emotional and moral fiber, criminal impulsiveness, tales that stage the clinical range of abnormalities among North Africans, the lack of synthetic capacity and cerebral laziness attributed to Africans, all signify the poverty, defectiveness, and, in a word, degeneracy of their subjectivity.

During the 1950s, the psychiatric hospital of Blida-Joinville was a colonial monument. Conceived in 1929 and opened in 1938, it was the work of psychiatrist Antoine Porot and architect Tony Garnier, both technical advisors to the government, who used the "favorable" context of the centenary of French presence in Algeria (1930) and the interest generated by the Colonial Exposition in Paris (1931) to push their project.

Antoine Porot, professor at the school of medicine in Algiers, had created the university psychiatric ward for the Mustapha hospital in Algiers after having built the first such ward for Tunis in 1912. His son Maurice also became a psychiatrist. The thesis topic he chose was *Les intoxications arsenicales par le vin et les produits viticoles* (*Arsenic Intoxications from Wine and Wine Products*). He oriented himself toward the European side of Algeria—its viniculture, its wine, its intoxications.

Colonial psychiatry, or what is known as the psychiatric school of Algiers, defends theses regarding "the morbid impulse among North Africans"—in other words, the criminal impulse of the native. In French thought, the criminalization of the Arab, staged in Camus's *L'étranger*, is ancestral. In 1896, for example, in his essay on "L'alienation mentale chez les Arabes," Meilhon affirmed that "the dominant feature of Arabs' madness is their tendency to violence":

> The important military contribution required of North Africa, the response of entire classes to recruitment campaigns, have made us aware of the real indigenous mass, a formless bloc of primitives who are for the most part profoundly ignorant and credulous, very distant from our mentality and our reactions and who have never understood the least of our moral concerns, nor the most elementary of our social, economic, and political preoccupations. All at once, we had to take stock of the entire moral resistance posed by certain simple souls, the powerful force of certain mental deficits and the deviancies imprinted by credulity and suggestibility.

There is no ambiguity in Porot's conclusions: "The colonizer's reluctance to give responsibility to the *indigène* is therefore not a matter of racism or paternalism but quite simply a scientific appreciation for the biologically limited possibilities of the colonized."[27]

The therapeutic failures at Blida-Joinville can therefore be explained. No linguistic or cultural pathway was put in place to comprehend the patients. The inmates were approached with one-size methods and entirely in the French language. They therefore remained foreign to anything that was proposed to them for their own good and imposed on them in the name of scientific universality. The practice itself, in widening the gap rather than filling it in and closing it up, confirmed once again the theory according to which "with these types, there is nothing to understand."

The hospital's inhabitants lived in madness, but neither could they avoid living in war and politics—in the history of their own world. How many of the few local psychiatrists were their allies? At the time, the best known were the Senegalese Seydo Tall and Amoussou as well as the Nigerian Thomas Adeoye Lambo.[28] The first to propose grounds for anticolonial psychiatry were Frantz Fanon in Algeria and then Henri Collomb in

Senegal. Collomb had also been able to observe neuroses among the *tirailleurs sénégalais*, a certain number of whom finished their careers in psychiatric hospitals.[29]

Explaining, Interpreting, Translating

The Time of Phantoms

Human subjectivity is historicized in many ways, in a range of relations that extend from the familial and personal universe to the political and public sphere. Developing a chronology is difficult, in this respect, because dates must be taken from multiple registers that are often objectively independent from one another. The birth of a brother or a sister can be placed on the same plane as a historical event that does not just involve an individual's siblings, but engages his or her entire world in one way or another.

Psychoanalytic practice is no stranger to these bizarre conjunctions in which facts having no subjective link between them nonetheless contribute as building materials to the psyche's very constitution. Freud's writings on the individual and the collective were completely misunderstood. He did not believe psychology stopped at the artificially created boundaries of private life. The barriers between individual and collective are superficial and illusory. In each of us, the common and the particular are mixed in different ways.

But even if historiography imposes the continuity of a possible storyline, this does not mean that subjects all belong to the same historical time. Thus, Dipesh Chakrabarty observes that "although the non-naturalness of the discipline of history is granted, the assumed universal applicability of its method entails the further assumption that it is always possible to assign people, places, and objects to a naturally existing, continuous flow of historical time. Thus, irrespective of a society's own understanding of temporality, a historian will always be able to produce a time line for the globe, in which for any given span of time, the events in areas X, Y, and Z can be named."[30] Instead of admitting that we do not all belong to the same historical time, we have wrongly claimed that not all belong equally to history.

Because it situates facts in a universal time, scholarly history generally gives more significance to ruptures and to periods. Having no need for a chronology that the entire planet could share, psychoanalysis privileges continuity and goes beyond temporal boundaries. Historiography, for its part, elaborates such boundaries and maintains them in the name of objectivity. It relies on distance and nonintimacy between the speaking subject and the object of which he or she speaks (even if this object is another subject), between the finished past and the present in the process of passing.

For the historian there are no phantoms. On the contrary, for the psychoanalyst as for any other subject, palpable, affective phantoms appear, but they do so on another stage and weave the very text of spoken subjectivity. On November 11, 1991, Moze attended commemoration ceremonies for the armistice of the First World War in his village of Oise. Then he went to drown himself. He was Zahia Rahmani's father. Having become a *harki* in 1958, he was arrested at the end of July 1962 and then "displaced" within France in 1967.

Zahia Rahmani observes that "certain families [of *harkis*] preferred to *drown themselves* in French society."[31] History structures subjectivity and forms a kind of architecture there because it is always interiorized. This is why war neuroses have a meaning even if they are not exclusively caused by war. This is why mental illnesses have a political signification even if they are not exclusively produced by politics.

One can therefore see things from two different angles and, following Michel de Certeau, differentiate between two ways of "distributing the *space of memory*."[32] Psychoanalysis recognizes the past in the present, in the mode of imbrication or of repetition, of equivocation or a quid pro quo. Historiography considers them as separate, in the mode of succession or correlation, effect or disjunction. Involvement, repetition, equivocation, and substitution versus succession, correlation, effect, and disjunction.

In Bergsonian terms, schematically, psychoanalysis is on the side of duration and its thickness; it interprets. Scholarly history finds itself on the side of time and its linearity; it explains. Psychoanalysis is translation; historiography is writing. Their common point is to actualize the past, to bring it to light and bring it up to date—but not using the same methods. The word, the sentence, and the text constitute historiographic discourse. This discourse is not entirely unproblematic.

Thus Dipesh Chakrabarty explains how historiography grasps the fact that Indian peasants invoke gods to explain their revolt. The historian will feel obliged to translate this declaration "into some kind of context of understandable (that is, secular) causes animating the rebellion." And to ask: "How do we conduct these translations in such a manner as to make visible all the problems of translating diverse and enchanted worlds into the universal and disenchanted language of sociology?"[33] Such translation involves signification and subjectivation.

Interpreting Rather Than Explaining?

A subject's relationship with history—in other words, a certain type of subjectivation—can be described in many ways. We must still determine which is most relevant. Each in his own fashion, Nietzsche, Freud, and Marx created new foundations for the possibility of a hermeneutic by proposing new kinds of interpretation. Three of these seemed noteworthy to Foucault.[34]

First, interpretation is a process fated to remain incomplete. Second, every sign is itself the interpretation of other signs. Finally, interpretation itself must be interpreted. "Interpretation," Foucault said, "does not clarify a matter to be interpreted, which offers itself passively; it can only seize, and violently, an already-present interpretation, which it must overthrow, upset, shatter with the blows of a hammer."[35]

Interpreting is not a linear process but a circular one that loops back on itself. It demands a return. It has no beginning; it does not lead to an end. It is reflexive. Interpretation has therefore exactly the same characteristics as translation. During the discussion that followed Foucault's lecture, Clémence Ramnoux was on the right track.[36] Indeed, religious interpretation is inscribed in a meaning more than in a sign. But, she also stresses, religious exegesis is nothing but a history of translations, adding judiciously that "there must have been some sort of medical relationship between Freud and Nietzsche by way of Lou Salomé."[37]

During the same discussion, Arion Lothar Kelkel very aptly raises the possibility that interpretive techniques may be therapeutic techniques of healing at their root.[38] To this remark, Foucault responds that, in fact, health has replaced salvation, thus linking Nietzsche (but also Freud and, in a different respect, Marx) in his concern for health and in his obsession with illness.

Nietzsche made historical culture into a distinctive morbid symptom of his time. Like translation, interpretation can also be revealed as a specific kind of treatment and care for the self. Like all subjectivity, but in a more acute fashion, postcolonial subjectivity is indecipherable at first glance. To be sure, it includes the specific signs linked to lived events and experiences, to singular interiorizations that, in the strong sense, determine ways of acting and thinking.

The opacity of this sort of subjectivity appears at two levels, colonial and local, which form it and inform it. Opacity is also an aspect of the inferiorization resulting from racialization. This is one of the chief arguments of *Peau noire, masques blancs*. Racial inferiorization cannot be reduced to inequality; not, above all, when it is manifest in the denial of subjects' symbolic status and their destitution as subjects. When subjects are not considered complete in and of themselves [*à part entiére*], one easily forgets what has happened to them, no matter how serious the facts.

For example, the concentration camp, made possible with the introduction of barbed wire, is a colonial invention. It was adopted by the Spanish in Cuba, during the war of independence (1895–98), with the name of *reconcentración*. The British used it in South Africa during the Second Boer War (1899–1902) opposing former settlers who wanted independence and new colonizers. The Spanish general Valeriano Weyler y Nicolau turned deportation and concentration into a military technique for struggling against rebellions.[39] He was followed by the English generals Frederick Roberts and Lord Kitchener, who locked up Boer women, children, and the elderly as well as "African natives."[40]

A photograph shows a skeletal young white Boer girl, Lizzie van Zyl, almost naked on a bed, with a distant gaze, before her death in Bloemfontein concentration camp. This girl did not understand English and was considered mentally deficient. Some detainees were burned. Broken glass, razor blades, and fishhooks were mixed into their rations. These cruel acts could be explained. But one might also interpret them: sadism ruled in these camps. The ordinary colonial practice of torture obeyed the same logic: it was not a matter of extracting information by violence but of showing the victims who was master.

Because methods circulated between colonies, the model of the camp was exported to Namibia. Starting in 1904, the Germans sought to exterminate the Hereros under the authority of General Von Bülow, who sent them to new concentration camps.[41] There "anthropological," "scientific," and "medical" experiments were carried out. Created for the colonies, the concentration camp became generalized and was then exported back to Europe. Though it went unremarked for a long time, this is not the only case in which a colonial apparatus was imported into Europe.

Subjectively speaking, the step of historical objectivation is necessary, for it allows things to be established that would otherwise remain in the limbo of imagination. But it is also insufficient, precisely to the extent that nothing but the self can ultimately take care of the self. As Paul Ricœur says, "the historian's profession has seemed to us to be sufficient to distinguish between the good and bad subjectivity of the historian. Perhaps the responsibility of philosophical reflection would be to distinguish between the good and the bad objectivity of history. For reflection constantly assures us that the *object* of history is the human *subject* itself."[42]

In this way, Ricœur distinguishes epistemological concern and ethical-cultural concern and clarifies what one ought to be able to expect from historiography: "We expect history to be a history of men, one which helps the reader who is instructed by the historian's history to achieve a high level of subjectivity—not just a personal subjectivity but that which is proper to mankind."[43]

The achievement of national independence is subjectively and empirically comparable to emigration. It is a kind of exile, a change of world. How can the reality of the old world be lived in the new one? How can one live and speak except using the imagination of that old world? How can its reality be spoken in the new world? Translation is doubly difficult because the colony is a multilingual space dominated by one language, a European language—it is the very language of domination.

Translating the Past into the Present

The work of decolonization includes freeing oneself from European languages, by abandoning them or by reappropriating them. In either case, discursively, the movement of passage from one world to another is an act of translation. A phenomenon once formulated linguistically can be understood in anthropological terms.

Translating is always complicated, involving multiple elements, and its grounds can be grasped in two ways. The first approach, put forward by Antoine Berman in *L'épreuve de l'étranger*, considers translation to be the transfer of a verbal message from one language to another.[44] The other, inspired by Georges Steiner in *After Babel*, regards translation as the interpretation of any meaningful set of elements within a single linguistic community.[45] According to Steiner's formula, the diversity of languages results in a harmful prodigality. One must continually avoid intoxication. To translate is to compare the incomparable, to find equivalence without identity. Thus, we can think about the very relationship of subjectivation to history using the language of translation and interpretation, rather than in terms of memory and recollection.

Translation moves from the whole to the part. This is why Paul Ricœur can say that the glossary manifests the impossibility of translating. The untranslatable exists only with respect to dictionaries. Likewise, one must approach the subject starting from history, rather than moving from the subject to a kind of history that, as in certain historical novels, all too often turns out to be a (prefabricated) theatrical setting. In the depths of any given language, transitions take place from one language to another language or from one word to another.

Meanwhile, tradition has given the scholarly historian the general role of a witness and judge, rather than that of a translator and interpreter. Perhaps this is because words, like principles, are invented by those who are dominant (in order to dominate). By contrast, it would be better for the translator or interpreter to figure out who he or she is than to become forgotten in his or her project, thereby reviving the ancient Delphic injunction to "know thyself."

Others have already observed the same, albeit in a different fashion and in other contexts. In fact, this is what motivates Gayatri Chakravorty Spivak's denunciation of "intellectuals [who] represent themselves as transparent" and whose position "valorizes the concrete experience of the oppressed, while being so uncritical about the historical role of the intellectual."[46] She challenges someone like Deleuze or Foucault on this point. In this context, the question *who* takes on primordial significance.

Foucault recognized this, even if he did not apply it to himself: "Interpretation will henceforth always be interpretation by 'whom?' One does not interpret what is in the signified, but one interprets after all; *who* posed the interpretation. The basis of interpretation is nothing but the interpreter, and this is perhaps the meaning that Nietzsche gave to the word 'psychology.'"[47]

Between science and fiction, according to Michel de Certeau, Freud "alters the historiographical 'genre' of writing by introducing the need for the analyst to *mark his place* (his affective, imaginary, and symbolic place). He makes this explicitness the condition of possibility of a form of lucidity, and thus substitutes for 'objective' discourse (a discourse that aims to express the real) a discourse that adopts the form of a 'fiction' (if by 'fiction,' we understand a text that openly declares its relation to the singular place of its production)."[48]

One might wonder what is said when the speaker does not know his or her situation, does not integrate that place, and does not work through it. An example a contrario: the American philosopher Michael Walzer opens his book *On Toleration* with some personal considerations.[49] He stresses that as an American Jew and as an object of toleration by others, he is nevertheless also subject to situations in which he can agree or refuse to tolerate someone else. With great simplicity, this explanation opens a perspective, namely of reciprocity. In doing so, Walzer places fiction at the heart of his analysis and in its interstices. But nothing is worse than listing off identities as alibis.

Historiography is a political science. For the historian, as for the political scientist, a war has its dead, its disappeared, its wounded. They are neither brothers nor sisters, neither parents nor children. Without names, their wounds remain wide open. The historian leaves them unburied—indeed, he digs them up. Thus, the facts, or whatever can be known of them, remain unsettled, with no interpretation or therapeutic translation to lift the weight that phantoms from the past impose on those still alive. New historiographical research, particularly the collection of testimony, strives ingeniously to repair this torn fabric, to integrate ordinary speech with erudite discourse. More and more frequently, historiography is constructed from below. Nonetheless, as Freud said, the novelist "has from time immemorial been the precursor of science."[50]

The Elementary Data of Unconsciousness

The unconscious is not found among the data of scholarly history. It is an elementary given of consciousness and the core of literature. Like psychoanalysis, literature has no proper or natural place. As Michel de Certeau observes, "When 'scientificity' creates a place for itself by eliminating what does not conform to it, Freudian analysis perceives the alterity haunting and without being aware, determining this appropriation; it demonstrates the contradictory games which occur in the same place, between the manifest and the hidden; between what is manifest and what is hidden; it diagnoses the ambiguity and plurality of this very place. From this point of view as well, it has more in common with the novel."[51] One's sensitivity to archival material changes depending on the place from which it was spoken or written. The very use of archives changes according to their implications.

These archives are also found in the folds and twists of subjectivity, forming a discreet and sometimes secret history whose outline is not visible from outside, whose chapters and paragraphs are not immediately provided with suitable titles. The lapses that may be produced by what is not said or is even denied may last a long time, with deleterious consequences. In the case of France, amnesty was also a significant factor in amnesia and therefore of "gangrene": public criminal law relied on and called for the forgetting of crimes. For example, on July 31, 1968, Parliament declared an amnesty regarding all violations of law committed during the Algerian War.

What a long road we have had to travel from the gangrene and forgetting of the Algerian War to its eventual exploration![52] The National Assembly's recognition of the very existence of a war on October 18, 1999, was hardly a small step. The "Algerian events" had long ago fizzled out. But undoubtedly it was less a matter of forgetting, as Ann Laura Stoler has pointed out, than of aphasia.[53] Elsewhere I have defended the idea that colonial history often functioned as a family secret, subjectively but also politically and individually.[54] The notion of family secret brings us back to the family complexes in which silences, denials, and lies are elaborated and transmitted, and which have their own relation to history (in the capital *H* sense).

In a way it is thanks to psychoanalysis that Ismaÿl Urbain's role in Algeria has been studied by his descendants.[55] Illegitimate son of a man from Marseille whose family name became his own first name and of a free woman of color from Guyana, he discovered Saint-Simonianism, converted to Islam, and gave himself a true first name. Having learned Arabic in Egypt, he became an interpreter in Algeria, and in 1840, he married an indigène woman, as his father had done previously. He became an advisor to Napoleon III and one of the architects of his Arab policy. The colonists, those who would later be called colonialists, considered him an enemy and regarded him as inventor of the "Arab kingdom."

To defend its status, historiography pushed affects outside its field of investigation, justifying this rejection first formally and then implicitly by reference to their subrationality and their individual character. Historiography also takes up the celebrated Latin maxim *minima non curat praetor* (leaders don't bother with the details). Acts of colonial violence, for example, were directed against people whose status as persons had disappeared into the mass of "race" or the "*indigénat.*" They contributed to the manufacture of an undifferentiated "body of exception," neither young nor old, neither man nor woman.[56]

This is why decolonization implies the restoration of subjectivities negated in the colony and left on the sidelines by historiography. The meaning of being colonized comes through in a portrait, not in a table or chart. Albert Memmi understood this well when, in 1957, he produced a *Portrait du colonisé* and a *Portrait du colonisateur*.[57] He tried to make subjects stand out from an ocean of racialized undifferentiation. Discussion must therefore begin with the processes of subjectivation proper to the subjects in question, rather than assuming at the outset a relationship whose elements are not examined with precision.

Under the term *colonizers* [*colonisateurs*], common sense throws the civilian and military colonials together with the settlers, all of whom occupy incomparable positions, just as it lumps their opponents together under the global category of *colonized subjects* [*colonisés*]. The differentiations can be approached only under certain circumstances. Even today, we are reluctant to get into distinctions whose mention seems inevitably to displace the point of view from which something is considered and render verdicts more difficult to pronounce. Lightness of tone and an imprecise manner of speaking are found in discourses that minimize the colonial phenomenon just as they are in efforts to dramatize it.

This manner of speaking and this tone are symptoms. Sometimes they equalize, in a "scientific" way, two incommensurate points of view: the standpoint of those who benefited from colonial domination and the standpoint of those who, quite to the contrary, suffered the devastating effects of this same domination. As a result, these points of view, along with their associated memories, are put on equal footing with the ease of someone who is neither committed to a side nor implicated by the colonial affair in any way, someone who treats its questions in books and scholarly discourses whose only outcome may well be a terminological quarrel. The deformation of plural memories so often invoked by specialists conceals the profound deformation of lives produced indirectly or directly by the colony.

The Retaliatory Cycle

The first vector of deformation involved the explicit promotion of violence. Colonial violence cannot simply be reduced to acts of aggression against persons. Following the reflections developed by Jacques Derrida in *Force de loi*, Achille Mbembe has traced "colonial sovereignty" back to three sorts of violence: violence that poses and authorizes the right of conquest and everything following from it, violence that legitimates this conquest and gives it a language, and finally, violence that assures its upkeep and preservation.[58] Massacre is widely employed in the last case: Sétif (May–June 1945), Haiphong (1946), Madagascar (1947), Casablanca (1947), Côte d'Ivoire (1949–50).

Having studied them extensively, Yves Benot does not try to do a history of the massacres perpetrated in the "Union française" between 1944 and 1950, but rather "to undertake a reflection that simultaneously addresses the persistence of colonialist ideology in France itself, even today, and on the equally contemporary resistance that this ideology provoked and continues to provoke in France."[59] Beginning with the first of these massacres, namely the one at Sétif in 1945, Benot follows the convention of trying to assess the number of victims on each side, but then he wonders: "In the end, is it useful to continue polemicizing on grounds that one might call strictly arithmetical? . . . After all, this is not a question in accounting."[60] Likewise, violence as such can be made to fade away by focusing on its functionality: rebellion, repression, prevention, precaution, and so on.

This violence lingers on. How many postcolonial wars have followed on the heels of anticolonial wars? In Nigeria, for example, the Biafran war raged from July 1967 to January 1970 in a country that had only been independent since 1960. How many military coups d'état? *Putsches* and their subsequent abuses are rife. In Togo, Gnassingbé Eyadéma deposed Sylvanus Olympio in 1963. In Algeria, in 1965, Houari Boumediene took power by force and replaced Ahmed Ben Bella. In Zaire, Mobutu Sese Seko pushed out Joseph Kasa-Vubu. In the Central African Republic, 1966, Jean Bedel Bokassa removed David Dacko. That same year in Nigeria, Johnson Aguiyi-Ironsi overthrew Nnamdi Azikiwe. He was immediately relieved by Yabuku Gowon. In Mali, Moussa Traoré pushed aside Modibo Keïta in 1968. These are just some examples—the days after independence are belligerent and militarized. A country abandoned to power relations, to every expression of force, to what Kateb Yacine called the retaliatory circle, has difficulty escaping this vicious pattern.

Literature is less obviously political and also less vulnerable to censorship and dogmatism than the writing of national histories. This is the reason why, as we have seen, it can give a more significant place the processes of subjectivation we previously analyzed in terms of translation and interpretation. Thus, Algerian literature in the French language has its versions of Antigone. Antigone, the paradigmatic tragic character, tries to bury her brother properly and to protect his corpse from wild animals despite the orders of her uncle Creon. In so doing, Antigone embodies the feminine attitude itself, by convention to be sure, but also in an exemplary way. In Max Weber's terminology, she incarnates the "ethic of conviction" with respect to the "ethic of responsibility."

Consider Assia Djebar.[61] She wanted to pursue philosophy before entering the École Normale Supérieure but later chose history, for political reasons. In essence, she passed from investigation of the real to analysis of the past, and from this to the elaboration of fictions. In the end, wishing to be a director, she could complete only two films in her mother country and finished by dedicating herself exclusively to literature. Here is how she speaks of Algeria as a "blank page": "A nation seeking its own ceremonial, in different forms, but from cemetery to cemetery, because, first of all, the writer has been offered as propitiatory victim: strange and despairing discovery!"[62] This text is a reflection on the murderous violence of the civil war that Algerians call "the black years," lit by the specter of the War of Independence, which was also fratricidal in its own way.[63]

The writer seems to have an action to realize, a mission to accomplish. Undoubtedly, she feels a duty or a debt. The attitude of the one who speaks, and speaks in the first person, reveals suffering that was directly or indirectly engendered by the colonial violence that she experienced. It proclaims a difficult birth. For the colony is a kind of society more or less entirely given over to a regime of ordinary violence, in this case a violence sponsored by the state.[64]

Violence cannot be presented exclusively in terms of the actions exercised by some over or against others. Neither can it be described uniquely from the side of the agent, unless, thanks to fiction, the author introduces a perspective permitting deeds to be imagined not only from the point of view of the armed party who exercises violence, but also from that of the one on whom it is exercised. This is what Didier Daeninckx tries to do, for example, in *Ceinture rouge* and in *Corvée de bois*. The writer thus effects a double displacement: first from the action to its consequences (to show exactly how they follow from the action), and second from the one who dominates to the one who is dominated.

Acknowledging the subjectivity of all those who suffered oppression is necessary if we are to understand that politics is a matter of human life and not of populations. In a state of exception such as the colonial state, norm and life come apart, and violence is confused with right or law. Giorgio

Agamben has shown that the state of exception provides government with a paradigm. For this reason he distinguishes between authority and power. He writes: "The juridical system of the West appears as a double structure, formed by two heterogeneous and yet coordinated elements: one that is normative and juridical in the strict sense (which we can for convenience inscribe under the rubric *potestas*) and one that is anomic and metajuridical (which we can call by the name *auctoritas*)."[65] The state of exception is a general regime of disconnection, particularly symbolic disconnection. This is why, as the philosopher puts it, "the only truly political action . . . is that which severs the nexus between violence and law."[66]

Violence, the key to decolonization, can be understood in many ways, as armed struggle, but also as internal combat against an interior enemy. Decolonization can thus be understood both as a healthy process and as a morbid phenomenon, naturally melancholic, leaving subjects without refuge and without shelter.[67] In fact, independence does not mean one miraculously feels back at home. As a political program, decolonization is also a matter of public health. However, mental health was far and away the most neglected task at the black dawn of independence.

For decolonization to succeed, one must therefore explore the interior architecture of subjects who found their existence, or that of their parents and grandparents, arbitrarily suspended by a foreign power. We will then discover postcolonial pathologies just as Fanon revealed colonial pathologies. Then too, it will be possible to understand certain objective difficulties. In so doing, we will also be able to leave room not just for the *historical dimension* but for *historicity*, and better grasp the temporalities by which we are driven. For example, the Maori think that the future is behind them. This is a way of saying that events, in the word's ordinary sense, are formed by our expectations, our experiences, our interests, and our hopes. It is also a way of saying that our life flows only in the present.

Notes

1. Garouste and Perrignon, *L'intranquille*, back cover.
2. Khadra, *L'écrivain*.
3. Khadra, *L'écrivain*, 117.
4. Khadra, *L'attentat*, 106.
5. The idea of subjectivation to which I am appealing is largely drawn from psychoanalysis. For Freud, the notion of the subject (*Subjekt*) is bound up with the (unconscious) destiny of the drives (notably their repression, reversal on the self, or reorientation

toward a new goal). For example, he will speak about the narcissistic subject (*narzisstische Subjekt*). To be sure, sublimation is doubtless the most socialized form of subjectivation, because it is a conscious act of symbolization. Denial, splitting, and derealization are also forms of subjectivation that render the subject of the drive a "subjected" subject (Lacan). The synthesis—*Wo es war, soll ich werden* (Freud), or "There where it was, I must come to be [*advenir*]"—is certainly the pithiest synthesis of the idea of subjectivation. Therefore, this idea refers both to an internal and largely unconscious elaboration and to an indefinite process—a becoming subject. Analysis, for Freud, participates in this process by permitting the subject to reach the kernel of his or her truth through the interpretation of his or her actions, thoughts, and affects—the disclosure of the relationship between the intrapsychic and the intersubjective. If psychoanalysis is a metapsychology, psychoanalytic work is a metasubjectivation. This singular work allows us to understand that, as the psychoanalyst René Major has stressed, "the unconscious is no longer simply outside of consciousness. It is parasitic on consciousness. Pleasure is no longer totally opposed to displeasure. It can be felt as suffering and suffering as a satisfaction. The subject seeks itself and finds itself; which is not, in itself, a contrary. It is not a pure present in relation to what has already passed. The past is present in the present and the present always already past. The origin is already delayed and the delay, therefore, is originary." From Major, "Derrida," 167.

6. Said, *Reflections on Exile*, 294.

7. See Lorcin, *Algeria, 1800–2000*; Giordano, *Autour de la mémoire*.

8. Personal communication. Malek Alloula (1937–2015) was an Algerian writer and poet who used the French language. He published numerous works, notably *Le harem colonial*, which opened the way to many studies of colonial eroticization.

9. See, later, Sigg, *Le silence*.

10. Fatma or Fatima is an Arab first name that became, under colonialism, a common noun: a *fatma* was a Muslim woman.

11. Ferenczi et al, *War Neuroses*. See also Winnicott, *Les enfants*. Karl Abraham (1877–1925) was a medical doctor and one of the founders of psychoanalysis. A surgeon during the First World War, he described both physical and psychic trauma syndromes. He worked on mania, melancholia, mourning, and war neuroses. Ernest Jones (1879–1958) introduced and institutionalized psychoanalysis in the United States by creating the American Psychoanalytic Association (1911) and in Great Britain by creating the London Psychoanalytic Society (1913). He was Freud's first biographer. He also took an interest in war neuroses after the First World War and made rationalization into a defense mechanism. Sandor Ferenczi (1873–1933) was a psychiatrist and psychoanalyst. He was particularly interested in narcissistic pathologies and introduced two fundamental concepts, those of introjection and identification with the aggressor.

12. "The range of things which are given symbolic representation in dreams is not wide: the human body as a whole, parents, children, brothers and sisters, birth, death, nakedness—and something else besides. The one typical, that is regular—representation of the human figure as a whole is a *house*, as was recognized by Scherner, who even wanted to give this symbol a transcendent importance which it does not possess." See lecture 10 of Freud, *Introductory Lectures on Psycho-Analysis*, 153.

13. In 2014 a very beautiful film was dedicated to these conflicts by the Swedish director Göran Hugo Ollsson, who drew on Swedish television archives and also on Fanon's *Wretched of the Earth*. At the start was this quotation: "Colonialism is not a machine capable of think-

ing, a body endowed with reason. It is naked violence and only gives in when confronted with greater violence." Fanon, *Wretched of the Earth*, 23.

14. The *harkis* (*haraka* means movement, activity) were drawn from the mobile groups of rural police put in place by Jacques Soustelle in 1955 among French of Muslim origin. After these "civilian goums", there were "military goums" active on the ground starting in 1955 and officialized the following year. The increase in the number of *harkis* reflected the psychological aspect of the war and was intended to show that the nationalists were still very much the minority. (Translator's note: A *goum* or *goumier* was a North African soldier under the command of French army officers, sometimes also nominally in the service of a local ruler.) See Hautreux, "L'engagement des harkis."

15. Leiris, *Phantom Africa*. In 1930, Michel Leiris was invited by the ethnographer Marcel Griaule to join the team that he formed for an almost two-year trip across Africa, from Dakar to Djibouti.

16. Ferenczi et al, *War Neuroses*.

17. Cooper, "Afrique: Équivoques indépendances," 40.

18. Translator's note: The *troisième* is comparable to the last year of middle school in the United States.

19. Derrida, *Monolingualism of the Other*, 11.

20. Khelifi, *Kateb Yacine*, 13.

21. Kateb Yacine, *Le cadavre encirclé*. "All the Arabs will wear wigs of black fiber. Their color will be swarthy, as one says."

22. Kateb, *Le cadavre encirclé*, 55.

23. Kateb, *Le cadavre encirclé*, 19

24. Kateb, *Le cadavre encirclé*, 51

25. Fanon, *Wretched of the Earth*, 16.

26. Foucault, *Abnormal*. See Berthelier, "L'homme musulman."

27. Porot, "Notes de psychiatrie musulmane."

28. These were the first Senegalese psychiatrists at the "central African hospital" of Dakar. Starting from 1951 and 1954, respectively, Seydo Tall and Amoussou arrived in a much-neglected ward. See Collignon, "La psychiatrie coloniale française." Thomas Adeoye Lambo (1923–2004) was another of the first African psychiatrists. He studied and worked as a surgeon in Britain and then returned to Nigeria as specialist in charge of the Aro psychiatric hospital in Abeokuta, where he employed both modern and traditional healing techniques. See Sadowsky, *Imperial Bedlam*.

After having met Fanon in 1956, the military psychiatrist and doctor Henri Collomb (1913–79) made the new Fann hospital, opened in 1956, the heart of ethnopsychiatry during the 1960s and 1970s. This was the start of the "School of Fann" or "Dakar school." Among his therapeutic techniques, Collomb included the *pénc*, a dialogue between the sick and their caretakers inspired by the model of a village within the confines of the hospital. He observes that "compensatory behaviors surge into the void and disorder of deculturation: the satisfaction of individual success, the possession of wealth, create and fill a lack of being. So does a return toward the most traditional forms, the call to magical practices and to ancient gods in order to overcome familial conflicts or personal difficulties." Collomb and Valantin, "Famille africaine." Today, Western therapies coexist with local practices, recourse to *sërin̄* (marabouts) or to *fajkat* (healers). See Bullard, "Critical Impact."

29. The *tirailleurs* (infantrymen) were a military body belonging to the colonial troops created in 1857 and dissolved in 1962. Their recruitment was not limited to Senegal. Until

1905, the *tirailleurs* were known for integrating slaves purchased from their masters. Léopold Sédar Senghor called them the empire's black Great Danes [*les Dogues noir de l'Empire*]. See Deroo and Champeaux, *La force noire*. As for the Algerian and Moroccan infantrymen, they made up the "African Army."

30. Chakrabarty, *Provincializing Europe*, 73–74.

31. Rahmani, "Le 'harki,'" 223 (my emphasis). Rahmani is the author of *Moze* (2003).

32. De Certeau, *Heterologies*, 4.

33. Chakrabarty, *Provincializing Europe*, 89.

34. Foucault, "Nietzsche, Freud, Marx."

35. Foucault, "Nietzsche, Freud, Marx," 275.

36. Clémence Ramnoux (1905–97) was a historian of ancient philosophy, specialist in the presocratics. She is known for *La nuit et les enfants de la nuit* (1959) and *Héraclite, ou Entre les choses et les mots* (1959).

37. Foucault, "Nietzsche, Freud, Marx," 606. Translator's note: The discussion after Foucault's talk, delivered at Royaumont in 1964, is not included in the English version of the text.

38. Arion Lothar Kelkel (1927–2015) was a historian of philosophy, specialist in Husserl and Heidegger. He is known for *Le legs de la phenomenologie* (2003).

39. During the Cuban War of Independence, hundreds of thousands of people, many of them women and children, were herded into camps under orders from Valeriano Weyler y Nicolau, governor general of the Philippines and Cuba. These camps were largely disorganized and unkempt, and disease and malnutrition spread rapidly. More than three hundred thousand people eventually perished under the Reconcentration Policy.

40. Boers and African natives were interned separately. Almost all of the Boer men captured by the English were sent overseas, so few remained in the local camps except women and children. More than 26,000 died there. The total black deaths in camps are officially calculated at a minimum of 14,154 but are estimated at 20,000. In fact, British records were incomplete and in many cases nonexistent, and many civilians died outside of the camps, increasing the final death toll. The average official death rate, caused by medical neglect, exposure, infectious diseases, and malnutrition inside the camps, was 350 per 1,000 per annum, peaking at 436 per 1,000 per annum in certain Free State camps. Eighty-one percent of the fatalities were children. See Spies, *Methods of Barbarism*; as well as Stanley, *Mourning Becomes*.

41. After the rebellion of the Hereros in 1904, Karl von Bülow (1846–1921) sent in General Lothar von Trotha, who had already proved himself in Tanganyika. The latter decided on the extermination (*Vernichtungsbefehl*) of all Hereros, not just the fighters. He intended to create an empty region: "They must leave or die. Such is my decision for the Herero people." "I believe that the Herero nation as such must be annihilated or, if this is not tactically feasible, expelled from the territory by all possible means." Finally, the Hereros were eliminated by forced labor in camps (*Konzentrationslagern*). The majority of the Hereros disappeared within seven years. This genocide was only recognized by Germany a hundred years later—in 2004. As for the Hereros of Namibia, the fact of their being a very small minority has not been without political consequences in that country. Kotek, "Le génocide des Herero." See also Erichsen and Olusoga, *Kaiser's Holocaust*; and, in French, Fontenaille-N'Diaye, *Blue Book*.

42. Ricœur, "Objectivity and Subjectivity," 40

43. Ricœur, "Objectivity and Subjectivity," 22.

44. "The *very goal* of translation opens a certain relation to the Other at the level of writing, making what is one's Own [*le Propre*] fruitful via the mediation of what is Foreign

[*l'Étranger*] . . . the essence of translation is to be an opening, dialogue, mixing, decentering." Berman, *L'épreuve*, 16.

45. Steiner, *After Babel*; Ricœur, *On Translation*, 24.
46. Spivak, "Can the Subaltern Speak?," 275.
47. Foucault, "Nietzsche, Freud, Marx," 277–78.
48. De Certeau, *Heterologies*, 6.
49. Walzer, *On Toleration*, xvi.
50. Freud, "Delusions and Dreams," 44. He also says of writers that "in their knowledge of the mind they are far in advance of us everyday people, for they draw upon sources which we have not yet opened up for science" (8). On the psychic plane, therefore, literary creation appears as a species of waking dream.
51. De Certeau, *Heterologies*, 24–25 (translation altered).
52. See Stora, *La gangrène*.
53. Stoler, "L'aphasie coloniale française."
54. See this volume, 80.
55. Levallois, *Ismaÿl Urbain*.
56. Translator's note: In the sense that we speak of a "state of exception." See Agamben, *State of Exception*, and Barkat, *Le corps d'exception*.
57. Memmi, *Portrait du colonisé*.
58. Mbembe, *On the Postcolony*, 25.
59. Benot, *Massacres coloniaux, 1944–1950*, 6.
60. Benot, *Massacres coloniaux, 1944–1950*, 31.
61. Assia Djebar (1936–2015) is her pen name. She was named Fatima-Zohra Imalhayène. She was the first French Muslim to integrate the École Normale Supérieure in 1955. In 1956, she participated in the exam strike called by UGEMA (Union Génerale des Etudiants Musulmans Algeriens) and was expelled from the École. In 1957, her first novel appeared: *La Soif*.
62. Djebar, *Algerian White*, 14.
63. The Islamic Salvation Front (Front Islamique du Salut, or FIS) won the first round of the 1992 legislative elections. The second round was then called off, which unleashed a civil war opposing Islamists (around twenty thousand terrorists) to the armed forces. There were around two hundred thousand victims of that war. The state of emergency was prolonged until 2011. Many intellectuals were assassinated: Omar Belhouchet, Tahar Djaout, Mahfoud Boubeci, Mohamed Boukhobza, Abdelkader Alloula—the list is long. Close to 71,500 university graduates would have fled between 1992 and 1996. This war resulted in a double amnesty (1999 and 2005). See Bennoune, *Fatwa Does Not Apply*.
64. Vergés, Zavrian, and Courrège, *Les disparus, le cahier vert*. At that time, and particularly during the Algerian War, lawyers or other third parties tried to publicize the colonial violence that was explicitly manifest in the numerous disappearances following people's arrest by agents of the French police. They tabulated the cases of disappearance and published these lists. The FLN legal team in France consisted of just five Algerians: Abdessamed Benabdallah, Mohamed Kebir Bendimerad, Nadjib Boulbina (attempted assassination), Mourad Oussedik, and Amokrane Ould Aoudia (assassinated).
65. Agamben, *State of Exception*, 85–86.
66. Agamben, *State of Exception*, 88.
67. See, for example, L. Gordon, "Décoloniser le savoir."

3

LANGUAGE, AN INTERNAL POLITICS

Language, Politics, State

Speaking in Another Language Than One's Own

It is not objectivity that one governs, teaches, or cares for, but rather subjectivity. This is why, at least since Freud, the three "professions" of government, education, and psychoanalysis have the reputation of being "impossible." To address the subjectivation of history and of politics we are therefore obliged to reflect on the overlapping of the borderlines to be found at work deep within those whose countries were once colonized. We must interrogate the situation of those who find themselves required by birth, which is to say by the greatest happenstance, to express themselves in everyday life using a language that is not "naturally" theirs, and one that they had to adopt in a postcolonial context. In fact, such people are inevitably confronted with a historical (past) and political (present) denigration of their original language, as well as of their culture, and finally of themselves—giving rise to splits that have not always attracted sufficient attention.

In his autobiography, *Out of Place*, Edward Said often comes back to the question of language. Spending summer vacations with his family in Lebanon, with his maternal relatives, he mentions that his father, Wadie, did not speak Lebanese but Egyptian with a Palestinian accent. In Cairo, although his father could express himself in Arabic, he preferred to resort to French, which was more fashionable, even if he could speak it less fluently than English. Said himself is always grappling with or in the grasp of questions regarding language. He took a wicked pleasure in speaking Arabic at high school where its use was forbidden.

In a more general sense, Said mentions a kind of linguistic mechanism and an automatism that made him pass from one language to the other in translation. "While speaking English," he writes, "I hear and often articulate the Arabic or French equivalent, and while speaking Arabic I reach out for French and English analogues, strapping them onto my words like luggage on an overhead rack, there but somehow inert and encumbering."[1]

Languages oblige us to speak or prevent us from speaking. Islam defends anyone whose defense of religion is also a defense of language. One finds an example of this in *Le soleil des indépendances*, by Ahmadou Kourouma. Fama, the main character, is at the mosque: "The prayer was in two halves like a kola-nut; the first, a plea for salvation, was recited in Arabic, the language consecrated by God. The second was spoken in Malinke, because it dealt with material things: giving thanks for sustenance, for health, for having eluded the bad luck and evil spells that scorch the black man blacker under the suns of Independence; asking for a mind and heart free of cares and temptations, and filled with peace today, tomorrow and always."[2] The separation between sacred and profane is enacted through the choice of a specific language. The division between public life and private life is also effected by linguistic means. For example, Kikongo will be spoken at home and French in the street.

Changing Names and Things

The postcolonial situation is truly paradoxical: at least in part, it consists in remaining a foreigner at home. Zairianization, Arabization—public policies implement nationalism within each country. Place names are changed. Léopoldville becomes Kinshasa, Stanleyville becomes Kisangani, Elizabethville becomes Lubumbashi, and the Congo itself, Zaire.[3] Annaba replaces Bône; Skikda is substituted for Philippeville; Bejaia abolishes Bougie. A whole symbolic geography is altered, down to the smallest villages of the countryside and the least-used alleys in the city. For a while, the signs are posted in one or the other language. The old people know the former names, and they continue to use them. Those who are younger do not know them and do not know which place is being discussed. The identity of places is unsettled by the diversity of names.

Countries themselves change names: Upper Volta becomes Burkina Faso; Dahomey becomes Benin. What should we think when all the places have been rebaptized in the postcolonial context? What mental images do all these nominations and denominations produce? This does not mean we would all get along if we simply shared the same vocabulary. One can give different names to the same terms, moreover, and endow them with different values or weightiness. Finally, currencies change, and so do their values.[4]

With some exceptions, what generally happens is that in the official work of a government or system of information or education, an imposed language substitutes for vernacular idioms that eventually become obsolete. This is the case today almost everywhere on the African continent because there one governs, one educates, one cares for others in a colonial language, whether this be English, French, or Portuguese. As Kafka's great swimmer put it, "I have to well admit that I am in my own country and that, in spite of all my efforts, I don't understand a word of the language you are speaking."[5] To write in a language, but also to speak, is to express oneself in a certain system of signs, in a unique semiotic field. Here enunciation is marked by the split and heterogeneity between types of statements.

In the Democratic Republic of the Congo, French is the official language. Four Bantu languages are national languages: Kikongo, Lingala, Tshiluba, and Swahili. In eastern Africa, to be sure, the Germans and the British made Swahili the common administrative language. Independent Tanzania, thanks to Julius Nyerere, made it the official language. The Institute of Swahili Research at the University of Dar es Salaam contributed to its promotion. In the Maghreb, standard Arabic (to speak loosely, because there are more and less standardized forms of Arabic) is the official language, although it was not a colonial language. It is sometimes doubled, as in Algeria, by French—which does not have the same status but in very many cases effectively performs the same role as an institutional language.

The difficulty is compounded by the phenomenon of diglossia in the Arabized regions. This is not the bilingualism that can be easily observed, even down to the giving of place names. For example, the birthplace of St. Augustine, Souk Ahras, owes its appellation to an Arabic term, *souk*, meaning "market," and to a word in Chaoui, a Berber language, *ahras*, plural of *aher*, which means "lion." We must remember that wild animals such as panthers, cheetahs, and lions said to be "of Barbary" did not disappear until the 1920s, pitilessly hunted down by the French. Just as with all colonial safari expeditions, the number of stuffed animals and skulls or horns brought back to Europe testified to the "courage" of hunters, explorers, and other colonial heroes, which is why they were preserved and exhibited—for example, in the Royal Museum of Central Africa in Tervuren.

In North Africa, diglossia refers to two varieties and two modalities of Arabic. As Abderrahim Youssi emphasizes in his defense of freedom for the Arab language, "the first is classical, unchanging, uniquely written and elitist. The second variety is vernacular. Despised, reduced to oral usage, marked by indigenous languages, it has evolved with time and its syntax has become simplified."[6] He also observes that the elitist path led, paradoxically, to illiteracy. At first, the Arabic language was learned through study of the Koran; then it was orally mastered by recitation; finally, only a tiny minority managed to memorize the totality of the Koran's 114 suras after a lengthy program. That was how one became a jurist, notary, or imam.

Later postcolonial linguistic policies were carried out by brute force and at a brutal pace. It was not for nothing that education was referred to as a "campaign." In the case of the Maghreb, "one single people, one single fatherland, one single language" translated into political projects aimed at Arabization. But in the Maghreb no less than in the Machrek (or Levant), the privileges of classical Arabic survived, forcing people to speak in one language and to write in another. Education was thus ineluctably accompanied by illiteracy. What is not written is not spoken. What is not spoken is not written, or rarely. Thus, Khaled Al Khamissi wrote his best seller *Taxi* in Egyptian. The persistent colonial concept of dialect prevented the variety of Arabic proper to each country from being promoted. Tunisian, Algerian, and Moroccan forms of Arabic are not supposed to be wholly different languages. They are "only dialects," and one speaks of them as distinct species of dialectal Arabic.

Are There National Languages?

The linguistic devaluation that was politically institutionalized by the colony did not end with accession to independence.[7] The monopoly over legitimate symbolic violence persisted. South Sudan became independent on July 9, 2011.[8] English is the official language there—it is the language of international politics, the one in which rulers interact with the UN representatives responsible for handing them the new state's start-up kit.[9] Arabic is the language of internal politics, which the rulers speak among themselves. Dinka, Nuer, Bari, Zande, and Shilluk are the languages into which the official speeches in Arabic must be translated by an interpreter if the local populations are to understand them.

The derealization produced by the nesting of these idioms and these languages can only lead to an even greater distance between rulers and those being ruled, who are already distant by definition. At this point, we cannot help but wonder what is meant by politics. Phenomena of linguistic domination have very profound effects on the way that politics itself can be defined. In Algeria, independence meant the end of French, not as a spoken language, but as a national language. And because it seemed impossible to teach and to govern in dialect, classical Arabic was asked to take its place. Arabization took place chiefly thanks to Syrians, Egyptians, and Iraqis who, it was said, knew "Arabic."

Starting on July 5, 1962, huge numbers acquired a new nationality, that of a country whose history they did not know (what was it?), whose rights and duties were no clearer, whose political nature was still unknown (Algeria became, and still remains, a "people's democratic republic"), whose own social life they had yet to discover, along with culture and eventually identity. For many reasons, language would be the crucial affair of this country. In a settler colony like Algeria, whose situation resembles that of an "old colony" like Martinique in many respects, the tongue had been cut.

At first, the colonial situation imposed a linguistic breach estranging two segments of the colony's population.[10] In making French not just the official language but also the dominant language, the imperial power relegated Algerian Arabic, spoken by the majority of Algerians, to the rank of an unwritten dialect that needed to be neither learned nor taught. It also turned Kabyle, the majority Berber language, into a local phenomenon and made it a matter of folklore. Kabyle, too, was denied the status of something that could be taught, which is to say something that could be shared.

To privilege writing over speech, the Algerian government turned toward the kind of Arabic said to be standard or classical and made it the country's official language, although this language could not yet be spoken by a population to which it was foreign. In fact, this standard Arabic was not Maghrebin, because it came from the Machrek or the Middle East. Even after independence, one was not born Algerian; one had to become so. How? In becoming Arabophone and nationalist, in being anticolonialist and anti-imperialist, in being nonaligned (for neither the United States nor the Soviet Union). There existed no linguistic neutrality.

Arabization produced considerable linguistic scrambling.[11] The political division between Arabizing Islamists and Frenchifying secularists was one of its effects. In Tunisia, after the fall of Ben Ali, the Ennahda party spoke of its adversaries as not really being true Tunisians, because they continued to use French. Classical Arabic and a "foreign" language such as

French were required for access to jobs and to positions with responsibility. As for the bourgeoisie, they preferred to speak colonial languages, French in the Maghreb and English in the Machrek. Colonial languages move one upward; local languages drag one down.

Mehdi, Fouad Laroui's young hero in *Une année chez les Français*, was ten years old in 1969.[12] Having won a scholarship, he left home to do his secondary education at the lycée Lyautey in Casablanca. He loved French. But he did not understand the Moroccan Arabic "dialect." At home, indeed, French was spoken. It was both his first language and the language of social mobility. Mehdi

> spoke French at school but also at home, with his brother and his sister—and it stopped there, because he never played outside with the neighborhood children. With his father and his mother, an unusual *modus vivendi* was established: he was most often spoken to in the dialect—which consisted of several sentences, always the same ("Eat!" "Go wash your hands!" "It is time for bed!" "Did you do your homework?")—and he answered in the French of the Comtesse de Ségur.[13] Certainly, in Arabic, he knew *chajra*, which means tree. But in French, he distinguished, at least linguistically, between the oak, the chestnut, the poplar, the plane tree.

Avoidance of the street is significant. It creates an in-between space [*un entre-mondes*]: neither France nor Morocco—a floating space between the local foreign language and the foreign language of the family.

These postcolonial political situations are reminiscent of colonial situations and linguistic policies themselves. Throughout the continent, colonial languages were imposed and dominated languages were apprehended in an administrative and military manner, not a properly political one. For example, in Algeria, it was through the Arab Offices, whose organization was fixed by a ministerial decree of February 1, 1844, that the French wanted to "know" those they were in the process of conquering and could hardly wait to colonize. In 1850 some forty offices, and by 1870 around fifty, were devoted to military exploration of the language, religion, and customs of Algeria's inhabitants. They symbolize a kind of preferred contact, apart from war in the proper sense, employing means as unique as they were symptomatic.

Learning to Talk in Official Jargon [Langue de Bois]

In a general sense, what the local people have, so to speak, assimilated, whether or not they fit into the strict category of the *indigénat*, is a certain

French, employed for a certain purpose and in light of certain policies. The *petit nègre* or *pitinègue* or "infantry French" is its caricature.[14] It can be considered a variety of jargon or officialese because it aims exclusively at matching the action of commanding with that of obeying. But it is also an in-between language fixed in a manual with the title *Le français tel que le parle nos tirailleurs sénégalais* (1916) teaching European officers how to communicate with their Senegalese infantrymen. It was a matter of the "natural and rational simplification" of French (a "complicated language") in order to "fix the mold into which the French sentence must be poured so that the infantrymen would know a few words of our language."[15] The incomplete and biased character of the vocabulary on which it was supposed to be grounded did not, as one might suspect, immediately disappear once independence had come.

Maurice Delafosse, colonial administrator and linguist, noted its recommendations: systematic recourse to the infinitive, employment of the term *là* (as in "that thing-there"), negation expressed uniquely by the foreclosive *pas*, and so on. The result: "To alert a thick-necked Black who, seated on his overturned canteens, is smoking a sooty short-pipe, [the Frenchman] speaks to him in telegraphic style—because his reading has taught him that Blacks speak only in the infinitive mode: 'You to carry my suitcases to customs, me to pay you.'" It is thus that Delafosse recalls his arrival in Africa, armed with his linguistic stereotypes "y a bon Banania."[16] In 1948—in *Hosties noires*—Senghor would later say: "I will tear off the *banania* grins from all the walls of France."[17]

A whole regime appreciating and depreciating human persons was fed by the hierarchization of tongues and languages and was exported by colonial powers such as France or England, who imposed forms of coloniality on their own soil, denigrating certain idioms along with their speakers. This was particularly true of France, whose unity was politically conceived on the model of uniformity. One may suppose that, *mutatis mutandis*, things on the ground were not fundamentally different for the English or the Portuguese. Meanwhile, today the provincialization of Portuguese and French renders linguistic confrontations inevitable, which is not the case for English, the linguistic vector of globalization.

For the Chadian writer Koulsy Lamko, the imposition of the French language destroyed "the very possibility of interrogating one's own imaginary in one's own words, of proposing scenarios for the analysis of one's society, of imagining adequate systems of organization, in other words policies, of proposing dreams, new visions taking cultural specificities into account. . . . This 'rape of the imaginary' mentioned by Aminata Traoré is not just a sociopolitical phenomenon; it is also linguistic."[18] For this reason, Algeria did not want to participate in the International Organization of Francophonie. It did this not in the name of "cultural identity" but rather to refuse what it perceived as the imperialism implicit in the politics of Francophonie initiated by France.

Political language, on the other hand, is everywhere distinctive: it has both its own syntax and its specific vocabulary. It aims at the production of consent through the use of euphemisms, legitimation, and many further tactics. But what happens when it is absorbed into an adopted language (as one speaks of an adopted child)? In a short text written in 1946, "Politics and the English Language," George Orwell attracted attention to the atrociously mechanical nature of political speech. He wrote:

> When one watches some tired hack on the platform mechanically repeating the familiar phrases—*bestial atrocities, iron heel, bloodstained tyranny, free peoples of the world, stand shoulder to shoulder*—one often has a curious feeling that one is not watching a live human being but some kind of dummy: a feeling which suddenly becomes stronger at moments when the light catches the speaker's spectacles and turns them into blank discs which seem to have no eyes behind them. And this is not altogether fanciful. A speaker who uses that kind of phraseology has gone some distance toward turning himself into a machine. The appropriate noises are coming out of his larynx, but his brain is not involved as it would be if he were choosing his words for himself. If the speech he is making is one that he is accustomed to make over and over again, he may be almost unconscious of what he is saying, as one is when one utters the responses in church. And this reduced state of consciousness, if not indispensable, is at any rate favourable to political conformity.[19]

Doublespeak has often been analyzed, notably because of its so frequent deployment of euphemism. Orwell's examples are illuminating:

> Defenseless villages are bombarded from the air, the inhabitants driven out into the countryside, the cattle machine-gunned, the huts set on fire with incendiary bullets: this is called *pacification*. Millions of peasants are robbed of their farms and sent trudging along the roads with no more than they can carry: this is called *transfer of population* or *rectification of frontiers*. People are imprisoned for years without trial, or shot in the back of the neck or sent to die of scurvy in Arctic lumber camps: this is called *elimination of unreliable elements*. Such phraseology is needed if one wants to name things without calling up mental pictures of them.[20]

The Imposition of a Language

How difficult it is to disentangle oneself from coloniality! What actually happens when this famous jargon is linguistically and not just socially distinct from the local spoken languages? It can still be diffused through channels of education and end by infiltrating almost every aspect of intellectual activity. This foreign tongue can be transformed into a language whose defect, at least as seen from the outside, is simultaneously to be abusively politicized and to be intellectually incongruous. Sometimes one can witness a postcolonial "return" of old practices, modified and displaced in service to some conflict—because the foreign languages have often been taught with an agonistic goal in mind.

To take but one example, the colonial policies on the African continent through which the French language was imposed were political offensives. Because attack is the best defense, the defense of French was implemented in the name of resistance to English. Thus, in an Inspection Report, a French functionary on a mission in Guinea (1902–3) considered the situation in these terms: "There are further reasons why Farmoréah, a significant Muslim center 40 km south of Benty, must be chosen as the location for a school directed by a European teacher. This will be the best way to throw up a barrier to the influence of the English language, because if one does not take care, English will soon be the only language employed for business transactions in eastern Guinea."[21]

To combat the influence of Islam on the one hand and Great Britain on the other, two distinct objectives could be pursued: on the one hand, to counteract Muslim education, dispensed in the madrassas and always in Arabic; on the other, to limit the range within which English was put to commercial ends. This is how schools became a leading edge of French colonial administration, schools for training auxiliary administrative personnel whose purpose was to support, from within, diverse colonial policies and to communicate its views.

Britain's colonial policies for India manifested the same ambition. As Thomas Macaulay formulated it in 1835, this is what was at stake in education in India: "We must at present do our best to form a class who may be interpreters between us and the millions whom we govern; a class of persons, Indian in blood and colour, but English in taste, in opinions, in morals, and in intellect. To that class we may leave it to refine the vernacular dialects of the country, to enrich those dialects with terms of science borrowed from the Western nomenclature, and to render them by degrees fit vehicles for conveying knowledge to the great mass of the population."[22]

This is why the French colonies, just like their English counterparts, did not imagine developing generalized schooling policies for the whole population. Women were largely excluded from schools, women who in the colonial language were considered "backward." The stakes were as much political as they were economic and social. In the case of Algeria's colonial system, Abdelmalek Sayad has analyzed the political meaning of the logic by which French schools were established, which might otherwise have seemed irrational on first glance.

Education, whose ends were opposed to colonial goals, was differentially and parsimoniously dispensed on the basis of property ownership. Schooling was introduced in inverse proportion to agricultural colonization. This educational distribution also obeyed other colonial divisions: ethnic, since, for example, the Berbers were colonially split between "assimilable" Kabyles and "unassimilable" Chaouis; and social, which is less surprising, since the poorest parts of the population were a priori excluded from schools.

For Sayad,

> it could be said that it was never in the nature of colonization to assure the emancipation of the colonized, even by means of the language, the school and the culture of the colonial society. . . . The whole history of schooling is marked by this hostility and, on the eve of independence, the structures of the school, its age, the density of its distribution or its general configuration were still narrowly dominated by the structures of colonization, above all property ownership. This is the only way to explain the curious disparities one observes from one region to another in rural Algeria; between the mountain for example where schools are relatively numerous and the plain where schools are almost totally absent and where, on the other hand, the interests of colonization are particularly powerful.[23]

The Diversity of Languages Put to the Political Test

The polyglossia in Africa is also enhanced, paradoxically, by emigration, in the sense that, as Kwami Appiah has observed in *Cosmopolitanism*, "thoroughgoing ignorance about the ways of others is largely a privilege of the powerful. The well-traveled polyglot is as likely to be among the worst off as among the best off—as likely to be found in a shantytown as at the Sorbonne."[24]

According to the studies, between 1,500 and 2,000 spoken languages can be counted on the continent.[25] By way of comparison, 1,635 languages are spoken in India, of which 37 are spoken by fewer than one thousand people. The Indian constitution recognizes 22 of them. One generally forgets that Gandhi gave his speeches in Hindi, of which he was not a terribly adept speaker. His first language was Gujarati. It was in South Africa, where he lived for more than twenty years between 1893 and 1914, that he took his first political steps.

Orality is an important factor of linguistic fragmentation. Most Africans are polyglots, even when one leaves the colonial languages out of the picture. We must recall that the French, the Spanish, and the Portuguese sought to develop a monolingualism for their own colonies, unlike the British, the Germans, or the Belgians. This is how Lingala, for example, became the official language of the army and the police of Congo-Kinshasa (DRC).

But are not the citizens of a single state who cannot communicate easily due to the diversity of languages, sometimes an extreme diversity as in the case of Cameroon, cut off from one another, at least relatively so? Are they, in this sense, foreigners among foreigners, even when close? What are the modalities of collective political life when one knows that politics does not exist apart from speech? Achille Mbembe has remarked that the social sciences shrug off local languages and knowledge of them in such a way that African politics and economics appear only as manifestations of lack. Thus, the field of theory is dominated by the incomprehensible.[26]

The states, however, can be monolingual, at least juridically. But in most cases their official language is a colonial language. Doesn't this cut the citizens off not only from one another but also from themselves? In Burkina Faso, for example, it is estimated that 50 percent of the population speaks Mooré, one of the national languages along with Bissa, and that only 10 to 15 percent of Burkinabés speak French, the official language of the country. In Morocco, the official language (particularly in administration and education) was first French; then classical Arabic became the language of administration. French subsequently became the formal professional language, while Moroccan served as the informal professional language. But about half of Moroccans are Berberophone.[27]

The political repercussions of the differential usage of these diverse idioms have occasionally been analyzed. Khaoula Taleb Ibrahimi emphasizes that the use of French spread in Algeria after the country's independence.[28]

This paradox, called "reverse Francization," is due to the intensive schooling policies of the young Algerian state. The global policy of Arabization carried out by the schools as well as in the administration, for its part, only began later (1978) and did not destroy the tacit bilingualism but merely attenuated its effects.

But Ibrahimi also shows that because culture and language are indissociable, polyglossia produces both a mix of codes on the linguistic plane and misunderstandings on the social plane. Finally, she shows how politically meaningful the choice of a language of expression can be. What is the real postcolonial meaning of using French? What meaning does the systematic use of Arabic convey? Political currents have been sheltered by the employment of some languages rather than others.

No one will be astonished that standard Arabic should be the privileged means of expression for Islamists. The defenders of secularism and male-female equality, for their part, have recourse to French. The written press itself is a sign of this. In what language does one work? In what language does one engage in politics?[29] These phenomena force us to ask ourselves what kind of consistency can be found in a public space entirely occupied by translation, given that in Europe this public space was conceived with relative linguistic homogeneity in mind.

In South Africa, for example, there are eleven national languages. But the provisional Constitution of 1993 was dedicated to an "untranslatable" term: *Ubuntu*. A central term from the Truth and Reconciliation Commission, it means "the quality of being one person with others," or, according to Antjie Krog's formula: "We are therefore I am."[30] Correlatively, the question is posed of knowing what content to give, in such a context, to the nation-state inherited from European colonization. The valorization of "ethnicities" has long made the linguistic dimension [*dimension linguistique*] of problems internal to the African continent's diverse countries more visible than the dimension of access to speech [*dimension langagière*]. The administrative and political borders are in fact doubled by other borders that are informal and less visible.

The Bambara-Diula-Mandika of the Mandé is spoken in Francophone countries (Burkina Faso, Guinea, Mali, and Senegal) but also in Anglophone (Gambia) and Lusophone countries (such as Guinea-Bissau). Thus, Rada Iveković wonders: "How do the facts of a language pass through speaking subjects without getting locked inside of them? Something passes from some to others in this transmissible *karma*."[31] Far from being a figure for destiny, karma designates "the generic and transgenerational solidarity of all forms of life, as much on the ontological plane as on the ethical plane. It is through others' history that our own non-state, non-official, people's history returns to the surface, transformed."[32]

Meanwhile, in comparing the two great colonial languages—namely, English and French, which one would also have to make comparable with Spanish and Portuguese—Rada Iveković notes the dissymmetry between the effects of English in India and those of French in Algeria. She writes, "In the case of English, language served to defuse the violence of (Indian) decolonization in important ways, something that was not possible for French (in Algeria)."[33]

English is a globalized language, in which local language and global language coincide. Its globalization detaches it from its colonial character. This is why the use of French and its organization, the Organization internationale pour la Francophonie (OIF), remain heavily politicized. Rada Iveković believes that no such detachment was produced for French, which, for her, complicates the relationship between France and its former colonies. In fact, French remains both a colonial language and a local language. The use of one language or another, consequently, does not favor the same type of sociality. The linguistic question haunts African writers.

Subject, Literature, People

Languages and Genres/Genders

"French will let me come and go; not just in multiple languages, but in all ways," said Assia Djebar in *Oran, langue morte*.[34] Literature is a practice of freedom. This is how the writer carries out the linguistic deterritorialization of which Deleuze and Guattari spoke in "What Is a Minor Literature?" For these two thinkers, "a minor literature doesn't come from a minor language; it is rather that which a minority constructs within a major language. But the first characteristic of minor literature in any case is that in it language is affected with a high coefficient of deterritorialization."[35] Djebar does this in a story about "women of the Algerian night" by uncovering their voices.

Women are leaving not only the colonial night but also an ancestral silence. These are two invisible borders. In Assia Djebar's works, the crossing of borders, particularly linguistic ones, is always being foregrounded. Not one book of hers, whether as a primary theme or in a more discreet but no less significant fashion, fails to evoke questions of language and the difficulties that language can carry along with it. Language is so closely imbricated with the proper name that writing, in the specific context of the Algerian War, required her to take on a pen name, an authorial name, what one usually calls a pseudonym. She says that she would not have chosen this situation and that it did not make her happy.

The friendly conversations between men and women in her novels unfold in French: "My friends spoke to me in French, in the past; each of the three, in fact, conversed with me in a foreign language; through humility, or austerity."[36] This recalls the observations of the anthropologist Tassadit Yacine, whose research on Kabyle society shows that not everything is expressed in a single given language. Honor is associated with men and fear with women, which leaves men no place to express their own fear in Kabyle, lest they lose their symbolic virility. Men's fears are thus difficult to study in their own language.

On the other hand, "What is said among the students through the mediation of a foreign language—as if to minimize its effects—will also be said through the mediation of an other voice (the voice of the dominated who are completely negated by the system). It is in fact the women, confronted with the task of caring for their men, who recognize the confused situation of their companions." From this we see how gender and language are interwoven. And she notes: "Students could only have conversations about the intimate aspects of their groups thanks to a doubly foreign language: Spanish. The relationship to the foreign language has an important function, one that would be interesting to study."[37]

Is the game changed in a different location? Or is Algerian even preferred when the protagonists find themselves in a foreign country? "I've already said that we speak French. Not in the old way. Not by cautiousness, nor by convention, to hide our imperceptible embarrassment, our common stiffness. There, on American soil, our French from before the dawn flows just as simply, after all, as the mother tongue we share. So, dear friends, before, did we find it so difficult to have an open dialogue? Our French was on parade, a ceremonial uniform . . ."[38]

Assia Djebar is never diverted—how could she be?—from the many paths that the use of several languages opens to her or closes off.

In practice, language also makes possibilities real. This is why Assia Djebar's writing flows from Arabic into French and French to Arabic even within French. An example:

> Then, in Arabic, she recites the well known *hadith*: "As said by our prophet, may the grace of God be on Him: *The best among the believers shall lead my people, even if it's a Sudanese slave!* You see," she concludes in a soft voice, "Islam promotes equality."
>
> But another starts up and interjects in French, "Then tell me—if the equality that you invoke is really without limits, what if it were a woman—yes, simply a woman? Would she lead "our"—she stresses the possessive pronoun with an ironic tone—"community"?[39]

It is in French that women's equality is put into words. Independence, however, chose Arabic to express itself. The complexity and the interlocking of languages in various life situations is one of the principal motifs of Assia Djebar's work. She thereby manages to raise awareness regarding the problems and the solutions that politics, understood here in a broad sense, encounters in the different languages of a single, formerly colonized country. But the cost of such a self-presentation in French is heavy: the writer lives in exile. She is sometimes considered blameworthy in her country. Many Algerian writers in the French language are considered by their fellow citizens to be "writing for the French." Contrary to what one might sometimes think, the "intercultural dialogue" starts off as an internal one.

Literary Politics

Thus, literature, in its linguistic incarnation, is political—because it is the literature of a minority. We know that Gilles Deleuze accords great significance to the notion of minor literature. There are three features that define it philosophically: the deterritorialization of language, the insertion of the individual into current political events, and the collective assemblage of enunciation.

In *Critique et clinique*, Deleuze clarifies: "Kafka said that in a minor literature, that is, in the literature of a minority, there is no private history that is not immediately public, political, and popular: all literature becomes 'an affair of the people,' and not of exceptional individuals."[40]

He proposes the following definition: "The literature of a minority is not defined by a local language that would be its defining feature, but by a treatment to which it subjects the major language."[41] It is in this sense that the greater part of African literature is a minority literature.

The reflections that Deleuze develops in the chapter of *Critique et clinique* titled "La littérature et la vie" deserve to be reviewed here. Indeed, as he emphasizes at the start, literature is bordered by nonliterature and particularly by politics. When he affirms that "the problem of writing is also inseparable from a problem of *seeing* and *hearing*," he immediately adds that "these visions, these auditions are not a private matter but form the figures of a history and a geography that are ceaselessly reinvented."[42]

We are already aware of Deleuze's refusal of the "papa-mama," which is reaffirmed in his conception of the relationship between life and literature as a kind of health. If literature is a kind of health, then inversely, health can take on a written form to the very extent that it invents a people, which is particularly the case for minor literatures in the sense that Deleuze, following Kafka, has defined them. "Health as literature, as writing, consists in inventing a people who are missing. It is the task of the fabulating function [*fonction fabulatrice*] to invent a people. We do not write with memories, unless it is to make them the origin and collective destination of a people to come still ensconced in its betrayals and repudiations."[43] This well-being has nothing to do with the writer's condition but rather with his or her task and what Deleuze calls "a possibility of life," which he associates with the "invention of a people" and with the "creation of a kind of health."[44] This is especially true in a postcolonial context.

From this perspective, the writer's task, or his or her proper work, consists in writing not "in the place" of a people whose enunciative position as subjects cannot be found, but rather in writing for a people to be invented or with them in mind. From this point of view, the people are those addressed and "literature is the people's concern."[45] This is why the modifications, metamorphoses, and other minoritarian becomings of the major language are so paramount. But does the address belong to its audience and, at the same time, to the sharing of tongues?

Do Writers and Political Actors Share the Same Language?

On the African continent, literature, like politics, is essentially carried out English, French, or Portuguese.[46] Writers, like political actors, but perhaps to an even greater extent, express themselves in a colonial language that they appropriate, reorient, and, each in their own way, render minor. Salman Rushdie puts it this way: "Those peoples who were once colonized by the language are now rapidly remaking it, domesticating it, becoming more and more relaxed about the way they use it—assisted by the English language's enormous flexibility and size, they are carving out large territories for themselves within its frontiers."[47]

The official valorization or privileging of some languages over others had effects on the literary as well as the political plane, thereby reinforcing the acuteness of problems raised by the existence and the consistency of a public space in a postcolonial context and in a polyglossic situation.[48] The greater part of Kenyan literature is in the English language. But if most Tanzanian writers express themselves in Swahili, it is due to the colonial institutionalization of this language.

The introduction of Latin or Arabic alphabets—historically progressive and not limited simply to the colonial period—was not synonymous with the development of literature in vernacular languages.[49] Taken as a whole, literature (as we understand it conventionally) in the vernacular language could appear and flourish on the African continent only in regions formerly colonized by the British and subject to Protestant evangelization.[50]

In the twentieth century, it was a religious perspective that led Americans to be concerned, politically and not cognitively, by the existence of autochthonic languages and the training of "elites." The Foreign Missions Conference of North America, financed by the Phels-Stokes Fund, was charged in 1922–23 with studying the improvement of educational systems in Africa. An International Missionary Conference was convened in Belgium in 1926 and was at the origin of the International African Institute, which, in 1930, created a literary prize destined to recognize texts in vernacular languages. For example, this is how James Mbotela (Swahili), Wast Ravelomoria (Malagasy), S. E. K. Mqhayi (Xhosa), and J. J. Adaye (Twi) were launched.[51]

The linguistic diversity of countries on the African continent produces inequalities. No career of any kind can be successful without some investment in the former colonial languages. This has been true since the struggle for independence. For example, Kwame Nkrumah (1909–72) spent time at the University of Pennsylvania, studied at the London School of Economics, and relied on the "veranda boys" who attended the British secondary colonial schools, to win in 1957 the independence of Ghana, name of one of the oldest West African empires, the former British Gold Coast. It was in London that his group was formed, notably with Kenneth Kaunda (Zambia), Jomo Kenyatta (Kenya), Joshua Nkomo (Zimbabwe), Julius Nyerere (Tanzania), Kojo Botsio (Ghana), and Harry Nkumbula (Zambia).[52]

Even the creative arts did not escape this restriction. Visual arts are also kinds of textualization. Such can be seen in the alphabetic creation of someone like Bruly Bouabré, who sacralized the triumph of writing. Bruly Bouabré (b. 1923) is an Ivoirian artist—and prophet—who, after a revelation in 1948, created a syllabary of 448 signs that he considers completely "African." He named this syllabary the "Bété alphabet" and gave himself the title of Cheikh Nadro—"the one who does not forget." Having taken courses at the French school of Daloa between 1931 and 1940, he later became a colonial functionary. It was after meeting with Théodore Monod that his work became internationally known.[53] Since 1970 he has limited himself to a postcard format (cardstock paper, colored pencils, ballpoint pen) for a body of work whose title is "World Knowledge."

From the same point of view, the "talking" paintings of Cheri Samba are equally meaningful. Cheri Samba (b. 1956) is an artist from the Congo (DRC). He has talked about wanting to introduce French texts into his canvases, despite certain compatriots' critiques regarding the "quality" of his French. The artist emblazons his images with commentaries, often political, and in his favorite self-portraits he does not hesitate to show himself beside Pablo Picasso, dressed, as one says, in "European" style. Questioned about this comparison, or this equalization, Samba responds: "It is to render homage to this great painter who was inspired by African art. It is also to thumb the nose a bit at these Western 'experts' who have spoken about African art in disdainful terms."[54]

A Curious Case of Tribalism

Disqualification versus valorization—if the formula is universal, its applications vary according to the situation. In the newly independent countries, the first postcolonial priorities were projects of requalification. Meanwhile, it is to be feared that the bases for such projects were all the more uncertain as they were colonial in origin, and all the more likely to have been misrecognized as they were historically masked. Joseph Tonda thus proposes "an impossible postcolonial rupture with colonial anthropology" since, for example, the anthroponymy taught in Brazzaville relates names to ethnicities.[55]

It is certainly more fruitful to carry out reflection in terms of linguistic facts than in terms of ethnic representations. The first refer indubitably to experience whereas the second are much more involved with tales and legends—in other words, myths—from which one tries to exhume intact a country's precolonial past. Such an approach would allow us to apprehend the cultural, social, and political condition of African countries apart from a binary logic opposing tribalism to the nation and tradition to modernity. Because there too, it can happen that distorted names create perennial misunderstanding.

Jean-Pierre Dozon, for example, has shown that the Bété were a kind of "colonial creation" whose birth certificate resulted from poor (French) colonial comprehension of the expression *bete o bete o*, which means "peace" or "pardon."[56] "The archives left by the colonial administration show readily," the author writes, "that this expression was used many times by the local population during the phase of intensive 'pacification' and designated, though misunderstood as an identity, a gesture of conciliation or of submission."[57] This is not a unique case. In Algeria, the city of Batna owes its name to the fact that, when Henri d'Orléans, duke of Aumale, stopped for the night in the massif of Aurès, on February 12, 1844, during his expedition to Biskra, the local guides told him, "N'bet H'na," or "We are spending the night here."

For Dozon, this vocable *bété* was used by colonial administrators despite the fact that almost nothing was known about the supposed Bété country. Colonial penetration began in 1908. The texts inventing the Bété were written between 1901 and 1904. Our perspective must therefore be reversed: ethnicity must be considered on the basis of discursive enunciation (qualification/disqualification), and statements must no longer be regarded as following from the existence of supposed ethnicities. To this day, and where politics is concerned, ethnicity is far more the product of political statements regarding the distribution of posts in the upper levels of the state than it is a substantial and ahistorical entity making populations into collective monads deaf to one another.

Tribalism is a colonial heritage whose artificiality and historicity are masked. Dozon continues: "as geopolitical configurations," tribalisms "are the product of European colonization (which is to say, from an arbitrary cutting up of national borders which broke ethnically coherent groups in two units, indeed more than two, thus creating conditions for tribalist claims and counter-claims)."[58] Ethnicity is at bottom a subcategory of race. When instituted differences must be abandoned, "combat identities" are employed for strategic reasons. But for how long? As for the languages that persist, they are the bearers of thoughts that we do not recognize.

Where the Child Who Read Is Going to Have to Reread Everything

The diverse supports for vernacular languages are generally exogenous to the societies in which they appear, inasmuch as rulers, for reasons of political and financial order, do not necessarily favor policies that are friendly to their countries' linguistic plurality (particularly in the matter of literature). The assets of local publishing houses are weak compared to their counterparts in the North—to such an extent that the very choice of a language for expression is heavy with stakes and consequences. When Kateb Yacine chose the theater, he picked Algerian.

The same thing happens when Assia Djebar or Sembène Ousmane decide to devote themselves to film: they write in a vehicular language and film in a vernacular language.[59] The very complex situation these writers share, according to Patrick Chamoiseau, is that of writing in a dominated country. In "The Upward Flight of Sleeping Books, or The Child Who Read Is Going to Have to Reread Everything," his first questions are the essential ones: "How then to write when your imaginary is watered, from morning til the moment of dreaming, with images, thoughts, and values which are not your own? How to write when what you are vegetates outside the forces that determine your life? How to write, dominated? What have literary works foreseen for you? What have they sedimented along the thread of time for you who are suffocating under this colonial modernity?"[60]

Deleuze defends the idea of pop philosophy, which resembles a schoolkid's prank, on the basis of his reflections on the major and minor, the territorialized and deterritorialized, the branch and the graft, but also the beauty of escape and mastery. He does this starting from an interrogation regarding languages: "How many people today live in a language that is not their own? Or no longer, or not yet, even know their own and know poorly the major language they are forced to serve?"[61] Because there, the question of the author is posed in a singular fashion. Although Deleuze never evokes the case of the colony, since his starting point is the case of Kafka, what he says still holds true in a colonial and postcolonial context.

In its Deleuzian theorization, the minor involves the persistent difficulty of making an individuated enunciation starting not from the subject but from the conditions in which he or she is found. From the inhospitable character of these conditions, he deduces the "rarity of talents" and the collective character of any enunciation whatsoever. What this brings to light is a de facto solidarity with neither intention nor emotion, an objective solidarity since "what each author says individually already constitutes a common action, and what he or she says or does is necessarily political, even if others aren't in agreement. The political domain has contaminated every statement (*énoncé*)."[62]

The difference in conditions of enunciation creates the fracture between major literature (literature of the masters) and minor literature because, after all, the latter cannot be an "individual (family or conjugal) affair." Individual affairs presuppose that the world has a certain stability and a certain transparency. The chaos, opacity, or trouble of the lived world make it into something other than an environment, a backdrop, or a setting that requires no caretaking. Thus, a minor literature establishes something *common*, a shared experience and not an individual one.

The implications are found in real possibilities of speaking and are complicated by the multiplicity of languages, because one does not pass from one language to another without transition as if everything could always be said in any language. It is a pipe dream to believe this could be done. It would presuppose political equality among languages and deny their different functions. Where Kafka is concerned, Deleuze distinguishes Czech as a vernacular language, German as a vehicular language when it is administratively and economically standardized, German as a language of reference when it is a matter of literature rather than of state bureaucracy, and finally Hebrew as mythic language.[63] This construction, characteristic of a European minority, is valid for the majority in the postcolonial world.

African literature has the status of a minor literature and says so. Algerian literature in the French language, for example, can be seen both as an internationalization of the language and of Algerian writing—because French is also an Algerian language—and as a form of resistance to the authoritarian politics of linguistic normalization, known as Arabization, that Algeria initiated on the French model right after independence. Since the end of the eighteenth century, France had effectively pursued an authoritarian politics of the French language, whose defense and illustration had already been handed over to an institution, the Academie Française, and which consisted not only in destroying the other languages of France to the best of its abilities—Breton, Basque, and Corsican could not be eradicated—but also in pitilessly stamping out regional accents.

Lapsus Linguae and Other Forgetful Notes

The unconscious dimension that language names and that it supports makes the social, political, cultural, and intellectual stakes of monolingualism and of postcolonial polyglossialism even more urgent. In *L'envers de la psychanalyse*, Jacques Lacan recalls the African patients whom he had encountered during the 1950s in these terms: "Their unconscious was not that of their childhood memories . . . but their childhood was retroactively lived out in our own familial categories. . . . This was the unconscious that had been sold to them along with the laws of colonization."[64]

Deleuze refers to the works of Georges Devereux, whose birth name was György Dobo. Devereux observed that the young Mohaves spoke easily of sexuality in their vernacular language but with difficulty in their vehicular language, English. Ethnopsychiatry thus appeared as a typically postcolonial enterprise inasmuch as it dealt with the passage from one language to another, both subjectively and objectively.

It is not irrelevant to recall that when Freud starts to write *Psychopathology of Everyday Life*, so he can say what he thinks about the forgetting of names, he immediately becomes interested in a name from a language that is foreign (to him)—a name that, as the reader will eventually understand, raises the question of borders and relations between the countries that they separate. When he reflects on forgetfulness and false memories, he explains that certain linguistic errors are inevitable. Put otherwise, the text shows the articulation of the frontier, of war, and of naming as if it were a watermark.

He writes: "When the war broke out with Italy in 1915 I was able to make the observation upon myself that a whole quantity of Italian place-names which at ordinary times were readily available to me had suddenly been withdrawn from my memory. Like so many other Germans I had made it my habit to spend a part of my holidays on Italian soil, and I could not doubt that this large-scale forgetting of names was the expression of an understandable hostility to Italy which had now replaced my former partiality."[65] But Freud, who has forgotten *Signorelli*, the name of an artist he had almost on the tip of his tongue, is not in a bilingual or polyglot context. Contrary to what the title of his book might lead you to believe, he has no need of Italian in his everyday life.

On the other hand, he missed many things that his patients were trying to say to him because he did not know certain languages. For words to suggest things and for things to escape words is not an exception but the rule. Meanwhile, polyglossia blurs the traces. When Nicolas Abraham and Maria Torok investigate the celebrated Wolf Man, one of Freud's patients, they approach the case from the standpoint of languages.[66] This patient spoke German with his psychoanalyst. But since childhood, he had spoken English with his nurse and Russian with his parents. What did he then say to Freud? In revisiting the analysis, the authors consider themselves archeologists tracking "archeonyms and cryptonyms," navigating signifiers using signifiers, sound images using sound images. The labyrinth is imagined with a single Ariadne's thread. Without doubt several bobbins are necessary to weave through it.

There exists no private language. If there was ever a strong bond between the individual and the collective, it is found in language. In this respect language is political. When Aristotle proposed definitions of man, he compared him to the animal and identified three specific differences. Man is an imitating animal who is pleased with images and finds himself able to create them. Man is a speaking animal because rationality cannot be manifest outside of language. For this reason, precisely, Aristotle considers man a political animal.

Still, we must make sure we are understood regarding language. Just because one governs, educates, and psychoanalyses in a certain language does not mean, as Derrida has emphasized, that it is necessarily one's own. But as Abdelader Khatibi puts it, "if there is no Language (*la langue*), if there is no absolute monolingualism, we must still pinpoint what makes a language maternal in its active division, and what is grafted from this language into one considered foreign and vice versa. Whatever is grafted there and is lost there, returns neither to the one nor to the other: the incommunicable."[67]

We find an interesting typo on page 29 of *Monolinguisme de l'autre*: "Among us, there are Francophone French speakers who are not Maghrebian; French speakers from *Fiance*, in a word, French citizens who have come here from France."[68] This error, a typographical lapsus, makes the Franco-Maghrebin of whom it is here a question into an incommunicable—a strange marriage announcement [*fiançailles*]. Between *Français* and *Fiancé*, an immaculate linguistic conception comes into the world, with one or several languages, nationalities, and citizenships.

Is not identity itself an Indo-European institution? All the postcolonial peoples of the world are affected by the identity trouble that Derrida pushes into the open with language. Like everyone else, such peoples are less the owners of their languages than they are owned by them. Languages are factors of dispossession and divestment. They are not possessions. No one holds them. Languages are not constitutive of communities. But they are the object of hegemonic threats.

They are hierarchized, put in the service of relations of force, of strategies of power. They are instrumentalized. Once again, the case of classical

Arabic is instructive. In a first step, this language, largely imaginary, was nationalized. In a second step, it was politically sacralized to such a point that to say nonreligious things implied a profanation of the Arabic language. *Al nahyy 'an al munkar, wal amri bil ma'rouf* ("the discouragement of what is hateful, and the injunction to obey what is virtuous") is understood to govern not just action but also language and the tongue itself.

In a way, monolingualism is a fiction. At the same time, the plurilingualism observed in Africa is a utopia. We can be content with neither "the tongue" [*la langue*] nor "the tongues." In fact, a language is an internal politics. It must neither be politically forbidden nor publicly suppressed. It is crucial that people be given access to speech. This is a lesson of the past; or at least, this is what the past teaches—from whence the problems posed by linguistic nationalism. Language sutures. It binds. Severed tongues are politically dangerous and personally toxic. Public or private aphasia is a form of alienation. But no language constitutes a homeland [*sol*]. Languages are all floating spaces of varied navigation. They are seas or oceans. The soil is a figure for rooting and uprooting. The sea and the ocean suggest the circulation and the instability of floating. To (re)politicize bonds, therefore, one must depoliticize languages.

Notes

1. Said, *Out of Place*, 198.
2. Kourouma, *Suns of Independence*, 16.
3. Zaire was the name of the Democratic Republic of the Congo between 1971 and 1997 under Mobutu Sese Seko. Under Mobutu's direction, a campaign of "Authenticité" was also launched to decolonize the country from Belgian colonialism. An example: the "Abacost" (an abbreviation for the French *à bas le costume*—literally, "down with the suit") was the distinctive wear for men promoted by Mobutu himself. In 1964, Tanganyika was renamed Tanzania. In the introduction to *Freedom and Socialism*, Julius Nyerere was convinced that throughout nearly the whole of Africa, "the first and most vocal demand of the people after independence was for 'Africanization.'" This is a narrative of return.
4. Heir to the franc of the French African colonies, created in 1945, the CFA franc, guaranteed by the French Treasury, has been since 1994 the official currency of the West African Economic and Monetary Union (UEMOA): Benin, Burkina Faso, Côte d'Ivoire, Guinea-Bissau, Mali, Niger, Senegal, and Togo. According to the former Togolese planning minister Kako Nubukpo, the CFA franc is "an instrument of voluntary servitude." See Nubukpo et al., *Sortir l'Afrique*. Its Central African equivalent is the franc of the Cooperation Financière in Africa for the Central African Economic and Monetary Community (CEMAC): Cameroon, the Central African Republic, Republic of Congo, Gabon, Equatorial Guinea, and Chad.

The Tunisian dinar and the Moroccan dirham have existed since 1958; the Algerian dinar, on the other hand, was instituted in 1964. None of these may be exported. Their convertibility is limited. The Euro and the dinar are exchanged on street corners in the black market. It would be interesting to examine the correlation between languages and currencies. As it happens, in a lecture given July 5, 2016, "Vertus de l'in-discipline," the great specialist in African literatures Alain Ricard related books, languages, and currencies, acknowledging that his ability to travel and collect books on foreign languages related directly to his relative purchasing power.

5. Cited in Deleuze and Guattari, *Kafka*, 94n25.

6. Youssi, AJDMR. See also Grandguillaume, "L'arabisation au Maghreb."

7. See Blommaert, *Language Ideological Debates*, particularly Stroud, "Portuguese as Ideology."

8. The disagreements between the north and the south of Sudan appeared as soon as Sudan became independent in 1956. Until then, it had been under Anglo-Egyptian domination since the nineteenth century. Two long civil wars tore the country apart.

9. English is also the official language in Botswana, Lesotho, Malawi (along with Chichewa), Namibia, Swaziland, Zimbabwe, Kenya (along with Swahili), and Zambia, where seventy Bantu languages are spoken, of which the most important are Bemba (23% of speakers) and Tonga (11% of speakers). Portuguese is the official language of Angola, Mozambique, and Guinea Bissau, where Bissau-Guinean creole, recognized as a regional language, is the vehicular language of the country.

10. The gulf between Europeans and indigenous peoples imposed by colonization was redoubled within the indigenous population itself. Linguistic breaks are, to be sure, always social breaks in their causes as well as in their effects. At first, the indigenous populations refused to attend French schools (1883–1922). However, because access to certain positions depended on ability in French, these populations ended up accepting education in French and even claiming it as their own (1922–62). A foreign language, French was taught to Algerians as if it were a "maternal" language, with programs and methods followed in France. Today, French enjoys a privileged status: it is a language at once foreign and familiar. Certain academic tracks in the university are always taught in French, including medicine, pharmacy, dental surgery, architecture, veterinary medicine, biology, agronomy, and mechanical engineering.

11. See Derradji, "Le français en Algérie."

12. Laroui, *Chez les Français*.

13. Sophie Rostopchine, Comtesse de Ségur (1799–1874), was a French writer of Russian birth. The novels for children of the Countess of Ségur were published from 1857 to 1872 in the Bibliothèque rose illustrée.

14. See Van Den Avenne, "Petit-nègre et bambara."

15. Fournier, *Le francais*, 6.

16. Delafosse, *Broussard*. Translator's note: Banania was an instant chocolate drink whose widespread and highly recognizable advertisements featured an African man grinning widely.

17. Senghor, *Hosties noires*; selected translations included in *Collected Poetry*. Among others, the book is dedicated to Léon Gontran Damas, from Guyane, and the Martinican Aimé Césaire. The book explicitly expresses Senghor's political solidarities and literary affinities. The citation is taken from "Liminary Poem," 39.

18. Lamko, "Un dilemme inépuisé," 63. See also, by the same author, "Comme un cœur obsédé."

19. George Orwell, "Politics," 362–63.

20. Orwell, "Politics," 362–63. Among other examples, see the inaugural speech of Denis Sassou Nguesso on April 16, 2016, at the Palais des Congrès in Brazzaville: "Discours d'investiture."

21. Cited by Diallo, "Langue et éducation."

22. Cited by Spivak, "Can the Subaltern Speak?," 282.

23. Sayad, "Bilinguisme et éducation," 208.

24. Appiah, *Cosmopolitanism*, xviii.

25. This is why so many are pleased at being able to speak an international African language (French, English, and, in a much smaller measure, Portuguese) enabling them to overcome the continent's intense linguistic fragmentation—or its prodigious diversity.

26. Mbembe, *On the Postcolony*, 7–8.

27. See Najab, "Multilinguisme et professions."

28. Ibrahimi, *Les Algériens*.

29. For a general approach to these questions, see articles in "Traduction et mondialisation," special issue, *Hermès*. One must be careful to distinguish "service language" (*langue de service*) and "cultural language" (*langue de culture*).

30. See Cassin, "Amnistie et pardon." See also Cassin, "Intraduisible et mondialisation"; and Gade, "Written Discourses on *Ubuntu*," where he writes, "It was during the period from 1993 to 1995 that the Nguni proverb '*umuntu ngumuntu ngabantu*' was often translated as 'a person is a person through other persons'" (313). For Gade, the first book to be written specifically on *ubuntu* is Samkange and Samkange, *Hunhuism or Ubuntuism*. Born into an Afrikaner family of writers, Antjie Krog is the author of *Country of My Skull*, a literary/journalistic account of the findings of the South African Truth and Reconciliation Commission.

31. Iveković, "Langue coloniale," 31.

32. Iveković, "Langue coloniale," 32.

33. Iveković, "Langue coloniale," 32–33.

34. Djebar, *Tongue's Blood*, 100.

35. Deleuze and Guattari, *Kafka*, 16.

36. Djebar, *Algerian White*, 15.

37. T. Yacine, "Anthropologie de la peur," 26.

38. Djebar, *Algerian White*, 19–20.

39. Djebar, *Tongue's Blood*, 116.

40. Deleuze, *Essays Critical and Clinical*, 57.

41. Deleuze, *Essays Critical and Clinical*, 55.

42. Deleuze, *Essays Critical and Clinical*, lv.

43. Deleuze, *Essays Critical and Clinical*, 4.

44. Deleuze, *Essays Critical and Clinical*, 4.

45. Deleuze and Guattari, *Kafka*, 18.

46. In 1940, the French publisher Gallimard published the French translation, made by Victor Ellenberger, of *Chaka* (1925), the famous Sesotho novel written by Thomas Mofolo. But despite Jean Paulhan's encouragement, Gallimard refused to publish more Sesotho books.

47. Rushdie, "Commonwealth Literature," 64.

48. For an overview of these questions, see Gérard, *Littératures en langues africaines*.

49. Many novels in local African languages were written because indigenous peoples were expelled from their lands and wanted to survive this ordeal. For example, in the Peul language, *Ndikkirijoom moolo (Ndikkiri the Guitarist)*, by Yero Doolo Jallo; in Akan, *Bere Adu* (*The Time is Gone*, 1913), by J. J. Adaye; in Boulou, *Nnaga Kon* (*The White Albinos*, 1932), by Jean-Louis Njemba Medou; in Ewé, *Amegbetoa alo Agbezuge le nutinya* (1949), by Sam Oblanim; in Xhosa, *USamson* (Samson, 1906), by Samuel Mqhayi; in Malagasy, *Raketaka Zandriko* (*Raketaka My Little Sister*, 1906), by Jean-Joseph Rabary; in Tamazigh, *Lwali n Wedrar* (*The Saint of the Mountain*, 1946), by Belaïd At-Ali; in Luganda, *Zinunula Omunaku* (1954), by Edward K. N. Kawere; and in Fon, *Bø gbæ ðie a?*, by Alidenu Vignondé. The French anthropologist Pierre Verger (1902–96) was a collector and an editor of Yoruba religious texts. For an overview of these questions, see Gérard, *Littératures en langues africaines*; or Ricard, *Le sable de Babel*.

50. Swahili is obviously a coproduction. By contrast, Yoruba was a local production.

51. According to Alamin M. Mazrui, Ibrahim Noor Shariff believes that *Uhuru wa Watumwa* (1934) was not written by James Mbotela because its level of Swahili is far too low, given that Mbotela was supposed to be a native speaker of Swahili. He believes the author is probably a European missionary who needed legitimacy among Africans with an African name. Shariff also suggests that Arabic rhymes and meters might be borrowed from the Waswahili instead of Swahili poetic conventions, which originated in Arabic. Swahili involves a cultural schizophrenia because this language is perpetually divided between its African and Arab sides. See Shariff, *Tungo Zetu*; and Mazrui, *Swahili beyond the Boundaries*, 174–75.

Attentive to the "duties of the Malagasy elite," according to the title of a lecture he delivered in 1932, Wast Ravelomoria (1886–1951) published several works including *Zaza niangarana* (1936) and *Boky mihidin' ny tanora, nosoratan'i* (1945). Samuel Edward Krune Mqhayi (1875–1945) defended Xhosa traditions in *Ityala lamawele* (*The Lawsuit of the Twins*, 1914).

52. Kenneth Kaunda (b. 1924) was the first president of Zambia (1964–91). Jomo Kenyatta (1890–1978), the first president of Kenya, studied anthropology at the London School of Economics. Joshua Mqabuko Nyongolo Nkomo (1917–1999), former vice-president of Zimbabwe, received a degree in social science from the Jan Hofmeyr School of Social Work in 1952 before founding the National Democratic Party (NDP) in 1960. The Ghanaian politician Kojo Botsio (1916–2001), who served in many top ministerial capacities in the government of Kwame Nkrumah, received a postgraduate degree in geography and education from Brasenose College, Oxford. Harry Mwaanga Nkumbula (1916–83) was a Zambian nationalist leader. After studying at Makerere University College in Uganda, he received a diploma from the Institute of Education, University of London, and later studied economics at the London School of Economics.

Julius Nyerere (1922–99), first president of Tanzania, was reported to have said "English is the Swahili of the world and for this reason must be taught and given the weight it deserves in our country." But his first minister of justice was Mathias Mnyampala, a Mgogo, a Catholic, and a great Swahili poet. See Roy-Campbell, *Empowerment through Language*, 100.

53. Théodore Monod (1902–2000) was a French naturalist, one of the greatest specialists in the Sahara.

54. See "L'esthétique et le message," interview with Chéri Samba conducted by Blada Mfukidi, May 5, 2004.

55. Tonda, "L'impossible décolonisation." See also Fardon, "'Destins croisés"; "Covering Ethnicity?"; and "Problem of 'Identity.'" The terminology—*ethnicities* (*ethnies*) in Africa or

castes in India—is a linguistic, textual, narrative, and discursive operation that must always be met with a critical interpretation.

56. Dozon, "Les Bétés."
57. Dozon, "Les Bétés," 60 (my quotation marks).
58. Dozon, "Les Bétés," 49.
59. *La nouba des femmes du mont Chenoua* (1979) and *La zerda et les chants de l'oubli* (1982) for Assia Djebar. In the filmography of Sembène Ousmane, one should particularly consider *Moolaadé* (2003), *Camp de Thiaroye* (1987), *Ceddo* (1976), and *Xala* (1974).
60. Chamoiseau, *Écrire en pays dominé*, 17.
61. Deleuze and Guattari, *Kafka*, 19.
62. Deleuze and Guattari, *Kafka*, 17.
63. Deleuze, *Kafka*, 23–25.
64. Lacan, *Other Side of Psychoanalysis*, 92 (translation altered).
65. Freud, *Psychopathology of Everyday Life*, 33–34.
66. Abraham and Torok, *Le verbier.*
67. Khatibi, *Du bilinguisme*, 10.
68. Derrida, *Monolingualism of the Other*, 12 (translation altered).

4

SEXED SPACE AND UNVEILED GENDER

Body, Veil, Sex

Violence Done to Women

COLONIZATION IS ONE OF THE CONTEXTS IN WHICH women are not mentioned except when they are raped, as if all violence done to women were concentrated in this crime, or as if one could not mention them at all outside of a passive situation. If rape is not of interest, then one studies prostitution, its images, its universe, its organization.[1] Meanwhile rape, symbol of violence, masks the apparatuses, particularly the colonial ones, that specifically target women.[2] It also leads us to miss the experiences of assault that can be recognized only if one first assumes that every colonized person has a personal life, emotional ties, and so on. Clearly the colony is not the only institution that engages in superficial indifferentiation ("all the same"); the colonial situation simply pushes it to the extreme.

At the same time, because colonial policies involve forced relocation and discrimination—indeed, segregation—their implementation necessarily depends on divisions and hierarchies supposed to render each person's lot entirely dependent on foreign powers, according to the category in which he or she is placed and according to the interests he or she serves. These policies are realized on the basis of sexual differentiations.[3]

Thus, the colony operates with a double standard. Women are both largely excluded from schooling and supposed to be protected by their male fellow citizens. Everything then happens as if, according to the old despotic way of talking, the distinctive mark of colonial politics were its benevolence toward women: they must be protected from their own people. But how? And in what sense? We must examine the conditions under which facts missed by ordinary observation become perceptible.

:h an inquiry allows subjects to be put back into a political process ıto a colonial history. It also allows us to illuminate, in the light of independence, present-day ways of talking (which are sometimes identical to remarks from the past) with respect to older attitudes. Finally, such an inquiry lets us draw lessons from anthropology and to give due credit to the diagnostic according to which, as Maurice Godelier says, "one cannot understand the nature of social relations without understanding the way they are thought and lived" because "these ways of thinking, of acting and of feeling constitute what one calls a particular 'culture,' and one sees that culture is inseparable from the social relations to which it gives meaning."[4]

A Law without Rights

Algeria was a unique colony. Claude Liauzu claimed that "in these experiences (of domination and control) Algeria occupied a specific place due to its importance, its role as a laboratory, the exceptional duration of its colonization and the gravity of the conflicts that marked its history, due to the final outbreak of violence, and also because of the exceedingly contradictory methods which were applied there."[5] Such a colony is an experimental terrain on which a colonial power believes it can do whatever it wants, with no regard for any principle whatsoever—transgressions are colonially constitutive.

The colony is not therefore a situation of simple political domination, leaving its natives free in most of their social activities. To the contrary, and particularly in Algeria, it affects every aspect of the country's social life to one degree or another. Starting on February 9, 1875, the French colonies were ruled by a set of dispositions foreign to French law, and a list of twenty-seven specific infractions was drawn up. One of them criminalized "negligence by the native agents of any category (adjuncts, cheikhs, oukaffs, kebirs and douars) to prevent crimes or infractions committed in their jurisdiction." This is the *code de l'indigénat*, more straightforwardly called the "billy-club code" (*code matraque*). In this state of exception, Algerian slavery was not suppressed by the decree of 1848, and polygamy was permitted there.

The colonial enterprise also attempts to destroy everyday ways of living. When corporations of artisans were prohibited in Algeria in 1884, this signified the death of artisanal manufacture. The only thing remaining were the rugs that, as long as anyone could remember, had been woven by women and were, ipso facto, not included in artisanal production properly so called. Although Morocco is known for its clay buildings, for a long time there has been no earth construction in Algeria, and the *ksours* are almost all in ruins.

This is the perspective from which we can observe the invasive character of colonial attitudes. Private life did not exist. The "respect for private life" was valid only for another world. In fact, if the domain of private life is first and foremost that of individual existence and of family life: then there can be no private life without there first being men and women, families, and children.

The colony imposes a right to surveillance over local peoples that is difficult for them to shake off. Concepts are at the forefront of this imposition. As Tzvetan Todorov remarked in his preface to the French edition of Edward Said's *Orientalism*, "the concept is the first weapon in making the other submit—because (although the subject cannot be reduced to the concept) it transforms him into an object; to delimit an object like 'the Orient' or 'the Arab' is already an act of violence."[6] One direct consequence of delimiting the object is the negation of personhood, both on the plane of thought and on the plane of action. To get away from the object and reach the subject, we must turn our backs on the other's submission and go over to his or her side. The operation is simultaneously subjective and objective. When it is simply objective, deceptive translations result [*"faux" amis*]. Some French have tried to stand out in this way. For example, to be friendly it does not suffice to give oneself a Muslim first name. Nor is it necessary.

But when it is subjective, this operation produces a real political friendship—in other words, an intimate solidarity and not an external indoctrination. In *Tout-Monde*, Édouard Glissant renders this homage to Fanon:

> In the military village, there were only proper married people. Sometimes there was a party, but it was within appropriate bounds. Most of the time, we Antilleans stayed among ourselves out of habit and were contented. Targin assures us that "there are Antilleans, students, who went over to the Arabs' side," I cannot believe that, that would really take nerve, but in the end, there might have been as many as two or three. "One even hears rumors over there," said Targin, "way down in the regions on the Sudan side, of a Martinican Algerian, he traveled for the Arabs, I believe he was called Frank Fanon."[7]

When Fanon arrived in the department of Algiers, he compared the situation he found to South African apartheid, so sharply did the colonial regime separate the European population, which, after the Crémieux decree of October 24, 1870, legally included the Jews of Algeria, from the Muslim population. Segregation in the matter of status or condition was at its peak. The possibilities of some corresponded to impossibilities for others.

He said this in *L'an V de la révolution algérienne*: "Algeria is a settlers' colony. The last settlers' colony to be talked about was South Africa. The points made are familiar to all."[8] It was this realization, and all the observations that he would make as he went along, that tipped him into political commitment and defense of the use of violence in the anticolonial combat. As he emphasized in his first book, it is the present that prepares the future, not the future that offers a model to the present. This is why he claimed no desire to "propose to prepare for the world coming after [him]."[9]

Apartheid is one figure for the content of political practices that prevailed in Algeria, as well as the heuristic path that allowed Fanon to gain a quick grasp on them and on the oppression reigning there. It was a mediation. He was already talking about it in 1952, in his chapter on "The Black Man and Psychopathology." He actually refers to an article on apartheid published in 1950 in *Les Temps Modernes*.[10] Thus he knows what the *code de l'indigénat* represents and has no mythological dreams before he sets foot on the African continent.

"Under the Act for Native Administration, the governor-general, as the supreme authority, has autocratic powers over the Africans. He can, by proclamation, arrest and detain any African considered a threat to disturbing the peace. He can prohibit meetings of more than ten people in any native sector. There is no *habeas corpus* for the Africans. Mass arrests without warrants are made at any moment."[11] Here one sees Fanon's understanding of how the colonial condition plays out in a settler colony, specifically South Africa, and how it oppresses a collectivity characterized as *indigène*, differing from Algeria only in being composed of black people. When Fanon approached Algeria and one of his psychiatric assignments, he was armed with this information about the country and with his reflection on racial alienation.

A Copernican Revolution

Because he paid attention both to racialization and to settler colonization, Frantz Fanon could approach the colony in an original manner, one that goes far beyond the simple anticolonialist fight and that has the merit of introducing sexuation into the analysis of colonial phenomena. He studied the various forms of colonial violence very attentively, whether in *Peau noire, masques blancs* or in *Les damnés de la terre*. Often accompanied by physical violence, forms of symbolic violence shape the subjectivities who, in any colony, are, ipso facto, partially or totally denied.

In *L'an V de la révolution algérienne* (1959), after having noted the resemblance between two African countries, Algeria and South Africa, Fanon goes on to carefully analyze the veil as a moving border between the colonizer's assaults and the passive resistance of the colonized.[12] This contrasted with the common practice then and even today of treating the veil as a manifest proof of backwardness from which only a few *évoluées*, as one said at the time, managed to escape.[13]

Indeed, to refuse the injunction was synonymous with stupidity. The Freud in the dream of "Irma's injection," recounted in *The Interpretation of Dreams*, considers Irma stupid because she did not accept his solution: she would be more intelligent if she followed his advice, because then, in opening her mouth, she would say about herself what Freud says about her. Sarah Kofman has spoken about this reference to the "suspended tongue."[14] On the other hand, intelligence consists in holding for one's own, as a woman, the views that the other would like one to hold and in saying with one's own mouth what he would like to hear. The supposed retardation of Algerian women thus refers at once to the (intellectual) stupidity proper to their (closed) sex and to the racialization that transforms this stupidity into (mental) backwardness.

In truth, Fanon's reinterpretation of this silent confrontation amounts to a Copernican revolution for two reasons. On the one hand, as with slavery, inertia will be understood as passive resistance. On the other hand, male-female relations will be perceived as a barrier to the project of colonial transformation, one that the colonizers would like to impose as indubitable testimony both to their victory and to its justifiability.

"We shall see," writes Fanon, "that this veil, one of the elements of the traditional Algerian garb, was to become the bone of contention in a grandiose battle, on account of which the occupation forces were to mobilize their most powerful and most varied resources, and in the course of which, the colonized were to display a surprising force of inertia."[15]

This would be the colonial strategy: "Get the women and the rest will follow."[16] It was supported by sociological analyses according to which Algerian society, beneath the patrilineal appearances, was supposed to be in reality an "essentially matrilineal structure." Fanon understood both sides simultaneously. From the side of the colonizer, indeed, it was a matter of a strategy beginning from the years 1930–35 of acting on men *via* women—using the women in order to dominate the men. Women represented an opportunity to devalue and to blame men so as to make them retreat.[17]

From the European side, men (employers) as well as women (technically called social assistants) were employed to unveil the *fatma.* To make the Algerian ashamed of the fate he reserved for his wife, "droves of social workers and women directing charitable works descended on the Arab quarters."[18] A colonial policy was set in action and carried out by numerous means, some of which seemed well intentioned. This is how the pressure was exercised not only more and more forcefully, but also more and more easily.

When bosses made social invitations to their employees, for example, they included their wives, thereby placing the men in an impossible situation: "If he comes with his wife, it means admitting defeat, 'prostituting his wife,' exhibiting her, abandoning a mode of resistance. On the other hand, going alone means refusing to give satisfaction to the boss; it means running the risk of being out of a job."[19] To unveil is "to attend the master's school."[20] The facts confirm his interpretation: "Servants under the threat of being fired, poor women dragged from their homes, prostitutes, were brought to the public square and *symbolically* unveiled to the cries of "Vive l'Algérie française!" ("Long live French Algeria!").[21] They were consequently shunned.

Starting from the colonizer's side, Fanon wound up on the side of the colonized, showing the profound stakes of the colonial relation among the colonized. This relation was violent because it was structurally and legally unequal and was differentiated on the basis of sex. Although they were made in another country and at a different moment, Guiliana Sgrena's observations in Bosnia are comparable. The wife of a man killed at Srebrenica in 1995 wore the veil to benefit from a certain kind of aid; others wore it to feel more secure in a war-torn country.[22] As a line of infranational distinction, the veil is supposed to indicate which side one belongs to, and this leads to its political instrumentalization.[23]

In this respect, the veil is a summons and a specific case of subjectivation in a situation of subjection, of constraint, but also in a situation where men are devalorized and thus their virility is disqualified. As stressed by the Egyptian Iqbal Baraka, director of the women's review *Hawaa*, the wearing of the veil "began to expand after the Arab defeat of 1967, when religious leaders attributed that loss to the fact that Muslims were becoming more distant from religion. According to them, the liberation of women was one of the principal reasons for it. Afterwards, terrible pressures began against the weakest and most marginal social stratum: women. It was a way of compensating for the deficit felt by Arab men who suffered repeated political defeats."[24] With the veil, the stakes of masculinity and the obsession with virility are all too clearly revealed.[25] Women's conduct appears to be derivative, almost as if in a trance, suspended, their situation under constraint. Thus, the wearing of the veil is not simply cultural and social; it is political.[26]

The Perversion of Relationships

Fanon was the first to illuminate the "sadistic and perverse character of these contacts and relationships" proper to the colonial system.[27] Even today we do not fully understand this character, not just insofar as it is a possible structure of political power but also as it plays a role in social relations. Nonetheless, we have discovered it under the rubric of "harassment," particularly in the workplace. "The tragedy of the colonial situation" is formulated not just in the language of politics, not just in the language of phenomenology or existential philosophy, but also in that of psychiatry.[28]

It is this truly tragic dimension that historiography, with its specific language, cannot express. But all the truth of the colonial situation is contained in this dimension. When it comes to expression, the language of politics is also relatively powerless, because either it is a (practically) agonistic language, or like the language of historiography, it is a (theoretically) neutralized language in which human flesh and life are not at stake.[29]

When it is not inquisitorial, however, psychiatry focuses on the subjectivity of individuals rather than attending to the personality of peoples. Psychiatry is capable of grasping what would otherwise escape notice, even among people considered "normal." The colonial military authorities did not overlook this: they exploited medicine as a spearhead of their politics of "pacification." What does it mean to focus on subjectivity? In the case that concerns us, as in every case, this means considering the question of reciprocity between colonizers and colonized and between men and women.

In fact, the question of reciprocity is not really a matter of persons or individuals, still less of peoples or populations, but first and most originally of subjects.[30] European men felt aggressivity and ambivalence with respect to Algerian women. "This woman who wants to see without being seen frustrates the colonizer. There is no reciprocity."[31] In fact, the desubjectivation of the subjected person is the fundamental logical operation carried out by the colonizers, their most basic syllogism. The colonial gaze prevents colonizers from becoming conscious of the fact that they are looked at, for then they would be required to apprehend the colonized or subjected person as a subject. This policy can backfire, as in the case at hand. "The history of the French conquest in Algeria," Fanon continues, "including the overrunning of villages by the troops, the confiscation of property and the raping of women, the pillaging of a country, has contributed to the birth and the crystallization of the same dynamic image. At the level of the psychological strata of the occupier, the evocation of this freedom given to the sadism of the conqueror, to his eroticism, creates faults, fertile gaps through which both dreamlike forms of behavior and, on certain occasions, criminal acts can emerge."[32]

Although the facts may occasionally conform to the colonial phantasies that one finds there, this is not always the case. But the colony is an extraordinary machine for phantasizing, insofar as the rules there are volatile, the laws unevenly applied, the regulations ad hoc. It is the explicit consideration of subjects that leads to sexual differentiation. Without subjects, there would be neither men nor women, but settlers and subject peoples, colonizers and colonized, indistinctly and indifferently. Without subjects, there would exist only bodies that can be assaulted in one way or another.

In general, the aggressions specifically reserved for women are highlighted in passing, without drawing attention to the simultaneously sexed and sexualized character of all colonial policy.[33] Consequently, to tell the truth about the colonial situation, we must not just investigate subjects and their lives, and therefore ask about women as well as men, but also open up our analyses (and our ears) to the hidden side of behaviors, choices, decisions, and policies.

Violence is meaningful starting from the moment that one hears the unthought and the unconscious that inhabit it. The language in which this can be formulated cannot, strictly speaking, be "scientific" in the sense that the academy defines this term. Indeed, this is why Fanon was not academically accepted when he presented his dissertation, *Peau noire, masques blancs*: his work did not appear to the academic authorities as being scientific. No one will miss the political dimension of this characterization.

Thus, Fanon was, we might say, sent almost ad patres, even if it were with his full consent, to a place figuring his academic death: the psychiatric hospital at Blida, in another colony than his own, which means, in the terms of that epoch, to another colonial department. He could thereby be confined to the periphery of knowledge. As a result, there are many respects in which Fanon is extremely well placed to understand the profound misdeeds of a multiform but unidirectional policy.

Body, Therefore Gender

Sensitive to the body, Fanon is also attentive to gender. One must recognize that it is not possible to speak immediately about the modification of the corporeal schema, to speak of musculature as the last personal refuge, to speak of subjective "abrasions" by colonialism. First one must be attentive to and implicated in a situation; one must be invested under one's own name. This allows one to observe things that few people pay attention to or take an interest in unless they have something to gain. It is also necessary to show that speaking of subjectivation is not the same as reducing colonial facts to subjective phenomena.

In one chapter of *Peau noire, masques blancs*, Fanon attacks the "so-called dependency complex of the colonized" and puts it through the same critique as Rousseau, in his own era, inflicted on the "right of the strongest."[34] Mannoni, originally a professor of philosophy, began to develop a *Psychologie de la colonisation* after having spent time in Martinique and then in Madagascar.[35] Fanon reproaches him for speaking the colonizer's idiom [*langue*] (in other words, his language [*langage*]) without ever being able to say even a few sentences or words in the idiom of the colonized.[36]

Mannoni is criticized for expressing himself in the language of psychiatry without being sufficiently knowledgeable to do the same in the language of politics. Mannoni reverses the order of causes and effects and, as a result, inadvertently denies the colonial phenomenon itself. With his "inferiority complex," he searches in people's subjectivity for explanatory elements that can be found only in the objectivity of their situation. Intellectual work in the colonial and postcolonial situation is, in this sense, necessarily bilingual and requires a constant work of translation and interpretation.

The problem is that this bilingualism is found far more often among the colonized than among the colonizers, due to the very fact of the colonial condition. From the colonizer's point of view, the colonized are closed up in their "maternal language." In fact, it is the colonizers who are monolingual: they do not know that the colony is a world cut in two. "After having imprisoned the Malagasy in his customs," Fanon writes, "after having unilaterally analyzed his vision of the world; after having drawn a closed circle around the Malagasy; after having said that the Malagasy has a dependency relation with his ancestors, characterized as being highly tribal, the author, in defiance of all objectivity, applies his findings to a bilateral understanding—deliberately ignoring the fact that since Gallieni the Malagasy has ceased to exist."[37] The colony is always a regime of violence on both the symbolic and physical planes, and these two types of assault are always closely correlated.

The colonized subject is presumed guilty—of ignorance, of a lack of culture, of savagery, of irrationality. Incapable of philosophy just as he or she is incapable of politics, this subject is reputedly mute, reduced to the inarticulate sounds of his or her voice and "dialect." It is not only colonial ideology that imposes this representation; above all, it is the colonial organization that transforms all those who would otherwise be equals into subalterns, rendered superficially uniform by their "personality" or their color and differentiated at the same time by their relative capacity for assimilation, their type of specific barbarism, the symbols of their backwardness, and many other things as well. Among the strongest, contempt and arrogance have the force of law.

Effacing the great division between the objective and the subjective, between what is historical and what is individual, proves rewarding. This strategy supposes that conditions of existence are subjectively determining. It supposes materialism. To comprehend all this, Fanon had to distance himself from his own original alienation as a young Antillean, with black skin and a white mask, and denounce the naturalization of differences in individuals' treatment according to their origin, their color, their affiliation, or as one said so often in Algeria, their personality.[38] His enterprise consisted in decolonizing psychiatric knowledge.

At that time, to speak schematically, he had to begin by relying on a classification of humanity into distinct and hierarchized kinds. "The normal African is a lobotomized European," said Dr. Carothers, an expert of the World Health Organization, in 1954.[39] Psychiatric knowledge was also based on an idealist conception of subjectivity in which, ultimately, the spirit or mind is always in charge. In this way, the colonial conditions of existence were eluded at the crucial moment. The expression of mental pathologies was subsequently attributed to the difference between cultures, not to the difference in conditions.

What makes Fanon a decolonial reference is his deconstruction both of the colonial vision and of the idealist and racist approach taken by the psychiatry of his time.[40] Decolonization thus appeared to him as the very opposite of a magical operation, a natural shock, or above all a private settlement: it was a form of combat. In a completely anachronistic way, one could say that Fanon was the first of the subalternists, so strong is his attention to discreet expressions, to insignificant facts, and to the weakest individuals.

Can the Subaltern(es) Speak?

Subaltern Studies is the work of a group of Indian researchers gathered around the historian Ranajit Guha and initially consisting of the historians Shahid Amin, David Arnold, Gautam Bhadra, Dipesh Chakrabarty, David Hardiman, Gyanendra Pandey, and Sumit Sarkar and the political scientist Partha Chatterjee. These specialists in modern India, working in India, Great Britain, Australia, or the United States, published ten volumes of *Subaltern Studies*, subtitled *Writings on South Asian History and Society*, between 1982 and 1989. Meanwhile, because the subalternists were united more by the positions they rejected than by those they actively supported, they were less a school than a forum for discussion. Their focus was the rewriting of history and the development of national consciousness.

To the question of knowing who makes history, the subalternists did not respond that it is the elite who direct the masses, but that it is the people who are the subject of their own history. Put otherwise, these are also the subaltern groups and the lower classes. Clearly these views were directly inspired by Marxism. This vision of things is found once again in the works on Algeria of Mohammed Harbi, who tries to study Algerian history from below and to show what it means for a movement like the struggle for Algerian independence to be a people's struggle.[41]

Gender, Speech, Writing

In this program, research is carried out retrospectively and in reverse, or, according to Guha's expression, against the grain. This is the standpoint from which they also tackled the question of gender. For this reason, Gayatri Chakravorty Spivak contends that the "historical" or "classic" Subaltern Studies was not informed by feminist theory and is no longer truly useful to feminist theory.[42] On the other hand, she believes that the new determinations of subalternity elaborated starting from the Foucauldian concept of biopower require that feminist theory be revised. The subalternists considered it important to know whether external perceptions of people's lives could also be conceived from the inside and expressed by a self—to know, in other words, whether the subaltern could speak.

Their preoccupation is shared by others. Thus, in *Orientalism*, Edward Said recounts that when Gustave Flaubert encountered Huchuk Hanem, an Egyptian courtesan, "*he* spoke for and represented her." Presenting the Balfour declaration, he notes: "It does not occur to Balfour, however, to let the Egyptian speak for himself, since presumably any Egyptian who would speak out is more likely to be 'the agitator [who] wishes to raise difficulties' than the good native who overlooks the 'difficulties' of foreign domination."[43]

The path by which Gayatri Chakravorty Spivak approaches this question in a renowned essay resembles in certain aspects the path taken before her by Fanon.[44] To this question, she responds firmly in the negative: "If, in the context of colonial production, the subaltern has no history and cannot speak, the subaltern as female is even more deeply in shadow."[45] No silent voice, in fact, can be restituted at a distance—sounded. The past is largely mute. It would seem that this is why we need literature.

A Child Is Being Beaten . . .

In the fourth part of her analysis, Spivak approaches the question on the basis of psychoanalysis, making reference to Freud and to Sarah Kofman, and concludes by constructing a problematic equation: "As a product of these considerations, I have put together the sentence 'White men are saving brown women from brown men' in a spirit not unlike the one to be encountered in Freud's investigations of the sentence 'A child is being beaten.'"[46] In 1919, Freud presented his text "A Child Is Being Beaten" as a "contribution to the study of the origin of sexual perversions" and focused on the difference between girls and boys in relation to this phantasy.[47]

In 1829, what were white men saving Indian women of color from? From the sacrifice of widows, *sati* (Sanskrit) or suttee (English transcription), which was abolished in that year. This case is the starting point for Spivak's demonstration that the colonizer's benevolence is the particular form taken by an imperialism, one that rests on an abusive reduction of what *suttee* means and on a profound misunderstanding of the ritual's internal stakes. Originally, *Sati* was not the proper noun meaning widow sacrifice but referred to the good wife. The British therefore committed a grave "grammatical error" that produced a constraint far greater than the injunction ordering a woman to burn herself on her husband's pyre.

Referring to the historian Pandurang Vaman Kane, Spivak then considers that "thus what the British see as poor victimized women going to the slaughter is in fact an ideological battleground."[48] Without entering into the complete details of her argument, we must stress the profound analogy between Spivak's interpretation of the British attitude toward suttee in India and the one Fanon proposes for the French attitude toward the wearing of the veil in Algeria. This is hardly surprising given that Fanon is a major reference for postcolonial thinkers—in other words, a source of inspiration.

In both cases, the position of the colonizers, the white men, rests on a crude vision. The historical, social, and political dimensions of the phenomenon are unknown. In the case of suttee, Spivak relates that in certain eras and in certain regions, this exceptional rule became a general rule with a specifically class dimension. The fact (veil, or suttee) is unconditionally tied back to tradition as well as to the alienation of the woman "of color" or "indigène." To be sure, this happens without calling into question the forms of British or French women's alienation; nor does it challenge the forms of emancipation internal and specific to women, according to the society in which they live; or for that matter the exact significations and the stakes of the positions at work there. We must add that unveiling, when it is not forced, is understood both literally and figuratively, or even materially and culturally.[49]

The relations between men and women are presumed heartily better on this score among Europeans, in this case British and French, than they are among non-Europeans, particularly Indians and Algerians. White men are not saving women of color but defending their own position. This means that women of color should expect nothing from white men, and above all not to be saved. To put it plainly, it is better to be an author in the colonies or a postcolonial intellectual from the Third World than a transparent thinker from the First World, which is to say one blind to himself or herself.

Spivak criticizes both Gilles Deleuze and Michel Foucault, but she relies on Jacques Derrida and Jean-François Lyotard. "I have attempted," she says, "to use and go beyond Derridean deconstruction, which I do not celebrate as feminism as such. However, in the context of the problematic I have addressed, I find his morphology much more painstaking and useful than Foucault's and Deleuze's immediate, substantive involvement with more "political" issues—the latter's invitation to 'become woman'—which can make their influence more dangerous for the U.S. academic as enthusiastic radical."[50]

Spivak refers to French philosophers. First she reconsiders the ideas defended by Derrida in *Of Grammatology*, which she translated into English, and takes her inspiration from his epistemological prudence.[51] In *Of Grammatology*, Derrida cautions against the frightful persistence of ethnocentrism and of the voluntary constitution of an Other to the "European subject": "Each time that ethnocentrism is precipitously and ostentatiously reversed, some effort silently hides behind all the spectacular effects to consolidate an inside and to draw from it some domestic benefit."[52] Spivak then borrows critical instruments from Lyotard. For, in this conflict over the interpretations of freedom, "the constitution of the female subject in *life* is the place of the *différend*."[53] For her, "what Jean-François Lyotard has termed the '*différend*,' the inaccessibility of, or untranslatability from, one mode of discourse in a dispute to another,' is vividly illustrated here."[54]

Widows: A Textbook Case

The British perceived suttee as a barbaric ritual. The French perceive the veil as a backward custom. What is more, the British interpreted the expression of a woman's free will as a crime. What should we think of a woman who, ready to be burned, recoils at the last moment? For the Indians, it is a culpable transgression that calls for penitence. But if the immolation must take place in the presence of a British policeman, as is sometimes the case, then it is a question of choosing freedom. Everything happens as if it were no longer the internal rule that prevailed, but a rule "imposed" by the colonial power.

What should we think of a woman who refuses to take off her veil after all this? It shows respect for the internal law, which testifies to a (relative) freedom to be herself and a guilty transgression of the exterior code of good conduct that the colonial power seeks to impose. This interpretive reversal is not just limited to the colonial situation. It is found again in the postcolonial situation when action, instead of being evaluated on its own merits relative to a given norm, is judged in relation to an exterior gaze bearing not on the action itself, but on the norm.[55]

The question of widowhood is no less crucial and central with respect to women than that of the veil in Algeria. It is not by chance that Spivak chose the case of suttee. In fact, when Dipesh Chakrabarty explores "domestic cruelty" and the "birth of the subject," it is on the basis of a certain type of literature, which even constitutes a literary genre. He also begins from an example, an article that appeared in the literary magazine *Ekshan* in 1991, devoted to a review of testimony by Bengali widows.

After the colonial scandal of suttee, in the years 1820–30, and after the 1856 law on the remarriage of widows, the fate dealt to these women captured everyone's attention and became a central subject for literature. The interesting aspect of this phenomenon for the historian is the question of knowing "what kind of a subject is produced at the intersection of these two kinds of memories, public and familial."[56] According to Chakrabarty, this subjectivation is due in part to the importation of a naturalist theory of compassion, and due in part to familial proximity, which is always one of the empirical factors of interest weighing on all those who, whatever their age, encounter the prohibitions of widowhood.

Closely examining the contributions of Hume and Smith, and their rational manner of thinking about sympathy toward others, Chakrabarty emphasizes that "the archive of the widow's interiority" was constituted by way of the novel, notably under the pen of Bankimchandra Chattopadhay (1838–94), Rabindranath Tagore (1861–1941), and Saratchandra Chattopadhyay (1876–1938). This is how intrafamilial affairs passed into the public domain. It is likewise thus that the woman's very body was displaced onto her "interiority."

Saratchandra Chatterjee (or Chattopadhyay, his Bengali birth name) offers an example of this phenomenon when he wonders, with respect to a young widow who was found in a man's company and who lost everything in one stroke, "Perhaps she has nothing called chastity left any more. Suppose I accept that. But what about her femininity? . . . Is the woman's body everything that matters, does her inside (*antar*) count for nothing?"[57]

This literature affected the self-understanding of its female readers. Quite often, fiction has served as a reference for the real itself. In the end, the distinction between the positions and voices of "agents" and "victims" of this cruelty toward widows became blurred—in such a way that, if there is a political subject emerging here, it is to the extent that "this single subject breaks up, on examination, into multiple ways of being human" and is ultimately irreducible to a given form of cruelty even if it is profoundly determined by it.[58]

Suttee functions a bit like the concept of the "stolen letter" that Lacan invented after having found it in Edgar Allan Poe.[59] It is a gaze that makes the invisible object into a piece of mail, something addressed and that can be read, if ultimately in multiple ways. This is really why Deepika Bahri, when she comments on Spivak's text, insists on the more or less critical ways that one can read the world in general and the postcolonial universe in particular.[60]

The postcolonial stakes of feminism are intense, because feminist struggles may appear as obstacles to national construction and to decolonization. Here the classic problem of prioritizing objectives is posed once again. Women's representation of themselves is neither uniform nor monolithic; to the contrary, it includes both positive and negative figures and can require, as Spivak has proposed, "representing" women, being their proxy.

"As soon as I must think about how I am going to speak as an Indian, or as a feminist, about how I am going to speak as a woman, I am actually trying to generalize myself, to make myself a representative."[61] This is to anticipate (but how?) the interlocutor's or receiver's reactions, without being able to predict any single result with confidence. It is also, secondly, to envisage her as not Indian, not feminist, not woman. Representation leads to aporias because it blocks speech without ever liberating it.

Position can only ever be understood politically, and not simply on the intellectual plane. It is only valid, if ever, in the context of a struggle or of a combat to impose a vision (which is always accompanied by material elements) on others who are either opposed to it or at least unfavorable. But one risks essentialization to the extent that one is supposed to embody "the Indian," "the feminist," "the woman." Now one is always "a" [*un* or *une*] male or female, never "the" [*le* or *la*]. Makeup is therefore indispensable for playing one's role properly. It corresponds to the prostheses enabling men to take up their own ceremonial roles.

The Conjugal Norm

The introduction of women in Gayatri Chakravorty Spivak's text differs in several ways from their presence in Frantz Fanon. Fanon is contemporary with the event; Spivak is not a direct witness. In suttee what is at stake are questions of succession. As for the veil, that is a matter of conjugality. Indeed, ever since *Peau noire, masques blancs,* Fanon had always proved very attentive to the types of desires and expectations that the colonial situation could foster in matters both of sexuality and of conjugality. He is even more attentive since the colony is a regime of sexual segregation, where endogamy prevails. "Legitimate" or "legal" mixed unions there are rare and, for this reason, remarkable.

When he comments on Mayotte Capécia's *Je suis Martiniquaise*, he shows how problematic the attitude of the "woman of color" can be in relation to the "white man." "Mayotte loves a white man unconditionally. He is her lord. She asks for nothing, demands nothing, except a for little whiteness in her life."[62] Fanon is familiar with a society that gives a specific name to the children of this mixed alliance: mulattos, indicating a status more than a quality of complexion. In Algeria, Fanon does not find that individuals are absolutely separated according to whether they are Europeans or Muslims. This is nothing new to him, but he deepens his examination of the phenomenon.

Objectively, rape stands for a transgression of the colonial code (the code that separates and divides), and subjectively, it stands for the colonial as transgressive ideal (the colonial state that permits, indeed authorizes). Indeed, perversion and total power [*toute puissance*] are marvelously wedded in a colony. What was called "marriage in the local style" [*mariage "à la mode du pays"*] in the French colonial empire, or at least in West Africa, meant quite simply that polygamy among the French themselves was rendered not legal but licit.[63]

The *signares* were well known in Senegal from the colonial times when Europeans whose wives remained in the metropole chose a concubine for the duration of their colonial stay. In the sixteenth century, Portuguese Jews, the *Lançados* (those who throw themselves—*se lancent*—into adventure) fleeing the Inquisition created comptoirs and married the daughters of the Sérère village heads. The mulatresses born of these unions, the *signaras* or *signares*, took over the business in leathers, cottons, indigo, spices, and sugar.

These women married only mulattos or Europeans. The Catholic Church endorsed these unions. Until the middle of the nineteenth century, at Saint-Louis or at Gorée, such Senegalese women enjoyed an enviable status in colonial society. Their position weakened with French colonization, after Faidherbe took over the region between 1854 and 1863, and his administration imposed juridical inferiority on women in keeping with the Napoleonic Code.[64] Nevertheless, their influence did not disappear. The custom remained.

Our interest here in the conjugal norm has nothing to do with its moral or social valorization but with the equal treatment that it presumes when it is respected. The norm is the mark of social and racial differentiation. This is why it attracted Fanon's attention. It refers to what is so well known that eventually one no longer interprets it: "There are an extraordinary number of mixed bloods in the colonies, in fact, even though there is no marriage or cohabitation between white males and black females. . . . Racial conflicts did not follow; they already existed. The fact that the Algerian settlers sleep with their little fourteen year old maids in no way proves there is no racial conflict in Algeria."[65]

Fanon's relevance, the reason he is of interest to postcolonial studies, has to do with his desire not to write in place of or to represent anyone except himself.

Speech Is Stolen

Nonetheless, it remains true that he wrote, according to Deleuze's apt phrase, "for the people who are missing." Fanon's texts have an audience in mind. They are not only addressed to the colonizers, omnipresent and loquacious. They are mostly addressed to those who are missing, the colonized, at best unacceptable interlocutors, and above all, the women among them, in their mute pseudofiguration (the silhouettes of cinema).

What Spivak denounced among the subalternists at the origin, Fanon realizes at his destination: writing does not replace a missing speech *ex post*, but to the contrary, permits it *ex ante*. Rather than seeking to *restitute* that absent speech, he strives to *institute* it. This marks a huge gap between the practices of historiography and those of psychiatry, or even more markedly, of psychoanalysis.

If the question of gender and that of speech are so intimately linked, it is because history from women's point of view (to differentiate it from what one calls the "history of women") is as much absent *in theory* as the feminine gender (the famous "second sex") is, in theory, mute. This is why the central question becomes one of theft—stolen history, hidden speech. Gender, one might say, happens on the quiet [*sans publicité*].

Reflecting on a "madman," Antonin Artaud, Jacques Derrida has truly grasped the way theft and speech are interwoven: "Theft," he writes, "is always the theft of speech or a text, of a trace. . . . The theft of speech is not a theft among others, it is confused with the very possibility of theft, defining the fundamental structure of theft."[66] In this chapter dedicated to *la parole soufflée* (whispered/stifled speech), the philosopher does not claim that there could be no theory of theft besides this one. He simply wants to bring "the essence of theft" into communication with the "origin of discourse."[67] It is not by chance, then, that Derrida—like Fanon, as we have already seen—directs his attention to dispossession, loss, separation, exile, and the flesh in Artaud.

We get a good example of stifled speech from Mayotte Capécia. In *Peau noire, masques blancs*, we know that Fanon dedicated his second chapter to "the woman of color and the White man." But this was much more a matter of "the woman of color and the European." When citing extracts from *Je suis Martiniquaise*, the novel that Mayotte Capécia published in 1948, he is exasperated. Even if it is both dated and derived from a youthful work, Fanon's position deserves to be made explicit:

> Every experience, especially if it turns out to be sterile, has to become a component of reality and consequently play a part in the restructuring of this reality. In other words, the patriarchal European family with its flaws, failings, and vices, in close contact with the society we know, produces about thirty percent of neurotics. On the basis of psychoanalytical, sociological, and political data it is a question of building a new family environment capable of reducing, if not eliminating, the percentage of waste, in the antisocial sense of the term. In other words, the question is whether the *basic personality* is a constant or a variable. All these frenzied women of color, frantic for a white man, are waiting.[68]

The scholarly language does not quite manage to conceal his irritation.

Nothing of the sort, meanwhile, when it comes to the man of color and the white woman, or the European woman. True, Fanon must be granted that the first interracial configuration is colonial while only the second is postcolonial. Fanon's remarks on Mayotte Capécia are examples of interpellation in the sense spoken of by Judith Butler. In *Giving an Account of Oneself*, Butler presents scenes of interpellation beginning with Nietzsche. She explains that a fundamental point of view on oneself emerges "only after certain injuries have been inflicted," as a result of the experience of suffering.[69] The scene of interpellation is the experience in which one is asked to "give an account" (*rendre compte*) of oneself.[70] "Telling a story about oneself," she adds, "is not the same as giving an account of oneself." The injunction redoubles, on a discursive ground, the suffering that one has empirically endured. "As we ask to know the other, or ask that the other say, finally or definitively, who he or she is, it will be important not to expect an answer that will ever satisfy. By not pursuing satisfaction and by letting the question remain open, even enduring, we let the other live, since life might be understood as precisely that which exceeds any account we may try to give of it."[71]

Mayotte Capécia

Mayotte Capécia, pseudonym of Lucette Ceranus Combette, wrote her book in an autobiographical mode.[72] Published in 1948, it was successful. Not everyone liked it. Jenny Alpha gave it a negative write-up in the journal *Présence Africaine*.[73] It was not so much a "report" or an "account" as a personal narrative or story [*récit de soi*], which responds to no injunction and does not follow from an interpellation.[74] This story goes back to childhood on the basis of "memories" that, singularly, make the young narrator simultaneously a "flawed *boy*" and a "*girl* of color."

Early on, the child tries to avenge an injury done to her by dumping black ink on the head of the one responsible, but Fanon does not pick up these kinds of signs. Ink (which serves for writing) is a reaction to the insult: "*négrillonne*." The author of this racist remark is struck in the head. Later, the child does not see in her future the classic schema giving the white man the (supposed) right to touch the black woman (*droit de cuissage/seigneur*). To the contrary, she sees a white woman (foreign—a Canadian woman) choosing a black man (Martinican). Fanon notes that she became a laundrywoman (*blanchisseuse*) but says not a word about her being the girl who led a gang.

The narrator depicts a situation familiar to everyone: the desire to get into a position where one need not be "in one's place." The act is a transgression. She turns it into a crucial experience that will determine her later conduct—to evade this type of place and situation.

> Among André's comrades, who like him were blockaded in the Antilles by the war, some had managed to have their wives come over. I understood that André could not remain apart; I also accepted not being admitted to this group, since I was a colored woman, but I couldn't help being jealous. It was useless for him to explain to me that his private life was something that belonged to him and that his social and military another, over which he had no control. I insisted so much that, one day, he took me to Didier. . . . I felt too heavily made-up, inappropriately dressed and that I didn't do justice to André, *perhaps simply due to the color of my skin*. Indeed, I spent such an unpleasant evening that I decided never again to ask André to accompany him.[75]

The lived experience of the black man leaves little place for the black woman's lived experience. Makeup, like clothing, appears displaced to the narrator. She is out of place. "Perhaps simply because of the color of my skin"—it is interesting that she expresses not an affirmation but a doubt. It comes back not to an *act* (making oneself up, dressing up) but to a *state*, not to an item of clothing but to a complexion. In the end, where one might have found a possible belief, this expression reveals an irreducible incredulity.

Henceforth identity (gender, race) appears as a reality in the Freudian sense of the term: a discourse that describes and creates a vision of the world for those who participate in it. Identity is not a reality in the empirical sense; it is a representation of one's life. As for discrimination, in other words the injury endured because of identity understood in this sense, it is like the very death of the subject. And as a death of the subject, it constitutes something both real and impossible—in other words, something unbelievable. But the subject is less in question than the world. Worlds must be undone.

The difference here between childhood and adulthood is remarkable. The combativeness of the narrator's first years gives way to the censorship of maturity.

> Of course, at times there were incidents between the white and black children, but it wasn't like in the United States. I, *a colored girl*, didn't mind at all when I provoked them. In any case, when a classmate failed to respect me—treating me like a *négrillonne*, for instance—I took out my inkwell and threw it, showering his head. This was my way of changing whites into blacks. The ink ran down his shirt and that caused a ruckus which at the end of school, degenerated into a fight between my followers and those of the ink-spattered one, sniveling in the corner and thinking about the spanking he was yet to receive at home.[76]

Mayotte keeps her inkpot at hand in the most incongruous situations. Her exit from childhood arrived with the chagrin of her friend Loulouze, driven from her home, who told her this: "Life is hard for a woman, you'll see, Mayotte, above all for a colored woman" ("*La vie est difficile pou' une femme, tu ve'as, Mayotte, su'tout pou' une femme de couleu'*").[77] The French *r* was never so well said; the accent, that phantom tongue, rolls it or forgets it, giving no respect to the letter.

It is on the basis of genealogy that she imagines the choice of a white man as lover:

> Surely, I was not the only one to have white blood, but a grandmother was less commonplace than a white grandfather. So then my mother was a *métisse*? I should have suspected this because of her pale complexion. I found

> her prettier than ever, more refined, more distinguished. If she had married a white man, would I, perhaps have been all white? . . . And would life have been less difficult for me? . . . How could a Canadian woman have loved a Martinican? I, who was still thinking about Monsieur the Curé, decided that I could only love a white man, a blond with blue eyes, a Frenchman.[78]

To make life easier? And what role does the curé play in her phantasy?

A Sexuality in the First Person?

"Mixed" postcolonial people share a concern about not only being legitimate but also, and above all, having an "indigène" father who never left the islands. Thus understood, interraciality [*mixité*] is a postcolonial phenomenon in which the places of men and women are reversed: women come from the former colonial powers; men are originally from the colonies. It involves a type of union prohibited by the colony, which explains its postcolonial success.

In fact, contrary to the charges advanced so often (in Algeria), the two groups did not live together in the colony (in harmony) but were side by side—they did not bond sexually. The Europeans and the indigènes, the whites and the blacks did not mix. They exchanged fluids without officializing their loves. The children were not recognized by their fathers. This had been the life of Lucette Ceranus Combette. From a liaison with a young French officer, she had a child. He himself never imagined marrying her or recognizing the child. "He had accepted the inevitable complications that were going to be created by this child of color that he could never recognize . . . the one who meanwhile would be born from his works and from his flesh."[79]

With *Je suis Martiniquaise*, it is no longer a matter of conjugality or of widowhood but of sexuality. This is expressed directly and actively. The character desires sexual relations and enjoys them. Thus, the woman expressing herself in the first person is not submitting to men of color from indigenous custom or from autochthonous tradition. She is a woman with a grip on herself who claims to prefer independence more than anything else. She is also someone who is confronted, by choice, with the "progressive" white or European who loses her despite the feeling that he is saving her.

In fact, the officer with whom Mayotte had an affair wrote his own memoir, one that allows us to discern his personal point of view from hers. The title of this text is "God Is Love." What did the officer say to his mistress? "Mulatto race, to be sure, but nothing negro about it; her face rather recalled those delicious dolls that are born from the guilty loves of robust French colonists and frail Annamites. Everything about her was attracting, intriguing, down to her simple and natural attitude, her air resembling a little girl fascinated by the telling of a marvelous tale."[80]

The ink and the writing are essential to Mayotte Capécia's character. But *Je suis Martiniquaise* appeared to have no author. It was thought to be composed of excerpts from elsewhere, that the author was illiterate, that it had been written by ghost writers (*nègres*), that the publisher had realized an editorial coup in adapting the text of Lucette Céranus Combette's lover. *Je suis Martiniquaise* was thought to be a fictionalized representation of her own life, but one she herself did not write. Treated with contempt in *Peau noire, masques blancs*, Mayotte Capécia testifies to the difficulty of escaping the suspended tongue and the stifled word.

The lactification Fanon denounced is not unrelated to the ventriloquism attributed to Mayotte Capécia. To be a ventriloquist is to be capable of speaking without moving the lips using a voice that seems to come from the belly. The voice is thus referred not to the mouth but to the belly, not to intelligence but to sexuality. Gender is not dissolved in color or race, and each must—someone will see to it—stay in his or her place. To some the pens, to others the inkwells. It is just one more form of violence. It is said that when she arrived in France, Lucette Céranus Combette barely knew how to read and write French.[81] After *Je suis Martiniquaise*, published in 1948, *La Négresse blanche* appeared with the same editor in 1950. Caribbean discourse was still a long way off. Can the subaltern(es) speak?

Notes

1. The first "Algerian" text on prostitution was written by Saadia-et-Lakhdar (Salima Sahraoui-Bouaziz and Rabah Bouaziz): *L'aliénation colonialiste et la résistance de la famille algérienne*. The chapter on prostitution articulated the commodification of Algerian women with the emasculation of men. See Taraud, *La prostitution coloniale*; Limoncelli, *Politics of Trafficking*, 123–32; Ferhati, "La danseuse prostituée"; Ferhati, "Enquêter sur la prostitution"; Ferhati, "Ambivalence des discours politiques"; and Ferhati, *La "tolérance" en Algérie*. Like the work of other Algerian academics, Berkahoum Ferhati's research has been the object of censorship in Algeria: the populations of the region concerned refused to be associated with prostitution, even in bygone times. It was a question of honor . . .

2. See Ighilahriz and Nivat, *Algérienne*; also, Lazreg, *Twilight of Empire*.

3. See Stoler, *La chair*. The author takes a detailed interest in the "racial incorporation of sexuality" (75), noting, in the plantations of Sumatra, the synonymy between domestic and sexual service. Thus, colonial sexualization led inevitably to a particular concern for the management of

mixed persons, or *métis*, who incarnated a border-body (both included and excluded), as well as impurity (nonpure blood). In fact, mixed persons jeopardized the very notion of reproduction, which is as much social as it is biological and therefore as much racial as it is sexual. The *métis* represents the failure of "reproduction" and the disturbance of the "community." This is how Stoler shows that fundamentally, and by the stakes he or she sets in motion, the *métis* is a "social good," a "political body" all by himself or herself. See also Stoler, *Carnal Knowledge*. In *Race and the Education of Desire*, the anthropologist observes that Foucault "links racism and the technologies of sexuality directly to biopower, without linking racism and sexuality explicitly to each other" (35). If so, an analysis of racisms is therefore necessarily a study of the ways sexualities are ordered, since research into sexual norms would have to include an interrogation of their racializing aspects.

4. Godelier, *Communauté, société, culture*, 28.
5. Liauzu, *Colonisation*, 124.
6. Todorov, "Preface à l'édition française," 23.
7. Glissant, *Tout-Monde*, 325–26.
8. Fanon, *Dying Colonialism*, 28.
9. Fanon, *Black Skin, White Masks*, xvii (translation altered).
10. Skikne, "Apartheid", cited by Fanon, *Black Skin, White Masks*, 162.
11. Fanon, *Black Skin, White Masks*, 161.
12. Fanon, "Algeria Unveiled," in *Dying Colonialism*, 35–67. For a contemporary point of view, see "Un livre sur la guerre d'Algérie" (author unknown), a review of Fanon's *L'an V de la Revolution Algerienne*. See also Fassin, "Fanon."
13. Only 4.5 percent of Algerian women were literate in 1954. Only three Muslim women were elected to the National Assembly in November 1958, including Nafissa Sid Cara (1910–2002). Elected as a *député* from Algiers, she was the first Muslim woman member of the French government and was secretary of state for Algerian affairs from 1959 to 1962. On May 25 1959, she said:

> Who are these Muslim women? For the most part, unknown people who did not count. Why? Because many of them were illiterate, poor. They were preoccupied with a totally material life and as a result were slaves to those concerns. What I am telling you is above all true for the women in the countryside, those from the mountains, those of the djebels who lead an archaic, medieval, extremely hard life. . . . Uneducated and poor, meanwhile (urban women) felt that it was necessary to send their students to the school and they sent them there. But when the girls reach the age of 12, 13, 14, they are closed off, cut from the external world, brought back home, veiled and married . . . they have had to fight against the hostility of older women, grandmothers, aunts who did not want to see them "do schooling," because schooling was emancipation, a rupture with traditions and consequently with the family. . . . They had to struggle against the hostility of numerous jealous neighbors. From the European side, they also had to struggle against reservations, because they were not completely accepted: there remained differences between the young Muslim girl and the young European girl who were sitting on the same bench to study. Differences of clothing, for example (for the young Muslim woman); her body . . . could not be exposed and thus her dress was too long, too large, she was never in fashion. . . . These girls . . . have suffered, in short, from having broken with the family environment and from the other side, from not feeling comfortable in the European environment.

See Debré, "Sid Cara, Nafissa."

14. Kofman, *Enigma of Woman*, 42–48. Here is someone who challenges the meaning of the French expression *avoir la langue bien pendue* (to have a sharp tongue).

15. Fanon, *Dying Colonialism*, 36–37. In keeping with these resources, French propaganda and the ideological fight must also be considered. Several documentaries have been made, such as *The Arab Women of the Bled*, *Women*, and *Blessing of God*. A film on the veil was thus produced for the consumption of the American public: *The Falling Veil*. According to Matthew James Connelly, "The narrator describes how de Gaulle appealed directly to women during his June 1958 visit to Algeria: 'His confidence in the women acted almost as an electric current for many of them, a kind of psychological shock . . .' Considering that electricity was the weapon of choice for French torturers, this metaphor could not have been more maladroit." Connelly, *Diplomatic Revolution*, 216. "This film clearly influenced an article in the *New York Times* in July 1958 called 'The Battle of the Veil.' According to the author, the forces of modernity . . . were pitted against the defenders of tradition, mostly elderly theologians." Scott, *Politics of the Veil*, 62.

16. Thus, the women become hostages. The system of "grandes concessions" of Haute-Sangha, formerly Oubangi-Chari and today the Central African Republic, gave rise to similar strategies—attacking women in order to get control over the men, with murderous results. Savorgnan de Brazza wrote the following to the minister of colonies (report no. 148 of August 21, 1905): "The most serious incidents took place between the Haute-Sangha and the Haut-Oubangi, because there was collusion between the private agents and certain administrators. . . . The kidnapping of women from the native villages was used in the usual way to requisition porters on the road from Fort-de-Possel to Fort-Crampel. . . . It is still considered the natural complement of all repression." De Brazza, *Mission d'enqête*. Brazza had already been horrified in 1869 by the French repression in Algeria. He was later accused of carrying out "philanthropy" rather than "colonization."

17. Fanon does not mention Zohra Drif, Hassiba Ben Bouali, or Djamila Bouhired, although they were so well known and so deeply implicated in the Battle of Algiers. See Reid, "Frantz Fanon's 'L'Algérie.'" "Algeria Unveiled" ("L'Algérie se dévoile") thus resembles—though only in certain respects—the chapter on "The Woman of Color and the White Man" in *Black Skin, White Masks*, which will be discussed later. But in "Algeria Unveiled," it is mostly a question of Algerian women fighters and of men's strong need for their participation. Finally—although this is often forgotten—Fanon was not writing from the depths of a university library in peacetime, and he produces the following note: "We are mentioning here only realities known to the enemy. We therefore say nothing about the new forms of action adopted by women in the Revolution. Since 1958, in fact, the tortures inflicted on women militants have enabled the occupier to have an idea of the strategy used by women. Today new adaptations have developed. It will therefore be understood if we are silent as to these." *Dying Colonialism*, 50.

18. Fanon, *Dying Colonialism*, 38.

19. Fanon, *Dying Colonialism*, 40.

20. Fanon, *Dying Colonialism*, 42.

21. Fanon, *Dying Colonialism*, 62.

22. Sgrena, *Le prix du voile*, 19.

23. Shepard, "La 'bataille du voile.'"

24. Interview on LBC-TV, May 28, 2006, cited in Sgrena, *Le prix du voile*, 183.

25. Note: The generator (*gégène*) used on male genital organs could lead to impotence. In *La gangrène*, Jérôme Lindon published the testimony of Bachir Boumaza (1927–2009), future minister of the Ben Bella government (1962–65) and future president of the National Council (1997–2001), who was imprisoned from 1958 to 1961 (he escaped). Tortured, he was rendered

impotent. See also, on torture, Sahnoun, *Mémoire blessée: Algérie 1957*. He became a diplomat and was notably Algerian ambassador to the United States (1984–89). See Cole, "Intimate Acts."

26. "It is the white man who creates the Negro. But it is the Negro who creates negritude. To the colonialist offensive against the veil, the colonized opposes the cult of the veil." Fanon, *Dying Colonialism*, 47. The veil is thus the analogue of negritude—a counteroffensive. It is to hold one's own. Does this mean that the question of the veil has found a solution? Fanon responds in the negative.

27. Fanon, *Dying Colonialism*, 40. An older example, in central Africa, of the sexualization of abuses: "A black person lying stretched on the ground and held by secure bonds, this involved making a cartridge of formidable explosive, that someone would have previously adapted for the purpose, on his back. . . . One of these miserable creatures had to go search for the cartridge. It was fixed between the patient's shoulder blades, when a new refinement of cruelty sprouted in the executioner's brain. They believed that the experience would be infinitely more conclusive if the copper tube were stuffed down his throat. The black screamed. A detonation echoed; bloody debris, limbs, and intestines were flung a very great distance." See "Les bourreaux des noirs."

28. Fanon, *Dying Colonialism*, 40.

29. Today this situation is counterbalanced by historians such as Ivan Jablonka for whom history is a form of contemporary literature. Thus, in 2012 he published *Histoire des grands-parents que je n'ai pas eus*.

30. See Studer, *Hidden Patients*. The author wonders if the small place reserved for "Muslim" women in the archives of the psychiatric wards in North Africa reflects their true place. In reality, if they were underrepresented in the hospitals, the doctors did not accord them the same interest as they did other patients. Their existence is in absentia, as in the film of Alain Resnais, *Muriel, ou Le temps d'un retour* (1963). Muriel is the fictional name of a real Algerian woman. See Branche, "Mémoire et cinéma."

31. Fanon, *Dying Colonialism*, 44. Precisely this argument could be found once again with respect to the wearing of the burqa in France.

32. Fanon, *Dying Colonialism*, 45.

33. This sexualization has persisted, particularly in the homosexual imaginary. The Front homosexual d'action révolutionnaire (FHAR), founded in 1971 by lesbian feminists (Christine Delphy) and gay activists (Guy Hocquenghem), was thus able to reproduce the most tired clichés about the "Arab"—the most racialist, most colonialist, and most shared by the extreme right: "What is great about them, it is that one can drink up virility. Sometimes it is said that we do not like heteros, because they are phallocrats, but we like Arabs quite a bit and they are phallocrats; we like to enjoy the virility"; "What are the Arabs? A knockout cock, nothing but." From "Les Arabes et nous," discussion among Patrice Finet, Guy Chevalier, and Michel Cressole in *Trois milliards des pervers*, 14. In the same volume, "Sex-pol en acte," which is the commentary on it attributed today to Gilles Deleuze, contains this observation: "The manner in which racist themes appear, manifesting a fascist and racist desire, crops up now and again—from the side of the men who are speaking, but also from the side of the Arabs who are absent and who are spoken about" (29). In these texts, as elsewhere, one also finds the development of an erotics regarding the Algerian War. Shepard speaks of an "eroticism of Algerian difference." See Shepard, *Mâle décolonisation*; and Idier, *Guy Hocquenghem*.

34. Fanon, *Black Skin, White Masks*, 64–88.

35. Mannoni, *Psychologie de la colonisation*. The text reworks and develops a set of articles that appeared in 1947–48 in *Psyché, Revue de psychologie des peuples, Chemin du monde*, and *Esprit*. Octave Mannoni (1899–1989) spent eighteen years in Madagascar, where he taught before becoming a psychoanalyst and which he left at the moment of the revolt of 1947. In his *Discourse on Colonialism*, Aimé Césaire critiqued him sharply. It was in response to this book that Fanon, who knew it well, wrote *Peau noire, masques blancs*. Mannoni's book is read more in the United States than in France, where its reception was mostly negative, although it influenced the anthropologist Georges Balandier—who eventually wrote, with reference to Mannoni, a "Sociologie de la colonisation." In speaking of this controversial book, in 1966 Mannoni wrote an article with an evocative title: "The Decolonisation of Myself." At bottom, far from Marxist theses, Mannoni sought to explain that race was more important than class and could not be reduced to it and that, consequently, an economic approach to colonization was inappropriate. "Economics explains to us how one can seek to dominate men in order to acquire superior wealth. But it has little to say about someone who makes use of his economic superiority simply to enslave someone. Now it is necessary to consider this sort of pleasure if one wants to understand colonial economics as colonial per se" (Mannoni, *Psychologie de la colonisation*, 218). See the detailed commentary of Vatin, "Octave Mannoni." See also "Fanon and Manonni: Conflicting Psychologies of Colonialism," app. 1 in McCulloch, *Black Soul White Artifact*.

36. Translator's note: The distinction between *langue* and *langage* is important in the theoretical work of Édouard Glissant. According to translator Betsy Wing, *langue*, which was translated as "self-expression" in *Caribbean Discourse* and which she translates in *Poetics of Relation* with "language-voice," refers to either national or dialectal spoken language, while *langage* refers to the way *langue* is used, particularly those ways that "can cross linguistic borders" and become culturally dominant. When written, language usually functions in the mode of *langage*. Glissant, *Poetics of Relation*, 173, 217n1.

37. *Black Skin, White Masks*, 74. Joseph Gallieni (1847–1916) was a soldier and colonial administrator, governor general of Madagascar (1896–1905), in charge of efforts to "pacify" the island. He immediately had Prince Ratsimamanga arrested along with his interior minister, Rainandriamampandry; they were executed. Queen Ranavalona III was arrested as well and deported first to Réunion, then to Algeria. Gallieni also established forced labor of indigènes. He applied a "racial politics" justified in terms of Gobineau. Taking inspiration from General Bugeaud in Algeria, in turn he was an inspiration to Hubert Lyautey (1854–1934) in Morocco, his future collaborator. On Gallieni and Lyautey, see Venier, "Une campagne."

38. In May 1951, the review *Esprit* opened with a text from Fanon, "La plainte du Noir, l'expérience vécue du Noir" (657–79), and concluded with an article by Mannoni titled "La plainte du Noir" (734–49).

39. Fanon, *Wretched of the Earth*, 227.

40. See Haddour, "Fanon."

41. An FLN expert during the negotiations at Évian, Mohammed Harbi (b. 1933) was later Ben Bella's adviser. Imprisoned without a trial, he escaped and went into exile in France, where he became a historian. In particular, he published *La guerre commence en Algérie* (1998), *L'Algérie et son destin: Croyants ou citoyens* (1992), and *Une vie debout, mémoires politiques, tome I: 1945–1962* (2001).

42. Spivak, "New Subaltern."

43. Said, *Orientalism*, 6, 33.

44. Spivak, "Can the Subaltern Speak?"

45. Spivak, "Can the Subaltern Speak?," 287.

46. Spivak, "Can the Subaltern Speak?," 296; Kofman, *Enigma of Woman*.

47. "In my patients' *milieu*," writes Freud, "it was almost always the same books whose contents gave a new stimulus to the beating-phantasies: those accessible to young people, such as what was known as the '*Bibliothèque rose*,' *Uncle Tom's Cabin*, etc. The child began to compete with these works of fiction by producing his own phantasies." As the production of phantasms, literature thus appears as a vector of subjectivation. The question of masculinity and femininity is particularly expressed in these lines from Freud: "The theory of the masculine protest seems to maintain its ground very much better on being tested in regard to the beating-phantasies. In the case of both boys and girls the beating-phantasy corresponds to a feminine attitude." Freud, "Child Is Being Beaten," 180, 202. With respect to another of Freud's texts, "The Taboo of Virginity," in which the psychoanalyst invokes three literary texts to confirm his hypotheses, Sarah Kofman writes that he "'enjoys' [*joue*] knowledge without possessing it." See Kofman, "Judith."

48. Spivak, "Can the Subaltern Speak?," 300.

49. See Gafaïti, "Histoire des femmes."

50. Spivak, "Can the Subaltern Speak?," 308.

51. Derrida, *Of Grammatology*. The philosopher was taught by psychoanalysis to suspect the transparency of statements, which makes him one of the first to transform philosophy on the basis of psychoanalysis and, in other terms, on the basis of the idea of the unconscious, which is what we find at stake in deconstruction. Of both deconstruction and psychoanalysis, René Major would later say that "what they have in common is being fundamentally and thoroughly tests of translation and of the untranslatable, therefore of transferences, transplants, and displacements." See Major, *Lacan avec Derrida*.

Derrida writes: "People would like to make us forget psychoanalysis. Will we forget psychoanalysis?" "Today, in the climate of opinion, people are starting to behave as though it was nothing at all, as though nothing had happened, as though taking into account the event of psychoanalysis, a logic of the unconscious, of 'unconscious concepts,' even, were no longer *de rigueur*, no longer even had a place in something like a history of reason . . . as though, finally, it were again legitimate to accuse of obscurity or irrationalism anyone who complicates things a little by wondering about the reason of reason, about the history of the principle of reason or about the event—perhaps a traumatic one—constituted by something like psychoanalysis in reason's relation to itself." Derrida, "Let Us Not Forget," 3, 4.

52. Derrida, *Of Grammatology*, 80.

53. Spivak, "Can the Subaltern Speak?," 301. See Lyotard, *Differend*: "A differend [*différend*] would be a case of conflict, between (at least) two parties, that cannot be equitably resolved for lack of a rule of judgment applicable to both arguments" (xi). "Is it up to the historian to take into account not only the damages, but also the wrong? Not only the reality, but also the meta-reality that is the destruction of reality?" (57).

54. Spivak, "Can the Subaltern Speak?," 300.

55. See Bouamama, "Ethnicisation et construction idéologique."

56. Chakrabarty, *Provincializing Europe*, 119.

57. Cited by Chakrabarty, *Provincializing Europe*, 139–40.

58. Chakrabarty, *Provincializing Europe*, 148.

59. "The Purloined Letter" (1845)–"a letter, a litter, une lettre, une ordure"—is a short story written by Edgar Allan Poe. Dupin, in Paris, enquires about a mystery. A certain princess

received a letter and opened it, but, because the Countess Deval came in, she put the envelope back on the table. Then, the dangerous letter could not be found. Translated into French by Baudelaire under the title "La lettre volée" ("The Stolen Letter"), it was rebaptised "La lettre en souffrance" ("The Purloined Letter") by Lacan. In his "Séminaire sur la letter volée," Lacan follows Marie Bonaparte's interpretation without mentioning her by name; he analyzes the novella by distinguishing between the gaze that sees nothing, the gaze that sees this blindness and believes that the letter is not in danger, and finally the gaze that observes the two others and understands that the letter is available for whoever wants to take it. Following Freud, he suggests that "the signifier's displacement determines subjects in their acts, in their destiny, in their refusals, in their blindnesses, in their success and in their fate; despite their innate gifts and their social assets, without regard to character or to sex, and that everything pertaining to the psychological pregiven will follow the signifying chain lock, stock and barrel." For Lacan, this letter is "like an immense female body." See "Seminar on 'The Purloined Letter,'" 21, 26 (translation altered). Jacques Derrida, who met Lacan in 1966, then reworked Lacan's analysis in his seminar *Le facteur de la verité* beginning from the question: "To inhabit fiction; is this, for the truth, to make fiction true or truth fictive?" For Derrida, it is a matter of enabling "the scene of the signifier to be reconstructed into a signified . . . writing to be reconstructed into the written, the text into discourse, and more precisely into an 'intersubjective' dialogue." This is why he invented the concept of the trace. See Derrida, *Post Card*, 421, 432.

60. Bahri, "Le féminisme."

61. Cited by Bahri, "Le féminisme," 311–12.

62. Fanon, *Black Skin, White Masks*, 25.

63. See Sankalé, *À la mode du pays.*

64. Louis Faidherbe (1818–89) was a soldier and colonial administrator. He participated in the conquest of Algeria (1849–52) and then became governor of Senegal (1854–61 and 1863–65). In 1857, he formed his first contingent of *tirailleurs* (infantry). Then he returned to Algeria once more (1867-70). He spoke Arabic and Wolof. See Hesseling, "L'annexion du Sénégal," 121–24.

65. Fanon, *White Skin, Black Masks*, 28–29n5.

66. Derrida, "La parole soufflée," 175. Antonin Artaud (1896–1948) was an artist and writer; he went through several stays in psychiatric institutions. He published a collection of poems: *L'ombilic des limbes* (1925). He invented the "theater of cruelty," which he theorized in *Le théâtre et son double* (1938). Already a lover of laudanum, he discovered peyote during a trip to Mexico (1936) among the Tarahumaras. In 1948, he published *Van Gogh le suicidé de la société*. The voice is not that of *logos* but of the flesh and of destruction. "Artaud's art, beyond art, rests on the shocking power of a force (the breath-voice) which tears language and destroys representation," said Derrida in "Forcener le subjectile," 70.

67. "Spirited [*soufflé*]: at the same time let us understand *inspired* by an *other* voice that itself reads a text older than the text of my body or than the theater of my gestures." Derrida, "La parole soufflée," 176. "Henceforth, what is called the speaking subject is no longer the person himself, or the person alone, who speaks. The speaking subject discovers his irreducible secondarity, his origin that is always already eluded" (178).

68. Fanon, *Black Skin, White Masks*, 31.

69. Butler, *Account of Oneself*, 10.

70. Butler, *Account of Oneself*, 12.

71. Butler, *Account of Oneself*, 42–43.

72. Lucette Ceranus Combette (1916–55). As Myriam Cottias and Madeleine Dobie stress, we owe the identification of Mayotte Capécia to Catherine Makward. See Cottias and Dobie, *Relire Mayotte Capécia*; Makward, *Mayotte Capécia*.

73. Jenny Alpha (1910–2010) was a Martinican singer and actress, playing on television, in cinema, and above all in theater. See Alpha, "Review."

74. This personal narrative was based on *Dieu est amour*, a text initially written by her French lover as his own memoir and confession to her. When Lucette Ceranus Combette left for Paris, she brought along his manuscript, which she had received by courier (once more a story of a "letter" and of "letters" [literature]). When the editor published *Je suis martiniquaise* in 1948, the cover ribbon read: "For the first time, a woman of color recounts her life." See Cottias and Dobie, *Relire Mayotte Capécia*, 16–18.

75. Fanon, *Black Skin, White Masks*, 26 (my emphasis, translation altered).

76. Capécia, *Martinican Woman*, 30 (my emphasis, translation altered).

77. Capécia, *Martinican Woman*, 37 (translation altered).

78. Capécia, *Martinican Woman*, 62–63 (translation altered).

79. See Arnold, "Mayotte Capécia," 39.

80. Arnold, "Mayotte Capécia," 39–40. Colonial traffic is such that one colony refers inevitably to another colony. We already observed this implicit principle with respect to the careers of colonial administrators. Here, Martinique is associated with French Indochina, the country of Annam.

81. See Makward, *Mayotte Capécia*, 158.

5

HAVING A GOOD EAR

MANY PEOPLE ARE STILL CONFUSED ABOUT THE RELATIONSHIP between decolonization and reception, preferring, for example, to make Fanon into a reader of Sartre rather than Sartre into a reader of Fanon. Fanon's reading of Sartre thereby appears essential, while Sartre's reading of Fanon appears inessential. Thus, the same division is reproduced, the same hierarchy, and in the end, the same coloniality. When Sartre reads Hegel, he is considered first as an author, even when he is visibly also a reader. One must therefore decolonize both gazes [*les regards*] and forms of knowledge [*les savoirs*].

The Alienation of Intellectuals

To speak about the decolonization of forms of knowledge is to interrogate knowledge transfers and to wonder what one has learned, what one is learning, what one can learn from the other—whoever he or she may be and wherever he or she may come from. The decentering implied by this attitude amounts to a new Copernican revolution. In this revolution, Europeans have to know what they are being offered by those other than themselves, non-Europeans. They need to know not how their own diverse and varied knowledges have been sown throughout the world, in a globalizing process that has not always been identified, but how they have integrated whatever has come from elsewhere into their ways of acting and thinking.

"Silence" is the name Edward Said has given to the singular universalism that can affirm itself as such only by effacing others who, no matter who they are or what they do, are relegated by nature and not by accident to a particularity from which they cannot free themselves. Thus, in *Culture and Imperialism*, Said notes that "the universalizing discourses of modern Europe and the United States assume the silence, willing or otherwise, of the non-European world. There is incorporation; there is inclusion; there is direct rule; there is coercion. But there is only infrequently an acknowledgement that the colonized people should be heard from, their ideas known."[1]

Freedom of expression belongs, de facto, to a prerogative.

It is easy to shut someone up by speaking. It is in fact tempting for Europeans or North Americans to try to have the last word in these matters. The last word is a way of trying to maintain world order and to immobilize subjects within it. For Said, to the contrary, it is necessary that "Western cultural forms . . . be taken out of the autonomous enclosures in which they have been protected, and placed instead in the dynamic global environment created by imperialism."[2] The world in motion is indeed disturbing and frightening because a position is meaningful only if it is stable, just as a place has no significance unless it is occupied. If others move, whoever sticks to his or her position or place is guaranteed to feel afraid. This is why mobility has always appeared as a figure of philosophical intelligence. Socrates shows this when chatting, armed with his misunderstandings about things, wandering the streets and alleys, stopping sometimes at the crossroads, going right up to the city's cultivated limits.

Asked about the "European intellectual," Edward Said emphasizes the authority and also the alienation that lurks within the jargon of specialists.[3] Comparative literature and anthropology are closely linked in some ways to imperialism, which is to say, at root, to the supposed absence of interlocutors. "I suppose," Said writes, "there is also some (justified) fear that today's anthropologists can no longer go to the postcolonial field with quite the same ease as in former times."[4]

Said prefers the autodidact to the authorized specialist. "I have," he says, "always been drawn to stubborn autodidacts, to various sorts of intellectual misfit."[5] The autodidact learns without a master. For this reason he or she is indifferent to authority. Having taught himself or herself, the autodidact is an orphan, intellectually speaking. This is why personal experience counts so much in the elaboration of his or her knowledge. It is also why he or she remains inimitable.

The autodidact is a bricoleur, a tinkerer. We are indebted to a migrant for the most beautiful possible tribute to bricolage. Leaving for Brazil, Claude Lévi-Strauss left philosophy. In French, as he recalls, "to 'bricoler'" was a matter of "ball games and billiards, . . . hunting, shooting, and riding. It was however always used with reference to some incidental movement: a ball rebounding, a dog straying or a horse swerving from its direct course to avoid an obstacle."[6]

These linguistic observations make clear that there is no migration without diversion or, to employ a normative term, subversion. Migrants have a "science of the concrete." They tinker with what they are, with where they come from and where they are going. Migration displays complicated trajectories far more than linear ones. When places are not the focus, such as departure or arrival points, one wonders where migrants have passed through or about the spaces they traverse. One ends up interrogating all these incidental movements that make up bricolage and the science of the concrete.

Migration Is a Bricolage

To migrate is to ramble, to avoid obstacles, to bounce. To migrate is to enter into mobility, not just that which creates distance from one place in order to approach something else more closely, but that which, in the head and in the body, in the symbolic and the imaginary, agitates the phantoms of the past, sometimes for a long while. From the standpoint of migration, the thinker is the one for whom this link to the past is broken, not the one who is born, lives, and dies in the same familiar environment. There is no migration without bricolage, which means without myth. There is no migration without art or "wild thought" [*pensée sauvage*]. Lévi-Strauss is a tinkerer who takes himself for an engineer. Inheritor of natural history, he undertakes to categorize and classify social relations, to begin with the "elementary structures of kinship." "It is common knowledge," he writes,

> that the artist is both something of a scientist and of a "bricoleur." By his craftsmanship he constructs a material object which is also an object of knowledge. . . . Let us now look at this portrait of a woman by Clouet and consider the reason for the very profound aesthetic emotion which is, apparently inexplicably, aroused by the highly realistic, thread by thread, reproduction of a lace collar. The choice of this example is not accidental. Clouet is known to have liked to paint at less than life-size. His paintings are therefore, like Japanese gardens, miniature vehicles and ships in bottles, what in the "bricoleur's" language are called "small-scale models" or "miniatures."[7]

We find here a remarkable gap between Lévi-Strauss's tools of analysis and his observations. It is why his digressions are so long, first drawing on bricolage, then on art, and in particular, this famous collar in the painting by Clouet. I do not know why this example comes to the researcher's pen because, instead of reflecting on the magic of the lace that moves him, he displaces his attention, turns away from the femininity of this object, and takes an interest in something more masculine. In this respect, the noteworthy thing is that Lévi-Strauss indicates that in art and the miniature "knowledge of the whole precedes knowledge of the parts"; put otherwise, synthesis precedes analysis instead of being its result.[8]

Migrations have their wild thoughts. They create an exile but can prove to be fertile. For Said, "exile can produce rancor and regret, as well as a sharpened vision. What has been left behind may either be mourned, or it can be used to provide a different set of lenses."[9] What is difficult at the affective level is intellectually stimulating. For anyone except Robinson, who recreates his universe wherever he finds himself down to the last detail, including the slaves, the response to new experiences is found in new ideas. Still one must already be prepared or equipped. Migrations are occasions or opportunities for thought.

Étienne Balibar has clearly seen the implications. Said, he writes, came as a result of his exile "to study the *condition of exile* in a privileged way, in its multiple modalities, as a situation which doubtless does not suffice to produce dissident interpretations, but which in the course of history has also facilitated the boldest realizations, in destabilizing subjects' adherence to a unique community that benefits from 'evidence' and 'authority,' and in installing them in some way at the very (unstable, uncomfortable) point where translation is at once necessary, everyday, and ill at ease."[10] Belonging [*adhésion*], in fact, is often a sign of allegiance [*adhérence*] to a place, a society, an institution. Inversely, a breakdown in allegiance leads to a lack of felt belonging. This is why slogans aim at belonging, or better, at allegiance.

Meanwhile, "to be an independent and postcolonial Arab, or Black, or Indonesian is not a program, nor a process, nor a vision."[11] Although they are a major postcolonial phenomenon, migrations toward the North are in themselves neither good nor bad. Far from the myth and its heroes, the stateless people are nothing per se, nothing exceptional. Said says: "Marginality and homelessness are not, in my opinion, to be gloried in; they are to be brought to an end, so that more, and not fewer, people can enjoy the benefits of what has for centuries been denied the victims of race, class, or gender."[12] There is never anything in Said that one could call particularism. The only things that interest him are the concrete universal and real equality.

Thus, exile can be heard in two ways in Said's work. In his eyes, it is both a real and a metaphoric condition: "Even intellectuals who are lifelong members of a society can, in a manner of speaking, be divided into insiders and outsiders: those on the one hand who belong fully to the society as it is, who flourish in it without an overwhelming sense of dissonance or dissent . . . and on the other hand, the nay-sayers, the individuals at odds with their society and therefore outsiders and exiles so far as privileges, power, and honors are concerned."[13]

When one compares Lévi-Strauss and Said, who do not come from the same horizons, who have neither the same projects nor identical perspectives, one recognizes that there is something twisted or wrenching [*déchirant*], in the strong and proper sense of the term, in the operation of thinking "between cultures" and not in one or the other. A decolonized or decolonial thought is a deterritorialized thought. The world between [*l'entre-monde*], or the interworlds [*les entre-mondes*], is the space in which decolonized thoughts move, detached from their chains, which is to say their common places. Ideas have no roots—this is truly why one could imagine a heaven of ideas. But they are sometimes incarnate in subjects, like toenails that turn inward and hurt one's feet. The text that Said devotes to interworlds is thus biographical (about Conrad) and autobiographical (about himself).[14]

Sometimes the interworlds are advantageous. "Marlow enters the heart of darkness to discover that Kurtz was not only there before him but is also incapable of telling him the whole truth; so that, in narrating his own experiences, Marlow cannot be as exact as he would have liked, and ends up producing approximations and even falsehoods of both which he and his listeners seem quite aware."[15] These lines from Said as a great reader of Conrad show how much autobiography, like history, can refer to fiction. The interworlds welcome a great deal of indetermination, instability, hesitation over spoken languages, common terrains, identities, and proximities.

Thus, the world is not conceived in the mode of conquest, of a grasp on virgin territories, of the mutual grip between spikes and rocks. It is not represented as a field of roots, an ancestral pantheon. It is an ensemble of movable and moving interworlds that make of seas and tides a style of self-figuring. Said was inspired by Conrad's maritime imaginary. The myth of Ulysses offers the image of a man who, having left Ithaca, lost it—a seafarer who, navigating with what he knows and, above all, thinks he knows, lives multiple adventures. His existence is wholly and completely journeying and exile. Today, instead of waiting indefinitely for her emigrant husband, Penelope herself can take off toward other lands. She need not feel the desire to return to her native country.

The Drift of Worlds Between

Genealogy is already a migration. It requires that there be foreigners, honorary siblings, who little by little weave a cloth, mostly of dreams, that one would be hard put to unravel. But often the false clarity of the family is confused with the true light of genealogy. The interworldly has no hearth. How many worlds are there—that is, how many societies, continents, cultures, and histories in an interworldly state? Conrad was a Pole who became English. From this drifting springs a worry that nothing can dissipate, neither in theory nor in practice. Far from being a defect in the theory, this tremor marks the excess of a practice always ahead of its mental elaboration.

This is why the interworldly is a challenge for thought. Thought rubs there and becomes sharper; it knows that this is the road to radicalization. Immersion profitably replaces the bird's-eye view and all the aerial perspectives that, dehumanizing the universe, are thought better equipped to seize it. In fact, to a great degree, reality is always immersed. One must therefore dive in to have any hope of glimpsing it. To dive—to give oneself, take one's time, let one's intentions dissipate. It is when advancing without protection that one has the best encounters, the most unforeseen and splendid.

Does this mean there are no phantoms, or no presences of a lost rather than absent past? To stray from history is not to forget it; it is merely to envisage it on the basis of a present, which is the only thing that matters, rather than from generally accepted beginnings. Interest is not speculative; it is vital. Terror, grief, and stupefaction are emotions that freeze us to the spot. One can prefer to wonder and to question, without crying and without laughing; one can let nothing be cause for surprise. Without a doubt, one must bury certain alphabets, only keeping those that let us cross borders.

Managing to designate and distinguish those among whom ethnically and culturally heterogeneous elements are merged is difficult enough. Displacement and migration, factors of change and transformation, are related for better or worse to the familiar, to the known, to what can be mastered. This is true from both sides, though differently. From the side of migrants, there is a great temptation to divide the self into several fragments. Among the autochthones, there is a fierce will to know who is arriving from outside, if not from elsewhere.

In fact, migrants force their way into a society. By their presence, they break the tacit evidences through which a common sense is forged and alliances cemented. By their existence, they disturb the stable arrangement thanks to which the world's order is credible. Their number is generally exaggerated, their importance overvalued. Migrants are the social spoilsports who prevent things from running smoothly, troublemakers who are always sent back to their margins. Instead of adding themselves or indeed multiplying themselves, they subtract themselves and become divided. Unity is forever lost, and an infinite regress rears its head.

Migrants are neither completely within what philosophers call percepts, nor completely within what they call concepts. Tinkering as they move, they inevitably function in a heterogeneous way and in the realm of the heteroclite. Thereby they call into question all those whose existence, at first glance, resembles an engineered product from which all accidents of transit, detours, and returns have been eliminated—a happy journey that distracts thought and captivates the eye, from port to port. The migrant is plunged into cultures; the autochthone has to do only with a single world or a unique universe. One consequence of the subordination of science to politics is the misrecognition of what migrants teach us about the universal—what we learn from those who are, by will or by necessity, bound to a particularity that might paradoxically not be their strength.

These relations to space and time, to countries and to history, show that space and the land, time and history are, in migration, themselves struck by mobility and uncertainty. One is reminded of the effective delocalization of haunted houses or the rooms of opium addicts. Delocalization produces fluctuating images, vacillating perceptions, misplaced thoughts. Curiously, and in a recurrent fashion, discourses produced about migrants mention their immobility (indeed their traditionalism) more than their mobility.

In Liverpool, they were long considered to all be opium smokers, which is to say immobile and asleep. This is how the *Liverpool Weekly Courier* once described the city's Chinese: "Strange silhouettes surge from the dusk, displacing dragging feet with a totally Oriental stiffness, and fixing their unmoving eyes, stretched in their yellow masklike faces, on incongruous surroundings. The street belongs to the Chinatown of Liverpool."[16]

This may illuminate the observation that Gregory Lee makes in another of his texts: "The modern lack of interest in sinology and the fact that the British occupation of Hong Kong, like the cultural practices of Chinese in Great Britain, were not the object of any attention on the part of British sinology, this lack of interest appeared to me as part of a process of dissimulation of China by the colonial West that this same West had produced over the course of the nineteenth century."[17]

Xenophobia is at work in the way the English represented to themselves the Chinese living on their territory (xenophobia has nothing to do with place but with territory)—Chinese opium addicts living in their deliria and their hallucinations. This representation may hold true not only for British Chinese but for all immigrants. The real space of existence is thus filled with shadows and phantoms; it is first a void evoking the kind of weightlessness that strikes all those who are away from their homes.

Portrait of Intellectuals as Potentates or as Travelers

One may quite rightly prefer travelers to despots. Edward Said has spoken of his admiration for Foucault. But, asked in 1985 about two fundamental books of the sixties, Foucault's *L'histoire de la folie* and Frantz Fanon's *Damnés de la terre*, he indicates that the second is more important for him, because it "comes out of the political struggles in progress, from the Algerian revolution."[18] The "collective struggle" in which Fanon's approach is inscribed takes precedence over the researcher's solitary work on his doctoral thesis. This means that theory interests him to the extent that it is rooted in practices. This is a position that not all share.

In their theoretical analyses, the great French thinkers of the sixties seem to have largely ignored anticolonial and anticolonialist struggles, with the notable exception of Jean-François Lyotard. A young agrégé in philosophy, he taught at the lycée in Constantine from 1950 to 1952. The "Algerian turn" was as important for him as it was for Pierre Bourdieu.[19] Lyotard's texts on Algeria were collected under the title *La guerre des Algériens.*[20]

Jacques Derrida, for example, never showed a specific interest in colonial questions on the theoretical plane although, and maybe even because, he was born in Algeria and spent his childhood in Algiers. Said, who is of the same generation, returns to the fundamental difference between Fanon and Foucault in emphasizing the fact that "the sense of active commitment" is absent from Foucault's first works but present in those of Fanon.[21]

For Said, Fanon represents "the end of a world." Said's attention to what happens practically is decisive. It is what allows him to grasp the effects of displacement and of migration implied by his readings. Thus, in another interview, he makes the comment that Conrad's celebrated novel, *Heart of*

Darkness, becomes very different when read by Europeans than when it is encountered by Africans.[22] Basically—for me—it involves reading over someone's shoulder something that one was not supposed to read. It means discovering a vision of which one is oneself the object. The archetypal difference between Foucault and Fanon can be envisaged thus: the first is in the position of the European reader of Conrad, the second in the position of the African or Antillean reader. A world separates them. The transparency of one is the opacity of the other.

Albert Camus is one of the most eminent examples of the European intellectual criticized by Said. Specifically, in his refusal to admit the existence of a Muslim Algerian nation, Camus fails to understand the emergence of a non-European point of view on the world. In the text titled "Identity, Authority, and Freedom: The Potentate and the Traveler," Said makes Camus into a potentate and Fanon into a traveler.[23] The potentate functions thanks to exclusion while the traveler functions thanks to inclusion.

Someone who would deny mixture, intermingling, and hybridity would in fact be on the potentate's side, not that of the traveler. "Like so many others," Said wrote, "I belong to more than one world. I am a Palestinian Arab, and I am also an American. This affords me an odd, not to say grotesque, double perspective."[24]

Intellectual mobility destroys ontology and ruins the notion of identity. It is better to reason in terms of the world than in terms of identity. This is already a remarkable displacement—a whole voyage. Stevenson's fable "The Citizen and the Traveller" maps the voyage onto the act of critique: "'Look round you,' said the citizen, 'This is the largest market in the world.' 'Oh, surely not,' said the traveller. 'Well, perhaps not the largest,' said the citizen, 'but much the best.' 'You are certainly wrong there,' said the traveller, 'I can tell you . . .' They buried the stranger at the dusk."[25] Stevenson's citizen, or the potentate, in this sense, considers the world as belonging to him. As for the traveler, he possesses no world. To one the authority, to the other the liberty.

This kind of travel may trouble Europe—or the West—may shake its theoretical authority and sovereignty. Meanwhile, the voyage brings conjunctions with it. While Camus proceeds by disjunction, Fanon tries to produce difficult conjunctions. However immaterial they may be, the operations of the mind do not in fact lack invisible imaginary and symbolic borders that, in thought, produce real effects from blind spots and biased perspectives. Voyaging creates worlds between.

What Is a Polyphonic Thought?

Despite what one might expect, "Between Worlds" is not a theoretical text.[26] It is an autobiographical account in which Said begins by identifying himself with Conrad. But Conrad's interworlds are intracontinental while those of Said are intercontinental. One passage highlights, albeit implicitly, what is involved with traveling: the absence of protection—in other words, exposure—and solitude.

In French, exposure belongs to the vocabulary of abandonment. The history of the term brings to mind children abandoned on the roadside or in a public home by mothers who could not feed them. It evokes the secret abandonment of the newborn in a place where he or she is likely to be picked up—a continual practice in antiquity. Exposure refers also to the lexicon of punishment: it is a penalty consisting in leading a convict before the crowd's gaze.

When one reads Said's memoirs, one is struck by the demands with which he was confronted in childhood, by the relative lack of support he received, by the gaze of which he was the object. His story is truly poignant. The absence of protection is evident with exposure, abandonment, resistance, retreat, solitude, reserve, and to end, with autodidacticism. Exile is not just geographic; it is also institutional.

The counterpoint follows between worlds. In an interworld, subjectivity is contrapuntal. Musical in origin, this term is fundamental in Said. The word *counterpoint* comes from the Latin *punctus contra punctum a morticulum*, literally "point against point," which is to say, note against note. Counterpoint is produced by the superposition of melodic lines. It is at the root of polyphony, the combination of multiple independent voices linked by laws of harmony. By extension, counterpoint means the capacity to play multiple notes at once. Said shows himself more sensitive to dialogue than to monologue. For this, one must have a good ear.

Polyphony is characteristic of a postcolonial moment. The line from the colonial past crosses that of the decolonized present; melodically independent languages intersect in counterpoint. Mikhail Bakhtin brought the category into literary analysis and described the phenomena whereby voices and enunciative sources were superposed in a single statement.[27] He wanted to found a "translinguistics" of the statement that would be both linguistic and pragmatic.

Never did Said propose a definition. To the contrary, he envelops and circumscribes his subject in a multiple and metaphoric fashion. It is a characteristic of his style of thinking. When we expect a definition, he proposes a metaphor; when we expect a story, he offers an analysis; and so on. Much like Fanon's, Said's text is composite.

Said always maps énoncés and enunciations onto one another. Indeed, reuniting énoncés and enunciations prevents us from falling back into the rut of ethnocentrism and of Eurocentrism. In fact, if the subject is not present in the énoncé, he or she is present in the enunciation. This is the conjunction that, at root, is generative of counterpoint and of polyphony. What characterizes intellectuals in the First World, as the subalternists would say, is the disjunction that they enact between enunciation and énoncé, between what they are (and where they are) and what they say. An institutional discourse is an énoncé totally disconnected from its enunciation, in which reflexivity fails [*fait défaut*]. This is what makes its repetition possible.

Colonial interworlds lead to invention rather than to repetition. And at the same time, repetition is the easiest thing, like a refrain or a melody that runs through one's mind without thinking. This is doubtless the source of Adorno's and Said's interest in the dodecaphonic music of Schoenberg. The dodecaphonic series is conceived as a series in which each of its twelve sounds may be heard, without allowing any of them to be repeated. This rule eliminates all hierarchy between pitches because, in the flux of melody, each has the same importance. It challenges the principles of tonal harmony. Dodecaphonic music is, according to Said's terms, "impertinent" and "intransigent"—making no concessions.

This Is Why We Sometimes Wonder If We Are Moving Forward

Said's proximity to Fanon is explained by the position that they occupy in colonial geography. For political reasons, both of them experienced exile. Said shares with Fanon the experience of the uninhabitable. "In the end, the writer is not even allowed to live in his writing," said Adorno. Said answers, "One achieves at most a provisional satisfaction, which is quickly ambushed by doubt, and a need to rewrite and redo that renders the text uninhabitable. Better *that*, however, than the sleep of self-satisfaction and the finality of death."[28]

Nomadism is inevitable to the extent that no textual dwelling place, no intellectual shelter is more than provisional. Said thus claims to have learned from Adorno, "better a lost cause than a triumphant one, more satisfying a sense of the provisional and contingent—a rented house, for example—than the proprietary solidity of permanent ownership."[29] Rental can be more profitable than ownership.

The postcolonial interworlds are certainly fruitful. They are not comfortable. The pleasure of living there gives way to torments such as doubt, the impression of being against the current, of belonging to the wrong side, "in a place," Said says, "that seemed to be slipping away from me just as I tried to define or describe it."[30] The feeling of relinquishing, of being unable to get a grip, and the impression of not mastering one's movements or one's path are revealed to be the most immediate effects of the absence of a proper place. Art, literature, and philosophy are the way that the right-handed have of being left-handed, or awkward.

Somewhere, indeed anywhere, resources may then be found to cross these moving expanses artistically, literarily, or philosophically without wrecking the ship. In so doing, writing banishes seasickness. "Autrefois," the first part of Assia Djebar's book *Les alouettes naïves*, which she published in October 1967, is placed under the sign of Kafka. She chose a passage from his journal for the epigraph: "If you were walking on a flat road, if you were determined to walk and you nevertheless walked backward, well, this would be a hopeless case, but if you are climbing a slope as steep as yourself seen from below, the steps backward would only result from the way the ground is configured and you should not despair."[31]

To climb back up to oneself, in fact, is no small affair—an arduous task. To escape this fatal reversal of "for" into "against" in the contrasting, antithetical, and in the end contradictory valorization between the past and the present, voluntarism is often the fatal weapon drawn as often by intellectuals as by political actors, a fake weapon whose effects can only be a self-fulfilling prophecy. This is insufficient. This is simply not enough.

Presenting the novel in *Jeune Afrique* upon its appearance, about five years after the independence of Algeria, Assia Djebar writes the following on the subject of "incessant lurching":

> Let us be frank: however sublime our present appears to us (the heroism of the liberation war), and however degraded the past becomes (colonial night),

to that same extent the present appears miserable (our insufficiencies, our uncertainties) and our past more solid (chain of ancestors, umbilical cord of memory). By this incessant lurching, and because we constantly make a wide gulf between the past, paralyzed in the present, and the present, giving birth to the future, we Africans, Arabs, and undoubtedly those from elsewhere, we walk with a limp when we believe we are dancing, and vice versa. This is why we sometimes wonder if we are moving forward.[32]

Notes

1. Said, *Culture and Imperialism*, 50.
2. Said, *Culture and Imperialism*, 51.
3. Said, "Europe and Its Others," 385.
4. Said, *Reflections on Exile*, 297.
5. Said, *Reflections on Exile*, 561.
6. Lévi Strauss, *Savage Mind*, 16 (translation altered).
7. Lévi-Strauss, *Savage Mind*, 22–23.
8. Lévi-Strauss, *Savage Mind*, 23–24.
9. Said, *Reflections on Exile*, xxxv.
10. Balibar, "Politique et traduction."
11. Said, *Reflections on Exile*, 379.
12. Said, *Reflections on Exile*, 385.
13. Said, *Representations of the Intellectual*, 52–53.
14. Said, *Reflections on Exile*, 554–68.
15. Said, *Reflections on Exile*, 554–55.
16. Lee, "L'opium."
17. Lee, "Textes, oublis, histoires."
18. Said, "Shadow of the West," 39.
19. It was in Algeria that Bourdieu, reading Lévi-Strauss with a critical eye, launched his theory, so to speak, with the publication of *Esquisse d'une théorie de la pratique*, in order, as he himself says, to "disconcert both those who reflect on the social sciences without practising them and those who practise them without reflecting on them" (Bourdieu, *Esquisse*, 155; cited by the translator on vii of his introduction to the English edition, *Outline of a Theory of Practice*). Here it was a matter of going beyond both structuralism (with its determinism) and phenomenology (with its attachment to free will).

Michel de Certeau saw clearly that Bourdieu was shooting between the poetic and the epistemological:

> In Bourdieu's work . . . Kabylia plays the role of a Trojan horse within a "theory of practice"; the three texts devoted to it (the three best that Bourdieu has written, especially "The Kabyle House or the World Reversed") serve as a multiple vanguard for a long epistemological discourse; like poems, these three "studies of Kabylian ethnology" lead into a theory (a sort of commentary in prose) and provide it with a fund of material that can be infinitely cited in marvelous fragments; in the end, at the point when Bourdieu publishes his three "early" texts, their referential and poetic

> locus is erased from the title (which reverts to commentary: *a theory*); and, scattered in the effects that it produces in the authorized discourse, this Kabylian origin itself gradually disappears, a sun obscured by the speculative landscape that it still illuminates: these traits are already characteristic of the position of practice in theory. (De Certeau, *Practice of Everyday Life*, 50)

In Algeria, Bourdieu cobbled together [*bricolé*] a new theory. This set the stage for the creation of the concept of *habitus*.

20. Lyotard, *La guerre des Algériens*. In 1997, Lyotard published a text with the title "La guerre des Algériens, suite." "Freud," he said,

> wrote that the "Wolf-man's" unconscious resembled Egypt. All the layers left one over the other by history remained visible, copresent, and intact in him. A common archeological metaphor in the Freudian representation of the unconscious. Meanwhile, it is strange when the materials supposedly piled up do not really constitute a subsoil but rather an immobile landscape. Every element is fixed where it appeared and it seems to escape the pressures, twists, condensations and erasures that the dream's interpretation depicts again and again. Two years in the region of Constantine gave me this sense that the deposits left by the community's past coexisted in its present rather than layering over one another. . . . It seemed to me in any case that, far from erasing the country beneath its weight, as I had sensed in Egypt, the remarkable heterogeneity that gives Algeria its socio-cultural complexity rendered it elusive and dancing. (Lyotard, "La guerre des Algériens," 67–68)

21. Said, "Shadow of the West," 40.
22. Said, "Between Two Cultures."
23. Said, *Reflections on Exile*, 395.
24. Said, *Reflections on Exile*, 397.
25. Stevenson, *Fables*, 12.
26. Said, *Reflections on Exile*, 554–68.
27. Mikhail Bakhtin (1895–1975) was a literary theorist who lived through the historical transition from the Russian empire to the Soviet Union. Bakhtin introduced the concept of polyphony to analyze the structure of Dostoyevsky's novels. In Dostoyevsky (1821–81), dialogue takes the place of action. For Bakhtin, to be is to communicate dialogically (*obščat'sja dialogičeski*). Polyphony is thus a principle used by Dostoyevsky to construct his literary work, which is marked by "plurivocality" (a plurality of voices). Fiction elaborates the presence, confrontation, and interaction of the author's and characters' voices from various angles. This is how Bakhtin develops the notion of dialogism, which is supposed to integrate the other both into the literary work and into the work's comprehension. Like Kafka, Bakhtin was influenced by Martin Buber, for whom the relation to the other is constitutive of personhood. For Bakhtin, finally, the word is "an essentially social phenomenon"—it is not a word-thing but a word-environment. See Bakhtin, *Problems of Dostoevsky's Poetics*.
28. Said, *Reflections on Exile*, 568.
29. Said, *Reflections on Exile*, 567.
30. Said, *Reflections on Exile*, 558.
31. Djebar, *Les alouettes naïves*, 13.
32. Djebar, *Les alouettes naïves*, 8–9.

CONCLUSION

THIS REFLECTION HAS BEEN ACCOMPANIED BY OBSERVATIONS AND interrogations regarding Frantz Fanon and Edward Said. The Algeria of yesterday and of today has constituted its center of gravity without being its exclusive object. In fact, this country is covered in imperial dust. The local characteristics are not, properly speaking, specificities. To identify a single difference, how many similitudes must be counted? Does it make good sense to isolate situations so that they can become textbook cases? Is it truly reasonable to divide North Africa from the Africa called sub-Saharan? Is it meaningful to dissociate colonial empires from one another when the circulations, exchanges, and borrowings between them were so intense? In my opinion, the decolonization of the African continent happens through the effacement of barriers, whether those of the North and the South or that of the Anglophone world and the Francophone world. This is why we have dealt with India and Martinique, Palestine and Egypt, but also with Kafka, a Czech Jew writing in German; and Conrad, Polish but writing in English; or even Derrida, a French Jew from Algeria; and Deleuze, a Frenchman from France. These are also the voices that batter me. The phantoms of Africa are multiple, and they are international.

> I write the language of the dead or my language who cares
> I write an offended language
>   machine gunned
>   a tongue of the orangerie
> I write French
>   living language
>   flayed sounds
> I write your voices so as not to smother
>   your voices raised in my palm
>   Raïs, Bentalha, I write the afterward[1]

To write the afterward—beyond the always particular circumstances, this reflection aims, above all, to make audible a kind of sound, a voice, a speech habitually concealed by the monotonous discourses that still colonize the French public and intellectual sphere. There the practice of eliding the subject still predominates. Instead of being the partner in a dialogue here and now, the recipient of remarks, the ex-colonized—always non-European—is still the largely excluded third of a discourse whose coloniality is unmistakable. Excluded third also means object. The third is thus subjectively cut from its history, from its languages, from its gender. Try never being able to speak about yourself and hearing yourself constantly spoken about by others. You'll see. Muteness is not a given; it's an experience.

By simple analogy in the mechanisms of ethnocentric assimilation/exclusion, let us recall with Renan that "in the most ancient languages, words used to designate foreign peoples are drawn from two sources: either words that signify to 'stammer,' to 'mumble,' or words that signify 'mute.'"[2]

The exit from this imposed muteness is therefore a kind of stuttering—in other words, a way of talking, of writing, of expressing oneself but also of repeating and at the same time of identifying what certain ears can hardly hear. It refers to the effective possibility of elaborating a thought for oneself, for one's own use. To make this normative would almost be nonsensical. It is not a prescription but a quest. Stuttering is thus like loving: a speech yearning to go beyond what exists. It means speaking to oneself like a foreigner in one's language, inventing new forces—a language that is not one's own. Socrates was reproached for stuttering like a child. He spoke not Athenian but philosophy; he questioned as much as—indeed more than—he affirmed; and above all, he did not answer any injunctions but his own. Deleuze, much later, took up stuttering to make it the sign of a becoming, a becoming mad, woman, animal, stammerer, foreigner.[3] It is not a matter of stammering in one's speech but a matter of turning language into one's own tongue. Today, I claim stuttering as the expression of decoloniality in action.

Notes

1. Djebar, *Ces voix*, 258. In the night of September 22–23, 1997, as at Raïs one month earlier, Islamists (from the Groupe Islamique Armé [GIA] or from the Armée Islamique du Salut [AIS]) committed a bloody massacre (involving decapitations, mutilations, and slashed throats) without any intervention from the army—against a population supposed to be in a "green belt" of Algiers reputed for its Islamism. More than two hundred deaths were reported. Today, former terrorists who received amnesty cohabit with victims.

2. Renan, *L'origine du langages*, cited by Derrida, *Of Grammatology*. Derrida adds: "The continuation of the text, that I cannot quote here, is most instructive in the origin and function of the word 'barbarian' and other related words" (123, 338n21).

3. See Deleuze, *Essays Critical and Clinical.* "But if the system appears in perpetual disequilibrium or bifurcation, if each of its terms in turn passes through a zone of continual variation, then the language itself will begin to vibrate and stutter" (108). "Creative stuttering is what makes language grow from the middle, like grass; it is what makes language a rhizome instead of a tree, what puts language in perpetual disequilibrium. . . . There are many ways to grow from the middle, or to stutter"—all the way to the breath-words of Artaud (111). "It is a painting or a piece of music, but a music of words, a painting with words, a silence in words, as if the words could now discharge their content" (112–3).

PART III

EPILOGUE

FROM FLOATING TERRITORIES TO DISORIENTATION

> Is it the charm of the impossible? Or are those beings who exist beyond the pale of life stirred by his tales as by an enigmatical disclosure of a resplendent world that exists within the frontier of infamy and filth, within that border of dirt and hunger, of misery and dissipation, that comes down on all sides to the water's edge of the incorruptible ocean, and is the only thing they know of life, the only thing they see of surrounding land—those life-long prisoners of the sea? Mystery!
>
> Joseph Conrad, *The Nigger of the "Narcissus"*

IN OUR REPRESENTATIONS, EARTH IS TO SEA AS certitude is to uncertainty, safety to danger—as theory, in sum, to experience. Floating suggests hesitation, doubt, indecision, the loss of bearings. Is being down-to-earth, *terre-à-terre*, tantamount to being prosaic? Actually, the dictionary reminds us that *terre-à-terre* was originally a maritime expression used to designate the act of sailing along the coast—that is, close to firm land. It's either that or the open sea. Maritime space, the open sea or ocean, is a figure for interworlds that coincide neither with a starting point nor with an end point.

At sea, we are somewhere. To know where, we must calculate our position (latitude and longitude) and use a compass to avoid losing our bearings. Those who sail know how complete the spatiotemporal disorientation of the sea can be; for the sailor, this is the source of great joy but also intense terror. We must reverse perspectives and envision the land from the sea, abandoning, in the process, the world vision enshrined by European modernity. Modernity isolates "Continental" Europe and elevates it above the rest of the world. But maritime space, which has historically been treated, charted, and divided as if it were land, is defined more by the acts of circulation traced on its surface than by its contours.[1] These circulations are not predetermined. They obey political and social "currents," as well as specific, and sometimes carefully recorded, "trajectories."

They also follow, in a very singular fashion, the vagaries of crossings. When Paul Gilroy invented the "Black Atlantic," what interested him was the specificity of a space—a space that could not, and cannot, be reduced to Europe or the Americas, any more than it can be reduced to Africa. That is why Gilroy makes the ship the symbol of the interworld, this "Middle Passage." He writes, "I have settled on the image of ships in motion across the spaces between Europe, America, Africa and the Caribbean as a central organizing symbol for this enterprise and as my starting point."[2] For Gilroy, the ship is "a living, micro-cultural, micro-political system in motion"; the ship is a "chronotope" of passage and a "central organizing symbol" of the diasporic condition.[3] He goes on to draw tight connections between the maritime universe and antislavery activists, liberators, and enthusiasts.

More by design than by accident, the Mediterranean Sea, conversely, has been a real colonial sea. From east to west and north to south, and vice versa, it transported not only goods and people, but also practices, cultures, and worldviews that could hardly avoid cross pollinating. The effect of Europe's imperial policies was, once again, to blur borders. France exported to the Maghreb its language and methods, its way of doing and forms of thinking. That is why, in the postcolonial universe, the political and aesthetical stakes of the overarching "distribution of the sensible" (*partage du sensible*) are revealed, if I may put it that way, in "the state of nature."[4] These stakes have been marked by extreme heterogeneity, excessive subordination, and intense conflicts. The political literary and artistic utterances that produce effects in the real, whether cohesive or divisive, are all the more complex for belonging to different worlds—worlds that have been set in opposition, both axiomatically and culturally. Doing, being, seeing, and saying are combined in complex and sometimes ambivalent ways.

The flow of French, Spanish, Italian, and Maltese citizens to North Africa in the wake of the French conquest, each with its place in a French hierarchy of humanity, had already—even if only on the European side of the Maghreb—produced an intensive cultural creolization (as we speak of intensive agriculture). More or less sidelined from the spaces reserved to the conquerors, the "indigenous" population acculturated themselves, sometimes willingly and sometimes not. In many respects, this acculturation resembled a migration, even if no geographic displacement was involved. Deep down, *migration* is a synonym for the *colony*. We could say, in effect, that to migrate is to live under a foreign law and to speak a language other than one's own, just as in a foreign country. It is to be obliged to live under new rules and in a different language. Migration is a process that generates uncertainty and floating—in other words, disorientation. In the colonies, one must live with foreigners who think they are in their own land.

Conversely, large segments of the so-called indigenous populations crossed and continue to cross the sea to reach the North, hoping to find in the metropolis living conditions that the colonial system could not offer them at home. These crossings to and fro accelerated and intensified in the twentieth century. After the struggles for independence, they further deepened the gap between the respective ethos of each region, while maintaining the passages and the circulation of people and goods. In some instances, independence itself created a new country, just as it sometimes brought about another language and system of laws. Thus, Europe, directly or indirectly, has irremediably blurred all (previous) maps. The situation is unique, at least insofar as a disquieting strangeness (*unheimlichkeit*) dominates relations—intimate and distant, familiar and foreign—between the ones and their others.

The innumerable events of displacements and uprootings resulting from colonization and the struggles for independence have produced an irreducible heterotopia and heterology to which the present attests.[5] Heterotopia and heterology irrigate, in equal measure, people living and working in the Maghreb and those of Maghrebin origin—or, as we say, of the "diaspora"—those who were born abroad and who live elsewhere, notably in Europe. Following Foucault's suggestion, we can say that a colony is not a proper space: like a cemetery or a brothel, or both at once, a colony is a counterspace. Completely apart from space, a counterspace is a localized utopia destined to efface, neutralize, and purify spaces. More than anything, Foucault's heterotopia juxtaposes, in one and the same place, spaces that are in principle incompatible, and thereby unsettles any and every geography (France is Algeria, and Algeria France). In this sense, we can draw an analogy between the way a heterotopia negates and disrupts space and the way transgender persons include, transform, and resist gender categories at a bodily level. What does *body* mean here? It means floating between two banks of the river and two genders, a corporeal in-between, a physical interworld. Something unclassifiable. A collage (of father and mother, masculine and feminine). A dream of freedom.

In 1997, Kader Attia began *Landing Strip* (*La piste d'atterrissage*), a diorama that in its final form consists of 160 slides of transgender Algerians living illegally in Paris—that is to say, Algerians who, in one and the same gesture, break gender and national borders and affirm a double identity in a space that is built on identity itself.[6] It is telling that this kind of phenomenon should open up the space for passages, because internal subjective migration and external objective migration, suffered or chosen by large segments of the population, accompany every instance of acculturation and creolization. That is why the sea, as a place of passage and perhaps as a counterspace, constitutes one of the (floating) centers of gravity of contemporary art in Africa, from Algiers to the Cape. Between dream and reality, the artist navigates by sight. Isn't Apollo, the god of song, music, and poetry, in Greek mythology, a navigator? Nietzsche writes, "With sublime gesture he shows us that the whole world of agony is needed in order to compel the individual to generate the releasing and redemptive vision and then, lost in contemplation of that vision, to sit calmly in his rocking boat in the midst of the sea."[7] Art is conceived as dwelling in the broad sense, in a floating interworld, amid two firm lands, one lost from sight and the other not yet seen. It is conceived as a migration, a crossing, an odyssey, a work of the imagination. By making the visual arts the arts of dreaming—whereas music is an art of intoxication [*ivresse*]—Nietzsche underlines the floating of appearances constitutive to the dream proper of the plastic arts. These include poetry, because, he says, "the veil of semblance is in fluttering movement and does not completely cover up the basic forms of the real."[8] Envisaging the plastic arts from the perspective of navigation and floating, Nietzsche conveys that the artist, like many others, plays with reality and with dream and political desire. This is what Said appreciated in Conrad's novels.

There is a term perfectly suited to describe it in the Arabic-Islamic world: *barzakh*. Henri Corbin translates it as *interworld*.[9] Philosophically, the term *barzakh* refers to imagination, to what can neither be perceived nor conceived but only dreamed and imagined. Geographically, this word means the *isthmus*, or the space [*espace intermédiaire*] between salted water (earth) and freshwater (heaven). *Barzakh* is more than a word. It is a concept, for it names the distinction between two intermingling things. It also names the difference between the present and the eternal or, put differently, their suspension and their intermingling. In its religious sense, *barzakh* is about thinking the "moment" that follows the disappearance and precedes the resurrection of those who will be judged. In other words, it allows us to think the time after departure and before arrival, the suspended time of the crossing, the *devenir*. Pronouncing the limit between the physical and the spiritual world, the real world and the possible world, *barzakh* leads us back to the voice of the subject expressing his or her interworld, his or her disorientation. This is one of the quintessential postcolonial endeavors. And last, the *barzakh* is a dynamic reality incarnated in people.

The decolonization of knowledge is less a process than a kind of labor. If I am interested in the decolonization of knowledge, this is insofar as it includes arts and literature. Arts and literature are forms of knowledge that do not intersect but are at the forefront of decolonization, because they are less subject to censorship than other symbolic activities such as, for example, philosophy. This is already a way of affirming that knowledge contains a failure to know. This failure is both an outside and an inside, and irreducibly so. For we do not know the processes by which we think, create, or write. This is the particular standpoint from which I reflect.

In addition, I think it is better to conceive of knowledge in terms of circulation and exchange rather than in terms of capital and property. The history of thought has showed us how ferocious was the fight for ownership of knowledge, starting with the "discovery" of America. The capitalization of knowledge led to botanical and ethnographic explorations, because, as some European thinkers so rightly observed, there is no power without knowledge. So the question "Who has knowledge?" appears more relevant than "What is it knowledge about?" or "What is knowledge?"—questions that are political and therefore epistemological. A decolonial perspective cannot avoid such moments of interrogation and reflection.

Here I would like to discuss only one aspect of the decolonization of knowledge, but one that seems to me decisive—namely, disorientation. Indeed, I believe that we must learn to become disoriented and thereby to become decentered—within oneself and from oneself—to properly or correctly reach regions of humanity long considered "backward" by Europeans.

We know how much value has been placed on orientation and how powerfully the North serves as the point of reference par excellence (can one travel without a compass?). We also know the extent to which philosophy has embraced this metaphor. This is why I was brought to recall the text published in 1786, now so famous, in which the German philosopher Kant poses the question of knowing "how to orient oneself in thinking."[10] Kant starts off by drawing our attention to the close relationship between space and one's own body, for the recognition of points on the compass supposes the physical distinction between left and right, between the left hand and the right hand. If this (subjective) difference is not felt, it is no longer possible to orient oneself spatially. The philosopher then remarks that orientation is linked to memory. He pictures himself in the dark, in his room, a space that is familiar to him, and he notes that remembering the location of objects is integral to his ability to get his bearings in this space once it has become invisible. Fixing the location of things is moreover the only way a blind person can live at home without too much difficulty. This is why, to finish, Kant imagines a wicked practical joker moving all the objects around—what was formerly on the right side is now on the left; what was on the left side is now on the right. If this (objective) change is not noticed, once night falls, one can no longer recognize oneself in an environment that was familiar a priori. It is therefore enough to confuse right and left for the sense of orientation to disappear.

Thus, I move from the figurative to the literal meaning, because all humanity, including Europe, organizes itself starting from the great difference between what is right and good and what is left and bad, a difference that is not truly physical but is still incarnate. This means that we all have a mental geography, sometimes mapped by scholars (circumstantial ethnographic studies on a particular "tribe," a dictionary of the ten most important figures in the intellectual world, exhibition catalogs that indicate countries or nationalities, panoramas presenting contemporary African art, etc.). This kind of physical geography, human, philosophical, and political, serves as our common sense or viewpoint [*table d'orientation*]. To put it differently, we all have a camera obscura (a dark room) in which, despite the darkness, we can locate objects on the condition that they have not been moved by some prankster without our knowledge.

Is there not, however, a colonial prankster who turned everything upside down? For is decolonization not a kind of epistemological reversal that puts on the right side what once was to the left and transforms—axiologically—left into right? Mapping seems to be a founding act that allows one to find a way out regardless of the circumstances and, once moving, to reach one's destination. Yet is the achievement of a cartographic objective consistent with a critical view? What happens if one does not have a destination? I have always been bothered by the cultivated posture that can perfectly date books and works, contextualize them historically, locate them socially and politically, and bring them to a definite biography. I always liked the margins of uncertainty, imperfectly listed fringes, the "thick brush." "Thick Brush"—the term comes from a colonial geographical map of 1845 that I have carefully preserved. It is a map of Algiers and its surroundings. Areas not yet completely dominated by reason and the colonial power are indicated on it using not place-names but labels for vegetation and its expansion—the bush with its bushmen. The "thick brush" designates what has not been surveyed, measured, leveled, and reduced to the span of the map.

The thickness introduces the third dimension (in addition to the length and width)—hence, reality itself. Salvation is therefore neither in the maps nor in the mapping. It is in the margins of philosophy.

In my view, orientation is linked to an evaluation (right/left) and to a colonization of space that always obeys this assessment: the modern is right, the traditional is left; the universal is right, the individual is left; language is right, the dialect is left; the people is right, the tribe is left; religion is right, belief and superstition are left. Finally, white is right; black is left. In this respect, Africa is fully left and hence far down. The primitive dualism that the West has swallowed metaphysically has polarized the entire world between right and left (top and bottom) to make of Africa a world not different but contrary to Europe, a world that is obscure to the very extent that it is magical. This contrariety is what the party defending disorientation tries to overcome. For it implies renouncing the right-left division that perpetuates a world order to be abolished by the decolonization of knowledge and power. This is not exclusive to Europeans but concerns us all. Can a right-handed person use the left hand to cook? This is, in some parts of Niger, equated with poisoning. Differentiation is unbalanced since it makes one side, the second, generally associated with women, the flip side of the first. When Lamyne Mohamed worked as an artist on the theme of African protective charms, it helped to break up the familiar geography of migration.[11] In fact, he revealed things that are rarely found in scholarly works because of their "world order"—for example, the importance of amulets for migrants that give them the courage to cross oceans and seas, when they do not necessarily know how to swim and face many dangers and perils in their journey. This is a blind spot of research and analysis that assumes disorientation—as I understand it, the loss of common sense and sense of orientation.

If orientation is a poison (due to the inherent hierarchy in the world order), disorientation is a cure. Choosing disorientation therefore amounts, in this sense, to choosing the left and the low, the poison rather than the remedy, knowing that any poison can be a medicine (vaccine) and that any remedy can become poison. In this sense the pharmakon holds great ambivalence, since it can both lose and save, heal and make sick.[12] The pharmakon is associated with magic, with chance more than with knowledge. A pharmakos is, in ancient Greece, a poisoner or one supposed to be such, often a prisoner of war or a person condemned to death (but also sometimes a disabled person or a slave), who can be sacrificed like a scapegoat. Expelled from the city or condemned to exile, this person becomes a migrant.

Decolonization requires specific pharmakons and original pharmakos—or pharmacists—who aim to treat the remains of colonial madness (and fury). The pharmakons are also artificial colors, makeup or costumes, artifacts, works (*ergon*) that, like writing, are detached from their author; hence, they are art works as well. They constitute what Derrida calls supplements. Disorientation is therefore both a pharmakon and a supplement—an elementary mixed milieu, impure, where differentiation occurs. This is why it is so important, for example, that the work of curating, criticism, and analysis of works from the South is performed by and for people from the South, who thereby lose their bearings. This is why it is also crucial that the works carried out by and in the countries of the South be acquired and collected in the countries of the South. This is still not really happening.

Disorientation should therefore not be understood as a failure or absence but as an action and posture. It should not occur by chance but should be sought as a desirable type of perennial indetermination that would not be interrupted by any term. Getting lost in a city as you get lost in a forest or a jungle is not a loss but a gain. The GPS, Global Positioning System, or geopositioning satellite speaks—"In less than fifty meters, turn right." From my point of view, the use of GPS in thought is rendered all the more superfluous by intra- and extracontinental migration, migration not only by artists from these continents but also by many other inhabitants—migration that creates a nebula, in its astronomical sense. A nebula (what one usually calls diaspora) is an interstellar cloud of dispersed material composed of gas and dust. Diffused, it produces light emissions (emission or reflection). Dark, or obscure, it blocks light. In this case, the shape of these astronomical clouds is very irregular: they have no defined external boundary, and their contours can be diffuse. Considering things this way allows us to pull back from the terrestrial geography within which high and low, left and right retain their power to the end. It is a way of not remaining locked up in the mental geography we learned or that has been transmitted to us; it is a pictorial way of saying that our symbolic universe is infinite. What is transmitted, in this respect, is more powerful than what has been learned and taught, because it is less noticeable.

This disorientation—here I continue to follow the story of the journey around my room that I told at the start—also involves forgetting. If memory is the sense of orientation, oblivion may be preferable. *Pharmakon kakon.* In what sense? It was understood that the spatial memory (crossing time and space) is made of the mental representation of an arrangement of objects—more or less distant from each other, more or less voluminous, and so on. When I get up half-asleep, I bump into things, having forgotten how the room is arranged. The calendar corresponds to time in the same way that mapping corresponds to space. Day and night correspond to right and left. Forgetting chronology, for me, means definitively bracketing teleology. Teleology orients historical processes to give them a meaning consistent with our implicit value judgments. It is at work particularly in what we call "art history"—that is, a temporally periodized cartography of artists and works in Western Europe. The only ones who enter into this field are classified on the model of the Eastern Chagall, who was eventually integrated into the grand narrative when he changed countries.

If history indeed is seen as progress, even, in a sense, within the arts, it is because time is considered first (and theoretically) as linear and because time is second (and virtually) conceived as pregnant with a better tomorrow. It could be conceived differently, like a progression without progress. Apart from the fact that modernity was at bottom an "à la carte" modernity in which "modern" elements were allowed to coexist with "traditional" elements, the periodization of political and cultural history leaves unthought the question of the present, of the "now" from which the periods of a chronological succession are determined. Decolonization was imagined more frequently as a process than as a labor. Often it was even inscribed in a philosophy of history that views it as historical evolution. After Bandung, decolonization? Decolonization, besides, is no sort of linear process. This is why decolonization must be envisaged not simply as a historical period but also as subjective labor on the self.

Any periodization of cultural history is problematic because it leaves unquestioned the position of the now, the present from which one is supposed to take a legitimate perspective on a chronological succession. Indeed, modernity thus conceived is a view of time taken from the perspective of God, or as Hegel would say, the end of history, the "ultimate now." There is thus no longer a worthwhile now. The present is not what really matters. What matters is to determine one's position in an evolution whose character is purely normative. Memory, therefore, is not necessarily good; it dresses today in yesterday's clothes. As a consequence, forgetfulness cannot be reduced to a dysfunction of memory or an accidental erasure of memory traces. Here too, forgetfulness is dynamic and decolonizing. One should, moreover, get out of one's room, even just in a mental sense, and head to unfamiliar places.

Nothing like waking up not knowing where we are. This is a metaphorical vocabulary. What does it say? It says that coloniality and the unthought are still at work; it says that literary writing and philosophical or artistic work are ways out. The god Thoth wants to offer writing to King Thamus.[13] Thoth promises him that writing (as a pharmakon) will give the Egyptians more science and memory than they have. But Thamus objects that, by dispensing men from exercising their memory, this invention will produce forgetfulness. Confident in writing, they will seek recollection outside and not inside. Indeed, writing is an uncontrollable externalization. Therefore, it is outside of oneself that one's own memories will be found. Writing empties the voice of its blood.[14]

To refuse the map and the memory—or the memory map—in other words, to refuse repetition, is not to say that the key to decolonization is lack of education. Quite the opposite—I would say that it is a matter of shedding an old skin. Because culture is also a lack of culture, in its boundaries and in its blind spots, in its parallax. In *Thus Spoke Zarathustra* (the text that Nietzsche saw as the peristyle of his philosophy), in the story of three metamorphoses, we find the description of the labor to be accomplished, the labor of mourning.[15]

The three metamorphoses indicate a singular process in which alienation is passed off as healthy self-affirmation. For the spirit does not, in fact, begin by fully enjoying its freedom and its talents: it is gripped by duty. It is, for Nietzsche, first a camel, bearing a burden that never lightens. Many things can weigh on the sprit. This is why the philosopher asks himself, Is it not burdensome "to love those who despise us and to offer our hand to the ghost that would frighten us? All these most difficult things the spirit that would bear much takes upon itself, like the camel that, burdened, speeds into the desert, thus the spirit hastens into its desert."[16] The desert is a path with no outlet. The second metamorphosis allows the spirit to pronounce a vigorous, beneficial "no." Having become a lion, the spirit enters into war with the dragon—it wants neither god nor master; it wants neither their values nor their prescriptions. What then is the last metamorphosis? Nietzsche's pen invents the child: "But say, my brothers, what can the child do that even the lion could not do? Why must the preying lion still become a child? A child is innocence and forgetting, a new beginning, a game, a self-propelled wheel, a first movement, a sacred 'Yes.' For the game of creation, my brothers, a sacred 'Yes' is needed: the spirit now wills his own will, and he who had been lost to the world now conquers his own world."[17]

The decolonization of knowledge is, in this sense, a rejuvenation [*devenir enfant*] of the mind, a way of losing the known world and of finding one's own world. The child is beyond good and evil, beyond right and left, beyond the "sense of orientation." He or she overcame the horrible values that were bequeathed to him or her. The child is thus disoriented and forgetful and can write an after(ward). Henceforth the road will be unknown and lined with dwellings. This is how I picture a decolonized gaze to myself.

Sometimes, I ask myself if this is not a generational story, given that our grandparents lived under the colonial regime of absolute obligation (without rights), our parents struggled through powerlessness for their independence and their rights, and perhaps thanks to them one has had the chance to become a child. The road is so unknown and lined with dwellings. It no longer follows the same steps and no longer takes the same path as before; but new ones have been created. Becoming a child (female, animal, clandestine, silly) is perhaps a minoritarian becoming (eternally minority), a perpetual transformation that does not institutionalize the good and the bad (beyond good and evil), that ultimately refuses to have the last word. The decolonization of knowledge is a massive labor of separation because one's bearings (one's north) are what must be lost.

Saying *labor* is not the same as saying *theoretical elaboration*, although the latter is without a doubt necessary. Decolonization refers simultaneously to the group and to the individual, not just objectively in the way I have indicated, but subjectively, in one's interiority. The more societies become individualist in the modern sense, the more this labor has fallen to the individual—the subject—rather than to the group. But we know that no society is completely divided up; the subject does not exist without the gathering of a society or of societies. This is the reason why the body is subjectively at stake in decolonization. How can a black skin be made into a neutral skin? Here we see who is participating in decolonization. Deracialization is included. How can we escape the monosexuation that characterizes postcolonial societies?[18] One sees this problem in particular among the postcolonial "thinkers" coming from Africa who are almost never "women thinkers" because such paths are closed to them.

The subalternization of women also takes place through bodies. A body in the grip of gender and race is a body that must doubly be decolonized. Only the subject can decolonize itself, along with other subjects. Once more, migration . . .

Notes

1. In his 1500 world map, Juan de la Cosa draws a blue line across the center of the Atlantic in order to figure the demarcating line established in the Papal bull known as "The Division of the World" (1493).

2. Gilroy, *Black Atlantic*, 4.

3. Gilroy, *Black Atlantic*, 4, 17.

4. I am thinking of the way Frantz Fanon speaks about colonial violence as "violence in a state of nature" (*violence à l'état de nature*) in *Wretched of the Earth*.

Le partage du sensible is the title of a book by Jacques Rancière. "It is a matter of knowing, first, how the world's order is pre-inscribed in the very configuration of the visible and the sayable, in the fact that it there are things one can see or not see, things one hears and one does not hear, things one hears as noise and other things that are heard as discourse" (see Palmiéri, "Interview with Rancière," 34). From Rancière, "Distribution of the Sensible," 12:

> I call the distribution of the sensible the system of self-evident facts of sense perception that simultaneously discloses the existence of something in common and the delimitations that define the respective parts and positions within it. A distribution of the sensible therefore establishes at one and the same time something common that is shared and exclusive parts. This apportionment of parts and positions is based on a distribution of spaces, times, and forms of activity that determines the very manner in which something in common lends itself to participation and in what way various individuals have a part in this distribution."

5. Foucault, *Le corps utopique*. Here is the list of heterotopias given by Foucault: gardens, cemeteries, asylums, brothels, prisons, retirement homes, museums, libraries, and finally and perhaps above all, boats. "Civilizations without boats are like children whose parents did not have a big bed on which one could play: their dreams dry up, espionage takes the place of adventure, and the ugliness of the police replaces the sun-gilded beauty of pirates" (36).

"Above all, heterology is opposed to any homogeneous representation of the world, in other words, to any philosophical system." Bataille, "D. A. F. de Sade," 97.

6. To live under a foreign law and speak a gender that is not its own—a singular acculturation, a migration in gender.

7. Nietzsche, *Birth of Tragedy*, 26.

8. Nietzsche, *Birth of Tragedy*, 119.

9. See, for example, Corbin, *Corps spirituel*.

10. Kant, "What Is Orientation?" This essay is Kant's contribution to the pantheism controversy, one of the eighteenth century's most famous and influential philosophical disputes. The principals in the dispute were Friedrich Heinrich Jacobi and Moses Mendelssohn, and its focus was the alleged Spinozism of Gotthold Ephraim Lessing. Might the principles of

Enlightenment rationalism in fact be morally and religiously subversive? Or was Spinozist pantheism a more formidable philosophical position than rationalist orthodoxy allowed?

11. See, for example, Beade, "Lamyne M."

12. Jacques Derrida offers an extensive study on the untranslatable concept of what is at once a remedy, recipe, drug, philter, etc.—namely, the pharmakon in "Plato's Pharmacy," from *Dissemination*, 63–172. "The *pharmakon* makes one stray from one's general, natural, habitual paths and laws." (70). It's a way to get out of the city. . . . According to Derrida, the god of writing is a "floating signifier," a "wild card." For Plato, if writings are memory (*mnémè*), that does not mean that memory (i.e., live memory) is supplanted by archives (*hypermnésis*)—a dead memory or a prosthesis. To solve the problem, Derrida invents the idea of *supplement*: "Conceived within this original reversibility, the *pharmakon* is the *same* precisely because it has no identity. And the same (is) as supplement. Or in differance. In writing." Derrida, *Dissemination*, 169.

13. This myth is reconsidered by Plato in the *Phaedrus*. The problem is that writings are silent; they cannot speak, answer questions, or come to their own defense. According to Socrates, "Any discourse ought to be constructed like a living creature, with its own body, as it were; it must not lack either head or feet; it must have a middle and extremities so composed as to suit each other and the whole work." Plato, *Collected Dialogues*, 510 (264c). "The dialectician selects a soul of the right type, and in it he plants and sows his words founded on knowledge, words which can defend both themselves and him who planted them, words which instead of remaining barren contain a seed whence new words grow up in new characters" (522 [276e–277a]).

14. "You have no more voice. You have given your blood. You have written." Jabès, *El, or The Last Book*, 10.

15. Nietzsche, *Thus Spoke Zarathustra*, 25–28. "To philosophize with a hammer. Zarathustra begins by asking himself if he will have to puncture them, batter their ears [*Muss man ihnen erst die Ohren zerschlagen*], with the sound of cymbals or tympani, the instruments, always, of some Dionysianism. In order to teach them 'to hear with their eyes,' too." Derrida, *Margins of Philosophy*, xii–xiii.

16. Nietzsche, *Thus Spoke Zarathustra*, 26 (translation altered).

17. Nietzsche, *Thus Spoke Zarathustra*, 27.

18. Translator's note: Here, *monosexuation* is being used to indicate the presumptive masculinity of many socially important activities and roles.

BIBLIOGRAPHY

Abraham, Nicolas, and Maria Torok. *Le verbier de l'homme aux loups*. Paris: Flammarion, 1999.

Adorno, Theodor. *Modèles critiques*. Translated by Marc Jimenez and Eliane Kaufholz. Paris: Payot, 1984.

Aeschylus. *Oresteia: Agamemnon; Libation-Bearers; Eumenides*. Translated by Alan H. Sommerstein. Cambridge, MA: Harvard University Press, 2009.

Affergan, Francis. *Critiques anthropologiques*. Paris: Presses de la Fondation Nationale des Sciences Politiques, 1991.

Agamben, Giorgio. *State of Exception*. Translated by Kevin Attell. Chicago: University of Chicago Press, 2004.

Ageron, Charles-Robert. *Histoire de l'Algérie contemporaine, Vol. 2, 1871–1954*. Paris: Presses Universitaires de France, 1979.

Aldrich, Robert. *Greater France: A History of French Overseas Expansion*. New York: St. Martin's, 1996.

Alloula, Malek. *Le harem colonial: Images d'un sous-érotisme*. Geneva: Slatkine, 1981.

Alpha, Jenny. Review of *Je suis Martinquaise*, by Mayotte Capecia. *Présence Africaine*, no. 5 (1948): 886–89.

Amselle, Jean-Loup. *Affirmative Exclusion: Cultural Pluralism and the Rule of Custom in France*. Translated by Jane Marie Todd. Ithaca, NY: Cornell University Press, 2003.

———. *Mestizo Logics: Anthropology of Identity in Africa and Elsewhere*. Translated by Claudia Royal. Stanford: Stanford University Press, 1998.

Amson, Daniel. *Adolphe Crémieux: L'oublié de la gloire*. Paris: Seuil, 1988.

Anzieu, Didier. *Le moi-peau*. Paris: Dunod, 1995.

Appiah, Kwame Anthony. *Cosmopolitanism: Ethics in a World of Strangers*. New York: W. W. Norton, 2006.

Aristotle. *Metaphysics*. In *The Basic Works of Aristotle*. Translated by W. D. Ross. Edited by Richard McKeon, 681–926. New York: Random House, 1966.

———. *Politics*. In *The Basic Works of Aristotle*. Translated by Benjamin Jowett. Edited by Richard McKeon, 1113–16. New York: Random House, 1966.

Arnold, A. James. "'Mayotte Capécia': De la parabole biblique à *Je suis Martiniquaise*." *Revue de littérature comparée* 305, no. 1:35–48.

Aron, Raymond. *Sur Clausewitz*. Brussels: Éditions Complexe, 1987.

Ashcroft, Bill, Gareth Griffiths, and Helen Tiffin. *The Empire Writes Back: Theory and Practice in Postcolonial Literatures*. 2nd ed. London: Routledge, 2002.

Bahri, Deepika. "Le féminisme dans/et le postcolonial." In *Penser le postcolonial: Une introduction critique*, edited by Neil Lazarus, translated by Marianne Groulez, Christophe Jaquet, and Hélène Quiniou, 301–30. Paris: Éditions Amsterdam, 2006.

Bakhtin, Mikhail. *Problems of Dostoevsky's Poetics*. Vol. 8 of *Theory and History of Literature*. Translated by Caryl Emerson. Minneapolis: University of Minnesota Press, 1984.

Balandier, Georges. "Sociologie de la colonisation et relations entre sociétés globales." *Cahiers internationaux de sociologie* 17 (July–December 1954): 17–31.

Balibar, Etienne. "Dissonances within Laïcité." *Constellations* 11, no. 3 (2004): 353–67.
———. "Politique et traduction: Réflexions à partir de Lyotard, Derrida, Said." In "Que veut dire traduire?" Special issue, *Revue Asylon(s)* 7 (2009–10). http://www.reseau-terra.eu/article932.html.
Ballanche, Pierre-Simon. "Formule générale de l'histoire de tous les peuples appliquée à l'histoire du people romain." *Revue de Paris*, September 1829.
Bancel, Nicolas, and Pascal Blanchard. "From Colonial to Postcolonial: Reflections on the Colonial Debate in France." In Forsdick and Murphy, *Postcolonial Thought*, 295–305.
Barel, Yves. *Le héros et le politique, le sens d'avant le sens*. Grenoble: Presses Universitaires de Grenoble, 1989.
Barkat, Sidi Mohammed. *Le corps d'exception: Les artifices du pouvoir colonial et la destruction de la vie*. Paris: Éditions Amsterdam, 2005.
Bataille, Georges. "The Notion of Expenditure." In Bataille, *Visions of Excess*, 116–29.
———. "The Use Value of D. A. F. de Sade." In Bataille, *Visions of Excess*, 91–102.
———. *Visions of Excess: Selected Writings, 1927–1939*. Edited by Allan Stoekl. Translated by Allan Stoekl, Carl R. Lovitt, and Donald M. Leslie Jr. Minneapolis: University of Minnesota Press, 1985.
Baubérot, Jean. "French Laicization in the Worldwide Context." *Religious Studies Review* 1, no. 1 (2007): 74–81.
Beade, Helene. "Lamyne M. The Artist with a Camera." Africanah. August 3, 2017. http://africanah.org/lamyne-m-the-artist-with-a-camera/.
Beaumont, Gustave de. "État de la question de l'Afrique." *Le Siècle*, November 26, 1832.
———. "État de la question de l'Afrique." *Le Siècle*, November 30, 1832.
———. "État de la question de l'Afrique." *Le Siècle*, December 3, 1832.
———. "État de la question de l'Afrique." *Le Siècle*, December 7, 1832.
———. "État de la question de l'Afrique." *Le Siècle*, December 11, 1832.
———. *Marie, ou L'esclavage aux États-Unis: Tableau des moeurs américaines*. Rev. 3rd ed. Paris: C. Gosselin, 1836.
Benjamin, Walter. "Franz Kafka: On the 10th Anniversary of His Death." In *Illuminations: Essays and Reflections*, edited by Hannah Arendt, 141–45. New York: Schocken Books, 1968.
Bennoune, Karima. *Your Fatwa Does Not Apply Here: Untold Stories from the Fight against Muslim Fundamentalism*. New York: Norton, 2013.
Benot, Yves. *La Révolution française et la fin des colonies, 1789–1794*. Paris: La Découverte, 2004.
———. *Massacres coloniaux, 1944–1950: La IVᵉ République et la mise au pas des colonies françaises*. Paris: La Découverte, 2001.
Benveniste, Émile. *Problèmes de linguistique générale*. Vol. 2. Paris: Gallimard, 1974.
———. *Problems in General Linguistics*. Translated by Mary Elizabeth Meek. Coral Gables, FL: University of Miami Press, 1971. First published as *Problèmes de linguistique générale*, vol. 1. Paris: Gallimard, 1966.
Berman, Antoine. *L'épreuve de l'étranger, culture et traduction dans l'Allemagne romantique: Herder, Goethe, Schlegel, Novalis, Humboldt, Schleiermacher, Hölderlin*. Paris: Gallimard, 1995.
Berthelier, Robert. "À la recherche de l'homme musulman." *Sud/Nord* 22 (2007): 127–46. https://www.cairn.info/revue-sud-nord-2007-1-page-127.htm.
Bettati, Mario. "Le droit d'ingérence: Sens et portée." *Le Débat* 67 (1991): 4–14.
Bhabha, Homi K. *The Location of Culture*. London: Routledge, 1994.
———. *Nation and Narration*. London: Routledge, 1990.

Birnbaum, Jean. "1914–1918: Guerre de tranchées entre historiens." *Le Monde*, March 11, 2006, 20–21.
Birnbaum, Pierre. *Les fous de la République: Histoire politique des Juifs d'État de Gambetta à Vichy*. Paris: Fayard, 1992.
———. "Sur l'étatisation révolutionnaire: L'Abbé Grégoire et le destin de l'identité Juive." *Le Débat*, no. 53 (January–February 1989): 172–88.
Blommaert, Jan, ed. *Language Ideological Debates*. Berlin: Mouton de Gruyter, 1999.
Bodin, Jean. *Les six livres de la république de I. Bodin Angeuin. A Monseignevr dv Favr, Seigneur de Pibrac, conseiller du Roy en son conseil priué*. Paris: n.p., 1576.
Bongie, Chris. "Édouard Glissant Dealing in Globality." In Forsdick and Murphy, *Postcolonial Thought*, 90–101.
Bouamama, Saïd. "Ethnicisation et construction idéologique d'un bouc émissaire." In Nordmann, *Le foulard islamique*, 38–49.
Bourdieu, Pierre. *Esquisse d'une théorie de la pratique précédé de Trois études d'ethnologie kabyle*. Geneva: Librairie Droz, 1972.
———. *Outline of a Theory of Practice*. Translated by Richard Nice. Cambridge: Cambridge University Press, 1977.
Bouvier, Pierre. "Ségolène Royal 'est de droite'. . . selon Pierre Bourdieu." *Le Monde (Société)*, October 5, 2006. http://www.lemonde.fr/societe/article/2006/10/05/segolene-royal-est-de-droite-selon-pierre-bourdieu_820078_3224.html#dUGj1hGCgUjv6sSf.99.
Branche, Raphaëlle. "Mémoire et cinema: À propos de 'Muriel' d'Alain Resnais." *Vingtième siècle*, no. 46 (1995): 191–94. http://www.persee.fr/doc/xxs_0294-1759_1995_num_46_1_3169.
Brunet, Elena, and Jérôme Hourdeaux. "Retour sur le Festival des Arts nègres." *Le Nouvel Observateur*, January 27, 2011. https://www.nouvelobs.com/culture/20110127.OBS7049/reportage-retour-sur-le-festival-des-arts-negres.html.
Buber, Martin. *I and Thou*. Translated by Walter Kaufman. New York: Scribner, 1971.
Buck-Morss, Susan. *Hegel, Haiti, and Universal History*. Pittsburgh: University of Pittsburgh Press, 2009.
Bullard, Alice. "The Critical Impact of Frantz Fanon and Henri Collomb: Race, Gender, and Personality Testing of North and West Africans." *Journal of the History of the Behavioral Sciences* 41, no. 3 (2005): 225–48.
Butler, Judith. "Can the Other of Philosophy Speak?" In *Undoing Gender*, 232–50. New York: Routledge, 2004.
———. *Giving an Account of Oneself*. New York: Fordham University Press, 2005.
Camus, Albert. *L'étranger: Roman*. Paris: Gallimard, 1942.
Capécia, Mayotte (Lucette Ceranus). *I Am a Martinican Woman* and *The White Negress*. Translated by Beatrice Stith Clark. Pueblo, CO: Passeggiata Press, 1998. First published in French as *Je suis martiniquaise* in 1948 and *La négresse blanche* in 1950.
Cassin, Barbara. "Amnistie et pardon: Pour une ligne de partage entre éthique et politique." *Le Genre humain*, no. 43 (2004): 35–58.
———. "Intraduisible et mondialisation: Interview with Michaël Oustinoff." *Hermés*, no. 49 (2007): 197–204.
Caussé, Bruno. "Zinédine Zidane, la légende ternie." *Le Monde*, July 11, 2006.
Césaire, Aimé. *Discourse on Colonialism*. Translated by Joan Pinkham. New York: Monthly Review Press, 2001.
Chakrabarty, Dipesh. *Provincializing Europe: Postcolonial Thought and Historical Difference*. 2nd ed. Princeton: Princeton University Press, 2007.
Chamoiseau, Patrick. *Écrire en pays dominé*. Paris: Gallimard, 1997.

Chow, Rey. *The Age of the World Target: Self-Referentiality in War, Theory, and Comparative Work*. Durham, NC: Duke University Press, 2006.

"Circulaire du 12 décembre 1989 du ministre d'Etat, ministre de l'Education nationale, de la Jeunesse et des Sports." *Hommes et Migrations*, no. 1129–30 (1990): 110–113. https://www.persee.fr/doc/homig_1142-852x_1990_num_1129_1_5014.

Clausewitz, Carl von. *De la guerre*. Paris: Éditions Payot et Rivages, 2006.

Coldefy, Capitaine. "Une éducation brusque: Le soldat nord-africain et les campagnes d'Europe." *Les Études*, February 1947.

Cole, Joshua. "Intimate Acts and Unspeakable Relations: Remembering Torture and the War for Algerian Independence." In *Memory, Empire and Postcolonialism: Legacies of French Colonialism*, edited by Alec G. Hargreaves, 125–41. Lanham, MD: Lexington Books, 2005.

Collignon, René. "Pour une histoire de la psychiatrie coloniale française: A partir de l'exemple du Sénégal." *L'Autre* 3, no. 3 (2002): 455–80. http://www.cairn.info/revue-l-autre-2002-3-page-455.htm.

Collomb, Henri, and S. Valantin. "Famille africaine." In *L'enfant dans la famille*. Paris: Masson, 1967.

Connelly, Matthew James. *A Diplomatic Revolution: Algeria's Fight for Independence and the Origins of the Post–Cold War Era*. Oxford: Oxford University Press, 2002.

Conseil d'État, Section de l'intérieur. "Avis 'Port du foulard islamique.'" n° 346893, November 27, 1989. Revue Actualité Juridique Française. Accessed January 20, 2019. http://www.rajf.org/spip.php?article1065.

Cooper, Frederick. "Afrique: Équivoques indépendances." Interview. *Le Monde Magazine*, July 3, 2010.

Coquery-Vidrovitch, Catherine. "The Rise of Francophone African Social Science: From Colonial Knowledge to Knowledge of Africa." In Martin and West, *Many Africas*, 39–53.

Corbin, Henri. *Corps spirituel et terre céleste: De l'Iran mazdéen à l'Iran shî'ite*. Paris: Buchet-Chastel, 1979.

Cottias, Myriam, and Madeleine Dobie. *Relire Mayotte Capécia: Une femme des Antilles dans l'espace colonial français (1916–1955)*. Paris: Armand Colin, 2012.

Curran, Andrew S. *The Anatomy of Blackness: Science and Slavery in an Age of Enlightenment*. Baltimore: Johns Hopkins University Press, 2011.

Cusset, François. *French Theory: How Foucault, Derrida, Deleuze, and Co. Transformed the Intellectual Life of the United States*. Translated by Jeff Fort. Minneapolis: University of Minnesota Press, 2008.

Daeninckx, Didier. *Ceinture rouge précédé de Corvée de bois*. Paris: Gallimard, 2003.

Davidson, Basil. *The Search for Africa: History, Culture, Politics*. New York: Random House/Times Books, 1994.

Davis, Angela. "Reflections on the Black Woman's Role in the Community of Slaves." In *Words of Fire: An Anthology of African-American Feminist Thought*, edited by Beverly Guy-Sheftall, 200–218. New York: New Press, 1995.

Davoine, Françoise, and Jean-Max Gaudillière. *History beyond Trauma: Whereof One Cannot Speak, Thereof One Cannot Stay Silent*. Translated by Susan Fairfield. New York: Other Press, 2004.

De Brazza, Savorgnan. *Mission d'enquête du Congo: Rapport et documents (1905–1907) de Pierre Savorgnan de Brazza, Commission Lanessan*. Preface by Catherine Coquery-Vidrovitch. Neuvy-en-Champagne: Le Passager Clandestin, 2014.

Debré, Jean-Louis. "Sid Cara, Nafissa (1910–2002)." In *Dictionnaire amoureux de la république*. Paris: Plon, 2017.

de Certeau, Michel. *Heterologies: Discourse on the Other.* Translated by Brian Massumi. Vol. 17 of *Theory and History of Literature.* Minneapolis: University of Minnesota Press, 1986.

———. *Histoire et psychanalyse entre science et fiction.* Rev. expanded ed. Paris: Gallimard, 2002.

———. *The Practice of Everyday Life.* Vol. 1. Translated by Steven F. Rendall. Berkeley: University of California Press, 1988.

De Gaulle, Charles. "Message radiotélévisé du général de Gaulle du 23 avril 1961." Jalons: Version Découverte, April 23, 1961. Accessed March 23, 2018. Video, 6:17. http://fresques.ina.fr/jalons/fiche-media/InaEdu00089/message-r.

Delafosse, Maurice. *Broussard, ou Les états d'âme d'un colonial.* Paris: Publication du comité de l'Afrique française, 1909.

Deleuze, Gilles. *Cinema 2: The Time-Image.* Translated by Hugh Tomlinson and Robert Galeta. Minneapolis: University of Minnesota Press, 1989.

———. *Essays Critical and Clinical.* Translated by Daniel W. Smith and Michael A. Greco. Minneapolis: University of Minnesota Press, 1997.

———. *Foucault.* Translated by Séan Hand. Minneapolis: University of Minnesota Press, 1988.

———. "Sex-pol en acte." In *Trois milliards de pervers: La grande encyclopédie des homosexualités*, 28–31. La Bussiere: L'Acratie, 2015. First published 1973.

Deleuze, Gilles, and Félix Guattari. *Kafka: Toward a Minor Literature.* Vol. 30 of *Theory and History of Literature.* Translated by Dana Polan. Minneapolis: University of Minnesota Press, 1986.

Deroo, Éric, and Antoine Champeaux. *La force noire: Gloire et infortunes d'une légende coloniale.* Paris: Tallandier, 2006.

Deroo, Éric, and Sandrine Lemaire. *L'illusion coloniale.* Paris: Tallandier Press, 2005.

Derradji, Yacine. "Le français en Algérie: Langue emprunteuse et empruntée." *Le français en Afrique*, no. 13 (1999): 71–82. http://www.unice.fr/bcl/ofcaf/13/derradji.html.

Derrida, Jacques. *Acts of Religion.* Edited by Gil Anidjar. New York: Routledge, 2002.

———. *Dissemination.* Translated by Barbara Johnson. Chicago: University of Chicago Press, 1981.

———. *Force de loi: Le "fondement mystique de l'autorité."* Paris: Galilée, 1994.

———. "Forcener le subjectile." In *Antonin Artaud, dessins et portraits*, edited by Paule Thévenin and Jacques Derrida. Paris: Gallimard, 1986.

———. "La parole soufflée." In *Writing and Difference*, 169–95. Translated by Alan Bass. Chicago: University of Chicago Press, 1978.

———. "Let Us Not Forget—Psychoanalysis." *Oxford Literary Review* 12, no. 1–2 (1990): 3–7.

———. *Margins of Philosophy.* Translated by Alan Bass. Chicago: University of Chicago Press, 1982.

———. *Monolingualism of the Other, or The Prosthesis of Origin.* Translated by Patrick Mensah. Stanford: Stanford University Press, 1998. First published in French as *Monolinguisme de l'autre, ou La prosthèse d'origine* in 1996.

———. *Of Grammatology.* Translated by Gayatri Chakravorty Spivak. Baltimore: Johns Hopkins University Press, 1976.

———. *Of Hospitality: Anne Dufourmantelle Invites Jacques Derrida to Respond.* Translated by Rachel Bowlby. Stanford: Stanford University Press, 2000. First published in French as *De l'hospitalité* in 1997.

———. *The Other Heading: Reflections on Today's Europe.* Translated by Pascale-Anne Brault and Michael B. Naas. Bloomington: Indiana University Press, 1992. First published as *L'autre cap* in 1991.

———. *The Post Card: From Socrates to Freud and Beyond.* Translated by Alan Bass, Trans. Chicago: University of Chicago Press, 1987. First published 1980.

———. *Specters of Marx: The State of the Debt, the Work of Mourning, and the New International.* Translated by Peggy Kamuf. New York: Routledge, 1994.

Descartes, Réné. *Meditations on First Philosophy: With Selections from the Objections and Replies.* Translated by John Cottingham. 2nd ed. Cambridge: Cambridge University Press, 2017. First published 1641.

Diallo, Mamadou Saliou. "Langue et éducation en Guinée." In *ACALAN Bulletin d'information,* edited by Adama Samassékou, 7–21. Bamako, Mali: Académie africaine des langues, 2007.

Diderot, Denis. *Essais sur la peinture: Salons de 1759, 1761, 1763.* Edited by Gita May and Jacques Chouillet. Paris: Éditions Hermann, 1984.

———. *Héros et martyrs: Salons de 1769, 1771, 1775, 1781; Pensées détachées sur la peinture.* Edited by Else Marie Bukdahl et al. Paris: Éditions Hermann, 1995.

Djebar, Assia. *Algerian White.* Translated by David Kelley and Marjolijin de Jager. New York: Seven Stories Press, 2001.

———. *Ces voix qui m'assiègent . . . en marge de ma francophonie.* Paris: Albin Michel, 1999.

———. *Les alouettes naïves.* Arles: Actes Sud, 1997.

———. *The Tongue's Blood Does Not Run Dry.* Translated by Tegan Raleigh. New York: Seven Stories Press, 2006. Originally published in French as *Oran, langue morte* in 1997.

Dorgelès, Roland. *Réveil des morts: Roman.* Paris: Albin Michel, 1923.

Douglass, Frederick. *My Bondage and My Freedom.* In *Bondage and Freedom,* vol. 2 of *The Frederick Douglass Papers, Series Two: Autobiographical Writings,* edited by John W. Blassingame, John R. McKivigan, and Peter B. Hinks. New Haven, CT: Yale University Press, 2003. First published 1885.

———. "What to the Slave Is the Fourth of July? An Address Delivered in Rochester, New York on 5 July 1852." In *1847–1854,* vol. 2 of *The Frederick Douglass Papers, Series One: Speeches, Debates, and Interviews,* edited by John W. Blassingame. New Haven, CT: Yale University Press, 1982.

Dozon, Jean-Pierre. "Les bété: Une création coloniale." In *Au cœur de l'ethnie: Ethnies, tribalisme et état en Afrique,* edited by Jean-Loup Amselle and Elikia M'Bokolo, 49–85. Paris: La Découverte, 1999.

Drousset, Claude. "Édito." *L'Équipe,* July 10, 2006.

Droz, Bernard. "Main basse sur les terres." In *L'Algérie des Français,* edited by Charles-Robert Ageron, 71–83. Paris: Seuil, 1993.

Erichsen, Casper, and David Olusoga. *The Kaiser's Holocaust: Germany's Forgotten Genocide and the Colonial Roots of Nazism.* London: Faber and Faber, 2010.

Fanon, Frantz. *Black Skin, White Masks.* Translated by Richard Philcox. New York: Grove Press, 2008. First published in French as *Peau noire, masques blancs* in 1952.

———. *A Dying Colonialism.* Translated by Haakon Chevalier. New York: Grove Press/Monthly Review Press, 1965. First published as *L'an V de la révolution algérienne* in 1959.

———. "La plainte du noir: L'expérience vécue du Noir." *Esprit,* 79 (1952): 657–78.

———. *Toward the African Revolution.* Translated by Haakon Chevalier. New York: Grove Press/Monthly Review Press, 1994. First published 1964.

———. *Wretched of the Earth.* Translated by Richard Philcox. New York: Grove Press, 2004. First published in French as *Les damnés de la terre* in 1961.

Fardon, Richard. "Covering Ethnicity? Or Ethnicity as Coverage?" *Contemporary Politics* 2, no. 1 (1996): 153–58.

———. "'Destins croisés': Histoire des identités ethniques et nationales en Afrique de l'Ouest." *Politique Africaine* 61 (1996): 75–97.

———. "The Person, Ethnicity, and the Problem of 'Identity' in West Africa." In *African Crossroads: Intersections between History and Anthropology in Cameroon*, edited by Ian Fowler and David Zeitlyn, 17–44. Providence, RI: Berghahn, 1996.

Fassin, Eric. "Fanon, du voile au viol, culture, genre et sexualité." In *Guerre d'Algérie, le sexe outragé*, edited by Catherine Brun and Todd Shepard. Paris: Éditions CNRS, 2016.

———. "'Good to Think': The American Reference in French Discourses of Immigration and Ethnicity." In *Multicultural Questions*, edited by Christian Joppke and Steven Lukes, 224–41. Oxford: Oxford University Press, 2004. https://doi.org/10.1093/0198296 10X.003.0011.

Febvre, Lucien. *Combats pour l'histoire*. Paris: Armand Colin, 1953.

Ferenczi, Sandor, Karl Abraham, Ernst Simmel, and Ernest Jones. *Psychoanalysis and the War Neuroses*. London: Psychoanalytical Press, 1921.

Ferhati, Barkahoum. "Ambivalence des discours politiques sur la prostitution (1962–2000): L'histoire bégaie!" In "Femmes et citoyenneté." Special issue, *NAQD*, no. 22–23 (2006): 67–79.

———. *De la "tolérance" en Algérie (1830–1962): Enjeux et soubassements*. Algiers: Dar El Othmania, 2007.

———. "Enquêter sur la prostitution en Algérie: Souvenirs de Bou-Saâda." *L'Année du Maghreb* 6 (2010): 253–68.

———. "La danseuse prostituée dite 'Ouled Naïl,' entre mythe et réalité (1830–1962): Des rapports sociaux et des pratiques concrètes." *Clio: Femmes, Genre, Histoire* 17 (2003): 101–13.

Ferro, Marc. *Histoire des colonisations*. Paris: Éditions de Seuil, 1994.

Finet, Patrice, Guy Chevallier, and Michel Cressole. "Les Arabes et nous." In *Trois milliards de pervers: La grande encyclopédie des homosexualités*, 10–27. La Bussiere: L'Acratie, 2015. First published 1973.

Fontenaille-N'diaye, Elise. *Blue Book: Récit*. Paris: Calmann-Lévy, 2015.

Forsdick, Charles. "Colonialism, Postcolonialism, and Cultures of Commemoration." In Forsdick and Murphy, *Postcolonial Thought*, 271–84.

Forsdick, Charles, and David Murphy, eds. *Postcolonial Thought in the French-Speaking World*. Liverpool: Liverpool University Press, 2009.

Foucault, Michel. *Abnormal: Lectures at the Collège de France 1974–1975*. Edited by Valerio Marchetti and Antonella Salomoni. Translated by Graham Burchell. New York: Picador, 2003.

———. *Aesthetics, Method, Epistemology: Essential Works of Foucault, 1954–1984*. Edited by James D. Faubion. Translated by Robert Hurley et al. New York: New Press, 1998.

———. *The Archaeology of Knowledge and The Discourse on Language*. Translated by A. M. Sheridan Smith. New York: Pantheon Books, 1972. First published 1969.

———. *Discipline and Punish: Birth of the Prison*. Translated by Alan Sheridan. New York: Pantheon Books, 1977. First published as *Surveiller et punir* in 1975.

———. *History of Madness*. Edited by Jean Khalfa. Translated by Jonathan Murphy and Jean Khalfa. London: Routledge, 2006. First published 1961.

———. "Il faut defendre la société (1976)." In *Dits et Écrits II, 1976–1988*, edited by Daniel Defert and François Ewald, 124–130. Paris: Gallimard, 1994.

———. *Le corps utopique, les hétérotopies*. Edited by Daniel Defert. Paris: Éditions Lignes, 2009.

———. "Nietzsche, Freud, Marx." In *Aesthetics, Method, Epistemology*, 269–78.

———. "Nietzsche, Freud, Marx." In *Dits et écrits I, 1954–1969*, edited by Daniel Defert and François Ewald, 564–79. Paris: Gallimard, 1994.

———. "Nietzsche, Genealogy, History." In *Aesthetics, Method, Epistemology*, 369–91.

———. "On the Ways of Writing History." In *Aesthetics, Method, Epistemology*, 279–95.

———. "The Order of Things." In *Aesthetics, Method, Epistemology*, 261–67.

———. *The Order of Things: An Archaeology of the Human Sciences*. Translated by Alan Sheridan. New York: Random House, 1970. First published 1966.

———. "The Thought of the Outside." In *Aesthetics, Method, Epistemology*, 147–70.

Fournier, L. *Le français tel que le parlent nos tirailleurs sénégalais*. Paris: Imprimerie-Librairie Militaire Universelle, 1916.

Frederickson, George M. "Identité nationale et codes d'altérité dans l'histoire de la France et des États-Unis." In *Les codes de la différence*, edited by Riva Kastoryano, 43–66. Paris: Presses de la Fondation Nationale des Sciences Politiques, 2005.

Freedman, Jane. "Secularism as a Barrier to Integration? The French Dilemna." *International Migration* 42, no. 3 (2004): 5–27.

Freud, Sigmund. "'A Child Is Being Beaten': A Contribution to the Study of the Origin of Sexual Perversions." In vol. 17 of *Complete Psychological Works*, 177–204. First published 1919.

———. "Delusions and Dreams in Jensen's *Gradiva*." In vol. 9 of *Complete Psychological Works*, 3–95. First published 1907.

———. "Fetishism." In vol. 21 of *Complete Psychological Works*, 149–57. First published 1927.

———. *The Interpretation of Dreams*. In vol. 4 of *Complete Psychological Works*, 1–630. First published 1900.

———. *Introductory Lectures on Psycho-analysis*. Vols. 15–16 of *Complete Psychological Works*. First published 1915–16.

———. *The Psychopathology of Everyday Life*. Vol. 6 of *Complete Psychological Works*. First published 1901.

———. "Screen Memories." In vol. 3 of *Complete Psychological Works*, 301–2. First published 1899.

———. *The Standard Edition of the Complete Psychological Works of Sigmund Freud*. Translated by James Strachey, Anna Freud, Alix Strachey, and Alan Tyson. London: Hogarth Press, 1959–1963.

———. "Thoughts for the Times on War and Death." In vol. 14 of *Complete Psychological Works*, 275–300. First published 1915.

Fyfe, Christopher. "The Emergence and Evolution of African Studies in the United Kingdom." In Martin and West, *Many Africas*, 54–61.

Gade, Christian B. N. "The Historical Development of the Written Discourses on *Ubuntu*." *South African Journal of Philosophy* 30, no. 3 (2011): 303–29.

Gafaïti, Hafid. "Histoire des femmes et dévoilement de l'écriture." In *La Diasporisation de la littérature postcoloniale, Assia Djebar, Rachid Mimouni*, 155–71. Paris: L'Harmattan, 2005.

Garouste, Gérard, and Judith Perrignon. *L'intranquille: Autoportrait d'un fils, d'un peintre, d'un fou*. Paris: Éditions L'Iconoclaste, 2009.

Gérard, Albert. *Littératures en langues africaines*. Paris: Mentha, 1992.

Ghemnour, Chérif. "La finale d'une legende." *Libération*, July 10, 2006.

Giesbert, Franz Olivier. *Mitterand, ou La tentation de l'histoire*. Paris: Éditions du Seuil, 1977.

Gilroy, Paul. *The Black Atlantic: Modernity and Double Consciousness*. Cambridge, MA: Harvard University Press, 1993.

Giordano, Rosario, ed. *Autour de la mémoire, la Belgique, le Congo et le passé colonial*. Paris: L'Harmattan, 2008.

Girault, René, Gérard Bossuat, and Seloua Luste Boulbina, eds. *Pierre Mendès France et le rôle de la France dans le monde.* Grenoble: Presses Universitaires de Grenoble, 1991.

Glissant, Édouard. *Caribbean Discourse: Selected Essays.* Translated by J. Michael Dash. Charlottesville: University Press of Virginia, 1992.

———. *Le discours antillais.* Paris: Gallimard/Folio, 1997.

———. *Poetics of Relation.* Translated by Betsy Wing. Ann Arbor: University of Michigan Press, 1997.

———. *Tout-Monde: Roman.* Paris: Gallimard, 1995.

Godelier, Maurice. *Communauté, société, culture.* Paris: CNRS Éditions, 2009.

Gordon, Avery. *Ghostly Matters: Haunting and the Sociological Imagination.* Minneapolis: University of Minnesota Press, 1997.

Gordon, Lewis R. "Décoloniser le savoir à la suite de Frantz Fanon." *Tumultes* 31 (2008): 103–23.

Graff, Gerald. *Professing Literature: An Institutional History.* Chicago: University of Chicago Press, 1987.

Grandguillaume, Gilbert. "L'arabisation au Maghreb." *Revue d'aménagement linguistique*, no. 107 (Winter 2004): 15–40.

Grégoire, Henri (Abbé). *Essai sur la régénération physique, morale, et politiques des Juifs.* Paris: Gallica Press, 1988. First published 1788.

Haddour, Azzedine. "Fanon dans la théorie postcoloniale." *Les temps modernes*, no. 635–36 (2005–06): 136–58.

Haneke, Michael. *Caché (Hidden).* Sony Pictures Classics; Les Films du Losange; Wega Film, Bavaria Film, BIM Distribuzione; with Arte France Cinéma, France 3 Cinéma, ORF Film/Fernseh-Abkommen Art/WDR, 2005.

Hanotaux, Gabriel, and Alfred Martineau. *Histoire des colonies françaises et de l'expansion de la France dans le monde.* Paris: Plon, 1929.

Hantel, Max. "Errant Notes on a Caribbean Rhizome." *Rhizomes* 24 (2012). http://www.rhizomes.net/issue24/hantel.html.

Harbi, Mohammed. *La guerre commence en Algérie: 1954.* Hydra, Algiers: Éditions Barzakh, 2005.

———. *L'Algérie et son destin: Croyants ou citoyens.* Paris: Arcantère, 1992.

———. "Pierre Mendès France, le FLN et l'Algérie." In Girault, Bossuat, and Luste Boulbina, *Pierre Mendès France*, 371–74.

———. *Une vie debout, mémoires politiques, tome I: 1945–1962.* Paris: La Découverte, 2001.

Harootunian, Harry D. "Postcoloniality's Unconscious/Area Studies' Desire." In *Learning Places: The Afterlives of Area Studies*, edited by Masao Miyoshi and Harry D. Harootunian, 150–74. Durham, NC: Duke University Press, 2002.

Harrison, Christopher. *France and Islam in West Africa, 1860–1960.* Cambridge: Cambridge University Press, 1988.

Hartog, François. *Évidence de l'histoire, ce que voient les historiens.* Paris: Éditions de l'École des Hautes Études en Sciences Sociales, 2005.

Hautreux, François-Xavier. "L'engagement des harkis (1954–1962)." *Vigntième Siècle, Revue de l'histoire* 90 (April–June 2006): 33–45. https://www.cairn.info/revue-vingtieme-siecle-revue-d-histoire-2006-2-page-33.htm.

Hesiod. *Theogony, Works and Days, Testimonia.* Edited and translated by Glenn W. Most. Loeb Classical Library. Cambridge, MA: Harvard University Press, 2006.

Hesseling, Gerti. "L'annexion du Sénégal." *Histoire politique du Sénégal: Institutions, droit et société*, 121–24. Paris: Karthala Editions, 1985.

Hiepko, Andrea Schwieger. "Europe and the Antilles: An Interview with Édouard Glissant." Translated by Julin Everett. In Lionnet and Shih, *Creolization of Theory*, 255–61.

Husserl, Edmund. *The Crisis of European Sciences and Transcendental Phenomenology: An Introduction to Phenomenological Philosophy*. Translated by David Carr. Evanston, IL: Northwestern University Press, 1970.

Ibrahimi, Khaoula Taleb. *Les Algériens et leur(s) langue(s): Éléments pour une approche sociolinguistique de la société*. Alger: Éditions El Hikma, 1997.

Idier, Antoine. *Les vies de Guy Hocquenghem: Politique, sexualité, culture*. Paris: Fayard, 2017.

Ighilahriz, Louisette, and Anne Nivat. *Algérienne*. Paris: Calmann-Levy, 2001.

Iveković, Rada. "Langue coloniale, langue globale, langue locale." In "Réflexions sur la postcolonie," edited by Seloua Luste Boulbina. *Rue Descartes* 58 (November 2007): 26–36.

———. *Le sexe de la nation*. Paris: Éditions Leo Scheer, 2003.

Jabès, Edmond. *The Book of Questions: El, or The Last Book*. Translated by Rosmarie Waldrop. Middletown, CT: Wesleyan University Press, 1984.

Jablonka, Ivan. *Histoire des grands-parents que je n'ai pas eus*. Paris: Seuil, 2012.

———. "L'Arche de Zoé ou le système du déracinement." *Humanitaire* 18 (2008). https://humanitaire.revues.org/198.

Jardin, André. *Alexis de Tocqueville, 1805–1859*. Paris: Hachette Littératures, 1984.

Jospin, Lionel. "De l'émancipation des Juifs de France à l'école du citoyen." *Cahiers Bernard Lazare*, no. 128–30 (1991).

———. "Le moment ou jamais: Entretien avec Lionel Jospin." *Le Débat*, no. 58 (January–February 1990): 3–17.

Kafka, Franz. *The Complete Stories*. Translated by Nahum N. Glatzer. New York: Schocken Books, 1983.

———. *Récits, romans, journaux*. Edited by Brigitte Vergne-Cain and Gérard Rudent. Paris: Librairie Générale Francaise, 2000.

Kant, Immanuel. *Kant's Political Writings*. Edited by Hans Reiss. Translated by H. B. Nisbet. 2nd enlarged ed. Cambridge: Cambridge University Press, 1991.

———. "On Perpetual Peace." In Kant, *Kant's Political Writings*, 93–130.

———. "What Is Orientation in Thinking?" In Kant, *Kant's Political Writings*, 237–49. Cambridge: Cambridge University Press, 1991.

Kateb, Yacine. *Abdelkader et l'indépendence algérienne*. Alger: Enag, 2009.

———. *Le cadavre encerclé*. In *Le cercle des réprésailles: Théâtre*. Paris: Seuil, 1959. First published in *Esprit* 221, no. 12 (1954): 689–706 and 222, no. 1 (1955): 74–100.

———. *Nedjma*. Paris: Seuil, 1981. First published 1956.

———. *Soliloques*. Paris: La Découverte, 1991.

Kechiche, Abdellatif. *Vénus noire*. France/Belgium/Tunisia: MK2 Productions, 2010.

Kelkel, Arion Lothar. *Le legs de la phenomenologie*. Paris: Kimé, 2003.

Kerner, Ina. "Postcolonial Theories as Global Critical Theories." *Constellations* (2018): 1–15. https://doi.org/10.1111/1467-8675.12346.

Khadra, Yasmina. *L'attentat*. Paris: Éditions Julliard, 2005.

———. *L'écrivain: Roman*. Paris: Éditions Julliard, 2001.

Khatibi, Abdelkader. *Du bilinguisme*. Paris: Éditions Denoël, 1985.

Khamissi, Khaled Al. *Taxi*. Translated by Hussain Emara and Moïna Fauchier Delavigne. Arles: Actes Sud, 2009.

Khelifi, Ghania. *Yacine Kateb*. Alger: Enag, 1990.

Kintzler, Catherine. "Aux fondements de la laïcité scolaire." In *La république et l'école*, edited by Charles Coutel. Paris: Agora/Presses-Pocket, 1991.

Kiouane, Abderahmane. *Débuts d'une diplomatie de guerre (1956–1962)*. Hydra, Algeria: Dahleb, 2000.

Kipling, Rudyard. "The White Man's Burden: The United States and the Philippine Islands, 1899." In *Rudyard Kipling's Verse, Inclusive Edition, 1885–1926*, 320–21. Garden City, NY: Doubleday, 1929.

Klein, Josephine. *Our Need for Others and Its Roots in Infancy*. London: Routledge, 1993.

Klein, William. *Festival panafricain d'Alger*. Office national pour le commerce et l'industrie cinematographique (ONCIC)/Centre national de la cinématographie et l'audiovisuel (CNCA) Algérie, 1969.

Kofman, Sarah. *The Enigma of Woman: Woman in Freud's Writings*. Translated by Catherine Porter. Ithaca, NY: Cornell University Press, 1985.

———. "Judith, ou La mise en scène du tabou de la virginité." *Littérature et psychanalyse*, no. 3 (1971): 100–116. http://www.persee.fr/doc/litt_0047-4800_1971_num_3_3_1934.

Kotek, Joël. "Le génocide des Herero, symptôme d'un *Sonderweg* allemande?" In "Violences," *Revue d'histoire de la Shoah* 189, no. 2 (2008): 177–97. https://www.cairn.info/revue-revue-d-histoire-de-la-shoah-2008-2-page-177.htm.

Kouchner, Bernard. "Le mouvement humanitaire." *Le Débat*, no. 67 (1991): 28–36.

———. "Introduction." *Action humanitaire, devoir d'ingérence: Naissance d'un nouveau droit. Les Cahiers de L'Express* no. 20 (1993).

Kourouma, Ahmadou. *The Suns of Independence*. Translated by Adrian Adams. London: Heinemann, 1981. First published 1968.

Krog, Antjie. *Country of My Skull: Guilt, Sorrow, and the Limits of Forgiveness in the New South Africa*. Johannesburg: Random House South Africa, 1998.

Kooijmans, Luuc. *Death Defied: The Anatomy Lessons of Frederik Ruysch*. Translated by Diane Webb. Leiden: Brill, 2011.

La Bruyére, Jean de. "Of Mankind." In *Characters*, translated by Henri Van Laun, 174–213. London: Oxford University Press, 1963. First published 1688.

Lacan, Jacques. *The Seminar of Jacques Lacan: Book XVII, The Other Side of Psychoanalysis*. Edited by Jacques-Alain Miller. Translated by Russell Grigg. New York: W. W. Norton, 2007.

———. "Seminar on 'The Purloined Letter.'" In *Écrits: The First Complete Edition in English*, translated by Bruce Fink, in collaboration with Héloïse Fink and Russell Grigg, 6–48. New York: Norton, 2006. First published 1966.

Lamko, Koulsy. "Comme un cœur obsédé: Leurres et lueurs de la francophonie." In *Retours du colonial? Disculpation et rehabilitation de l'histoire colonial*, edited by Catherine Coquio, 359–70. Paris: L'Atalante, 2008.

———. "Un dilemme inépuisé." In "Cette langue qu'on appelle le français." Special issue, *Internationale de l'imaginaire* 21 (March 2006).

Laroui, Fouad. *Une année chez les Français*. Paris: Julliard, 2010.

Latour, Bruno. *We Have Never Been Modern*. Translated by Catherine Porter. Cambridge, MA: Harvard University Press, 1993.

Lazarus, Neil. *The Postcolonial Unconscious*. Cambridge: Cambridge University Press, 2011.

Lazreg, Marnia. *Torture and the Twilight of Empire: From Algiers to Baghdad*. Princeton: Princeton University Press, 2008.

Le Bras, Hervé. *Le sol et le sang*. First edition. Paris: Les Éditions de l'Aube, 1994.

Le Cour Grandmaison, Olivier. *Coloniser/exterminer: Sur la guerre et l'état colonial.* Paris: Fayard, 2005.

———. *De l'indigénat: Anatomie d'un "monstre" juridique: Le droit colonial en Algérie et dans l'empire français.* Paris: Zones (La Découverte), 2010.

———. "Du droit colonial." *Droits* 1, no. 43 (2006): 123–40.

———. *Le 17 octobre 1961: Un crime d'état à Paris.* Paris: La Dispute, 2001.

Lee, Gregory. "L'opium et le Chinois dans le discours colonialiste." *Nouvelles du Sud*, no. 33 (2003): 35–47. https://papers.ssrn.com/sol3/papers.cfm?abstract_id=1030900.

———. "Textes, oublis, histoires." *Vacarme* 11 (2000) 56–57. http://www.vacarme.org/article758.html.

"Le festival des arts nègres de 1966: Événement culturale d'importance mondiale." In "Sénégal: Terre du dialogue." Special issue, *Le Monde Diplomatique* 6 (June 1965).

Lefeuvre, Daniel. *Pour en finir avec la repentance coloniale.* Paris: Flammarion, 2006.

Le Garrec, Jean. *Rapport fait au nom de la Commission des Affaires Culturelles, Familiales, et Sociales sur le proposition de loi, adoptée par le Senat, relative à la restitution par la France de la dépouille mortelle de Saartjie Baartman à l'Afrique du Sud.* No. 3563, January 30, 2002.

Legendre, Pierre. *De la société comme texte, linéaments d'une anthropologie dogmatique.* Paris: Fayard, 2001.

Legifrance. "Loi du 9 décembre 1905 concernant la séparation des Eglises et de l'Etat." Accessed January 26, 2019. https://www.legifrance.gouv.fr/affichTexte.do?cidTexte=LEGITEXT000006070169&dateTexte=20080306.

———. "Loi no. 2005-158 du 23 février 2005 portant reconnaissance de la Nation et contribution nationale en faveur des Français rapatriés" [. . . bearing on the nation's recognition of the contribution made by repatriated French]. Accessed November 3, 2018. https://www.legifrance.gouv.fr/affichTexte.do?cidTexte=JORFTEXT000000444898&dateTexte=&categorieLien=id.

Leiris, Michel. *Phantom Africa.* Translated by Brent Hayes Edwards. Calcutta: Seagull Press, 2017. First published 1934.

Le procès de Raoul Salan: Compte-rendu sténographique. Paris: Albin Michel, 1962.

"Les bourreaux des noirs: Un crime colonial." *Le Matin*, no. 7662, February 16, 1905.

Le Sueur, James D. *Uncivil War: Intellectuals and Identity Politics During the Decolonization of Algeria.* 2nd ed. Lincoln: University of Nebraska Press, 2005.

Levallois, Michel. *Ismaÿl Urbain: Une autre conquête de l'Algérie.* Paris: Maisonneuve et Larose, 2001.

Levisse-Touzé, Christine. *L'Afrique du Nord dans la guerre, 1939–1945.* Paris: Albin-Michel, 2000.

Lévi-Strauss, Claude. *The Savage Mind.* Chicago: University of Chicago Press, 1966.

———. *Tristes Tropiques.* Paris: Union Générale d'Éditions, 1965.

Liauzu, Claude, ed. *Colonisation: Droit d'inventaire.* Paris: Armand Colin, 2004.

Liauzu, Claude, and Thierry Le Bars. "Les insultes d'un ministre de la République." *Le Monde*, May 12, 2005.

Limoncelli, Stephanie. *The Politics of Trafficking: The First International Movement to Combat the Sexual Exploitation of Women.* Palo Alto, CA: Stanford University Press, 2010.

Lindon, Jérôme, ed. *La gangréne.* Paris: Minuit, 1959.

Lionnet, Françoise, and Shu-mei Shih, eds. *The Creolization of Theory.* Durham, NC: Duke University Press, 2011.

Loomba, Ania. "Postcolonialism—or Postcolonial Studies." *Interventions: International Journal of Postcolonial Studies* 1, no. 1 (1998): 39–42. https://doi.org/10.1080/13698019800510121.

Lorcin, Patricia M. E., ed. *Algeria, 1800–2000: Identity, Memory, Nostalgia*. Syracuse, NY: Syracuse University Press, 2006.

Luste Boulbina, Seloua. "Le deuxième sexe en politique." *La Mazarine* (December 1998).

———. *Les Arabes peuvent-ils parler? Suivi de "Dans l'ombre de l'Occident" et autres propos de Edward W. Said*. Paris: Editions Blackjack, 2011.

Lyotard, Jean-François. *The Differend: Phrases in Dispute*. Translated by Georges Van Den Abbeele. Minneapolis: University of Minnesota Press, 1988.

———. *La guerre des Algériens: Écrits, 1956–1963*. Paris: Galilée, 1989.

———. "La guerre des Algériens, suite." *Lignes* 30 (1997): 66–76.

Macey, David. *Frantz Fanon: A Biography*. New York: Picador, 2001.

Magnin, André. *J'aime Chéri Samba*. Arles/Paris: Actes Sud/Fondation Cartier pour l'art contemporain 2004.

Major, René. "Derrida: Lecteur de Freud et de Lacan." *Études françaises* 38, no. 1–2 (2002): 165–78. https://www.erudit.org/fr/revues/etudfr/2002-v38-n1-2-etudfr686/008398ar/.

———. *Lacan avec Derrida: Analyse désistentielle*. Paris: Mentha, 1991.

Makward, Catherine. *Mayotte Capécia, ou L'aliénation selon Fanon*. Paris: Karthala, 1999.

Manceron, Gilles. *Marianne et les colonies—une introduction à l'histoire coloniale de la France*. Paris: La Découverte, 2003.

Mannoni, Octave. "The Decolonisation of Myself." *Race and Class* 7 (April 1966): 337–45.

———. *Psychologie de la colonisation*. Paris: Seuil, 1950.

———. "La plainte du noir." *Esprit* 179, no. 5 (1951): 734–49.

Martin, William G., and Michael O. West, eds. *Out of One, Many Africas: Reconstructing the Study and Meaning of Africa*. Urbana: University of Illinois Press, 1999.

Martin, William G., and Michael O. West. "The Ascent, Triumph, and Disintegration of the Africanist Enterprise, USA." In Martin and West, *Many Africas*, 85–122.

Mauco, Georges. *Les étrangers en France. Leur rôle dans l'activité économique*. Paris: Armand Colin, 1932.

Mazrui, Alamin M. *Swahili beyond the Boundaries: Literature, Language, and Identity*. Athens: Ohio University Press, 2007.

Mbembe, Achille. "De la scène coloniale chez Frantz Fanon." In "Réflexions sur la postcolonie," edited by Seloua Luste Boulbina. *Rue Descartes* 58 (2007): 37–55.

———. *On the Postcolony*. Berkeley: University of California Press, 2001.

———. "Regard: Images coloniales sur l'Afrique noire." In *Images et colonies: Iconographie et propaganda colonial sur l'Afrique française de 1880 à 1962*, edited by Nicolas Bancel, Pascal Blanchard, and Laurent Gervereau, 280–85. Nanterre/Paris: BDIC-ACHAC, 1993.

———. "What Is Postcolonial Thinking? An Interview with Achille Mbembe." Translated by John Fletcher. *Eurozine*, January 9, 2008, 1–3. https://www.eurozine.com/what-is-postcolonial-thinking/. First published in *Esprit*, December 2006.

McCulloch, Jock. *Black Soul White Artifact: Fanon's Clinical Psychology and Social Theory*. Cambridge: Cambridge University Press, 1983.

Mehta, Uday Singh. *Liberalism and Empire: A Study in Nineteenth Century British Liberal Thought*. Chicago: University of Chicago Press, 1999.

Meilhon A.-J. "L'aliénation chez les Arabes: Études de nosologie comparée." *Annales médico-psychologiques* 3 (1896): 17–32, 178–207, 365–77.

Mékachéra, Hamlaoui. "Colonisation: Réconciler les mémoires." *Le Monde*, May 7, 2005.

Memmi, Albert. *The Colonizer and the Colonized*. Boston: Beacon Press, 1991. First published as *Portrait du colonisé—portrait du colonisateur* in 1957.

Mendès France, Pierre. *Oeuvres Complètes*. 4 vols. Paris: Gallimard, 1985–87.

———. "The Radio Talks of Pierre Mendès France." Radio program recorded October 20, 1954. Paris: Parisian Program.

Merleau-Ponty, Maurice. *Phenomenology of Perception*. Translated by Colin Smith. London: Routledge and Kegan Paul, 1962. First published 1945.

Mignolo, Walter. "I Am Where I Think: Remapping the Order of Knowing." In Lionnet and Shih, *Creolization of Theory*, 159–62.

Mohanty, Chandra Talpade. "'Under Western Eyes' Revisited: Feminist Solidarity through Anticapitalist Struggles." In *Feminism without Borders: Decolonizing Theory, Practicing Solidarity*, 221–51. Durham, NC: Duke University Press, 2003.

Montesquieu, Charles de Secondat (Baron de). *The Spirit of the Laws*. Translated by Anne M. Cohler, Basia Carolyn Miller, and Harold Samuel Stone. Cambridge: Cambridge University Press, 1989. First published as *L'esprit des lois* in 1748.

Morrissey, Lee. "Derrida, Algeria, and 'Structure, Sign, and Play.'" *Postmodern Culture* 9, no. 2 (January 1999). https://doi.org/10.1353/pmc.1999.0004.

Mosès, Stéphane. "Émile Benveniste et la linguistique du dialogue." *Revue de métaphysique et de morale* 32, no. 4 (2001): 509–25.

———. *Exégèse d'une légende: Lectures de Kafka*. Paris: Éditions d'Éclat, 2006.

Mouffe, Chantal. *The Democratic Paradox*. London: Verso, 2005.

Mudimbe, Valentin Y. *The Invention of Africa: Gnosis, Philosophy, and the Order of Knowledge*. Oxford: James Currey Press, 1988.

Musil, Robert. *Désarrois de l'élève Törless*. Translated by Philippe Jaccottet. Paris: Seuil, 1995.

Naïr, Sami. "Ce morceau de ténèbres." *Le Monde*, November 10, 1989.

Najab, Fayçal. "Multilinguisme et professions au Maroc." In "Francophonie et mondialisation." Special issue, *Hermès*, no. 40 (2004): 166–72.

Ngũgĩ wa Thiong'o. *Decolonizing the Mind: The Politics of Language in African Literature*. London: James Currey, 1986.

Nietzsche, Friedrich. *Beyond Good and Evil*. In *Basic Writings of Nietzsche*, edited and translated by Walter Kaufman, 191–435. New York: Modern Library, 1968.

———. *The Birth of Tragedy*. In *The Birth of Tragedy and Other Writings*, edited by Raymond Geuss and Ronald Speirs, translated by Ronald Speirs, 1–116. Cambridge: Cambridge University Press, 1999.

———. *Daybreak: Thoughts on the Prejudices of Morality*. Edited by Maudmaire Clark and Brian Leiter. Translated by R. J. Hollingdale. Cambridge: Cambridge University Press, 1997.

———. *La généalogie de la morale*. 3rd ed. Translated by Henri Albert. Paris: BNF/Gallica Press, 1900.

———. *Oeuvres Philosophiques Complètes*. Vol. 1, pt. 1, *La naissance de la tragédie: Fragments posthumes (automne 1869–printemps 1872)*. Edited by Giorgio Colli and Mazzino Montinari. Paris: Gallimard, 1977.

———. *On the Genealogy of Morals* and *Ecce Homo*. Translated by Walter Kaufman and R. J. Hollingdale. New York: Vintage, 1989.

———. *Thus Spoke Zarathustra*. Translated by Walter Kaufmann. New York: Penguin Books, 1978. First published 1883.

———. *Untimely Meditations*. Translated by R. J. Hollingdale. Cambridge: Cambridge University Press, 1983.

Noiriel, Gérard. "Le jugement des pairs: La soutenance de thèse au tournant du siècle." *Genèses* 5 (September 1991): 132–47.

Nordmann, Charlotte, ed. *Le foulard islamique en questions.* Paris: Éditions Amsterdam, 2004.

Nubukpo, Kako, Bruno Tinel, Martial-Ze Belinga, and Demba Moussa Dembélé, eds. *Sortir l'Afrique de la servitude monétaire: À qui profite le franc CFA?* Paris: La Dispute, 2016.

Nyerere, Julius. *Freedom and Socialism.* Oxford: Oxford University Press, 1968.

Odutula, Toyin. "Toyin Ojih Odutula." Accessed October 2, 2017. http://toyinodutola.com.

Ollsson, Göran Hugo. *Concerning Violence: Nine Scenes from the Anti-Imperialistic Self-Defense.* Helsinki Filmi Oy / Final Cut for Real, 2014.

Orwell, George. "Politics and the English Language." *The Orwell Reader: Fiction, Essays, and Reportage by George Orwell*, 355–66. New York: Harcourt Brace Jovanovich, 1956.

Ozouf, Mona. *L'homme régénéré: Essai sur la revolution française.* Paris: Gallimard, 1989.

Palmiéri, Christine. "Interview with Rancière." *ETC*, no. 59 (2002): 34–40. https://www.erudit.org/fr/revues/etc/2002-n59-etc1120593/9703ac.pdf.

Pascal, Blaise. *Pensées and Other Writings.* Translated by Honor Levi. Oxford: Oxford University Press, 1995. First published 1670.

Péguy, Charles. *Oeuvres en prose completes.* Paris: Gallimard, 1987.

Pervillé, Guy. *De l'empire français à la décolonisation.* Paris: Hachette/Littératures/Pluriel Histoire, 1991.

Peyrefitte, Alain. *C'était de Gaulle.* Paris: Fayard, 1994.

Plato. *The Collected Dialogues of Plato.* Edited by Edith Hamilton and Huntington Cairns. Princeton: Princeton University Press, 1961.

Porot, Antoine. "Notes de psychiatrie musulmane." *AMP*, 10th series, vol. 9 (May 1918): 377–84.

Rahmani, Zahia. "Le 'harki' comme spectre ou l'écriture du 'déterrement.'" In *Retours du colonial? Disculpation et rehabilitation de l'histoire coloniale française*, edited by Catherine Coquio, 221–37. Nantes: L'Atalante, 2008.

———. *Moze.* Paris: Sabine Wespieser, 2016.

Ramnoux, Clémence. *Héraclite, ou Entre les choses et les mots.* Paris: Les Belles Lettres, 1959.

———. *La nuit et les enfants de la nuit.* Paris: Flammarion, 1994.

Rancière, Jacques. *Disagreement: Politics and Philosophy.* Translated by Julie Rose. Minneapolis: University of Minnesota Press, 1999.

———. "The Distribution of the Sensible: Politics and Aesthetics." In *The Politics of Aesthetics*, translated by Gabriel Rockhill, 12–41. London: Continuum, 2004.

———. *Le partage du sensible.* Paris: La Fabrique, 2000.

Ratzel, Frederick. *Der Lebensraum: Eine biogeographische Studie.* Tübingen: H. Laupp, 1901.

Redeker, Robert. "Face aux intimidations islamistes, que doit faire le monde libre?" *Le Figaro*, September 19, 2006.

Reid, Donald. "The Worlds of Frantz Fanon's 'L'Algérie se dévoile.'" *French Studies* 61, no. 4 (2007): 460–75. https://doi.org/10.1093/fs/knm128.

Ricard, Alain. *Le sable de Babel: Traduction et apartheid: Esquisse d'une anthropologie de la textualité.* Paris: Éditions du CNRS, 2001.

———. "Vertus de l'in-discipline: Langues, textes, traductions." Opening lecture of 4th REAF. Accessed November 3, 2018. http://www.lam.sciencespobordeaux.fr/sites/lam/files/ricard_vertus_reaf_juillet_2016_0.pdf.

Richards, David. "Postcolonial Anthropology in the French-Speaking World." In Forsdick and Murphy, *Postcolonial Thought*, 173–84.

Ricœur, Paul. "Objectivity and Subjectivity in History." In *History and Truth*, translated by Charles A. Kelbley, 21–40. Evanston, IL: Northwestern University Press, 1965.

———. *On Translation*. Translated by Eileen Brennan. London: Routledge, 2006.

Rivet, Daniel. *Le Maghreb à l'épreuve de la colonisation*. Paris: Hachette Littératures/Pluriel Histoire, 2002.

Robert, Marthe. "Kafka in France." *Obliques*, no. 3 (1973): 3–10.

Robin, Marie-Monique. *Death Squadrons: The French School [Escadrons de la mort]*. Ideale Audience, in association with Canal+, Arte France, and Televisió Catalunya-TV3, 2003.

Romilly, Jean-Edmé. "Tolérance." In vol. 16 of *Encyclopédie ou Dictionnaire Raisonné des Sciences, des Arts, et des Métiers*, edited by Denis Diderot and Jean-Baptiste Le Rond d'Alembert. New facsimile printing of the first edition of 1751–1780. Stuttgart/ Bad Cannstatt: Friedrich Frommann Verlag, 1967.

Roudinesco, Elizabeth. *Jacques Lacan and Co.: A History of Psychoanalysis in France, 1925–1985*. Translated by Jeffrey Mehlman. Chicago: University of Chicago Press, 1990.

Rousseau, Jean-Jacques. "On the Social Contract (1762)." In *Basic Political Writings*, edited and translated by Donald A. Cress. Indianapolis: Hackett, 1987.

Roy-Campbell, Zaline. *Empowerment through Language: The African Experience—Tanzania and Beyond*. Trenton, NJ: Africa World Press, 2002.

Rushdie, Salman. "'Commonwealth Literature' Does Not Exist." In *Imaginary Homelands: Essays and Criticism, 1981–1991*, 61–70. New York: Viking Press, 1991.

Saadia-et-Lakhdar (Salima Sahraoui-Bouaziz and Rabah Bouaziz). *L'aliénation colonialiste et la résistance de la famille algérienne*. Lausanne: La Cité Éditeur, 1961.

Sade, Donatien Alphonse Francoise (Marquis de). *Les cent vingt journées de Sodome, ou L'école du libertinage*. Paris: Éditions 10/18, 1998. First published 1785.

Sadowsky, Jonathan. *Imperial Bedlam: Institutions of Madness in Colonial Southwest Nigeria*. Los Angeles: University of California Press, 1999.

Sahel, Claude. "L'Abbé Grégoire, les patois et les Juifs." *Cahiers Bernard Lazare* (1989): 123–24.

Sahnoun, Mohamed. *Mémoire blessée: Algérie, 1957*. Paris: Presses de la Renaissance, 2007.

Said, Edward W. "Between Two Cultures." In *Power, Politics, and Culture*, 233–47.

———. *Culture and Imperialism*. New York: Alfred A. Knopf, 1993.

———. "Europe and Its Others: An Arab Perspective." In *Power, Politics, and Culture*, 385–93.

———. "In the Shadow of the West." In *Power, Politics, and Culture*, 39–52.

———. *Orientalism*. New York: Vintage, 1979.

———. *Out of Place: A Memoir*. New York: Vintage, 2000.

———. *Power, Politics, and Culture: Interviews*. New York: Pantheon Books, 2001.

———. *Reflections on Exile and Other Essays*. Cambridge, MA: Harvard University Press, 2000.

———. *Representations of the Intellectual: The 1993 Reith Lectures*. New York: Vintage, 1996.

Samba, Chéri. "L'esthétique et le message doivent aller de pair." Interview with Blada Mfukidi. May 5, 2004. Republished on Congo-Forum. August 23, 2007. http://www.congoforum.be/fr/interviewsdetail.asp?id=32885.

Samkange, Stanlake, and T. M. Samkange. *Hunhuism or Ubuntuism: A Zimbabwe Indigenous Political Philosophy*. Salisbury: Graham, 1980.

Sankalé, Sylvain. *À la mode du pays: Chroniques saint-louisiennes*. Paris: Riveneuves, 2007.

Sarkozy, Nicolas. "Le discours de Dakar de Nicolas Sarkozy." Speech given July 27, 2007, in Dakar. *Le Monde*, November 9, 2007. http://www.lemonde.fr/afrique/article/2007/11/09/le-discours-de-dakar_976786_3212.html.

Sassou Nguesso, Denis. "Discours d'investiture du Président Denis Sassou Nguesso." *Les Echos du Congo Brazzaville*, April 17, 2016. http://lesechos-congobrazza.com/politique/982-discours-d-investiture-du-president-denis-sassou-nguesso.

Saunders, David. "France on the Knife-Edge of Religion: Commemorating the Centenary of the Law of 9 December 1905 on the Separation of Church and State." In *Secularism, Religion, and Multicultural Citizenship*, edited by Geoffrey Brahm Levey and Tariq Modood, 56–81. Cambridge: Cambridge University Press, 2009.

Sayad, Abdelmalek. "Bilinguisme et education en Algérie." In *Education, développement et démocratie*, edited by Robert Castel and Jean-Claude Passeron, 205–16. Paris: Mouton, 1967.

Schmitt, Carl. *The Concept of the Political*. Translated by George Schwab. Chicago: University of Chicago Press, 1996. First published in German 1932.

———. *La notion de politique: Théorie du partisan*. Translated from German by Marie-Louise Steinhauser. Paris: Calmann-Lévy, 1972.

———. *Theory of the Partisan: Intermediate Commentary on the Concept of the Political*. Translated by G. L. Ulmen. New York: Telos Press, 2007. First published in German 1962.

Scott, Joan W. *The Politics of the Veil*. Princeton: Princeton University Press, 2007.

Senghor, Léopold Sédar. *Hosties noires*. Paris: Seuil, 1948.

———. "Liminary Poem." In *The Collected Poetry*, translated by Melvin Dixon, 39–40. Charlottesville: University Press of Virginia, 1991.

Sgrena, Giulina. *Le prix du voile*. Translated by Maria Assunta Mini. Algiers: Mille Feuilles, 2008.

Shaftesbury, Anthony Ashley Cooper. *Principes de la philosophie morale or Essai de M. S*** sur le mérite et la vertu, avec des réflexions* . . . Translated by Denis Diderot. December 14, 2015. https://fr.wikisource.org/wiki/Essai _sur_le_mérite_et_la_vertu. First published Amsterdam: Zacharie Chatelain, 1745.

Shariff, Ibrahim Noor. *Tungo Zetu, msingi wa mashairi na tungo nyinginezo*. Trenton, NJ: Africa World Press/Red Sea Press, 1988.

Sharpley-Whiting, T. Denean. "Femme Négritude: Jane Nardal, *La dépêche Africaine*, and the Francophone New Negro." *Souls*, Fall 2000, 8–17.

Shepard, Todd. "La 'bataille du voile' pendant la guerre d'Algérie." In Nordmann, *Le foulard islamique*, 131–41.

———. *Mâle décolonisation, "l'homme arabe" et la France: De l'indépendance algérienne à la revolution iranienne*. Paris: Payot, 2017.

Sigg, Bernard W. *Le silence et la honte: Névroses de la guerre d'Algérie*. Paris: Messidor/Editions Sociales, 1989.

Skikne, I. R. "Apartheid en Afrique du Sud." *Les Temps Modernes*, July 1950, 122–37.

Smouts, Marie-Claude, ed. *La situation postcoloniale: Les postcolonial studies dans le débat français*. Paris: Les Presses Sciences Po, 2007.

Spieler, Miranda Frances. *Empire and Underworld: Captivity in French Guiana*. Cambridge, MA: Harvard University Press, 2012.

Spies, S. B. *Methods of Barbarism: Roberts and Kitchener and Civilians in the Boer Republics January 1900–May 1902*. Cape Town: Human and Rousseau, 1977.

Spivak, Gayatri Chakravorty. "Can the Subaltern Speak?" In *Marxism and the Interpretation of Culture*, edited by Cary Nelson and Lawrence Grossberg, 271–313. Basingstoke, UK: MacMillan Education, 1988.

———. *A Critique of Postcolonial Reason: Toward a History of the Vanishing Present*. Cambridge, MA: Harvard University Press, 1999.

———. "The New Subaltern: A Silent Interview." In *Mapping Subaltern Studies and the Postcolonial*, edited by Vinayak Chaturvedi, 324–40. New York: Verso, 2000.

Stanley, Liz. *Mourning Becomes . . . : Post/memory, Commemoration, and the Concentration Camps of the South African War, 1899–1902*. Manchester, UK: Manchester University Press, 1996.

Starobinski, Jean. "Sur la flatterie." *Nouvelle revue de psychanalyse*, no. 4 (Fall 1971): 131–51.

Steiner, George. *After Babel: Aspects of Language*. 3rd ed. Oxford: Oxford University Press, 1998.

Stevenson, Robert Louis. *Fables*. New York: Scribner, 1910.

Stoler, Ann Laura. *Carnal Knowledge and Imperial Power: Race and the Intimate in Colonial Rule*. Los Angeles: University of California Press, 2002.

———. *La chair de l'empire: Savoirs intimes et pouvoirs raciaux en régime colonial*. Paris: La Découverte, 2012.

———. "L'aphasie coloniale française: L'histoire mutilée." In *Ruptures postcoloniales: Les nouveaux visages de la société française*, edited by Nicolas Bancel, Florence Bernault, Pascal Blanchard, Ahmed Boubeker, Achille Mbembe, and Françoise Vergès, 62–78. Paris: La Découverte, 2010.

———. *Race and the Education of Desire*. Durham, NC: Duke University Press, 1995.

Stora, Benjamin. *Algeria, 1830–2000: A Short History*. Translated by Jane Marie Todd. Ithaca: Cornell University Press, 2004.

———. *La gangrène et l'oubli: La mémoire de la guerre d'Algérie*. Paris: La Découverte/Poche, 2005.

Stroud, Christopher. "Portuguese as Ideology and Politics in Mozambique: Semiotic (Re) constructions of a Postcolony." In Blommaert, *Language Ideological Debates*, 343–80.

Studer, Nina Salouâ. *The Hidden Patients: North African Women in French Colonial Psychiatry*. Köln: Böhlau Verlag, 2015.

Sullivan, Shannon, and Nancy Tuana, eds. *Race and Epistemologies of Ignorance*. Albany: SUNY Press, 2007.

Taïeb-Carlen, Sarah. *Les Juifs d'Afrique du Nord: De Didon à de Gaulle*. Saint-Maur: Sepia, 2000.

Táíwò, Olúfẹ́mi. *How Colonialism Preempted Modernity in Africa*. Bloomington: Indiana University Press, 2010.

Taraud, Christelle. *La prostitution coloniale: Algérie, Tunisie, Maroc, 1830–1962*. Paris: Payot, 2003.

Thucydides. *History of the Peloponnesian War, Books I and II*. Translated by Charles Forster Smith. Loeb Classical Library. Cambridge: Harvard University Press, 1991.

Tocqueville, Alexis de. *Democracy in America*. Translated by Harvey C. Mansfield and Delba Winthrop. Chicago: University of Chicago Press, 2000. First published in French as *De la démocratie en Amérique* in 1835.

———. *Lettres choisies: Souvenirs (1814–1859)*. Edited by Françoise Mélonio and Laurence Guellec. Paris: Gallimard, 2003.

———. *Oeuvres*. La Pléïade. 3 vols. Edited by André Jardin. Paris: Gallimard, 1991.

———. *Oeuvres Complètes*. Edited by Jacob Peter Mayer. 18 vols. Paris: Gallimard/NRF, 1952–98.

———. *Souvenirs*. Paris: Gallimard, 1999. Translated as *Recollections*. Translated by George Lawrence. Edited by Jacob Peter Mayer and A. P. Kerr. Garden City, NY: Doubleday, 1970. First published 1893.

———. *Sur l'Algérie*. Edited by Seloua Luste Boulbina. Paris: Garnier Flammarion, 2003.

———. *Sur l'esclavage*. Edited by Seloua Luste Boulbina. Algiers: Éditions Barzakh, 2008.

———. *Writings on Empire and Slavery*. Edited and translated by Jennifer Pitts. Baltimore: Johns Hopkins University Press, 2001.

Todorov, Tzvetan. "Preface à l'édition française." In *L'orientalisme: L'orient crée par l'occident*, by Edward Said, 21–25. Paris: Seuil, 2003.

Tonda, Joseph. "L'impossible décolonisation des sciences sociales africaines." *Mouvements* 72, no. 4 (2012): 108–19.

"Traduction et mondialisation." Special issue, *Hermès* 49. Paris: CNRS Éditions, 2007.

Turlais, Pierrette. "Alfred Dreyfus, cahiers de l'Île du Diable." *Malaise dans le capitalisme. Cahiers Sens Public* 11–12 (2009): 93–101.

"Un livre sur la guerre d'Algérie." Review of *L'an V de la Revolution Algerienne*, by Frantz Fanon. *Informations et liaisons ouvrières*, no. 19 (March 1960): 10–12. http://archives autonomies.org/IMG/pdf/ico/ilo/ILO-019.pdf. Cited with commentary by Nedjib Sidi Moussa at http://sinedjib.com/index.php/2016/09/08/un-livre-guer/.

Valverde, Juan. *L'anatomia del cuerpo humano*. Rome: Per Ant. Salamanca and Antonio Lafrerj, 1560.

Van Den Avenne, Cécile. "Petit-nègre et bambara: La langue de l'indigène dans quelques œuvres d'écrivains coloniaux en Afrique occidentale française." In *Citer la langue de l'autre: Mots étrangers dans le roman: De Proust à W. G. Sebald*, edited by Danielle Perrot-Corpet and Christine Queffélec, 77–95. Lyon: Presses Universitaires de Lyon, 2007.

Van Eeckhout, Laetitia. "Une disposition adoptee avec l'aval du gouvernement français." *Le Monde*, June 11, 2005.

Vatin, François. "Octave Mannoni (1899–1989) et sa *Psychologie de la colonisation*: Contextualisation et décontextualisation." *Revue du Mauss* 37, no. 1 (2011): 137–78. https://www.cairn.info/revue-du-mauss-2011-1-page-137.htm.

Venier, Pascal. "Une campagne de propangande colonial: Gallieni, Lyautey et la defense du régime militaire a Madagascar (1899–1900)." *European Studies Research Institute*. Manchester: University of Salford, 1997.

Vergès, Françoise. *Abolir l'esclavge: Une utopie colonial, les ambiguities d'une politique humanitaire*. Paris: Albin Michel, 2001.

Vergés, Jacques, Michel Zavrian, and Maurice Courrégé. *Les disparus, le cahier vert*. Lausanne: La Cité, 1959. First published in *Les Temps Modernes* as "Le 'cahier vert' des disparitions en Algérie," September 1959, no. 163.

Vesalius, Andreas. *De humani corporis fabrica libri septum*. Translated by William Frank Richardson and John Burd Carman. San Francisco: Norman, 1998. First published 1543.

Veyne, Paul. "Foucault Revolutionizes History." Translated by Catherine Porter. In *Foucault and His Interlocuters*, edited by Arnold I. Davidson, 146–82. Chicago: University of Chicago Press, 1997.

Vives, Jean-Michel. "Pulsion invocante et destins de la voix." 2008. http://www.insistance .org/news/42/72/Pulsion-invocante-et-destins-de-la-voix/d,detail_article.html. Page no longer available.

Voltaire (François-Marie Arouet). *Essai sur les moeurs et l'esprit des nations et sur les principaux faits de l'histoire depuis Charlemagne jusqu'a Louis XIII*. Paris: Garnier frères, 1992. First published 1756.

———. *Philosophical Dictionary*. Adelaide: University of Adelaide Library, 2014. https://ebooks.adelaide.edu.au/v/voltaire/dictionary/. Derived from *The Works of Voltaire: A Contemporary Version*, vols. 5–14. Translated by William F. Fleming. New York: E. R. DuMont, 1901. First published in French as *Dictionnaire Philosophique Portatif ou raison par l'alphabet (de Abraham à vertu)* in 1764.

———. *Traité sur la tolérance*. Geneva: Fréres Cramer, 1763. http://tolosana.univ-toulouse.fr/fr/notice/075853078.

———. *The Works of Voltaire: A Contemporary Version*. Translated by William F. Fleming. New York: E. R. DuMont, 1901.

Walker, David. *Appeal to the Coloured Citizens of the World*. Edited by Peter P. Hinks. University Park: Pennsylvania State University Press, 2000. First published 1829.

Walzer, Michael. *On Toleration*. New Haven, CT: Yale University Press, 1997.

Weil, Patrick. *La France et ses étrangers*. Paris: Calmann-Lévy, 1991.

———. "Le statut des musulmans en Algérie coloniale: Une nationalité française dénaturée." *Histoire de la Justice* 16 (2005): 93–109.

———. *Qu'est-ce qu'un Français? Histoire de la nationalité française depuis la Révolution*. Paris: Gallimard, 2004.

Wiedorn, Michael. *Think Like an Archipelago: Paradox in the Work of Édouard Glissant*. Albany: SUNY Press, 2018.

Winnicott, Donald. *Les enfants et la guerre*. Translated by Madeleine Michelin and Lynn Rosaz. Paris: Payot, 2004.

Yacine, Tassadit. "Anthropologie de la peur: L'exemple des rapports hommes-femmes en Algérie." In *Amour, phantasms et sociétés en Afrique du Nord et au Sahara*, edited by Tassadit Yacine. Paris: Awal/L'Harmattan, 1992.

Young, Robert. *White Mythologies: Writing History and the West*. London: Routledge, 1990.

Youssi, Abderrahim. AJDMR. Accessed June 30, 2014. http://www.ajd-mr.org/modules.php?name=News&file=article&sid=5171. Page no longer available.

Zinn, Howard. *A People's History of the United States, 1492–Present*. Revised and updated edition. New York: Harper Perennial, 1995.

INDEX

SELOUA LUSTE BOULBINA is an *agrégée* in philosophy, with doctorate degrees in political science and philosophy, and program director of courses on "Decolonization of Knowledges" at the Collège International de Philosophie in Paris. She teaches political theory at the Institut d'Études Politiques in Paris and is a research associate and PhD supervisor at the Laboratoire de Changement Social et Politique (Laboratory for Social and Political Change) at l'Université Paris VII–Denis Diderot. She is author and editor of many books, including *Les Arabes peuvent-ils parler?* (Can the Arabs speak?), *Grands travaux à Paris* (The great urban projects of Paris), and, most recently, *Les miroirs vagabondes* (Wandering mirrors). Luste Boulbina has also held visiting positions in Beijing and Senegal.

LAURA HENGEHOLD is Professor of Philosophy at Case Western Reserve University in Cleveland, Ohio. Her previous books include *The Body Problematic: Kant and Foucault on Political Imagination* and *Simone de Beauvoir's Philosophy of Individuation*. She is editor (with Nancy Bauer) of the *Blackwell Companion to Simone de Beauvoir* and editor and translator of Jean Godefroy Bidima's *Law and the Public Sphere in Africa: La Palabre and Other Writings*.